PLANT PROJECTS FOR YOUNG SCIENTISTS

Salvatore Tocci

FRANKLIN WATTS
A Division of Grolier Publishing
New York ▪ London ▪ Hong Kong ▪ Sydney
Danbury, Connecticut

Photographs ©: Corbis-Bettmann: 88 (Grant Smith); David R. Frazier: 8; Dwight R. Kuhn Photography: 44, 55, 57, 67 right, 87, 111; Frederick D. Atwood: 30, 41, 67 left; H. Armstrong Roberts, Inc.: 28 (T. Dietrich), 25 (R. Krubner), 33 (M. Thonig), 31; Photo Researchers: 20 (Archive), 78 (James Bell/SS), 79 (Biophoto Associates), 56 (Richard L. Carlton), 104 (Omikron/Carolina Bio Supply), 61 (J. H. Robinson), 101 (Science Photo Library); Randy Matusow: 18; Rob Simpson Nature Stock: 23 (R. & A. Simpson); Tom Sack & Associates: 36 (Greg Vaughn); Visuals Unlimited: 54 (John D. Cunningham), 93 (Robert E. Lyons); Wisconsin Fast Plants: 50 (Paul H. Williams/Department of Plant Pathology); Wolfgang Käehler: cover.

NOTE TO READERS:

Throughout this book, most measurements are given only in metric units because that is the system of measure used by most professional scientists. Words in *italics* appear in the Glossary at the back of this book.

Some of the projects described in this book are loosely based on experiments in *Botany Projects for Young Scientists* (Franklin Watts, 1992) by Maurice Bleifield.

Diagrams created by Bob Italiano

Visit Franklin Watts on the Internet at:
http://publishing.grolier.com

Library of Congress Cataloging-in-Publication Data

Tocci, Salvatore
      Plant projects for young scientists/Salvatore Tocci.
      p.   cm. — (Projects for young scientists)
Includes bibliographical references and index.
Summary: Provides instructions for and explains the principles behind a variety of plant projects and experiments for home or school.
ISBN 0-531-11704-9 (lib. bdg.)
1. Plant projects Juvenile literature. 2. Plant—Experiments Juvenile literature.
[1. Plant projects. 2. Plant—Experiments. 3. Botany—Experiments. 4. Science projects. 5. Experiments.]
QK52.6.T63   2000
580'.78—dc21   99-15454
                                                                                CIP

©2000 Franklin Watts, a division of Grolier Publishing
All rights reserved. Published simultaneously in Canada.
Printed in the United States of America.
1 2 3 4 5 6 7 8 9 10 R 09 08 07 06 05 04 03 02 01 00

GROLIER
PUBLISHING

C O N T E N T S

PLANT PROJECTS FOR YOUNG SCIENTISTS

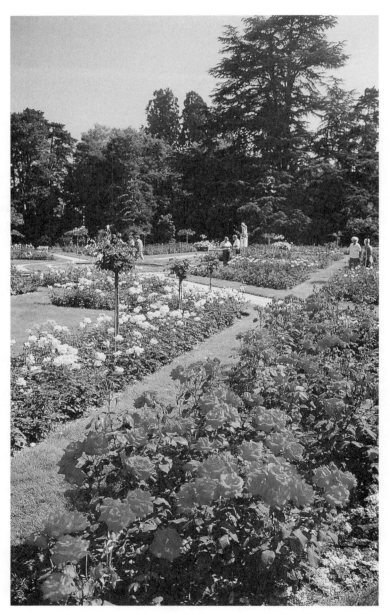

This rose garden is full of beautiful flowers.

CHAPTER

HOW TO START

Is there a flower garden in your yard or at a local park? Do you enjoy the bright, beautiful blossoms that plants produce each year?

Many people enjoy growing plants in their yards or inside their home. Some people also have a vegetable garden where they grow peas, cucumbers, string beans, lettuce, tomatoes, and peppers. Herb gardens with basil, thyme, oregano, dill, rosemary, and parsley are also very popular.

Most people like plants. Since you are reading this book, you are probably one of them. Are you looking for an idea for a science project that involves plants? Perhaps you are searching for a project to complete a class assignment. Or maybe your school is sponsoring a science fair, and you want to enter it. It is also possible that you want to do a project to earn some extra credit. And there is always the chance that you are looking for project ideas just because you are interested in learning more about plants. By performing some or all of the projects in this book, you will learn a lot about botany—the study of plants.

Before you can begin your project, you need to make some decisions. At this point, you may not even know what type of plant you would like to use in your project. Even if you do, you may not know exactly what you are going to do with the plant. Read on for some helpful suggestions.

CHOOSING YOUR PROJECT

After completing a science project, most students look back and find that one of the hardest parts was choosing and designing the project. You should begin by thinking about your interests and hobbies. If you like growing vegetables, you may want to do a project that investigates how seeds grow and develop. You can find such a project in Chapter 3. If you love food, you can examine how plants manufacture nutrients. See Chapter 5. If you are interested in the environment, Chapter 8 includes a project that explains how to determine whether a sample of water is polluted. If you'd like to work with one of the major structures that make up a flowering plant—roots, stem, and leaves—check out Chapter 4.

Take a look at the contents and index of this book. Do any of the topics listed there interest you? If you still aren't sure, you may want to start reading and stop when you come across something that intrigues you. As you look through the book, you will notice that each section includes background information to give you some basic knowledge about the project that follows.

Each project has a "What You Need" section that lists the materials and equipment required. This book does not provide instructions about how to use specific types of equipment or how to prepare solutions. If you need this kind of help, check a science reference book or ask your science teacher for guidance.

If you would like to expand on a project or if you are looking for a greater challenge, look at the "Doing More" sections that follow each project. Most of these suggestions will require additional research—both for more detailed information about the topic and for techniques required to carry out the project. Some of the resources listed at the back of this book may help you. If not, ask your science teacher or a librarian for help, or search for information on the Internet.

RESEARCHING YOUR PROJECT

Once you have chosen a topic, read as much as possible about it. All good scientists read everything they can about their field. Reading will provide you with important background information and help you narrow your topic to a specific question or problem. It may even help you come up with ideas for taking your investigation in new and exciting directions.

Do not feel restricted to conducting projects exactly as they are described in this book. Be inventive. Try new things. Think of the projects in this book as a place to start, then use your imagination.

Begin your research in your school library. Read a few books on your topic, then look for articles in science magazines, such as *Discover* or *Scientific American*, and professional journals, such as *Journal of Plant Physiology* or *Plant Science*. If your school doesn't have all the resources you need, check with a librarian at a local college.

Because articles in professional journals are written by scientists and are intended for other scientists, many of them will be too technical for you to understand. However, you can scan these journals for ideas and information. If you come across an article that seems relevant to your topic, ask your science teacher to help you understand it.

Be sure to check the multimedia encyclopedias and science reference sections that are available through on-line computer services such as America Online and Microsoft Network. These services also provide access to the Internet, an extremely valuable resource for obtaining information to help you with your botany project.

In effect, the Internet is the world's largest "information mall," earning it the title "The Information Superhighway." The part of the Internet that many people find most useful in searching for information is the World Wide Web. Searching or "surfing" the Web can be somewhat intimidating. Using a directory, which consists of hundreds of thousands of documents sorted into various categories, can make your search much easier. Among the most popular directories are Yahoo (*http://www.yahoo. com/*) and Magellan (*http://www.mckinley.com/*).

For a more focused search, you can use an index with the help of a tool known as a search engine. Several search engines and their Web addresses are listed in Table 1. To use an index, all you do is type in one or more keywords. The more specific your keywords are, the more focused your search will be.

For example, if your keyword is "plant," you will probably get millions of hits. Each hit represents a Web site that contains information about the keyword(s) you entered. In many cases, a Web site will have "links" that can connect you to additional sites with similar information.

Obviously, you could spend more time going through these Web pages than you will on the project itself. But if

TABLE 1: Accessing an Index on the Web

Search Engine	Address
Alta Vista	*http://altavista.digital.com/*
Excite	*http://www.excite.com/*
Go2	*http://www.goto.com/*
HotBot	*http://www.hotbot.com/*
Infohiway	*http://www.infohiway.com/*
Infoseek	*http://guide.infoseek.com/*
Lycos	*http://lycos.cs.cmu.edu/*

you type in the keywords "plants + nutrients + growth," the list of documents will be much shorter and will focus on the topic of nutrients that are needed for plant growth.

It is important to realize that each search engine uses its own techniques. Some require you to put quotation marks around the words to show that they go together. Others may require that you insert the word "and" or the sign "+" between words to indicate that you are looking for documents containing all the keywords. Check out the search engine's instructions for the most efficient way to conduct a search.

CARRYING OUT YOUR OWN PROJECT

As you design your project, be as creative as possible. Can you think of an investigation that no one has ever done before? By incorporating your own ideas and perhaps even your own experimental design, you will greatly improve your project.

When most people hear the words "experimental design," the first thing they think of is the scientific method. The scientific method is usually described as a set of steps—collecting information, forming a hypothesis, carrying out an experiment, and drawing a conclusion. In reality, the scientific method is not a set routine, and scientists do not depend solely on one method in their work. They rely upon a wide variety of methods known as scientific processes. See Table 2.

An accurate definition of the term "scientific method" includes a variety of scientific processes that are used to answer a specific question. For example, if a scientist wants to determine whether a specific insecticide can prevent a plant disease, his or her scientific method would

TABLE 2: Scientific Processes

Step	Methods for Accomplishing Step
Collecting information	Observing, conducting field studies, measuring, sampling
Hypothesizing	Forming a hypothesis, predicting
Experimenting	Conducting a controlled experiment, problem solving, analyzing data, evaluating data, communicating
Drawing conclusions	Modeling, inferring, forming a theory

most likely involve forming a hypothesis, carrying out an experiment, evaluating the results, drawing a conclusion, and communicating the findings. However, the scientific method used by a scientist studying the relationship between various flowering plants might include collecting and analyzing data in the field, examining collections at botanical gardens, sharing findings with other scientists, and forming a hypothesis. Whatever scientific processes you decide to use will constitute the scientific method for your botany project.

If one of the processes you decide to use involves conducting an experiment, be sure to include a *control group* whenever necessary. A control group serves as a standard of comparison. Scientists carrying out an experiment often set up two groups that are identical in all respects but one. One group—the *experimental group*—is subjected to the factor being investigated; the other—the control group—is not.

For example, if you wish to find out how adding a particular chemical to the soil affects the growth of pea plants, you would grow plants in the experimental group in soil that contains the chemical. But you would grow pea plants in the control group in regular soil. All other growing conditions would be identical for both groups of plants. They would be exposed to the same amount of sunlight and receive the same amount of water. If the chemical affects plant growth, you should observe a noticeable difference between the plants in the experimental group and those in the control group.

Experiments also involve variables—something that changes. In the preceding example, the chemical additive acts as the *independent variable*—the factor you can change in any way you wish. For example, you can decide how much chemical to add, how many times to add it, and the time of season it is applied. The growth of the pea plants is known as the *dependent variable*. It changes based on what you do with the independent variable. For example, you may find that when more chemical is added (the independent variable), the plants produce larger peas (the dependent variable).

No matter what scientific processes you use, be sure to record all your data in a neat and organized manner. It is best to keep all your written observations, drawings, photographs, and numerical data together in one notebook. You may find it helpful to make graphs and tables to organize your numerical data. A computer spreadsheet program can help you organize your data. Some will even create tables and graphs for you.

If you enjoy working with computers, you may decide to use one for other parts of your project too. For example, you can develop a program to simulate a real-life situation that shows how a pollutant might affect the distribution of a certain plant. As you read this book, think of other ways to use a computer to enhance your project.

SCIENCE COMPETITIONS

You may decide to enter your project in a science fair. This is an ideal opportunity to show off your project and have it judged by professionals, perhaps even by a botanist whose interests parallel yours. Science fairs are often sponsored by schools and local organizations. Each science fair has its own rules and specifications, so read the entry form and application carefully before planning your project.

Projects that win at local competitions are usually entered in regional, state, or even national competitions. The last step would be the Intel International Science and

SAFETY FIRST

All projects should be done under supervision, either from a parent, a teacher, or a scientist. The more complicated the project, the more knowledge you will need about proper procedures and safety factors. Before you begin your project, discuss all the safety aspects with the person supervising you. If any doubt arises, seek advice from someone knowledgeable, perhaps even a botanist, about the topic you are investigating.

- Always work under the supervision of an adult.

- Wear protective eye goggles, especially when working with chemicals or a heat source.

- Do not wear contact lenses when working with chemicals. Wear protective gloves and a laboratory apron when working with corrosive chemicals like acids.

- Do not taste any chemicals or inhale any fumes they emit.

- Keep your hands away from your face and mouth while you are working on your project. Do not eat or drink anything in the area where you are carrying out your project.

- Keep your work area as clean and neat as possible.

- Do not use chipped or broken glassware in your experiments.

- Report any problems or injuries to the adult supervising your work.

- When in doubt, ask your parent, a science teacher, or a professional scientist for advice.

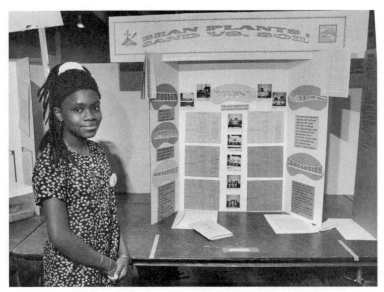

Anokye Blisset did a science project to find out whether bean plants grow better in sand or soil.

Engineering Fair, held annually at various locations throughout the United States, or the Intel Science Talent Search. If your biology project gets you all the way to one of these prestigious competitions, remember that this book may have been the first step to your success.

CHAPTER 2

NONFLOWERING PLANTS

When people hear the word "plant," they usually think of a rose or a daisy or an apple tree. But not all plants produce beautiful flowers. Just think of a 105-meter-tall redwood tree or a giant ragweed—a plant that causes an allergic reaction in many people. Feathery ferns and the moss that forms thick green carpets on shady forest floors are plants too. What do roses, daisies, apple trees, redwood trees, ragweed, ferns, and mosses all have in common?

To answer this question, you need to know something about the system scientists use to identify, classify, and name living things. This system, developed in the 1700s by a Swedish naturalist named Carolus Linnaeus, organizes living things based on their physical appearance and patterns of behavior. Although Linnaeus placed all living things into two major categories—plants and animals—most scientists now divide Earth's creatures into five

Carolus Linnaeus developed the system
most scientists use to name, identify, and
classify plants and other living things.

major categories, or *kingdoms*—animals, plants, fungi,
protoctists, and bacteria.

For an organism to be included in the plant kingdom,
it must be composed of many cells and manufacture its
own nutrients through *photosynthesis*. Every plant cell is
surrounded by a cell wall made of cellulose. Just as the
earthworms, eagles, elephants, and eels included in the
animal kingdom are quite different from one another, so

are the mosses, mistletoe, marigolds, and mango trees included in the plant kingdom. Each of the five kingdoms contains a wide array of diverse organisms.

THE FIRST PLANTS

Earth is more than 4.6 billion years old. Some studies suggest that the first life forms appeared about 3.9 billion years ago. The first photosynthesizers lived in watery environments about 3 billion years ago. Over time, these creatures added huge quantities of oxygen first to the oceans and then to the atmosphere.

By about 450 million years ago, the atmosphere contained enough oxygen to support life on land. Some of the oxygen had undergone chemical changes to form an ozone layer in the upper atmosphere. This protective layer blocked some of the sun's ultraviolet (UV) rays, preventing them from reaching Earth's surface. Shielded from UV rays that would otherwise destroy them, small plants appeared in the muddy waters at the edges of ponds, lakes, and streams.

Eventually, plants moved onto land where they could absorb more sunlight and have access to more nutrients. But life on land brought some dangers. To survive in this harsh, dry habitat, plants had to develop mechanisms for extracting water and nutrients from soil. These plants also had to find ways to reproduce on land. The plants that adapted in ways that allowed them to overcome these challenges thrived in their new environment.

The first land plants were small because they did not have an efficient system for transporting water and nutrients throughout their bodies. Nevertheless, they successfully colonized land, and many species still survive today. The following project will explore two of these plants—liverworts and hornworts.

SEARCHING FOR LIVERWORTS
AND HORNWORTS

What You Need	
Magnifying lens	Peat pellets
Trowel	Water
Pint-sized jars with lids	

Did you ever wonder how the liverwort got its name? "Wort" is an Old English word meaning "herb." At one time, people believed that liverwort contained substances that could cure diseases of the liver.

Search for liverworts in wooded areas. They usually grow in moist, shady places, so you should look along the edges of streams or ponds and on the sides of shaded roadways. A female liverwort plant resembles a palm tree, while a male plant looks like a mushroom. Liverworts are not very large. The smallest ones are less than 2.5 centimeters (cm) high, while the tallest grow no higher than 20 cm.

Use a magnifying lens to examine the plants you find. Search for coconut-like structures under the "leaves" of a female plant. These structures, called *sporophytes*, play a role in the life cycle of the plant. To find out more about how liverworts reproduce, check your local library or conduct an Internet search.

Hornworts are much less common than liverworts, so they may be more difficult to find. Hornworts are small and flat. When you locate a hornwort, dig it up carefully. Notice that it is anchored to the ground by rootlike structures. These structures are called rhizoids. They help both liverworts and hornworts attach to the surfaces on which they grow.

Liverworts are primitive plants. They lack many of the structures found in more advanced plants.

You can use pint-sized jars with lids and peat pellets to set up a "greenhouse" for your liverworts and horn-worts. Place a peat pellet in each lid and cover it with water. After the pellet swells, place a plant in the peat and loosely screw on the jar. Do not tighten the lid all the way. If you do, the plant will not be able to get the gases it needs from the air. Watch your plants for several days or weeks. Be sure to always keep the peat moist. Prepare a report summarizing your observations and findings.

Doing More

- The New York Botanical Garden (NYBG) is in the process of cataloging its collection of primitive plants. The first phase, which involved cataloging its collection from Alaska, Canada, and Greenland, has been completed. The NYBG is currently cataloging primitive plants from the continental United States. Their Web address is *http://www.nybg.org/bsci/hcol/bryo/*. Does anything about their collection surprise you? You can also find links to numerous other sites dealing with liverworts, hornworts, and other primitive plants at *http://www.helsinki.fi/kmus/botcryp.html*.

- Liverworts and hornworts often grow where they are not wanted, especially under warm and humid conditions. These plants may crop up on roofs, patios, fences, and walkways. They may also grow in greenhouses. Commercial products that thwart the growth of these unwanted plants are made from chemical substances known as fatty acids. These substances are extracted from plant and animal sources. They are effective and environmentally safe. Find out how these products work. Design a project aimed at developing an even more effective product for preventing the growth of primitive plants.

THE MOSSES: VASCULAR OR NONVASCULAR?

Liverworts and hornworts are known as nonvascular plants. They are considered more primitive than most of the plants now on Earth. That is because, as time passed, plants developed *vascular systems* to transport materials throughout their bodies. The cells and tissues that make up a vascular system are specialized to conduct water and other materials throughout the plant.

Plants are not the only organisms with a vascular system. The heart, arteries, and veins in our bodies perform the same important function. The vascular system serves as a supply line, allowing an organism to spread out or grow larger.

In most plants, a vascular system transports water and dissolved materials from the tip of the roots up the stem to the leaves. Materials also move in the opposite direction through the vascular system. Nutrients manufactured in the leaves during photosynthesis move down the stem and to the roots.

Not all vascular plants have well-developed transport systems. For example, mosses have only a simple con-

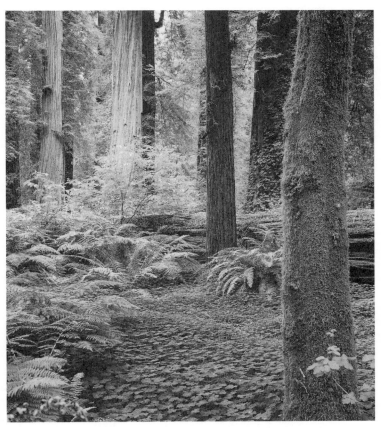

Mosses can grow in a variety of places, including on the bark of trees.

ducting channel made of cells specialized for transport. These cells cannot conduct water very far. In fact, the vascular system in mosses is so simple that some botanists classify mosses as nonvascular plants.

Mosses are known as pioneer organisms. As this name implies, mosses are among the first living things to thrive in barren areas. Once soil begins to form in an area, mosses spread quickly and form a thick carpet on the ground. Because mosses hold water, other plants can then begin to grow in the area.

One kind of moss—sphagnum moss—usually grows in wet, boggy areas. When this moss dies, it forms peat. In many northern European and Asian countries, people dig up the bogs, gather the peat, dry it out, and burn it to warm their homes.

During World War I, sphagnum moss was also used as a dressing to bind soldiers' wounds. The following project will show you why sphagnum moss makes a good medical dressing and why it is often added to potting soil.

HOW MUCH WATER CAN SPHAGNUM MOSS ABSORB?

What You Need	
Sphagnum moss	Large container
Weighing paper	Water
Balance	Clock or watch

Place a small sample of sphagnum moss on weighing paper and use a balance to determine its weight. Place the moss in a large container. Add water very slowly. Occasionally use your hand to stir up the mixture. Notice what happens to the water. The moss plant is filled with tiny tubes and spaces that allow the moss to absorb water and retain water like a sponge.

Continue adding water until the moss is saturated. Be sure to allow enough time—at least 15 minutes—for the moss to absorb the water. Carefully pour off any water that is not absorbed.

Determine the weight of the moss, and calculate how much water the moss absorbed by subtracting the weight of the moss from the weight of the moss and water. Divide this value by the weight of the moss to determine how many more times its own weight it absorbed. You should now be able to explain why sphagnum moss can be used as a surgical dressing and why it is added to potting soil. Experiment with ways of increasing the absorbency of the moss. Compare the absorbency of sphagnum moss to that of other materials such as cotton, paper towels, and diapers.

Doing More

- During World War I, doctors also used garlic to treat soldiers' wounds. Hospitals were supplied with the raw juice, which was then diluted with water. This solution was applied to swabs of sterilized sphagnum moss and then used to bandage wounds. This treatment, which prevented infections from developing in wounds, saved thousands of lives. Design a project that proves the effectiveness of this treatment. You will have to learn how to grow bacteria on culture dishes.

- Mosses are more susceptible than other plants to air pollution. The sudden and unexplained destruction of a large area of moss is an indication that the air may be polluted. Botanists believe that the gas sulfur dioxide is responsible. Mosses readily absorb this gas. As a result, they are unable to absorb all the carbon dioxide they need to conduct photosynthesis. Design a project that demonstrates how increasing sulfur dioxide concentrations can affect mosses. Determine if some types of mosses are more susceptible to air pollution than others.

SIMPLE VASCULAR PLANTS

As plants evolved more and more efficient vascular systems, they were able to grow taller. The first plants to develop efficient vascular systems had two types of conducting tissues, just as today's vascular plants do. Cells

Some American pioneers used a kind of simple vascular plant called horsetails to scrub their pots and pans.

that transport water up from the roots make up a tissue known as *xylem*. Cells that conduct sugars and other nutrients throughout a plant form a tissue called *phloem*. Together, xylem and phloem allow simple vascular plants—ferns, horsetails, and club mosses—to grow more than 25 m tall.

Unlike nonvascular plants and mosses, ferns, horsetails, and club mosses have a true vascular system. They also have specialized body parts, such as roots, stems, and leaves. The most common simple vascular plants are the ferns. Although they grow best in the tropics, ferns can be found throughout the world, including the Arctic region and deserts. Most ferns have an underground stem called a rhizome. The tough strands that form a rhizome provide a surface on which a variety of orchids can grow. The leaf of a fern is known as a frond. In the following project, you can explore the structure of ferns and attempt to grow them "from scratch."

EXAMINING AND GROWING FERNS

What You Need	
Ferns	Pint-sized jars with lids
Magnifying lens	Peat pellets
White paper	Water
Pencil eraser	

You can find ferns growing in most wooded areas, especially in the spring. You can also purchase them at a nursery, a greenhouse, or even a supermarket that has a garden section.

Ferns grow in many North American forests. These cinnamon ferns are common in New England.

Use a magnifying lens to examine a frond. Do you see any capsule-like structures on the underside? Each of these structures is known as a sporangium. Spores are produced within each sporangium. A *spore* is a reproductive cell that can develop into an adult plant. Carefully remove a sporangium from a frond and place it on a piece of white paper. Use an eraser to crush the sporangium and release the spores.

Use the pint-sized jars with lids and peat pellets to set up a "greenhouse." Place a peat pellet in each lid and cover it with water. After the pellet swells, sprinkle some of the spores on the peat and screw on the jar loosely. Be sure to keep the peat moist. How many different kinds of ferns can you grow in your "greenhouses"? Don't worry if very few spores develop into plants. Growing ferns is not easy. You may want to check the Internet for helpful hints and suggestions.

When a spore develops, the first thing you will see is a little green, heart-shaped body called a *gametophyte*. A gametophyte is the stage that alternates with a sporophyte in the life cycle of plants. If you have not already done so, check the library or search the Internet for information about the life cycle of plants. Prepare a report summarizing your observations and findings.

Doing More

- The earliest leaves to develop on a fern are called fiddleheads. The young fiddleheads of some ferns are edible. Search the Internet for recipes that use fiddleheads. Buy some fiddleheads at a reputable supermarket and try one of the recipes. Test it on your fam-

A quick look at the tightly coiled leaves of a young fern plant will help you understand how fiddleheads got their name.

ily and friends. Just be sure not to tell them what they are eating until after they have tasted it!

- Scientists have identified more than 12,000 species of ferns. Botanists use various criteria to determine if two ferns belong to the same species. For example, they extract proteins from the plants and compare them using a process called *electrophoresis*. This technique separates the proteins based on their size and electrical charge. If the proteins are stained with dye, scientists can compare banding patterns to see how closely related the fern plants are. Select two fern plants that look similar and carry out an electrophoresis project to see if they belong to the same species.

VASCULAR PLANTS WITH SEEDS

Despite their differences, all the plants you have read about so far have one feature in common—they do not produce seeds. A seed is a plant embryo surrounded by a protective coat. Like a human embryo, a plant embryo slowly develops into an adult. An embryo's protective coat prevents it from drying out. When conditions are too hot or too dry, a seed will remain inactive. When conditions are favorable, a seed will begin to sprout, or germinate. The seed will grow into a young plant known as a seedling. While it develops into a seedling, the embryo depends on nutrients stored in the seed.

There are two main groups of vascular plants that bear seeds—*gymnosperms* and *angiosperms*. Gymnosperms were the first vascular, seed-bearing plants to evolve. They appeared on Earth about 380 million years ago. Modern examples of gymnosperms include such conifers as pine, spruce, redwood, sequoia, cedar, cyprus, juniper,

Some gymnosperms grow up to 60 meters tall.
These pine trees are growing on a bluff
overlooking the ocean.

and fir trees. They produce seeds in cones. The needles of these trees are modified leaves. Because needles have a small surface area, they limit the amount of water that is lost to the air. This is an important characteristic for these trees because most grow in the north where some seasons are quite dry.

A conifer bears two kinds of cones. One is known as a female or *seed cone*. A female cone produces spores that develop into eggs. The second kind of cone is the male or *pollen cone*. A male cone is usually smaller and less woody than a female cone. Spores produced by a male cone develop into *pollen grains*. A pollen grain is a plant's male sex cell, so it contains a sperm. Conifers produce huge quantities of pollen grains. When pollen grains are released by a male cone, they are swept away by the wind. If they land on a female cone, the sperm can fuse with the eggs. A fertilized egg cell is called a *zygote*. The zygote becomes the embryo of a seed. When the female cone releases its seeds, they too may be dispersed by the wind.

The following project looks at one of the factors that causes a female cone to release its seeds—a forest fire. The heat of a forest fire can open up the woody scales on a female cone so that the seeds are released. At one time, people saw only the destructive nature of forest fires. As a result, every effort was made to put them out as quickly as possible. We now know that forest fires are a necessary part of a forest's development. Today, managed forest fires are deliberately started and carefully controlled.

SUBJECTING PINE CONES TO HEAT

Collect cones from a number of different conifers. Be sure to choose cones that are closed and contain seeds. Use a field guide to identify the type of tree each cone grew on. Keep in mind that conifers are not the only gymnosperms that produce cones. Large cones are also produced by a

What You Need	
Pine cones from different gymnosperms	Pint-sized jars with lids
Field guide to trees	Peat pellets
Stove	

group of gymnosperms known as the cycads. Cycads are not native to North America, but some people plant them for ornamental purposes. Still another group of cone-bearing gymnosperms are the gnetophytes.

To determine which of the cones you collected are the most heat-sensitive and which are the most heat-resistant, place them in an oven. Gradually increase the temperature until the first cone opens. Carefully remove that cone from the oven. When it has cooled, carefully remove any seeds you find inside the female cones. Continue to heat the remaining cones until the last one has opened. Record the temperature at which each cone opens.

Using the pint-sized jars with lids and peat pellets, set up a "greenhouse" for each seed. Place a peat pellet in each lid and cover it with water. After the pellet swells, place a single seed on the peat and loosely screw on the jar. Be sure to keep the peat moist. How many different kinds of gymnosperm seedlings can you grow? Carefully watch each plant as it grows. Record all your observations and findings in your notebook.

Doing More

- People use pine needles as mulch, as an ingredient in tea, and as a groundcover to inhibit the growth of other plants. Search the Internet for information on different ways to use pine needles. Carry out a project that demonstrates each of these uses.

- Taxol, a chemical substance found in the bark of the Pacific yew tree, is effective in treating some forms of cancer. However, environmentalists are concerned that these trees, which are already scarce, may become extinct if they are used to obtain taxol. Due to this controversy and because scientists found it difficult to

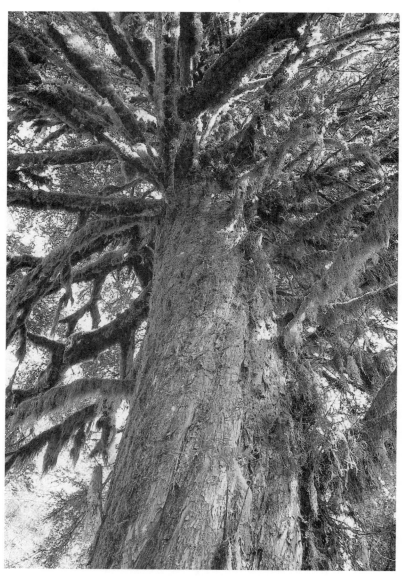

A drug prepared from the bark of this Pacific yew tree is used to treat ovarian cancer, breast cancer, and some types of lung cancer.

extract taxol from yew bark, they developed ways to make synthetic derivatives of taxol.

Check the Internet for information on the concerns raised by environmentalists and the latest developments in the search for effective derivatives. You could do a project that examines how these chemical compounds are prepared and how they work to kill cancer cells. Check with a local research center, university, or hospital to see if they use taxol derivatives in their cancer-treatment programs.

CHAPTER 3

FROM FLOWER TO SEED TO FLOWER

As you know, wind transports the pollen produced by gymnosperms. Some of the pollen settles on female cones, allowing sperm to fertilize egg cells. The transfer of pollen from the place where it is produced to the site where eggs are located is called *pollination*.

Because the wind is unpredictable, so is pollination in gymnosperms. If there is little wind one year, there may be no pollination. If there is too much wind, pollen grains may be blown too far and never land on female cones.

About 144 million years ago, a new group of plants—the angiosperms—evolved. Although some angiosperms rely on the wind or water for pollination, most use a much more reliable kind of pollination. Instead of producing cones, angiosperms produce flowers. Figure 1 shows the parts of a flower. The stamens, which consist of an anther and a filament, are the male reproductive structures of a

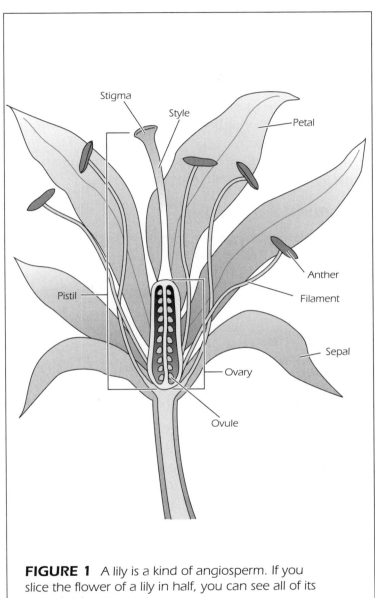

Stigma

Style

Petal

Anther

Filament

Pistil

Sepal

Ovary

Ovule

FIGURE 1 A lily is a kind of angiosperm. If you slice the flower of a lily in half, you can see all of its reproductive structures.

flower. The pistil, which consists of a *stigma*, a style, and an ovary, are the female reproductive structures of a flower.

The colors, shapes, and scents of flowers attract insects, birds, and other small animals. When these animals visit flowers, pollen sticks to their bodies. When they move to another flower, some of the pollen rubs off. As a result, these animal pollinators transfer pollen from one flowering plant to another.

In the following project, you can begin your study of angiosperms by taking a closer look at pollen.

EXAMINING POLLEN

What You Need	
Variety of flowering plants	Methylene blue stain
White paper	Medicine dropper
Camel's-hair brush	Coverslips
Glass microscope slides	Microscope
	Petroleum jelly

Place a flower, such as lily, on a piece of white paper. Using a clean camel's-hair brush, gently brush the *stamen*—the male reproductive structure—to gather pollen. Pollen is powdery and usually white or yellow.

Gently wipe an area of the brush covered with pollen over a microscope slide. Add a drop of methylene blue to the sample and apply a coverslip. Search for pollen grains under the low power objective of the microscope. Then, switch to the highest power objective and focus on a single pollen grain.

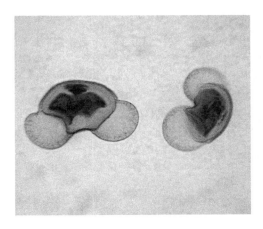

Compare the pollen grains you see under the microscope to these pine pollen grains, which have been stained and magnified 600 times.

Compare the pollen grains from several different kinds of flowers. Sketch each one in your notebook. Be sure to label each drawing so you know what kind of plants each pollen grain came from. How are the pollen grains similar? How are they different? Are they different shapes? Are the surfaces of all the pollen grains smooth, or do some have tiny spines or indentations? Do you think the differences you see play a role in pollination?

Some angiosperms, such as grasses, maples, poplars, and birches, rely on the wind for pollination. Compare the pollen of these plants to pollen produced by plants that have large showy flowers and are pollinated by animals.

You may also want to study the pollen floating in the air. Cover several glass microscope slides with a very thin film of petroleum jelly and expose them to the air for 24 hours. Place each slide in a different setting. Using a microscope, count the number of pollen grains that settle on each slide. How many different types do you observe on one slide? Which areas have the highest pollen count? If possible, expose slides to different weather conditions. How does weather affect the quantity of pollen in the air?

Doing More

- For pollination to be successful, pollen must land on a flower's stigma—the female reproductive structure. When a pollen grain sticks to a stigma, it develops a pollen tube that grows down to reach an egg cell deep inside the flower.

  To grow pollen tubes, place some pollen grains on a microscope slide. Add a drop of a 10% sucrose (table sugar) solution to the pollen and place a coverslip over the sample. Next, cover the slide with a wet paper towel to keep the sample moist. After 20 minutes, examine the slide under the high power objective of a microscope. You should be able to see the pollen tubes growing. Determine the length of ten pollen tubes. Repeat your observations and measurements at 10-minute intervals. Plot the average growth rate of the pollen tubes over time.

- Determine the best concentration of sugar for growing pollen tubes. Start with a 1% sugar solution. Compare the optimum sugar solution for each type of angiosperm that is available. Prepare a chart of your results.

- Some angiosperms are capable of self-pollination. In this case, pollen from a plant lands on a stigma of the same plant. The sweet pea is one example of an angiosperm that self-pollinates. Examine one of these flowers carefully, and then gently remove the brightly colored, leaf-shaped petals. Explain how the arrangement of petals on a sweet pea plant favors self-pollination rather than cross-pollination—pollination with another plant. Design and carry out a project that shows how cross-pollination could be favored in sweet pea plants. Extend your findings to other angiosperms that self-pollinate.

SEED DISPERSAL

If pollination is successful, a pollination tube will grow, a sperm will fertilize an egg cell, and a seed will develop. Many angiosperms produce seeds that are enclosed in fruits. After an animal eats the fruit, it often tosses out the seeds. In many cases, the seeds are deposited some distance away from the parent plant. This helps angiosperms spread out over a wider geographic area.

If a seed lands in a place with favorable weather and soil conditions, the seed will sprout. If conditions are not favorable, the seed will remain dormant. Some seeds can remain dormant for thousands of years. When scientists planted seeds they found trapped in the stones of ancient pyramids and other monuments, many of the seeds grew.

The angiosperms' pollination and seed dispersal techniques have helped them to become extremely successful on land. In the following project, you will examine how easily the wind spreads the seeds of some angiosperms. Your findings should make it clear why nearly 95 percent of the species of vascular plants alive today are angiosperms. These include the grasses, shrubs, vines, herbs, and many of the trees you encounter every day.

DISPERSING DANDELION SEEDS

What You Need	
Dandelions	Forceps
Magnifying lens	Measuring tape

If it's spring or summer, you should have no problem finding dandelions. No matter how conscientious someone has been in taking care of their lawn, dandelions always seem to appear among the grass. You can also find dandelions growing in fields.

Pick a dandelion that has gone to seed and examine it with a magnifying lens. Blow into the seed cluster, and notice how the feathery structures float away.

Pick another dandelion. Use forceps to gently remove one of the fine hairs on the seed cluster. Look for the seed attached to the end of the hair. Examine the opposite end of the hair with a magnifying lens. You should see an arrangement of fine tufts called a parachute.

Gently remove all the seeds from the dandelion. How many seeds grow in one dandelion head? Why does a dandelion produce so many seeds?

On a windless day, blow a dandelion seed cluster and follow it as it floats through the air. Measure the distance it travels. Repeat this procedure with nine more dandelion seed clusters. Calculate the average distance traveled by a seed cluster. Repeat this procedure on a windy day. On average, how much farther does a seed cluster travel?

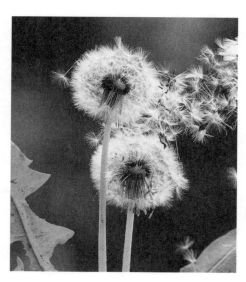

The feathery structures of a dandelion seed cluster can be carried away by even a gentle breeze.

Count the number of tufts in one parachute. Repeat this procedure with several parachutes. Determine the average number of tufts contained in a seed cluster. Then find the average number of tufts in seed cluster from a dandelion in a different lawn or field. If the average number of tufts is different, determine if this has an effect on the distance traveled by a dandelion seed.

If possible, extend your project to find out how the wind disperses other kinds of lightweight seeds. Possibilities include seeds produced by maple trees or tumbleweed plants. Do these seeds have any special features that enhance their ability to be transported by the wind? Contrast the structures of these seeds to those of seeds that are dispersed with the help of a fruit.

Doing More

Dandelions have a number of practical uses. For example, they are sometimes used in salads and wine. Dandelions are also used as an herbal medicine. In fact, the dandelion is one of the six most widely used medicinal herbs. Chinese healers sometimes use dandelions to treat diseases of the liver, dissolve kidney stones, relieve constipation, eliminate acne, purify the blood, and reduce acid indigestion. Check the Internet for information about the medicinal uses of dandelions. Design and carry out a project to test whether such claims are justified.

GERMINATION

If a seed lands in a good spot, it will start to grow and develop, or *germinate*. For a seed to germinate, it must be exposed to the proper temperature and amount of moisture. The following project examines the early stages of plant growth.

OBSERVING GERMINATION

<table>
<tr><td colspan="2" align="center">What You Need</td></tr>
<tr>
<td>
Bean seeds

Corn kernels

Small beakers or glass jars

Water

Razor blade or sharp knife

Stereomicroscope
</td>
<td>
Book on plants that includes a diagram of a seed

Lugol's iodine

Paper towels

Rubber bands

Glass microscope slides

Permanent marker

Metric ruler
</td>
</tr>
</table>

Soak a bean seed and a corn kernel in water overnight. The next day, cut each one in half, and observe them under a stereomicroscope. Compare the seeds, and write your observations in your notebook. Identify the various parts of each seed by referring to a book on plants. Determine if starch is present by covering the cut seeds with Lugol's iodine.

Place six corn kernels along one end of a folded paper towel. Roll up the paper towel and secure it with a rubber band. Stand the towel in a beaker or glass jar with some water in the bottom. Be sure that the end of the towel with the kernels is at the top, as shown in Figure 2. The paper towel will soak up the water and keep the kernels moist. Repeat this procedure with six bean seeds. Keep the corn and bean seeds moist for 3 days. Replace any water that evaporates from the glass jar.

Seed

Paper towel

Paper towel

Rubber band or string

Water

FIGURE 2 You can germinate seeds by wrapping them in a paper towel that is partially submerged in a beaker or jar of water. Be sure the seeds are not covered with water. If they are submerged, they will rot.

After 3 days, remove the corn and bean seeds from the paper towels. Observe the roots and shoots that have started to grow. Starting at the seed, use a permanent marker and ruler to make a small dot every 0.5 cm along the shoot and root. Rewrap the seeds in fresh paper towels, secure them with a rubber band, and place them in water.

After 3 more days have passed, remove the seeds from the paper towels. The first leaves that appear on a growing plant are called cotyledons. The cotyledons store food for the growing embryo. Measure the distance between the marks you made on the shoots and roots. In what region does growth occur in the shoot and in the root? Extend your project by examining the growth of other types of seeds. Note any similarities and differences you observe.

Doing More

- The seeds of some flowering plants contain substances similar to antibiotics. Design a project to detect these substances. You could begin by spreading bacteria onto nutrient agar and then placing cut seeds on it. After a few days, look at the samples. If you notice areas near the seeds that are free of micro-organisms, then a microbial agent is most likely present. Next, try to isolate the substance and identify its chemical nature. Could the seeds be an economical source for the antimicrobial chemical? How would you find out?

- Design a project to find out how the age of a seed, *acid precipitation*, or radiation affect the germination rate of seeds.

- Many scientists have expressed concern about human exposure to electromagnetic fields. Obtain information from your library and the Internet about studies related to this topic. To investigate how an electromagnetic field affects germination, you could magnetize a piece of metal by passing an electric current through a wire that is wrapped around the metal. You could also expose seeds to an electromagnetic field by placing them near an electric motor. The seeds should be exposed for at least a month before they are planted.

- If grass seeds are not watered daily, they will not germinate. Some scientists believe that the water dissolves a substance in the seed coat that inhibits the seed from germinating. Design a project to test for the presence of an inhibiting substance in the seed coat of grass. You may decide to soak seeds in water for 24 hours before you plant them.

    The liquid remaining from the first soaking should be used to soak additional seeds. If an inhibitory substance was dissolved in this water, how might this affect the germination of the second group of seeds? If the second group germinates as well as the first group, how might you extend this project to continue testing for an inhibitory substance?

    You can also use high-pressure liquid chromatography (HPLC) to perform a chemical analysis on the liquid that is used to soak the seeds. Use HPLC to isolate and purify a chemical compound from the liquid. Then test its possible inhibitory effect on seed germination.

FAST PLANTS

After almost 20 years of experimenting, Dr. Paul Williams at the University of Wisconsin developed a new variety of plants. These plants are known as Wisconsin Fast Plants, or simply as Fast Plants. As their name implies, these

Fast Plants germinate and produce flowers
in a very short period of time.

plants develop very quickly. Rather than taking the usual
6 months to grow from a seed to an adult plant with flowers, these plants blossom after just 5 weeks. Because Fast
Plants develop so quickly, they are ideal for classroom use.
Students can easily observe all aspects of plant growth and
development in a very short time period.

The scientific name of these Fast Plants is *Brassica
rapa*. Along with radishes, broccoli, cauliflower, and cab-
bages, Fast Plants are members of the mustard (crucifer)
family. These plants are easy to grow and develop quite
well when exposed to the fluorescent lights found in most
classrooms. They are hardy and easy to manage. In addition, they are available in a wide variety of traits. You can

obtain more information about Fast Plants at *http://fast plants.cals.wisc.edu/biofastplants.html*.

In the following project, you will experiment with Fast Plants. You can order Fast Plant seeds at the Web site listed above or by contacting Wisconsin Fast Plants, University of Wisconsin-Madison, Department of Plant Pathology, 1630 Linden Drive, Madison, WI 53706.

GROWING FAST PLANTS

What You Need	
Fast Plant seeds	Sharp knife or razor blade
Metric ruler	
Camel's-hair brush	Magnifying lens or stereomicroscope

Follow the instructions for planting the seeds. Observe their growth through an entire life cycle—from seed to seed. Note the day on which the following occur: seed germination, development of the cotyledons, appearance of the first leaves, development of the first flower buds, appearance of the first flower, and development of seeds by the adult plant.

Use a ruler to measure the height of six seedlings each day for a period of 18 days. Plot the results, placing the height of each seedling on the *y*-axis and the number of days on the *x*-axis. Calculate the seedlings' average growth rate per day.

Once flowers have fully developed, use a camel's-hair brush to transfer pollen from one plant to another. Observe how long it takes for seeds to start developing in their pods. Use a sharp knife or razor blade to carefully cut a pod lengthwise. This will expose the ovules within the pod. An *ovule* is the structure in which egg cells are produced.

When sperm from a pollen grain fertilizes an egg cell inside the ovule, an embryo will form and develop. Cut open an enlarging ovule every 2 days to observe the development of the embryo. Use a magnifying lens or stereomicroscope to observe the embryos. Draw diagrams to show the changes that an embryo undergoes.

Doing More

- The short life cycle of a Fast Plant makes it ideal for studying the effects of environmental factors on growth and development. Devise a project to investigate the impact that an environmental factor such as acid precipitation has on Fast Plants. You could also investigate how pesticides and herbicides affect plant growth and development.

- Another plant that has a short life cycle is a fern with the scientific name *Ceratopteris richardii*. This fern completes its life cycle within 10 to 12 days. These ferns come in two distinct sexes—males and *hermaphrodites*. A hermaphrodite produces both sperm and eggs. The sperm of *Ceratopteris richardii* are easily visible when the pollen is mixed with water and then observed under a microscope. These characteristics make *Ceratopteris richardii* an ideal organism for a project involving the life cycle of plants. Are the sperm from a male plant as effective in fertilizing egg cells as the sperm from a hermaphrodite? For more information on this plant, contact *http://www.carosci .com/tips/jan98/0198a.htm.*

CHAPTER 4

PLANT STRUCTURES

The evolution of a vascular system allowed plants to move onto land, increase in size, and develop highly specialized structures, such as roots, stems, and leaves. In most plants, the roots grow underground and help to anchor the plant in the soil. They absorb water and dissolved nutrients that are then transported by the vascular system to the rest of the plant. Tiny *root hairs* along the edges of a root increase the root's overall surface area and increase the amount of water and dissolved nutrients that a root can absorb.

TYPES OF ROOTS

Have you ever dug up a root and noticed that it had one large *taproot* with other smaller roots growing out of it? Not all plants have this type of root system. Some plants,

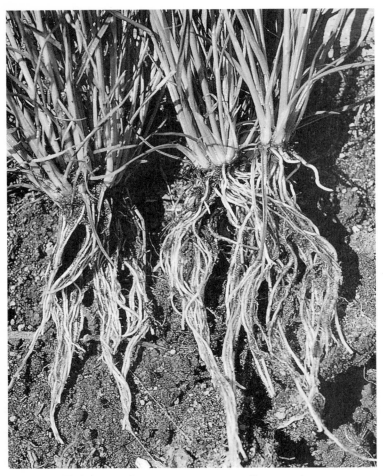

This grass has numerous small roots that branch to form a fibrous root system.

such as the grasses, have fibrous root systems made of many small roots that branch out to form a network.

Obviously, a plant with a large or extensive root system can absorb more water and nutrients than a plant with a small root system. The roots of most plants grow

The prop roots at the base of a corn plant provide additional support for the plant.

no more than 5 m long. But some plants, such as mesquite and cottonwood trees, have roots that extend more than 50 m in length. These plants live in dry areas and need long roots to reach underground water supplies. Regardless of their length, a plant's roots make up about one-third of its dry mass.

Some plants have *adventitious roots*—roots that grow aboveground. A corn plant has a kind of adventitious root called prop roots. As the name implies, prop roots help

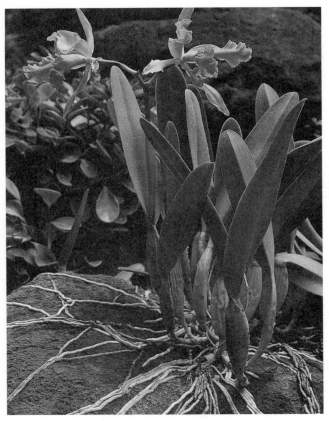

The air roots of an orchid plant obtain moisture and nutrients from the air.

the stem hold the corn plant upright. An orchid and some vines have a kind of adventitious root called air roots. These roots obtain water and dissolved nutrients from the air. This kind of root system makes it possible for vines to climb walls and trees.

Some types of roots store nutrients. That is why we eat them. The roots of carrots, sweet potatoes, radishes, turnips, beets, and the cassava plant store large quantities

Many people like the crisp, sharp taste of radish roots.

of carbohydrates or starches. Although the cassava is largely unknown in the United States, more than 500 million people throughout the world depend on it for nourishment. In Africa, the cassava root provides more than one-third of the calories consumed daily by most people.

GROWTH OF ROOTS

Roots grow in three ways—*mitosis*, elongation, and maturation. Mitosis is the mechanism by which one cell divides to produce two new cells. You will have the chance to examine mitosis in roots in Chapter 7. Cells produced by mitosis undergo a process called elongation to increase in length. When cells mature, they become specialized to carry out a particular function. For example, cells on the surface of a root develop root hairs to facilitate water and nutrient absorption. The following project will take a closer look at elongation.

MEASURING THE GROWTH OF ROOTS

What You Need	
Lima beans	Metric ruler
Small beakers or glass jars	Fine-tipped permanent marker
Water	9-cm × 13-cm glass plate
Paper towels	Tape
Rubber bands	Glass jar large enough to hold the glass plate
Facial tissue	

Soak several lima beans overnight in a jar of water. Germinate the seeds as shown in Figure 2 on page 47. Once the seeds have germinated, select five seedlings with straight roots that are 2 to 3 cm long. Carefully blot each root with facial tissue. Place each root alongside a metric ruler. Using a fine-tipped permanent marker, gently draw lines at 2-millimeter (mm) intervals along the length of each root. Start at the tip, as shown in Figure 3a.

Cover a 9-cm × 13-cm glass plate with a paper towel. Secure the paper towel in place with tape. Place the five seedlings on the paper towel and use a rubber band to secure them to the glass plate. Place the glass plate with the seedlings in a jar that contains about 3 cm of water. Be sure the seeds are not covered with water. Cover the jar with wet paper towels to create a moist chamber for the seedlings. See Figure 3b. After 2 days, remove the glass plate and measure the distance between the lines on each root. Prepare a graph that shows how each interval

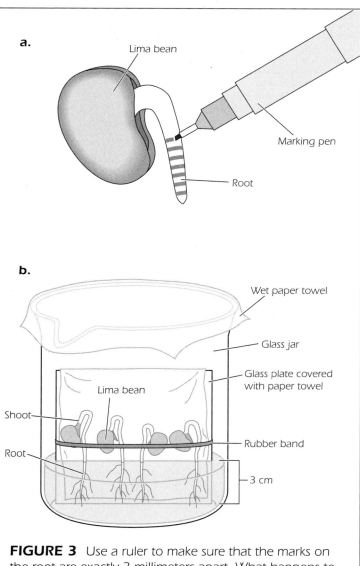

FIGURE 3 Use a ruler to make sure that the marks on the root are exactly 2 millimeters apart. What happens to these marks as the root grows? How can you tell where elongation has occurred?

marked off on the root grew over the 2 days. Where does most of the growth occur? This part of the root is known as the region of elongation. Extend your project by measuring root growth in other types of plants.

Doing More

- As roots grow, they help anchor soil in place. Thus, roots play a major role in preventing soil erosion. You can determine which part of a root binds the soil by gently pulling up a plant and examining the roots with a magnifying lens. Calculate how much soil a root system can bind in terms of its own weight. Determine which plants have roots that can bind the most soil.

   Extend your project by observing a wooded area where the trees have been cut down or a field that has been overgrazed by animals. What happens to the soil when all the plants in an area are removed? Design a project to determine how much soil gets eroded from such an area. You will have to contact a local environmental agency for information on how to determine whether an area has been overgrazed and suggestions for measuring soil erosion.

- Determine how much water a plant's root system can absorb in a given time period. You could do this by using toothpicks to suspend a plant in a jar of water and then measuring the amount of water lost from the jar over a period of time. Some of the water loss will be due to evaporation, so be sure to include a control in your experiment. The difference between the total water lost and the amount that evaporated represents the amount absorbed by the roots. Extend your project to compare the amount of water that the roots of various plants can absorb. Be sure to include examples of taproots and fibrous roots.

A LOOK AT STEMS

The main job of a stem is to transport materials between the roots and leaves. A stem also supports the plant's leaves and branches. Trees often have woody stems that can support the weight of many leaves and branches. The stems of smaller plants often remain soft and flexible, and are usually green. These stems are known as *herbaceous stems*.

The herbaceous stems of some plants are modified for special purposes. For example, the stems of strawberry plants grow horizontally along the ground. These stems form new plants, allowing the strawberry plant to spread. The stems of cactus plants store water. Some stems, like

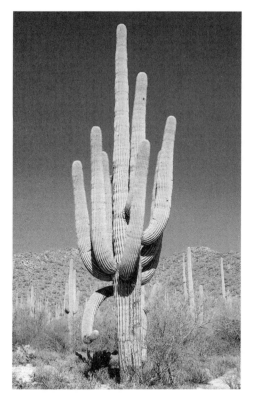

A single saguaro cactus can hold up to 1,000 kilograms of water.

those of a rose plant, grow thorns that protect the plant from animals. The swollen underground stems of a potato plant store starch, making potatoes a carbohydrate-rich source of nourishment.

Scientists do not know exactly how water, dissolved materials, and nutrients are transported through stems, but they do have some ideas. One explains how water is transported upward through the xylem, and the other accounts for the transport of nutrients to all parts of a plant through the phloem. Both ideas are based on the strong attraction that water molecules have for one another.

To observe this attractive force, use a medicine dropper to add water to the surface of a penny. Are you surprised by how many drops stick together before the water flows away? The water does not fall off the penny until the force of gravity exceeds the attractive force between the water molecules. Scientists had this idea in mind when they suggested the *cohesion-tension theory* to explain how water is able to move up a very tall tree.

The attraction between water molecules is called cohesion. This attractive force accounts for a continuous column of water that extends through the xylem—from the roots to the leaves. As water evaporates from the leaves, this column of water is subjected to great tension.

If you are having trouble envisioning this process, imagine that you are strongly attracted to someone. You and your friends run into that person at the mall. What would you do if that person left? You would probably want to leave too. If someone else is attracted to you, he or she might want to follow you if you leave the mall.

This behavior is similar that of water molecules. When one water molecule evaporates from the leaf, another one takes its place. Eventually, this second molecule will also leave through evaporation. In effect, the first water molecule pulls the second molecule along. This pull extends all the way to the bottom of the plant's water column. As water molecules are pulled up the column, more water is absorbed by the roots to replace the water molecules that have evaporated. Thus, water is transported in an unbroken column up through the xylem.

Transport through the phloem is more complicated. Because the xylem is made of dead cells, the water moving through these long channels meets no resistance. The phloem, however, is made of living cells. The interior of each cell is filled with materials. Nutrients that pass through these cells must "push aside" the materials. As a result, transporting nutrients through the phloem is more difficult than transporting water through the phloem.

Transport through the phloem is explained by the *pressure-flow hypothesis.** It states that the pressure exerted by water molecules as they move through the xylem pushes sugars and other nutrients through the phloem. This pressure can push nutrients through the phloem in different directions at different times. The following project will explore how water is transported through plant stems. Do you think this movement helps to carry materials through the phloem?

EXAMINING TRANSPORT THROUGH THE STEMS

Cut a celery stalk into a 15-cm length. Add red food coloring to the pitcher of water until the water is dark red. Add colored water to the glass until it is about three-

---

* Notice that this idea is a hypothesis, not a theory. What is the difference between a hypothesis and a theory? Do you think scientists are less certain about the mechanism by which materials are transported through the phloem than the method used to transport water through the xylem? Why?

quarters full. Place the celery stalk in the glass, and place it in direct sunlight. Every 30 minutes, measure how high the colored water has risen in the celery stalk. Calculate the rate at which the water is transported in terms of distance traveled per minute.

Test how temperature affects water transport by repeating the procedure with the glass in a refrigerator. Next, try placing the celery stalk in warm water of varying degrees. Do you notice any differences? Why must you be sure to use the same length of celery stalk and the same volume of water in every case?

Use a fan to check how the rate of evaporation affects the rate of water transport. What other factors can you test to see how they affect the rate of water transport?

Extend your project by comparing the rate of water transport in various plants. Plants you can test include carnations, rhubarb, or any other long-stemmed angiosperm. If you use a carnation, experiment with ways to change the color of the flower. Carefully slice the stem in half lengthwise with a razor blade. Spread the cut stem apart, so you can immerse each half in a different color of food coloring. See Figure 4. What different color combinations can you produce?

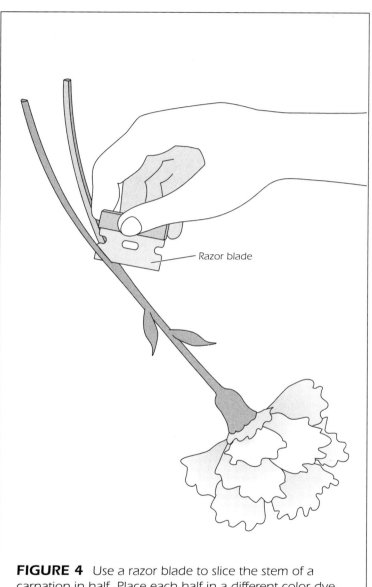

Razor blade

FIGURE 4 Use a razor blade to slice the stem of a carnation in half. Place each half in a different color dye and watch what happens.

Doing More

- As a result of evaporation, more than 90 percent of the water that travels through the xylem is lost through the leaves. Evaporation of water from leaves is known as *transpiration*. Transpiration plays a role in the cohesion-tension theory. But water lost by transpiration is never used by the plant for any of its functions. Design and carry out a project that demonstrates how much of the water that passes through the xylem is eventually lost through the leaves. Check the Internet for information on factors that control transpiration.

- The transport of nutrients through the phloem involves a process known as *active transport*. As a result of active transport, materials are moved against a concentration gradient. In other words, rather than moving as they naturally would from an area of high concentration to an area of lower concentration, materials move in the opposite direction. According to the pressure-flow hypothesis, a molecule binds to a nutrient and transports it against the gradient. The system is powered by an enzyme—a molecule that speeds up the rate of a chemical reaction—called ATPase.

  Check the Internet for details on how the pressure-flow hypothesis operates. You will need to know how sources and sinks in plants function during transport through the phloem. Develop a computer model that demonstrates the operating basis of the pressure-flow hypothesis. Your model should take into account what happens when nutrient and water concentrations change.

WHY PLANTS HAVE LEAVES

When someone says the word "leaf," you probably think of maple or oak leaves, or maybe you envision the leaves of a geranium or a marigold. All these leaves are broad

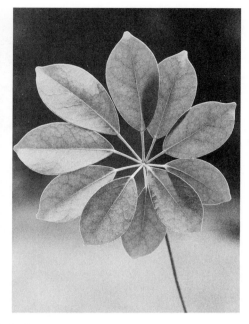

The leaf of a white oak (left) is called a simple leaf because it has only one blade, which is broad and flat. Other plants have a compound leaf (right) in which the leaf blade is divided into a number of distinct leaflets.

and flat. Each one has a wide surface area to capture the sunlight needed for photosynthesis.

Some plants have leaves that look quite different. Cactuses have spiny leaves that protect the plant from predators and avoid too much exposure to sunlight. The leaves of other plants are shaped like long tubes and trap insects that land on them. Even broad, flat leaves can vary. Some are round, while others are heart-shaped. Some consist of a single blade, while others are divided into smaller parts called leaflets. The following project will introduce you to the variety among leaves.

PRESSING LEAVES

What You Need	
Variety of leaves	Double-sided tape
Small plastic bags	White paper
Telephone book	Field guides
Several large books	

Begin by collecting leaves from a variety of plants in your area. Keep them in a plastic bag until you get home. To preserve your leaf samples, place each one between the pages of a telephone book, close the telephone book, and place six or seven heavy books on top of it. After 1 or 2 weeks, the leaves will be flat and dry.

Using a narrow strip of double-sided tape, attach each leaf to a sheet of white paper. Label each leaf with the common and scientific names of the plant it came from. Check both your school and local library for field guides. If possible, collect additional information about each specimen in your collection.

You can extend this project by comparing the leaves taken from different locations on a tree. For example, are the leaves on the north side of a tree different from those on the south side? Are leaves close to the trunk different from those at the tip of a branch?

To expand your collection, use e-mail to contact students who live in other parts of the United States or in other countries. Ask them to send you leaves from interesting plants that do not grow where you live. The students should pack the leaves in way that will prevent them from drying out. See how many different specimens you can add to your collection.

Doing More

Most people who press flowers and leaves to use in artwork rely on a plant press. Check the library and the Internet for information about plant presses. Design and build your own plant press and use it to prepare a collection of roots, stems, and leaves.

PHOTOSYNTHESIS

Powered by energy from sunlight, plants use two simple chemicals—carbon dioxide and water—to manufacture sugar and oxygen. This process is called photosynthesis. Photosynthesis is responsible for producing the *organic compounds* that serve as the food supply for almost every organism on Earth. Without photosynthesis, life on Earth would consist of nothing more than a few kinds of bacteria that use a different process to manufacture the nutrients they need to survive.

In addition to light energy, photosynthetic organisms require two additional materials—enzymes to speed up chemical reactions and *chlorophyll*, a green pigment that absorbs the light energy used to drive photosynthesis. Although chlorophyll is the main pigment required for photosynthesis, several other pigments are also involved. These include red, yellow, and orange pigments.

PLANT PIGMENTS

Because chlorophyll is the most abundant pigment in plants, it masks all the others. That is why most plants appear green to us. When the temperature falls in autumn, the chlorophyll in leaves begins to break down and the other pigments become visible, creating the beautiful fall foliage. The following project will show you how to make a plant's red, yellow, and orange pigments show up at any time of the year.

SEPARATING PLANT PIGMENTS

What You Need	
Spinach leaves	Acetone
Glass beaker	Petroleum ether
Ethanol	Graduated cylinder
Hot plate	Large test tube
Watch glass	Wooden cork to fit test tube
Toothpick	
Chromatography strip	Large paperclip
Metric ruler	Paper towels

Caution: Because you will be working with flammable liquids, be sure to carry out this project under adult supervision.

Break a few leaves of spinach into small pieces. Place the pieces in a beaker and cover them with ethanol. To remove pigments from the plant, boil the leaf pieces until the solution turns dark green. Do not allow all the ethanol to evaporate. Carefully add more as needed. *Caution: Ethanol is flammable, so be careful when heating the leaves.*

When the solution is dark green, allow the beaker to cool. Cover the beaker with a watch glass so the ethanol does not evaporate. If you plan to keep the pigment extract for any length of time, cover the beaker tightly and store it in a refrigerator. Plant pigments break down rapidly upon exposure to light, heat, and oxygen.

Using a toothpick, apply a thin line of pigment extract 2 cm from the end of the chromatography strip. (You can substitute a piece of filter paper that is 15 cm long and 1.5 cm wide.) After the extract has dried, apply another layer of extract directly on top of the first one. Repeat this step at least once more after the second layer has dried. By applying extract several times, you will increase your chances of seeing all the different pigments in spinach leaves. The finer and darker the line, the better the pigment separation will be.

Prepare a mixture of 5 parts acetone to 95 parts petroleum ether. Pour 10 milliliters (mL) of this solvent into a large test tube. Slowly lower the chromatography strip into the test tube, making sure that the pigment line remains above the level of the liquid in the test tube. Use a wooden cork and paperclip to keep the paper from touching the sides of the test tube. See Figure 5. Position the test tube so that it remains upright.

Observe the strip as the liquid moves up the paper. Notice what happens to the dark green pigment line. When the liquid is close to the top of the strip, carefully remove it from the test tube and let it dry on a piece of paper towel. The different pigments in the spinach leaves should become visible as the strip dries.

Wooden cork

Test tube

Paper clip

Chromotography strip

Pigment extract

Acetone/ petroleum ether solvent

FIGURE 5 Notice that the pigment line is above the solvent level in the test tube. The paper strip should be removed when the leading edge of the solvent approaches the top of the paper.

At the upper end of the strip, look for the yellow bands of pigment. These are known as carotenes and xanthophylls. Below these, you should see the blue-green pigment chlorophyll a. Toward the bottom of the strip, you should see a yellow-green pigment representing chlorophyll b. If the pigments did not separate as well as you would like, try adjusting the proportions of acetone and petroleum ether. For example, you might want to mix 8 parts acetone with 92 parts petroleum ether.

Test different types of leaves. You can extract the pigments from the leaves of both flowering and non-flowering plants. Do different plants contain different pigments? Compare the pigments you can separate from the leaves of maple, poplar, and oak trees over a 2-week period during the fall.

Next, try comparing the chromatography bands from plants that grow under different conditions. For example, do plants that grow in a dense forest where there is little light have the same pigments as plants that grow best in direct sunlight?

Doing More

- Observing plant pigments is a qualitative analysis. To obtain some quantitative data, keep track of the number of pigments that are green, red, and yellow or measure the distances traveled by the pigments and the liquid solvent. The ratio of these two distances is known as R_f value. Figure 6 explains how to calculate an R_f value.

  Separate the pigments from different plants and calculate the R_f value for each one. Which pigments have the largest R_f values? The smallest R_f values? If separated under the same conditions, each pigment,

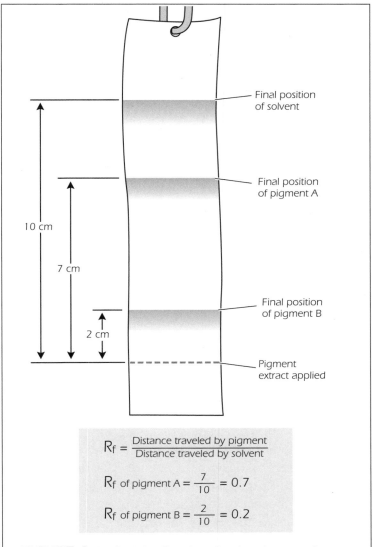

$$R_f = \frac{\text{Distance traveled by pigment}}{\text{Distance traveled by solvent}}$$

$$R_f \text{ of pigment A} = \frac{7}{10} = 0.7$$

$$R_f \text{ of pigment B} = \frac{2}{10} = 0.2$$

FIGURE 6 To find the R_f values for the pigments in spinach leaves, divide the distance each pigment travels by the distance the solvent travels. Be sure to measure from the leading edge of each pigment.

such as chlorophyll a, should have a set R_f value. Do your results support this?

- Ask your science teacher if your school has the equipment and materials needed to carry out thin-layer and column chromatography. If so, use these techniques to separate the pigments in a plant. How do these results compare to those you obtained with paper chromatography?

- During the mid-1970s, a technique known as high pressure liquid chromatography (HPLC) was developed and refined. With the help of automation and computers, HPLC quickly became a popular technique for isolating substances from a mixture.

  Today, scientists also use a technique known as gas chromatography. This process is useful for separating a mixture that contains hundreds of substances. For example, gas chromatography has been used to isolate and identify the various chemical compounds in wine. Some of these substances are present in only a few parts per trillion. Include information about both HPLC and gas chromatography as part of your project.

- Chlorophyll absorbs wavelengths of light associated with all colors except green. Because chlorophyll reflects green light, it looks green to us. The absorption pattern of a pigment is known as its absorption spectrum. A spectrophotometer measures the quantity of light that is absorbed by a substance. If a spectrophotometer is available, estimate the chlorophyll content of one or more plants.

  Begin by washing and blotting dry about 5 grams (g) of spinach leaves. Use a razor blade to chop the leaves into small pieces. Place the pieces in a mortar containing 10 mL of cold methanol, a pinch of magnesium carbonate, and a pinch of sand. Grind the leaves until they are thoroughly pulverized.

Filter the pulverized leaves and collect the filtrate—the liquid that passes through the filter paper. Use a vacuum filter if possible. Wash out the mortar with another 10 mL of cold methanol and filter the liquid. The filtrate should have a dark green color. Add more cold methanol so that the final volume of filtrate is 25 mL. Use a spectrophotometer to take readings at 650 nanometers (nm) and 665 nm. Be sure to take readings at each of these values using methanol that does not contain any pigment. The chlorophyll content of spinach leaves can be calculated from the following formulas.

$$\text{chlorophyll a} = 16.5 \times \begin{array}{c}\text{absorbance} \\ \text{value at} \\ 665 \text{ nm}\end{array} - 8.3 \times \begin{array}{c}\text{absorbance} \\ \text{value at} \\ 650 \text{ nm}\end{array}$$

$$\text{chlorophyll b} = 33.8 \times \begin{array}{c}\text{absorbance} \\ \text{value at} \\ 650 \text{ nm}\end{array} - 12.5 \times \begin{array}{c}\text{absorbance} \\ \text{value at} \\ 665 \text{ nm}\end{array}$$

The chlorophyll content will be expressed in the units milligrams/liter (mg/L). Use this same procedure to extract the chlorophyll from a variety of other plants and to carry out absorbance readings. How do their chlorophyll contents compare to those of spinach?

CHLOROPLASTS

If you look at a plant's cells under a microscope, you can see that they contain tiny structures called *chloroplasts*. The number and shape of chloroplasts varies from plant to plant. In some plants, each cell contains more than fifty

The cells of an Elodea plant contain many chloroplasts.

chloroplasts. The cells of other plants contain fewer than five chloroplasts. Chloroplasts may be spherical, football-shaped, or star-shaped.

Chloroplasts are the site of photosynthesis. Inside, energy from the sun's rays is converted into the chemical energy in organic compounds. In the following project, you will observe chloroplasts in two very different organisms.

OBSERVING CHLOROPLASTS

What You Need	
Glass microscope slides	Elodea leaf
Coverslips	*Euglena*
Medicine dropper	Microscope

Using the glass microscope slides, coverslips, and a medicine dropper, prepare wet mounts of an Elodea leaf and *Euglena*. Elodea plants are common in freshwater ponds. You may also purchase Elodea at an aquarium supply store or pet shop. A leaf from this plant is only two cells thick. *Euglena* is neither a plant nor an animal. It belongs to a group of microscopic creatures called protoctists. It can be found in ponds, puddles, birdbaths, ditches, and aquariums. You can also purchase it from a science supply company. *Euglena* can move around using its powerful flagellum and often ingests smaller organisms. However, *Euglena* also contains chloroplasts and can carry out photosynthesis.

Examine the Elodea first. Use the low power objective to focus on the top layer of cells. Then switch to the

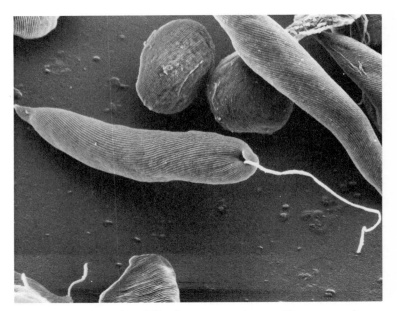

This photograph of *Euglena* was taken with a scanning electron microscope and magnified 2,000 times. Notice the long flagellum that each individual uses to move.

highest power objective. Slowly turn the fine adjustment knob until you see the chloroplasts, which are located along the edges of the cell. Observe their movement. Because the cell's *cytoplasm* is constantly in motion, the chloroplasts move around the periphery of the cell.

Next, take a look at the *Euglena* sample. Can you see the chloroplasts inside?

Doing More

- Design a project that creates the optimal conditions for *Euglena* to function like a plant cell rather than an animal cell. Expose it to different intensities and wavelengths of light and count the average number of chloroplasts that form in a *Euglena* under these different conditions.

  Develop a way of measuring the photosynthetic activity of the chloroplasts you see. Can you think of a way to measure the volume of oxygen gas that is given off as a result of photosynthesis?

  Researchers have recently reported that *Euglena* is capable of synthesizing beta-carotene, vitamin C, and vitamin E. Design a project that investigates whether *Euglena* can also synthesize other vitamins.

- Some researchers believe that chloroplasts were once independent, simple unicellular organisms. These organisms were captured by more complex unicellular organisms where they proceeded to live and divide. The process by which cells take up large particles, such as chloroplasts, is known as endocytosis.

  Scientists have found that isolated chloroplasts can be taken up by fibroblast cells in mice and gut cells in sea slugs. Can other kinds of cells be induced to take up chloroplasts? Check the Internet for other information that supports this endosymbiotic hypothesis.

PHOTOSYNTHESIS: THE DARK SIDE

Photosynthesis is powered by energy from sunlight. Chloroplasts and chlorophyll are involved in the part of photosynthesis known as the light reaction. During the other part of photosynthesis, known as the dark reaction, carbon dioxide changes into sugar. The carbon dioxide required for the dark reaction is a product of the light reaction. In turn, the dark reaction makes products that keep the light reaction operating. So the light and dark reactions of photosynthesis are mutually dependent. This means that when carbon dioxide is in short supply, the rate of photosynthesis drops. The following project investigates the dark reaction of photosynthesis.

OBSERVING THE DARK REACTION

What You Need	
Very wide-mouthed jar (battery jar is suitable)	Large test tube
	Wooden splint
Water	Matches
Elodea	
	Straw
Funnel	Stopwatch
Glass marking pen	Bottle of seltzer water
Metric ruler	

Fill the jar with water. Allow the water to stand overnight at room temperature so that any unwanted gases in the water can escape. Place several healthy strands of an Elodea plant in the jar. Cover the plants with a funnel. The tip of the funnel should be below the level of the water. Make sure that the cut ends of the stems point upward toward the neck of the funnel.

Use the glass marking pen to draw a line around the large test tube 3 cm from the bottom. Fill the test tube with water from the jar. Place your thumb over the top of the test tube, flip it upside down, and lower it over the stem of the funnel. Do not remove your thumb until the last possible moment. The test tube should rest loosely against the stem of the funnel as shown in Figure 7.

Carefully move the jar so that it is exposed to either natural or artificial light. (A light designed for growing houseplants provides wavelengths that are most effective for stimulating photosynthesis.)

If you see bubbles of oxygen gas, you will know that the plant is carrying out photosynthesis. These bubbles will pass through the tip of the funnel, collect in the test tube, and displace the water. The more oxygen gas that collects in a given time period, the higher the rate of photosynthesis. Determine the length of time required to collect enough oxygen to displace the water up to the 3-cm line on the test tube.

You can perform a simple test to prove that the gas collected in the test tube is oxygen. Allow the gas to displace all the water in the test tube. Carefully remove the test tube and place your finger over the opening. Hold one end of a wooden splint in your other hand and ask a friend to light the other end of the splint with a match. Then blow it out. Remove your finger from the opening and quickly insert the glowing splint into the test tube. Notice what happens to the splint. Because oxygen supports combustion, the splint begins to burn again.

Repeat the experiment, but first use a straw to blow exhaled air into the water for 1 minute. The carbon dioxide in the exhaled air will dissolve in the water. Use the

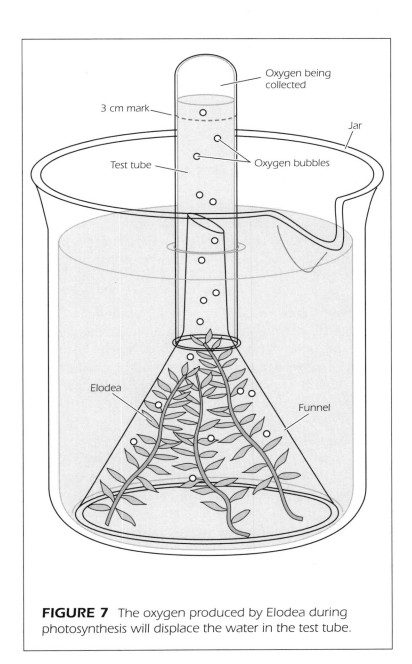

FIGURE 7 The oxygen produced by Elodea during photosynthesis will displace the water in the test tube.

stopwatch to measure how long it takes to produce enough oxygen gas to reach 3 cm of the test tube. Next, exhale into the water for longer periods of time. Does it take more or less time to produce enough oxygen gas to reach 3 cm of the test tube? Make a graph that plots the results you obtain for each procedure.

Replace the tap water with seltzer water. Seltzer water contains so much carbon dioxide under pressure that bubbles of the gas are given off when the bottle is opened. How does water with such a high concentration of carbon dioxide affect the rate of photosynthesis? Be sure to set up a control so you can calculate how much of the gas you collect is carbon dioxide from the seltzer water.

Doing More

- If you would like to use water containing a known quantity of carbon dioxide, add various amounts of baking soda to carbonate distilled water. Using distilled water will ensure that no other chemicals are present in the solution. Baking soda contains a chemical compound called sodium hydrogen carbonate, $NaHCO_3$. This compound reacts in water to produce carbon dioxide gas.

  Begin with a 0.25% solution of NaHCO3. Then repeat the experiment with successively greater concentrations of $NaHCO_3$. You might want to compare 0.50%, 0.75%, 1.0%, 2.0%, and 3.0% solutions. Plot the results you obtain. Next, see what happens to the rate of photosynthesis in the total absence of carbon dioxide. Ask a chemistry teacher to help you design a method for removing all the carbon dioxide from a solution.

  You can use a manometer to measure the quantity of oxygen gas produced in this experiment. Record the original and final positions of the syringe plunger. The difference between the two readings represents the volume of oxygen gas that caused the fluid to move in the tube. You can use a manometer to test several variables. Try different temperatures, light intensities, and wavelengths of light to see how they affect the rate of photosynthesis. Determine the light intensity and temperature beyond which no further increase is possible.

CHAPTER 6

HORMONES

All animals, including humans, respond to *stimuli*. A stimulus is anything that causes a reaction or a response. Stimuli can come from either an individual's environment or its own body. For example, when you see a ball hurtling toward your head (stimulus), you raise your hand (response), so that it will not hit you in the face. You might be surprised to hear that plants respond to stimuli too.

Plants respond to several different kinds of stimuli, including light, temperature, gravity, and water. Their response varies, depending on the nature of the stimulus. Plants that grow in a warmer environment may grow taller or produce larger fruit than plants that grow in a cooler environment.

In some cases, a plant may even move in response to a stimulus. For example, the leaves of a plant may turn

This tomato plant is displaying phototropism—it is moving toward the light.

toward a light source. Plant movement is known as *tropism*. When a plant moves toward a stimulus, the response is said to be a positive tropism. When a plant moves away from a stimulus, it is said to be a negative tropism. Tropisms can be caused by four different kinds of stimuli—light, direct contact with an object, gravity, and chemicals.

In animals, nerve cells or a nervous system are responsible for the response to most stimuli. Plants do not have nerve cells or a nervous system, but they do have chemical messengers called *hormones*. Hormones determine a plant's ability to respond to its environment. Hormones, which are also present in animals, are effective in very low concentrations.

Because plant hormones can stimulate or inhibit plant growth, they are also known as plant regulators. Botanists have been able to extract and study hormones from a variety of plants. As a result, they can now synthesize these hormones in the laboratory. Plant hormones can be grouped into five major categories: auxins, gibberellins, cytokinins, ethylene, and abscisic acid. Researchers are still looking for a group of hormones called florigens, which control the development of flowers. Here's your chance to carry out a project with plant hormones.

A LOOK AT AUXINS

In 1880, Charles Darwin, a pioneer in the study of evolution, wrote a book in which he described the effects of light on the movement of a species of grass. Darwin

Charles Darwin, best known for suggesting that species evolve over time, also investigated a number of other science areas, including botany.

demonstrated that the tip of the plant produces a substance that signals it to bend toward the light. In 1926, a botanist named F. W. Went isolated this substance from the tips of oats. He named the substance auxin, which means "to grow" in Greek. Auxins are plant hormones that can stimulate cell elongation, lateral root development, or growth of flower parts. They can also suppress growth of lateral buds, delay fruit ripening, and inhibit the aging of leaves.

In recent years, scientists have synthesized several compounds that are similar to auxins. These include 2,4-dichlorophenoxyacetic acid (2,4-D), which is used as a weedkiller, and naphthalene acetic acid (NAA). When NAA is sprayed on olive and apple trees, some of the immature fruits drop off the trees, so the remaining ones can grow larger than normal. Later, the remaining fruit is sprayed directly with NAA to prevent them from dropping. In the following project, you will examine one of the many effects auxins have on plants.

STIMULATING PLANT GROWTH

What You Need	
Potting soil	Single-edged razor
Fifteen small plant containers	Agar
	A small shallow tray
Oat seeds	Metric ruler

Add moist potting soil to each of the fifteen containers and plant one seed in each one. Keep the containers in the dark until the seedlings are at least 2 cm high. Select two healthy seedlings and use a single-edged razor to remove the top 2 to 3 mm of each plant's *coleoptile*—the pale sheath that surrounds the shoot of the seedling. See Figure 8a. Replace the tip on one seedling, and leave the stump of the other coleoptile uncovered. Place both seedlings back in the dark. After a minimum of 6 hours, remove the seedlings and compare the length of both coleoptiles. Explain the difference in their lengths.

Prepare some agar according to the directions on the container. Carefully pour hot agar into the tray until it is about 1 cm thick. Allow the agar to cool. Carefully cut the tips off five oat coleoptiles and place four of them on the agar. Leave the tips on the agar for 1, 2, 3, and 4 hours respectively. Then cut the agar into small blocks so that each block is exposed to only one of the tips. Discard the tips and place the agar blocks on the coleoptile stumps. As a control, place an agar block that was not exposed to a tip on the fifth coleoptile stump.

Place each seedling in the dark for at least 6 hours. Be sure that all the blocks are in contact with the stumps for the same amount of time. Why do you think this is important? Remove the seedlings and measure the length of each coleoptile. Explain any differences in their lengths.

Repeat the procedure, but this time cut the tips off eight oat coleoptiles. Place the tips on a new agar block. Leave two tips on the block for 1 hour, another two for 2 hours, two more for 3 hours, and the last two for 4 hours. After the agar has been in contact with the coleoptile tips for the appropriate amount of time, cut the agar into blocks, and place each block on one side of a stump, as shown in Figure 8b. Use an untreated agar block as a control. Keep the seedlings in the dark, again making sure that all the blocks remain in contact with their coleoptile stumps for the same amount of time. Remove the

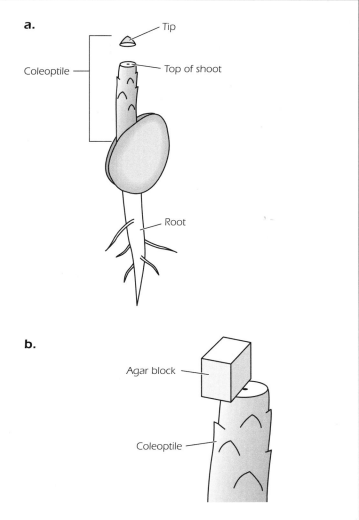

a.

Tip

Coleoptile

Top of shoot

Root

b.

Agar block

Coleoptile

FIGURE 8 Use a single-edged razor to remove the top of the coleoptile. Carefully place the agar block on one side of the coleoptile stump. Auxin stimulates plant cells to grow longer. Cells that grow longer will cause that side of the seedling to bend in the opposite direction.

seedlings and observe how they have grown. Explain your observations.

Can you see any connection between your results and the positive phototropism that occurs in response to a light source coming from one side of the plant. Do library research or an Internet search to find out how light affects the distribution of auxins in the stem of a plant.

Repeat the procedure using corn seedlings in place of oat seedlings. A corn seedling has a larger coleoptile than an oat seedling. Would you expect the results to be the same? Do your results confirm or reject your hypothesis?

Doing More

- You can also explore the effect of auxins on root development. Obtain a commercial auxin compound such as Rootone and follow the directions to induce root formation in various types of cuttings. You can use geranium, coleus, lilac, or forsythia plants. Be sure to include a control in each case. Prepare a table summarizing your results. You may also want to investigate how auxins affect the germination of seeds. The project on pages 46–48 includes instructions for germinating seeds. Vary the auxin concentration of the solution used to water the germinating seeds.

- Have you ever wondered why bananas, navel oranges, and certain kinds of grapes are seedless? With the help of auxins, these seedless fruits are the result of a process called parthenocarpy. Search the Internet to find out more about parthenocarpy. You can find a report that describes how seedless summer squash was developed at *http://www.nysaes.cornell.edu/pubs/press /1998/whitaker.html*. Try to design a project in which you use parthenocarpy to develop a new kind of seedless fruit.

GIBBERELLINS PROMOTE GROWTH

In the 1920s, Japanese scientists discovered that rice plants infected by the *Gibberella* fungus grow abnormally tall. Scientists isolated the disease-causing substance from the fungus and named it gibberellin. They later discovered that healthy plants also produce gibberellins.

Gibberellin is a plant hormone that promotes growth. For example, grapes grow larger when they are sprayed with gibberellins. All California raisins come from grapes that have been sprayed with this hormone. Gibberellins also promote uniform germination of seeds, and they are used to increase the alcohol content of beer by boosting the amount of sugar produced during the malting process.

Although gibberellin is found in all parts of a plant, the highest concentrations are found in seeds that have not yet started to germinate. To date, more than ninety gibberellins have been isolated from mosses, ferns, gymnosperms, and angiosperms. To learn more about gibberellins, try the following project.

Can you tell which plant was treated with gibberellin?

GROWING TALLER PLANTS

What You Need	
Two flower pots	Metric ruler
Potting soil	Cotton swabs
Marking pen	Water
Labeling tape	Gibberellic acid solution
Bean seeds	

Fill two flower pots with potting soil. Be sure that both pots are filled to the same level. Label one pot "A" and the other "B." Plant five bean seeds in each pot, spacing them evenly around the edge. Be sure that each seed is placed at least 1 cm below the soil surface. Allow the seeds to germinate in the dark and grow until they are at least 3 cm tall.

Measure the height of each seedling. Average the height for the five seedlings in each pot and record these values in a data table in your notebook. For the next 10 days, measure the height of each seedling and calculate the average height of the seedlings in each pot.

On the tenth day, wet a cotton swab with gibberellic acid solution, which sells under the brand names Gibrel or Wonder-brel and is available at most garden centers. Gently rub the swab over the leaves and shoot tips of each seedling in pot A. *Caution: Be careful when working with gibberellic acid. It is flammable and can irritate your eyes and skin. If you get any gibberellic acid on your skin, wash it off immediately.*

Wet a second cotton swab with water and rub it on the seedlings in pot B. Place both pots in direct sunlight. Be sure that the seedlings in both pots receive the same amount of light, water, and air circulation. Why?

For the next 10 days, measure the height of each seedling and calculate the average height of seedlings in each pot. Record the data in your table. On the tenth day, calculate the percentage increase in the average height of the two groups of seedlings. Plot your data on a graph, placing number of days on the *x*-axis and the average height of the plants on the *y*-axis. Did the seedlings treated with gibberellic acid show the same percentage increase each day during the course of your project?

Next, test the effect of gibberellins on the germination and development rate of seeds. Soak some bean seeds in a gibberellic acid solution overnight. Compare their germination and growth to seeds that have been soaked overnight in water. You can also test the effect of gibberellins on flower development. Spray a gibberellic acid solution on a geranium plant that has no flowers. Be sure to include a control.

Doing More

- Certain commercial products contain chemicals that stunt plant growth by blocking the synthesis of gibberellins. Examples include Phosphon D, Cycocel, and Amo-1618. Carry out a project to find out which of these products is most effective in inhibiting the growth of plants. Include information on how these chemicals work.

- The synthesis of a gibberellin by a plant involves a series of chemical reactions, or biochemical pathway, that begins with a substance called acetyl coenzyme-A.

This compound is involved in other biochemical pathways, including one that operates during respiration.

Check the Internet for information on biochemical pathways involving acetyl coenzyme-A. Carry out a project that summarizes the importance of this compound, especially in the synthesis of gibberellins. You may want to use a computer drawing program to construct molecular models that illustrate the major steps in the synthesis of gibberellins.

CYTOKININS PROMOTE CELL DIVISION

Cytokinin is a plant hormone that stimulates cell division. It was first discovered when scientists observed that coconut milk stimulates the division of plant cells. The researchers isolated the substance responsible for the increased rate of cell division and named it cytokinin. Since that time, more than 200 natural and synthetic cytokinins have been identified.

Today, many of these cytokinins are used to culture plant tissues in the laboratory. Scientists also expose the tissues to a high ratio of auxins to cytokinins to stimulate the formation of roots. A low ratio of auxins to cytokinins is used to stimulate the development of shoots. In the following project, you can test the effect of cytokinins on cell division in germinating seeds.

STIMULATING CELL DIVISION

Use a cork borer to remove one of the three "eyes" on a coconut. The tissue in this area is softer than the rest of the coconut. Puncture one of the other "eyes" with a hammer and large nail. *Caution: Be careful when puncturing the coconut. You may want to ask an adult to carry out this step.*

What You Need	
Coconut	Small pan
Cork borer	Stove
Hammer	Filter paper
Large nail	Bean seeds
Cheesecloth	Graduated cylinder
Two glass beakers or jars	Distilled water

Pour the milk out of the coconut and allow it to filter through several layers of cheesecloth. Collect the filtrate in a glass beaker or jar. Pour the milk into a small pan and boil it for 10 minutes. Heating will cause the proteins in the milk to form a solid mass.

After the liquid has cooled to room temperature, pour it through filter paper. Collect the filtrate in a clean beaker or jar. Discard the solids trapped by the filter paper. (If you are not going to use the coconut milk extract immediately, you can freeze it. Thawing and freezing have no effect on the activity of the cytokinins in the extract.)

To germinate the seeds, follow the instructions given in the project on pages 46–48. Soak a few beans in distilled water to establish a control group. Soak the rest of the seeds in various concentrations of milk extract that has been diluted with distilled water. Compare the rates of germination and development among seeds exposed to different concentrations of coconut milk. You may also want to examine the effect of gibberellins on the germination and development of other types of seeds. Which kind of seed shows the greatest response to the cytokinins in coconut milk?

Doing More

Although the first cytokinin was isolated in 1955, scientists have done relatively few studies on the effect of this hormone on root systems. One study showed that when cytokinin was applied to roots at very low concentrations, the rate of root growth and photosynthesis increased. However, if the roots were exposed to more than 0.47 parts per million (ppm) of cytokinin for longer than 2 days, both root growth and photosynthesis were inhibited. Carry out a project to determine how increasing concentrations of cytokinins affect the root growth in a plant.

ETHYLENE STIMULATES FRUIT RIPENING

The ancient Egyptians accelerated fig ripening by exposing the fruit to a gas. When the ancient Chinese burned incense in closed rooms, the resulting gas stimulated the ripening of pears. In 1901, a Russian scientist showed that ethylene was responsible for ripening the figs and pears. Ethylene can also be used to ripen tomatoes, bananas, oranges, lemons, grapefruits, and apples.

Ethylene is produced only by flowering plants. Besides accelerating ripening, this plant hormone stimulates seeds to sprout and flowers to bloom. The following project will show you another function of ethylene.

A ROTTEN APPLE

Place a plant in each jar. Add the apple to one jar and screw the lids onto both jars. Observe the jars daily for several days. The rotting apple gives off ethylene. How does it affect the plant?

Explain why ethylene is sprayed on fruits just before they are harvested. Why can exposure to ethylene be critical to the survival of *deciduous trees* in the winter?

Doing More
*   If possible, grow vegetables in a field and cover them with a transparent material that lets in light, but does not permit any gases to escape. Place some fruit among the crops as a source of ethylene gas. Does the fruit affect your crop in any way? Be sure to set up the proper control.

*   Ethylene is also emitted by automobiles and industrial sites. Scientists do not know the long-term effects of high levels of ethylene in the atmosphere. Some researchers are concerned that plant growth and crop yields might be negatively affected. Scientists in Alberta, Canada, are currently studying this phenomenon. To find out more about this research project, contact *http://www.arc.ab.ca/ethylene/topic1.html*. Include the information you obtain as part of a project that examines the long-term impact of increasing ethylene levels.

CHAPTER

HEREDITY

People have long recognized that physical traits are passed from one generation to the next. For example, you may have the same color eyes as your mother or be as tall as your father. For years, scientists searched for the mechanism behind *heredity*—the transmission of traits from parents to their offspring. In the mid-1800s, an Austrian monk named Gregor Mendel performed a series of experiments with pea plants and gained an understanding of heredity.

Over the course of almost 9 years, Mendel grew thousands of pea plants, collected the seeds, and carefully recorded their characteristics. Then he planted the seeds. Mendel kept track of the characteristics of the plant produced by each seed.

Mendel knew nothing about the inside of a cell. He reasoned that each sex cell—sperm and egg—carries two

Gregor Mendel carried out his plant breeding
experiments in this garden at Brno Monastery
in the Czech Republic.

"factors" for each trait. The two factors may or may not
have the same information. If they do have the same
information, the pea plant is *homozygous* for that trait. If
the two factors have different information, the pea plant
is *heterozygous* for that trait. Alternate forms of a factor are
called *alleles*.

Mendel did not know exactly what the factors are
made of or where they are located inside the cell. Today,
scientists use the word "genes" to describe Mendel's "factors." They know that genes are located on *chromosomes*.
In most organisms, chromosomes are found in a cell's
nucleus. The nucleus acts as the control center of a cell,
directing most of its activities.

In effect, chromosomes form the basis of heredity. Most of your cells contain forty-six chromosomes. The cells of a pea plant contain fourteen chromosomes.

COPYING CHROMOSOMES

During mitosis, one cell divides to produce two cells that have the identical genetic material as the original cell. For this to happen, each chromosome must makes a copy of itself. The nucleus breaks down, the chromosome pairs line up along the middle of the cell, and each copy of the chromosome pair moves away from the other—toward opposite ends of the cell.

In this way, the original chromosome is parceled out to one of the new cells, and the copy ends up in the other new cell. As a result, each of the new cells has genetic information identical to that of the parent cell. The following project looks at the stages of mitosis.

OBSERVING MITOSIS

Place an onion or garlic bulb in a container with water. After the roots sprout, select one that is at least 3 cm long. Using a single-edged razor blade, cut off a section 1 cm from the bottom of the root. Place the tip on a clean glass microscope slide, and cover it with a few drops of 1 N HCl. *Caution: HCl is a dangerous acid. Work in a well-ventilated area and wear protective eye goggles, gloves, and an apron or smock. You may want to work under the supervision of an adult. If so, be sure the adult also follows these safety precautions.*

After putting on your protective eye goggles, pass the slide over a low flame two or three times. Using a piece of paper towel, blot off any remaining acid. Cover the tip

Onion or garlic	A bunsen burner or alcohol burner
A container with water	
Single-edged razor blade	Metric ruler
	Paper towels
Glass microscope slides	Toluidine blue O or aceto-orcein stain
Protective eye goggles	
1 N HCl	Coverslips
Matches	Microscope

with a few drops of toluidine blue O or aceto-orcein stain. Again pass the slide through the flame and blot it dry. Add a drop of fresh stain, apply a coverslip, and place the slide between two paper towels. Press gently with your thumb using a steady, firm pressure to crush the root tip. Examine the slide with a microscope. You can also use a prepared slide of a root tip.

As you look at the root cells, notice the darkly stained structures near the center of the cells. These are the chromosomes. Individual chromosomes will not be visible in most of the cells you examine because they are in a stage that occurs between cell divisions. The cells that do contain visible chromosomes are undergoing mitosis.

Mitosis consists of four stages. During *prophase*, the chromosomes become visible. During *metaphase*, the chromosomes organize near the middle of the cell. During *anaphase*, the chromosomes move away from one

The darkly stained, rod-shaped structures in these cells are chromosomes undergoing mitosis.

another. During *telophase*, two distinct cells start to form. The stages of mitosis are shown in Figure 9.

Examine fifty cells that are undergoing mitosis. Identify the stage of mitosis for each cell. Keep a tally of your observations. In onion cells, mitosis takes about 80 minutes. You can calculate the length of a particular stage by multiplying the percentage of cells in that stage by 80. For

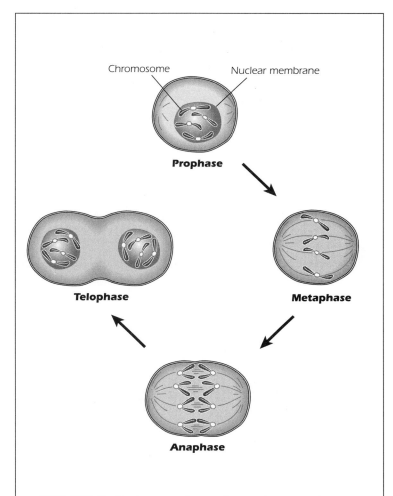

Chromosome   Nuclear membrane

Prophase

Telophase

Metaphase

Anaphase

FIGURE 9 During prophase, the nuclear membrane begins to break down and the chromosomes become visible. During metaphase, the chromosomes line up along in the middle of the cell. During anaphase, chromosomes move toward opposite sides of the cell. During telophase, the cell begins to split into two new cells.

example, if five of the fifty cells are in prophase, then the length of this stage would be calculated in the following manner:

$$5 \div 50 = 0.10$$
$$0.10 \times 80 = 8 \text{ minutes}$$

Doing More
- Prepare your slides at different times of the day to see if there is a peak period for mitosis. Expose the onion or garlic to different light and temperature cycles. A project that determines the optimum conditions for mitosis would have practical applications for growing the plant.

- Experiment with ways of affecting cell division by adding various substances to the water used for rooting. Look for any obvious abnormalities: broken or damaged chromosomes, changes in their number, or irregular arrangements. Test the effects of such plant products as nicotine, caffeine, and quinine. Experiment with colchicine, a chemical that allows chromosomes to double but prevents the cell from dividing. As a consequence, the cell ends up with an extra set of chromosomes.

    Scientists have used colchicine to produce plants with larger flowers and fruits. Find out if any of these changes are reversible—can you restore the chromosomes to their original condition?

FROM MITOSIS TO CLONING
In the early 1960s, scientists placed small pieces of carrots in Erlenmeyer flasks containing a culture medium that included coconut milk. The flasks were sealed to prevent

contamination and gently shaken. The carrot cells grew rapidly. Next, the scientists grew individual carrot cells in culture. The cells divided rapidly to form large fragments, which developed into small plants when transferred to agar containing coconut milk. These early cloning experiments, produced complete organisms from single cells. A *clone* is an organism that is produced from a single cell and is genetically identical to its parent.

Mitosis makes cloning possible. Because mitosis is at work, all the cells in an adult contain the same genetic information as the cells that existed when the individual was a zygote—a fertilized egg cell. If a zygote has all the information necessary to develop into a adult, then any cell within the zygote should be able to develop into an adult too.

If the cells of a zygote are separated and allowed to develop under ideal conditions, each one will become an adult. And all the adults that develop from cells taken from a single zygote will be identical. In other words, they will be clones. The following project will show you how to produce a clone.

CLONING AN ORGANISM

For a tissue-culture cloning project to be successful, it must be done under aseptic conditions. That means you must make sure that no bacteria or molds contaminate your equipment or materials. Because air currents can introduce bacteria and mold into your cultures, avoid working near an open window or door. Wash your hands thoroughly with soap and hot water and dry them with paper towels. Next wash all the surfaces you will work on with soap and water. Dry the surfaces, and then wipe them down with a paper towel that has been soaked with rubbing alcohol.

What You Need

Paper towels	Sterile distilled water
Rubbing alcohol	Graduated cylinder
Pressure cooker	#4 cork borer
Culture medium	Bunsen burner or alcohol burner
Six 150-mL Erlen-meyer flasks	
Cotton swab	Dissecting needle
African violet plant	Methylene blue stain
Sterile petri dishes	Medicine dropper
Forceps	Glass microscope slides
Bleach	Coverslips
	Microscope

Sterilize all the equipment you will use in a pressure cooker. *Caution: Working with a pressure cooker can be dangerous. Perform this step under adult supervision.* After you sterilize the equipment, store it in a jar containing rubbing alcohol. Before using each item, shake off any excess alcohol and then carefully pass the object through a flame to kill any bacteria that are still present. Allow the object to cool before using it.

Pour 50 mL of culture media into each of six flasks. You can purchase culture media for African violets at a garden-supply store or one of the scientific supply companies listed at the back of this book. Seal each flask with a cotton plug. Sterilize the flasks by placing them in a pressure cooker. Set the temperature at 250°F and the pressure at 15 pounds per square inch.

When steam begins to flow from the escape valve, close the valve. This will begin the sterilization process. After 20 minutes, turn off the heat and allow the pressure cooker to cool very slowly. ***Caution: Do not remove the escape valve or the lid until the pressure cooker has cooled to room temperature!***

While you are waiting for the pressure cooker to cool, remove three healthy leaves from an African violet plant. Wipe them with a cotton swab that has been soaked in rubbing alcohol. Place the leaves in a sterile petri dish and cover them with a 20% bleach solution. Prepare the bleach solution in a sterile graduated cylinder. Dilute 20 mL of household bleach in 80 mL of sterile distilled water. After 10 minutes, use forceps to remove the leaves and rinse them three times with sterile distilled water. Use a sterile #4 cork borer to punch out two disks from the central portion of each leaf.

Remove the first flask from the pressure cooker, remove the cotton plug, and quickly pass the mouth of the flask through a flame. Then use forceps to transfer one leaf disk to the flask. Be sure the disk makes good contact with the surface of the culture medium. Repeat this procedure with each of the other five flasks. Set the flasks aside at room temperature. Be sure that they are not exposed to direct sunlight.

Keep a weekly record of your observations. Within 30 days, a mass of unspecialized cells called a *callus* should develop around each disk. Open one of the flasks and use a dissecting needle to gently scrape a tiny section of the callus onto a glass microscope slide. Apply a drop of methylene blue stain, add a coverslip, and examine the cells under a microscope. Describe the appearance of the cells.

Watch what happens in the other five flasks for the next 4 to 6 months. You should see roots and shoots develop, and eventually the African violet should bloom.

Don't get discouraged if your flasks become contaminated. If this happens, you can always begin the project again. Once you have mastered this technique, you can try cloning tomatoes, petunias, or other plants. You may also want to see what happens to your plants when you add a small amount of a plant hormone, such as auxin.

Doing More

- You can also clone some plants by cutting a portion of a stem or root and placing it in a container of water or moist soil. Try placing a leaf from a *Bryophyllum* plant on moist soil in a flower pot. After a short time, new plants should begin to form on the leaf. Farmers often propagate raspberries and blackberries by burying a stem underground. The stem forms root and, eventually, a whole new plant grows. Design and carry out a project that involves producing a clone using one of these two methods.

- Since the early 1960s, scientists have cloned a variety of organisms. But this kind of research makes many people nervous. In 1997, President Bill Clinton issued an order banning any federally funded project that involved cloning humans. Italy, Denmark, and several other countries enacted similar bans.

  To find out more about this controversial topic, check the library and search the Internet for books and articles that present both sides of this bioethical issue. Prepare a position statement outlining your views on this issue. Be sure to support your position with facts and scientific knowledge. Your project could also take the form of a video documentary. Watching the movie *The Boys from Brazil* may give you ideas about how to develop a documentary of your own.

HOW INHERITANCE WORKS

In all, Mendel investigated the inheritance of seven characteristics in pea plants. Sometimes he got the results he expected—but not always. For example, he found that

Mendel showed that when tall pea plants are crossed with short ones, all of the offspring are tall.

when a tall pea plant is mated, or crossed, with a short pea plant, all the offspring are tall.

Mendel realized that some forms of a trait must take precedence over others. Thus, he referred to tall as the *dominant allele*, and short as the *recessive allele*. A dominant allele for a trait masks a recessive allele. Mendel went on to show how dominant and recessive alleles are inherited. The following project will give you the opportunity to see how genetic traits are inherited.

SIMULATING A GENETIC CROSS

What You Need	
Package of dried yellow split peas	Two wide-mouth jars
	Marking pen
Package of dried green split peas	Three empty plastic or glass containers

Open the packages of peas and count out fifty of each kind. Mix the peas and place them in one of the wide-mouth jars. Label this "Jar A." Count out fifty more peas of each kind, mix them, and place them in the other wide-mouth jar. Label this "Jar B." You now have 100 peas in each jar.

Assume that Jar A represents the stamen of a flower and that each split pea in this jar is a sperm in a pollen grain. Assume that Jar B represents an ovule and that each pea in this jar is an egg cell. Label one of the empty containers Yellow/Yellow, the second Yellow/Green, and the third Green/Green.

Without looking, randomly select a pea from Jar A with your right hand. Using your left hand, randomly select a pea from Jar B. These two peas represent a *genetic cross*. Place the two peas in the container with the appropriate label. Continue removing peas from Jar A and Jar B until there are none left. Count the number of peas in each of the three containers. Divide each number by 2 to obtain the number of genetic crosses. Record your results.

What ratio of Yellow/Yellow: Yellow/Green: Green/Green did you obtain? If you assume that a yellow pea is dominant, and a green pea is recessive, how many of the "offspring" of these genetic crosses will be yellow? How many will be green? Do some research to find out how your results compare to those of Mendel.

When an organism is heterozygous, or has two different alleles for a specific trait, it is called a *hybrid*. Thus, a dihybrid cross involves two parents that are both heterozygous for a specific trait. Mendel's understanding of dihybrid crosses helped him formulate his Principle of Segregation.

Do some research to find out what this principle states. Were your findings consistent with Mendel's Principle of Segregation? If not, why should you repeat the experiment using more peas?

Doing More
- Buy seeds for tall and dwarf pea plants. Plant them 2.5 cm deep in a local garden or in the bottom halves of half-gallon milk containers. Be sure to keep the soil moist. When flower buds appear, cross-pollinate the plants. To do this, gently force open the buds of one dwarf plant and snip out the unripe stamens, as shown

in Figure 10. Cover the plant with a plastic bag to prevent stray pollen from reaching it. When the buds of a tall plant open, use a camel's-hair brush to transfer pollen from the ripe stamens of the tall plant to the stigma of the dwarf plant that you prepared.

When you are done, cover the plant with a plastic bag. Allow the pods to remain on the plant until they have thoroughly dried and have begun to split open. Then collect the seeds.

Plant these seeds and measure them as they grow. Cross-pollinate their flowers using the same technique. Collect the second-generation seeds and plant them. Measure them as they grow. Do your results agree with Mendel's Principle of Segregation?

- Mendel also observed that traits in his pea plants were inherited independently of one another. This phenomenon is known as Mendel's Principle of Independent Assortment.

  For example, the inheritance of the trait for seed color is not affected in any way by how the trait for seed shape is inherited. To see this for yourself, label four jars "A-1," "A-2," "B-1," and "B-2." Place fifty yellow peas and fifty green peas in jars A-1 and B-1. Place fifty wrinkled peas and fifty smooth peas in jars A-2 and B-2. Assume that jars A-1 and A-2 each represent the stamen of a flower and that each pea inside the jars is a sperm in a pollen grain. Assume that jars B-1 and B-2 each represent an ovule and that each pea inside the jars is an egg cell.

  Randomly withdraw a pea from each of the jars. In this case, you will assign letters to each pea that you choose. Dominant alleles will be assigned a capital letter, while recessive ones will be assigned the same letter but in lower case. Because yellow is dominant over

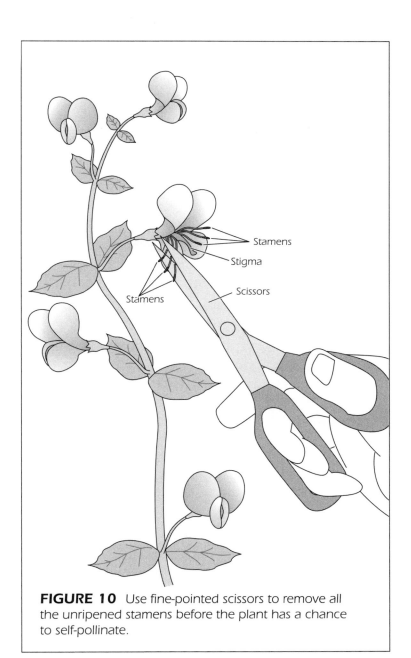

Stamens

Stigma

Scissors

Stamens

FIGURE 10 Use fine-pointed scissors to remove all the unripened stamens before the plant has a chance to self-pollinate.

green, assign *Y* for yellow and *y* for green. Round is dominant over wrinkled, so you should assign *R* for round and *r* for wrinkled.

When you combine the four peas from each draw, you should assign four letters that represent the offspring produced by this genetic cross. There are a total of nine possible groupings. Combine the groupings that produce plants with the same traits. For example, both *YYrr* and *Yyrr* will produce yellow, wrinkled seeds. What are the ratios of yellow/round, yellow/wrinkled, green/round, and green/wrinkled "plants" that result from your simulated genetic crosses? Do your findings agree with Mendel's Principle of Independent Assortment?

PATTERNS OF HEREDITY

Not long after the importance of Mendel's work was recognized, scientists discovered that heredity did not operate solely on the basis the Principle of Segregation and the Principle of Independent Assortment. In fact, the mechanism by which organisms inherit traits is quite complicated.

In some cases, traits are controlled by groups of genes. In other cases, one allele for a trait is not dominant over the other, so scientists say the alleles are *codominant*. For example, when a snapdragon with red flowers is crossed with a snapdragon with white flowers, the offspring will have pink flowers.

The intricacies of heredity do not end here. Do some research to learn how linkage, jumping genes, epistasis, and multiple alleles can influence patterns of inheritance. In some cases, even the environment can affect how genes are expressed. Any one of these topics would make an excellent topic for a project that investigates heredity in plants.

CHAPTER 8

ECOLOGY

Like all other living things, plants interact with their environment. In Chapter 6, you learned that plants respond to stimuli such as light, water, and gravity. Plants also interact with animals and other organisms. In Chapter 5, you learned that photosynthesis produces the chemical energy and oxygen that most living things need to survive. In turn, other organisms produce the carbon dioxide that plants need to carry out photosynthesis. Thus, all living things are dependent on one another and on their environment. The study of relationships between living things and between living things and their environment is called *ecology*.

In recent years, the field of ecology has become increasingly important. Many people today are concerned about the effects of soil, water, and air pollution on the environment. Plants are often the first organisms to suffer from pollution, but over time the effects travel throughout an ecosystem. For example, if the soil in a particular area is polluted, the grasses there may die. As a result, the rabbits that feed on the grasses will die too. And, eventually, the snakes that eat the rabbits and the hawks that eat the snakes will be affected. All this can happen as the result of soil pollution.

SOIL POLLUTION

One of the most serious forms of soil pollution is caused by acid precipitation—acid rain or acid snow that contains very high levels of acid. An acid, such as lemon juice, tastes sour and reacts with metals to produce a gas. The *pH* of a solution is a quantitative expression of its acidity. The pH scale ranges from 0 to 14, with 7 being neutral. Any solution with a pH less than 7 is acidic. The lower the pH, the more acidic the solution. See Figure 11.

Any solution with a pH higher than 7 is said to be basic. The higher the pH, the more basic the solution. A base, such as baking soda, is a chemical substance that tastes bitter and feels slippery. Normally, the pH of rain and snow is 5.5. Thus, both are slightly acidic.

When we burn fossil fuels, such as coal and oil, carbon dioxide gas is released into the atmosphere. This gas reacts with water in the atmosphere to produce acids. The acids fall back to Earth when it rains or snows. Acid precipitation often has a pH of 3. The most acidic rain ever measured in the United States had a pH of 1.5. It fell in Wheeling, West Virginia. A drop in pH from 5.5 to 1.5 may not seem that significant, but keep in mind that each unit on the pH scale represents a ten-fold change in concentration. Thus, rain with a pH of 1.5 is 10,000 times more acidic than rain with a pH value of 5.5! The following project will show you how acid rain can affect plant life.

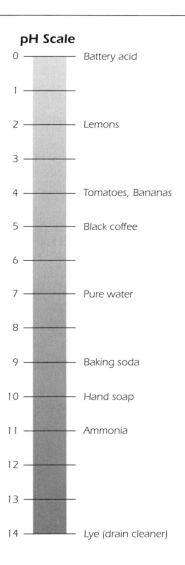

pH Scale

pH	Substance
0	Battery acid
1	
2	Lemons
3	
4	Tomatoes, Bananas
5	Black coffee
6	
7	Pure water
8	
9	Baking soda
10	Hand soap
11	Ammonia
12	
13	
14	Lye (drain cleaner)

FIGURE 11 Is a banana more acidic than ammonia? Look at the scale above to find out.

ASSESSING THE IMPACT OF ACID RAIN

What You Need	
Radish seeds	Distilled water
Twelve small pots	pH 3 and 5 buffer capsules
Potting soil	
Marking pen	Metric ruler

Plant a few radish seeds in each of the twelve pots. Separate the pots into three groups of four pots each. Label the pots in the first group "A," the pots in the second group "B," and the pots in the third group "C." Follow the instructions on the buffer capsules to prepare two solutions—one with a pH of 3, the other with a pH of 5. Water the seeds and seedlings that develop in the A group with the pH 3 solution, those in the B group with the pH 5 solution, and those in the C group with distilled water. Be sure that all the pots get the same volume of solution and that they are all exposed to the same light and temperature condition. Why is this important?

When the seedlings are 4 weeks old, measure the width and length of at least four leaves on each plant. Calculate the leaf ratio by dividing the width (in millimeters) by the length (in mm). Record your results in a table or use a computer spreadsheet to keep track of your data. Compare the average leaf ratios of the three sets of plants. Explain any differences you observe.

Doing More
- Test the effect of your acid solutions on the development of other kinds of plants. Use the seeds of flow-

ering plants and herbs. How are their leaves affected by the acid solutions?

You can also investigate how the acid solutions affect the growth of cuttings. Cut several 15-cm-long pieces of geranium stems. Dip the lower end of each stem in a root hormone powder and then insert it into a pot of soil. Divide the cuttings into different groups and water each one with a different pH solution. After 4 weeks, compare the size and appearance of the stems. Repeat the procedure with cuttings from other kinds of plants. Try coleus, African violet, and begonia plants. Do all plant cuttings react the same way to the acid solutions?

- In the Pacific Northwest, acid fog is a serious threat. Test the effect of "acid fog" on a geranium. Use a spray bottle or plant mister to wet the leaves of a geranium plant with a fine mist of a pH 3 solution every day for 2 weeks. Be sure to set up a control. Water the soil regularly with distilled water, and keep each plant covered with a bell jar. Place the plants in indirect light and make daily observations on the condition of the leaves. Photographs are a good way to keep track of your observations. Try to make quantitative observations, too. For example, measure the length of the leaves each day.

WATER POLLUTION

Acid precipitation can also pollute the waters of oceans, lakes, streams, rivers, and ponds. These waterways are polluted in other ways too. Industrial companies sometimes dump chemicals and toxic wastes into them.

Only in the last few decades have we begun to recognize water pollution as a major problem. As the pioneers moved across North America, they could drink water from the rivers and streams without worrying about possible health hazards. But today most of these waters are not suitable for drinking. In fact, some rivers are so polluted that nothing can survive in them.

In 1959, the Cuyahoga River in Ohio was so polluted that oil slicks on the surface caught fire and burned for 8 days! Two years later, the river burned again. This ecological disaster spurred the U.S. Congress to pass the Clean Water Act in 1972. As a result, the quality of water in the Cuyahoga River, and in many other bodies of water throughout the United States, has improved significantly. But we still have a long way to go before we can drink water as freely as the pioneers did.

How can you tell whether a body of water is polluted? In some cases, it is obvious. The water looks dirty and may even contain trash. In other cases, however, it's not so easy to tell whether the water is polluted. That's when the *Allium* test can come in handy. (*Allium cepa* is the scientific name for an ordinary white onion.)

This test was first used 60 years ago to find out how a drug called colchicine affects the chromosomes in onion root cells. It can also be used to determine how water pollutants affect root development. Researchers like this test because they can obtain results in less than a week and because it does not require any fancy equipment.

CHECKING FOR WATER POLLUTION

Onion bulbs that measure between 1.5 and 2.5 cm in diameter work best. If they are not available, larger ones can be used, but you will also need larger beakers or jars. Remove the loose outer layers of the onions and cut a 2-mm slice off the base of each bulb to expose the primary root cells.

What You Need	
Ten small white onion bulbs	Ten small glass beakers or jars
Sharp knife	Toothpicks
Large container with a lid	Metric ruler

Fill the large container with a water sample from a local river, pond, or stream. Pour some of the water into five of the beakers or jars. Place an onion on the top of each beaker or jar. Only the base of the onion should be touching the water. If the beaker or jar is too wide to keep most of the onion above the water level, use toothpicks to suspend the onion. See Figure 12 on the next page. Fill the other five beakers or jars with tap water and add an onion to each one.

Store the onions in the dark at room temperature. Observe the water levels daily and add more if necessary. If the water becomes cloudy, replace it with a fresh sample. This will prevent contamination by bacteria or molds. Around the fifth day or when you see roots at least 1 or 2 cm long, remove the onions with roots, cut off the roots, and carefully measure each one. If some onions have not grown roots, replace them with fresh onions. (They may have been treated with a growth inhibitor to prevent roots from sprouting while the onions were on display.) Be sure that all bulbs are left in the solution for the same amount of time. At the end of your experiment, calculate the average root length for each bulb. Account for any differences that you observe.

You can repeat this procedure using water samples from different bodies of water. Does any one water sam-

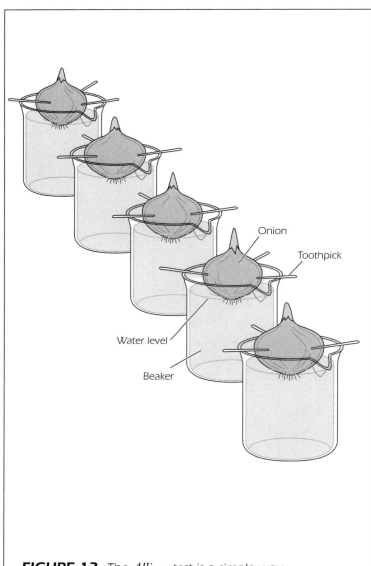

Onion

Toothpick

Water level

Beaker

FIGURE 12 The *Allium* test is a simple way to find out whether water from a local pond or stream is polluted.

ple inhibit the growth of roots more than the others? What does this tell you about the condition of this water sample? For more information on the *Allium* test, contact *http://embryo.ib.amwaw.edu.pl/~dslado/invittox/prot/8.htm*.

Doing More

- Water pollutants can affect the rate of mitosis in cells. To see this for yourself, use the procedure described in the Observing Mitosis project on pages 102–106 to prepare slides of onion cells from the ten onions you used in your project. Observe 100 cells from each onion. Keep track of the number of cells undergoing mitosis, and calculate the mitotic index (MI) by using the following formula.

$$MI = \frac{\text{number of cells undergoing mitosis}}{100}$$

  Compare the MI of the onions exposed to water samples to those exposed to tap water. Explain any difference that you observe.

- You can use the *Allium* test to determine whether a substance is toxic at a certain concentration. Place onion bulbs in solutions containing various concentrations of NaCl (start with 0.5% NaCl solution). At what salt concentration do the roots show some sign of being affected? You could also try testing the effect of household chemical substances, such as pain relievers, cleaning solutions, and plant-treatment products. Keep in mind that the *Allium* test is highly sensitive. Just because root development is inhibited doesn't necessarily mean that the solution will be harmful to other organisms. It merely indicates a potential health hazard.

AIR POLLUTION

Earth's atmosphere is 0.035 percent carbon dioxide. Like the glass in a greenhouse, the carbon dioxide in Earth's atmosphere allows sunlight to pass through, but it does not allow heat to escape. Thus, carbon dioxide is referred to as a *greenhouse gas*, and the impact it has is known as the *greenhouse effect*.

Carbon dioxide, along with a few other gases in the atmosphere, helps keep the average temperature of Earth's surface at 17°C. Without these gases, scientists estimate that the average temperature would be −25°C. That's cold!

For the past 150 years, the amount of carbon dioxide in the atmosphere has been gradually increasing. Some of the increase is the result of burning fossil fuels. Additional carbon dioxide has been added by burning vegetation, especially large areas of forest. Many people are now concerned about the possible long-term impact of adding so much carbon dioxide to the atmosphere. Will the greenhouse effect warm Earth too much? Some people suggest that global warming is already occurring.

Temperature records for the past 140 years support this idea. Eight of the warmest years on record occurred between 1980 and 1992. If this warming trend continues, the average global temperature might increase by as much as 3.5°C. This increase may not seem significant, but even this small increase would have a serious impact on rainfall patterns, sea levels, and soil moisture. It could cause massive droughts inland and catastrophic floods in coastal regions.

It is impossible to carry out an Earth-wide experiment to examine the long-term impact of an escalation in the greenhouse effect. Instead, scientists must rely on computer models. But developing a model that considers all the possible variables is no easy task. Keep in mind that these models are really attempting to predict weather patterns hundreds of years from now. To find out about the immediate impact of the greenhouse effect on plants, try the following project.

INVESTIGATING THE EFFECT OF RISING TEMPERATURES

What You Need	
Seeds	Two small thermometers
Potting soil	
Four small plastic containers	Plastic wrap
	Rubber bands
Water	Metric ruler

Plant some seeds in each of the four plastic containers. Water the soil, and place a thermometer in two of the containers. Using plastic wrap, cover one container with a thermometer and one container without a thermometer. Secure the plastic wrap with a rubber band.

Place all four containers in indirect light. (Direct light may burn the seedlings in the containers covered with plastic wrap.) Add water to the containers as needed. After watering the covered containers, be sure to re-secure the plastic wrap with the rubber bands. Since the plastic wrap will retain moisture, you may have to water the uncovered containers more frequently.

Each day, record the temperature in both the uncovered and covered containers. Which seeds germinate first? As the seedlings develop, measure their heights each day. Determine the average height of the covered and uncovered seedlings. Repeat the procedure with different kinds of seeds? Do they react in the same way to growing in covered versus uncovered containers? Redesign the procedure so that you study how carbon dioxide concentrations influence seed germination. To do this, poke a small hole through the plastic wrap and insert a drinking straw. Periodically blow through the straw to expose the plants to a higher carbon dioxide concentration. If you try this procedure, keep all four containers in a shaded area. Why?

Doing More

- To combat the greenhouse effect, people are planting new trees in areas where forests have been cut down. Because carbon dioxide is required for photosynthesis, more trees means more photosynthesis to remove carbon dioxide from the air. Search the Internet for information on reforestation programs. Use the information as the starting point for initiating a similar project in your area.

- Carbon dioxide passes through a chemical cycle known as the *carbon cycle*. As you can see in Figure 13, four processes make up this cycle. Only one of these processes—photosynthesis—reduces the amount of carbon dioxide in the atmosphere; the other three processes increase it. Develop a computer program that illustrates how the carbon cycle operates. Design your program to show how an increase in any one process can affect the entire cycle.

- Carbon dioxide is not the only dangerous pollutant in our atmosphere. For many years, we pumped vast

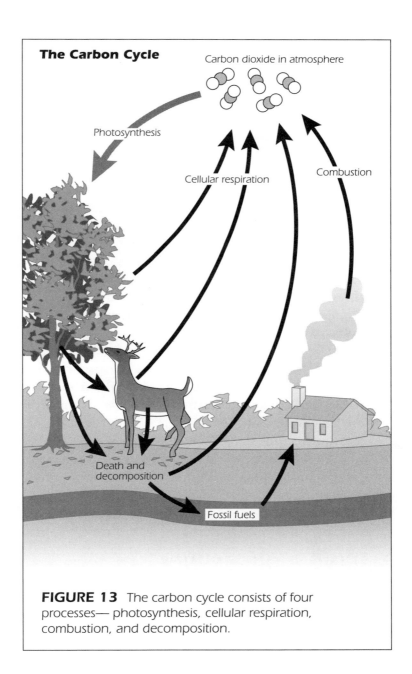

FIGURE 13 The carbon cycle consists of four processes— photosynthesis, cellular respiration, combustion, and decomposition.

quantities of *chlorofluorocarbons* (CFCs) into the air. These gases, used primarily as coolants in air-conditioning systems and refrigerators and to power aerosol spray cans, slowly began to destroy Earth's ozone layer. The ozone layer is a portion of the atmosphere that blocks harmful ultraviolet radiation from entering the lower atmosphere. Ultraviolet radiation is classified as a *mutagen*—a substance that can cause a change, or mutation, in an organism's genetic material. Mutations can lead to cancer, especially various kinds of skin cancer.

Between 1977 and 1984, scientists found that the amount of ozone above Antarctica decreased by more than 40 percent. By 1993, the ozone "hole" was almost as large as the continent of North America. As the ozone hole becomes larger, the incidence of skin cancer will increase.

To date, 165 nations have signed the Montreal Protocol, which requires industries in participating countries to stop manufacturing chlorofluorocarbons (CFCs). Hopefully, this ban will give the ozone layer the time it needs to repair itself. Do a project to find out more about the ozone layer, the mechanism by which CFCs destroy the ozone layer, and efforts to protect and preserve this important part of the atmosphere.

MAKING A DIFFERENCE IN YOUR COMMUNITY

If you have reached this point in the book and have yet to discover a project that you would like to undertake, ask a local elected official what pollution-control measures have been enacted in your community. Carry out a project to determine how these measures have affected your community, especially the local plant life. As part of your project, try to increase community awareness. If you discover that no local measures have been enacted, think of ways to convince people you know to take steps to reduce soil, water, and air pollution in your community.

GLOSSARY

acid precipitation—rain, snow, or any other form of precipitation that has a higher acid content than normal

active transport—a process in which materials move into or out of a cell against the concentration gradient. In other words, they move from an area of low concentration to an area of higher concentration.

adventitious root—a root that grows aboveground

allele—one of the two alternate forms of a gene

anaphase—the stage of mitosis in which members of each chromosome pair move toward opposite ends of a cell

angiosperm—a seed-bearing plant that produces flowers

callus—a mass of unspecialized cells that develops from a single cell

carbon cycle—the process by which carbon and carbon compounds circulate through an ecosystem

chlorofluorocarbon (CFC)—one of a group of compounds that break down ozone when released into the atmosphere

chlorophyll—the green pigment that absorbs light energy used to drive photosynthesis

chloroplast—the structure inside a plant cell where photosynthesis occurs

chromosome—a rod-shaped structure that carries the genetic information of an organism. In most cases, chromosomes are located in the nucleus of an organism's cells.

clone—an organism that is produced from a single cell and is genetically identical to its parent

codominant—sharing dominance

cohesion-tension theory—a theory that accounts for the movement of water and dissolved materials through stems *coleoptile*—a pale sheath that covers the primary shoots of grains and grasses

control group—in an experiment, a group that serves as a standard of comparison to another group that is identical in all respects but one

cytoplasm—excluding the cell nucleus, the contents that make up the interior of a cell

deciduous tree—a broad-leaved tree that loses its leaves in the autumn

dependent variable—the factor in an experiment that depends on how the independent variable is manipulated

dominant allele—the form of a gene (allele) that masks, or dominates, the other form

ecology—the study of an area, the organisms that live there, and the weather and soil conditions that affect it

electrophoresis—a process in which the molecules of a substance are separated according to their molecular weight

experimental group—a group that is subjected to the factor being tested in an experiment

gametophyte—a plant or the stage in the life cycle of a plant in which sexual reproduction occurs

genetic cross—choosing two individuals to mate and produce offspring

germinate—to grow and develop from a seed

greenhouse effect—a process in which the surface and lower atmosphere of a planet warms up because carbon dioxide and other gases in the atmosphere absorb and hold heat from the sun

greenhouse gas—a gas that contributes to the greenhouse effect

gymnosperm—a vascular, seed-bearing plant that does not produce flowers

herbaceous stem—the soft, flexible, green stems of most plants. Trees have wood stems.

heredity—the transmission of traits from one generation to the next

hermaphrodite—an organism that has both male and female reproductive organs

heterozygous—inheriting a different form of a gene (allele) for a trait from each parent

homozygous—inheriting the same form of a gene (allele) for a trait from each parent

hormone—a chemical produced in one part of the body that acts on another part of the body to stimulate or inhibit a function

hybrid—heterozygous; an organism that has inherited a different form of a gene (allele) for a trait from each parent

independent variable—a factor in an experiment that a researcher is free to manipulate

kingdom—one of the divisions into which all living things are classified

metaphase—the stage of mitosis in which chromosome pairs align themselves along the equator of a cell

mitosis—the process by which a cell divides to produce two genetically identical cells

mutagen—a substance that can cause a change, or mutation, in the genetic material of an individual

nucleus—the part of a cell that directs most of its activities

organic compound—a compound that contains carbon and hydrogen

ovule—the structure of a plant in which an egg cell is produced

pH—a measure of a solution's acidity

phloem—a group of cells that conducts nutrients down a plant

photosynthesis—the process by which organisms turn water and carbon dioxide into organic compounds, such as sugar, and water

pollen cone—the "male" cone of a gymnosperm

pollen grain—the "male" sex cell of a plant

pollination—the process of transferring pollen from stamen to stigma

pressure-flow hypothesis—a hypothesis that explains the movement of nutrients such as sugar through stems

prophase—the stage of mitosis in which the chromosomes shorten and become visible

recessive allele—the form of a gene (allele) that is masked, or dominated, by another form of that same gene

root hair—one of the many tiny projections that cover a root and increase its total surface area

seed cone—the "female" cone of a gymnosperm

spore—a reproductive cell that can develop into an adult plant

sporophyte—a plant—or the stage in the life cycle of a plant— that bears spores and reproduces asexually

stamen—the male reproductive structure of a flower

stigma—the female reproductive structure of a flower

stimulus (pl. stimuli)—anything that causes an organism to react or respond

taproot—a large primary root that grows straight down and has many smaller roots growing out of it

telophase—the stage of mitosis in which the original cell begins to divide to form two cells

transpiration—the process by which water evaporates from the leaves of a plant

tropism—plant movement in response to a stimulus

vascular system—the structures within an organism that transport materials from one part to another

xylem—a group of cells that conducts water and dissolved materials up a plant

zygote—an egg cell that has been fertilized by a sperm

RESOURCES

BOOKS

Aaseng, Nathan. *Meat-Eating Plants*. Springfield, NJ: Enslow Publishers, 1996.

Bonnet, Robert L. and G. Daniel Keen. *Botany: Forty-Nine Science Fair Projects*. New York: McGraw, 1989.

Bonnet, Robert L. and G. Daniel Keen. *Botany: Forty-Nine More Science Fair Projects*. New York: McGraw, 1990.

Dashefsky, H. Steven. *Botany: High School Science Fair Experiments*. New York: McGraw, 1995.

Gardner, Robert. *Science Project Ideas About Trees*. Springfield, NJ: Enslow Publishers, 1997.

Gardner, Robert and Richard Adams. *Ideas for Science Projects*. Danbury, CT: Franklin Watts, 1997.

Hershey, David R. *Plant Biology Science Projects*, New York: Wiley, 1995.

Jackson, Denny and Gary Hanna. *Botany: A Laboratory Manual*. Dubuque, IA: Kendall Hunt, 1996.

Smith, Robert A. *Plant Tissue Culture Studies*. Reston, VA: National Association of Biology Teachers, 1997.

Tocci, Salvatore. *How to Do a Science Fair Project*. Danbury, CT: Franklin Watts, 1997.

INTERNET SITES

Access Excellence
http://gene.com/ae/
Take a look at the "What's New" (science update), "Let's Collaborate"(on-line projects), and "Activities Exchange" (activities-to-go) sections.

The Access Indiana Teaching & Learning Center
http://tlc.ai.org/botanidx.htm
This site features links to sites dealing with all aspects of botany. Some of these links include information about backyard gardens, plant fossils, aromatic herbs, and a plant database that is maintained by the U.S. Department of Agriculture. You can also connect to several botanical gardens including the Brooklyn Botanical Garden and The Morton Arboretum.

Awesome Library
http://www.neat-schoolhouse.org/science.html
The botany link on this site takes you to a Web page where you can access information on botany materials, papers, and projects. You can also search the library by typing in one or two words.

Botanical Society of America
http://www.botany.org/
This society promotes research and teaching in all fields of botany. Links take you to articles about recent findings in plant research and to back issues of the society's publications.

Botany: A Helpful Index for All
http://www.bergen.org/AAST/Projects/Botany/
This site has all kinds of instructional information about plants.

Hands-On-Science Organization
http://www.hands-on-science.org/
One section is devoted to "Kids" with information on projects to do at home and an opportunity to get feedback.

i-Explorer
http://isleuth.com/botany.html
This site allows you to search for information on eleven specific topics, including botanical literature and an annotated index of botany sites.

Medical Botany Library
http://www.floridaplants.com/medical.htm
This homepage has links to sites dealing with herbal medicine, books on botany, and poisonous plants.

Online Journals
http://spock.tnstate.edu/library/journal/onjbotany.htm
This site connects to three professional journals: *Journal of Experimental Botany*, *The Plant Cell*, and *Plant Physiology*. Some of the articles are accessible without a fee.

SciCentral
http://scicentral.com
This site is a science and engineering megadirectory that is maintained by professional scientists. One section leads to a K–12 science page with a science fair project resource guide. Another section is titled "Today's Research Highlights."

SCIENCE SUPPLY COMPANIES
Many science supply companies sell their merchandise only to schools—not to individuals. If you need chemicals or equipment that are not readily available, your science teacher may let you borrow them from the school. If not, ask your teacher for a catalog from one of the following companies. By looking through the catalog, you may be able to think of a way to substitute available materials for scientific equipment. Coming up with these types of substitutes shows ingenuity and will impress anyone who takes the time to look at your project. If there seems to be no substitute, ask your teacher to order the equipment for you.

Carolina Biological Supply Company
2700 York Road
Burlington, NC 27215-3398
http://www.carolina.com/

Connecticut Valley Biological Supply
P.O. Box 326
Southampton, MA 01073

Edmund Scientific
101 E. Gloucester Pike
Barrington, NJ 08007
http://www.edsci.com/
This company will mail any item they carry directly to your home. They have a variety of items that can be valuable for carrying out a biology project. Write them for a copy of their catalog.

WARD's Natural Science Establishment
P.O. Box 92912
Rochester, NY 14692-9012
http://www.wardsci.com/

INDEX

THE
IMPOSTER
BRIDE

Also by Nancy Richler
Your Mouth Is Lovely

THE
IMPOSTER
BRIDE

NANCY RICHLER

St. Martin's Press

New York

THE IMPOSTER BRIDE. Copyright © 2012 by Nancy Richler. All rights reserved. Printed in the United States of America. For information, address St. Martin's Press, 175 Fifth Avenue, New York, N.Y. 10010.

First stanza (5l.) of "Dedication" from *The Collected Poems 1931–1987* by Czeslaw Milosz. Copyright © 1988 by Czeslaw Milosz Royalties, Inc. Reprinted by permission of HarperCollins Publishers.

www.stmartins.com

Library of Congress Cataloging-in-Publication Data

Richler, Nancy, 1957–
The imposter bride / Nancy Richler.
    p. cm.
Also published in Toronto, Ont. : HarperCollins Publishers, c2012.
ISBN 978-1-250-01006-3 (hardcover)
ISBN 978-1-4299-9998-4 (e-book)
1. Brides—Fiction. 2. Impostors and imposture—Fiction. 3. Runaway wives—Fiction. 4. Mothers and daughters—Fiction. 5. Jews—Québec (Province)—Montréal—Fiction. I. Title.
    PR9199.3.R5115I46 2012
    813'.54—dc23

2012038670

First published in Canada by HarperCollins Publishers Ltd

First U.S. Edition: February 2013

10 9 8 7 6 5 4 3 2

For Janet and Martin
And for Vicki

CHAPTER 1

In a small room off a banquet hall in Montreal, Lily Kramer sat in silence with her new husband. It was summer and the room was hot. There were no windows and no door, only a curtain beyond which the guests—almost none of whom she knew—washed down sponge cake and herring with shots of schnapps and vodka. Lily and her husband sat on either end of the couch on which she assumed they were meant to consummate their marriage.

In front of the couch was a table laid with fruit and hard-boiled eggs. Her husband picked up a plum and rolled it in the palm of his hand. His name was Nathan and she had known him for a week. It was his brother, Sol, she had been meant to marry, a man she had corresponded with but hadn't met, who had caught one glimpse of her as she disembarked at the station and decided he wouldn't have her. Lily watched Nathan roll the plum in his hand and wondered what his brother had seen in her that made him turn away.

Nathan picked up a knife and began scoring the skin of the plum into sections. They had not yet touched, not even a brush of hand or lip upon becoming husband and wife. She could still count the number of glances they had exchanged, the first when she'd sat on the couch at the house where she was staying, so ashamed by the rejection at the station that she'd had to struggle to meet his gaze while he apologized on behalf of his brother and entire family.

"Your brother cannot even apologize on his own behalf?" she asked. She was surprised by her shame. Disappointed. She had no time to waste—no strength—on a man who fled at the mere sight of a woman. Or so she would have thought.

"Not even that," Nathan replied.

"No great loss, then," she said, forcing a lightness she didn't feel into her voice. She had crossed two oceans to marry this Sol. She had nothing and no one to return to.

"The loss is his," Nathan said quietly.

She had thought he would leave then, beat a hasty retreat from his brother's misdemeanour, but he didn't. He remained standing before her, shifting his weight from foot to foot.

"Would you like to sit down?" she asked finally.

His eyes were warm and brown; there was no pity in them. And he seemed to like what he saw. Already there was heat in his gaze.

He returned the next day to formalize their engagement. Why the rush? Lily wondered when he reappeared at the door. It was not as if she were fielding other offers, would be taken by another if he didn't quickly stake his claim. But then she knew, thought she knew. It was the rush of colour to her face when he had first entered the room, the lowered gaze that she'd had to force upwards, her chin raised in defiance of what

she felt. He had returned to banish her shame. He brought witnesses and brandy—and the same heat in his gaze. He was a lucky man, Lily thought at that moment. His desire inclined him to acts of goodness.

"Do you speak English?" he asked her that day. They'd been speaking Yiddish until then.

"Ticket," she answered. "Bread. Cousin. Suitcase."

Her English was good, near fluent, in fact. It was her anger at that moment that made her conceal it, sudden anger at his assumption that it was she who was the more ignorant of the two—she who spoke five languages and could get by in several others, who had smuggled lives across borders he wouldn't be able to find on a map. Rage, in fact, that it should have come down to this: if Nathan Kramer would have her, she would have him and be grateful. She, who had held all of life and death between her two hands before dying and washing up into this pale afterlife of her own existence.

"Freedom," she continued. "Buttons. Train."

"Buttons?" he asked, smiling.

"Eisenbergs," she said, naming the family that was hosting her, Sol's employer, whose business was buttons.

"Yes, yes, I understand," Nathan said, still smiling.

He knew she spoke English, had known from the expressions on her face as she'd followed his earlier conversation with the Eisenbergs—all in English. He had met greenhorns before, knew their nodding at wrong moments, their delayed smiles, awkward laughter, baffled eyes. There was none of that in her. She was tired, yes, after the long journey she had made, and certainly confused and distressed by his brother's behaviour at the station, but she was not a woman who didn't understand what was being said all around her. She

understood perfectly. And yet pretended she didn't. That intrigued him.

He had wanted her at once, had decided the moment he'd first stepped into the room. It was not her beauty that drew him. Not merely her beauty. He saw it, of course—how could one not? The fine bones of her face, the smoky blue eyes . . . But it was the tension in her, a feral tension, part hunger, part fear. It was that which had quickened his blood, that—not her shame—which had made him return the next day with his witnesses and brandy. He had not expected to find such tension in the living room of Sam Eisenberg, the Button King of Montreal. He had met many girls already in the living rooms of Jewish Montreal. Nice girls and not-so-nice, intelligent girls, beautiful girls, wily, witty, hopeful girls, but this . . . no, not this.

"Please," he said now, holding out a segment of the plum, the first exchange of their married life.

He watched her—his new bride—as she took a bite of the fruit. Her eyes filled with tears.

"What?" he asked.

"Nothing." She shook her head, closed her eyes briefly. "It's a good plum, not too sweet."

They had both fasted that day, in accordance with tradition. Should they have broken that fast on something else, Nathan wondered now, begun their marriage with a bite of egg, perhaps, symbolic of new life? A slice of melon, wholly sweet, without the tart edge of a plum?

"It's many years since I tasted a plum like that," Lily said in her near-perfect English. She handed the remainder of the segment back to him, took a long drink of water, then held the glass against her cheek to cool her skin.

"It's warm," he said, and she agreed.

She moved the glass to her other cheek, though it was no longer cool on her skin. Nathan handed her a napkin and she smiled her thanks as she wiped the sweat from her brow and upper lip. He had not seen her smile until then.

LILY AZEROV KRAMER. She was not who she said she was.

No one really is, I suppose, but Lily's deception was more literal than most. Her name before . . . she'd left it there, in that beaten village where the first Lily had died, freeing, among other things, an identity card to replace the one she'd discarded, an identity that could propel a future if someone would just step into it.

Someone would, of course. The village was in Poland, 1944. Nothing went unused.

And here are some of the things that that someone acquired when she stole the identity of a girl she hadn't known at all in life: the name, first of all, Lily Azerov; the identity card; a pair of woollen socks; a notebook filled with dreams and other scribblings; a single frosted stone.

She pulled the socks over the threadbare ones she was already wearing. The identity card and notebook she stuffed inside the waistband of her trousers, but not before memorizing the only item of practical worth in the notebook's pages: *Sonya Nemetz, Rehov Hayarkon 7, Tel Aviv.* The stone, which she knew to be a diamond, she slipped inside her body.

It was only then that she hesitated, only as she was ready to leave that something as strong as her will to survive overtook her. She knew she should flee. Every instinct prodded her to leave that village at once and make her way back to the

forest, where she could wait until it was safe to start moving again. And then to move, to join the mass of refugees flooding west in the wake of the liberating army, to fold herself into that mass and begin the life that might, in time, become her own. Move, she told herself, as she had so many times over the past three years, her instincts always keeping her a few inches beyond death's grasp. But something other than instinct rose in her that day. She hesitated. Her eye lingered. Was it the angle of the dead girl's body, limbs slightly askew as her younger sister's had once been in sleep? A fragment of the girl's dreams that had floated up and entered her as she quickly leafed through the notebook? The shadow of the rat skittering, the smell of its next meal luring it closer?

She stayed. She placed her open hand on the smooth, cold brow, passed it over sightless eyes—greyish blue like her own—and brought down the lids. The eyes would be covered. That was the least and most she felt she could do. She could bring down the lids of the eyes and hold them for a moment. This she did for the girl whose future she was stealing. And then she fled.

SOL KRAMER was among the guests at the wedding. The wedding that should have been his. Throughout the evening he could be seen toasting the bride and groom and lifting his brother high above his head in dancing more frenzied than joyous. His voice boomed louder than that of any other guest, his face shone with sweat.

"*L'chaim,*" he shouted, downing shot after shot of whisky. He already regretted his decision.

That was the sort of man Sol Kramer was. If he ate brown bread for breakfast, he later wished he'd eaten white. Didn't merely wish, spent good time wondering how his day would have gone, how much better he would have felt—his gut, his entire being—had he only eaten white bread instead of brown.

The bride looked good to him now. There was a boldness in her expression that he hadn't noticed before, that hadn't been there, he could swear, when she first stepped off the train. She'd looked bewildered then, glancing around, waiting anxiously for someone to claim her. Pathetic is how she'd looked, a woman alone with no one to greet her. A piece of unclaimed baggage.

She couldn't be expected to look otherwise, he realized, after all she'd been through. And he, in turn, wasn't expected to love her, just to marry her and stay married for as long as it took to slip her through a crack in Canada's doors, which had not yet reopened to refugees who were Jewish. The marriage, Sol's first, was to be an act of charity. An act of charity for which he'd receive a small payment, a token of appreciation, nothing lavish, just enough to give him the start he'd been needing, the leg up that other young men, through no merit of their own, had received from family or other lucky breaks. Sol Kramer had had no lucky breaks. This marriage was to have been his first. But when he saw the bride he recoiled.

Damaged goods. That's what he saw. A broken life, a frightened woman, a marriage that would bind him—however briefly—to grief.

Let someone else marry her, he decided on the spot. He was a charitable man, no one would dispute it. He would never deny the widows and orphans of the world. But neither, it turned out, did he want to have to marry them. And

why should he have to, with his looks and his smarts and the future that hummed just beyond his fingertips? Let someone else marry her, he told the busybody who'd arranged it. His charity did not extend to his marital bed.

But the woman he had left at the station was gone now, had disappeared entirely within the beautiful bride that his brother had taken. She was being lifted in her chair at the centre of the room. As the dancers beneath her struggled to get a solid grip, she sank briefly and her chair tilted, first one way, and then so far to the other that it looked as if she might slide off. A collective gasp went out, a few shrieks from the women, but Lily held on. Laughing, no less. More guests rushed in to help lift her, more muscled arms than were needed, and an instant later Sol watched as she rose straight out of the crowd. The woman who could have been—should have been—his.

She was radiant as her bearers transported her on her elevated throne across the room towards her bridegroom. Triumphant, she seemed to Sol. She didn't bother to hold onto the sides of her chair, which still dipped and bobbed perilously. With both hands free she waved a handkerchief in the direction of her bridegroom—Sol's own brother—who reached to grab the other end. Her eyes never lowered to the crowd beneath her; she spared not so much as a glimpse in Sol's direction.

She noticed him, though, his attempts to draw her gaze with his own. So now he wants me, she said to herself. I know you now; I've met your type before. He was a man who could only want what another had wanted first, she thought, a man whose own appetite for life was so meagre that he relied on parasitic yearnings to sustain him. She met his eyes briefly, then looked away.

I'm nothing to her. Less than nothing. A coward, Sol

thought as he sank into the nearest available chair. He watched his brother stretch to reach her handkerchief, heard her laughter as Nathan caught hold briefly before the dancers beneath him bore him away.

"It won't last," said a voice beside him, a voice that emanated from the throat of a woman but had the weight and gravity of a man's.

Sol turned and saw that he had joined the table of a guest he didn't recognize, a middle-aged woman who either was or thought herself to be a cut above the rest of the guests. Her dress, a blue satin, was more formal than those of the other women, her bearing more upright and severe. Her hair was pulled back from a pale, wide brow and lacquered into a shell. She had not left her table the entire evening and had placed a restraining hand on the arm of the teenage girl beside her—her daughter, Sol assumed—every time the girl tried to rise to join the dancing.

"It can't possibly last," the woman said. "Already it's emitting that inimitable smell."

"Mother, please," the daughter hissed. She was clearly mortified. She twisted a napkin between her fingers and stared down at the table, refusing to look up.

"The stench of a bad match is unmistakable," the woman said.

"I see," Sol responded, though of course he didn't. He just didn't know what else to say. He was good in social situations—smooth, some would say—but this particular situation, the woman's peculiar rudeness, was beyond the range of his skills. The daughter, exuding sullenness, continued twisting her napkin. She kept her face down towards the table, showing nothing of herself but the straight part in her dark, wavy hair.

The mother looked at Sol, awaiting his response.

He thought for a moment, then smiled brightly and extended his hand. "Sol Kramer," he said. "Brother of the groom."

The woman didn't return his smile, but she did take his proffered hand. "Ida Pearl Krakauer," she said. "And this is my daughter, Elka."

The girl looked up from her twisted napkin. She was pretty as well as sullen, Sol noted with pleasure.

"Ida Pearl Krakauer," Sol repeated. He didn't recognize the name.

"So tell me," Ida said. "Where did your brother find that ring?"

"The ring?"

"That piece of chipped glass he thinks is a diamond."

Sol felt his colour rising on his brother's behalf. A full month's earnings had gone into what this woman was now calling a piece of chipped glass.

"Grinstein's," she said, not waiting for his response. "I recognize the style. Lack thereof."

"It's been a pleasure, I'm sure," Sol said as he rose to leave the table. He wasn't about to listen to his brother's taste and judgment being insulted. Nor would he lower himself by answering the woman's rudeness with his own.

"Sit down, sit down. I didn't mean to offend you. If I had known you were such a hothead I would have kept my mouth shut, I'm sure."

Elka smiled slightly at her mother's mimic of Sol—Sol's turn of phrase which he had thought elegant but now knew to be ridiculous.

"And anyway," Ida Pearl continued, "I'm a competitor of Grinstein's, so you shouldn't take me so seriously."

"With all due respect, Mrs. Krakauer, I don't believe you're someone to be taken lightly."

At this Ida Pearl smiled, an actual full and genuine smile.

"Instead of rushing off in a huff, why don't you take my daughter for a spin? I don't approve of mixed dancing at weddings, but . . ."

Elka was already on her feet, smiling invitingly if somewhat shyly at Sol.

" . . . as you can see, my disapproval is of no consequence."

An odd bird, to say the least, Sol thought as he led Elka into the mixed circle of dancers of which Ida Pearl disapproved. But the daughter was adorable, there was no disputing that. Especially when she smiled up at him and two endearing dimples formed at the corners of her mouth.

A boor, Ida thought as she watched Sol manoeuvre Elka through the crowd. A man who was in love with his own brother's wife and didn't even have the decency to hide it.

"Here. Smell me," Elka said, thrusting her arm under Sol's nose.

Smell her? Sol wondered. But it was a lovely young arm, slender and well formed. Sol took the wrist between his thumb and forefinger, turned it so that the soft underside was exposed, and inhaled.

"Mmm . . ." he sighed. "Lilac." Though, in truth, his sense of smell was so saturated with herring, sweat and the perfume of the other guests that the delicate floral scent he thought he detected might well have been imagined.

"Rosewater," Elka corrected. "But that's just my perfume. Can you really not smell it?" She smiled slyly at him.

"Smell what?" he asked, also smiling, but uneasy.

"It's not their stench she smells." Elka pointed in the direction

of the bride and groom. "Anyone can see they're well matched. Just look at his face, how he loves her."

But Sol couldn't bear to look at his brother right then, at the happiness that should have been his.

"It's her own marriage to my father that my mother smells. It leaks out through my pores, she can't escape it."

"You smell nice to me," Sol murmured as he cast about for a way to change the subject. What was it with this mother–daughter pair and their bizarre talk of odours? And what kind of girl talked about her parents' marriage in that way to a man she'd barely met?

A pity, thought Ida Pearl, looking in the direction her daughter had pointed. For it wasn't happiness she saw on Nathan's face. It was longing. A longing suffused, at that moment, with hope, but a hope that wouldn't last, couldn't last, Ida knew. And he seemed a decent young man, nice to look at and well mannered. A young man whose future, if not for his bride, might have held the promise of happiness.

IDA PEARL AND ELKA had not actually been invited to the wedding, a fact Sol might have figured out for himself had he given the matter any thought. All the guests were from the Kramer side. They had to be. The bride had no friends or relatives in Montreal. She knew no one except the Eisenberg family that had agreed to host her.

But Sol wasn't thinking about the guest list that night, hadn't thought to wonder about the provenance of the only two strangers in the room. His mind was on himself, his own failings. How could he have turned away from a woman like

Lily? How could his first instinct about her have been so wrong? He was a man who set great store on instincts. He had to. His future, lacking education or family connections to support it, rested entirely and solely on his astuteness. And now this failure. The bright future that had flashed just ahead flickered and faded in his mind. In its place, a sepia-washed vision: a shapeless woman in a sundress, watering tomato plants on the balcony of a walk-up; a man in an undershirt, chewing sunflower seeds on that same balcony and spitting out the husks on the floor. It was a repellent vision, shocking in its clarity. One in which Sol immediately recognized himself and his future wife.

Was it that vision that impelled him to invite Elka to step outside the hall with him, a need for distraction from his own darkening thoughts?

Elka glanced worriedly towards her mother. She didn't need to ask to know she was forbidden. "I guess if it's just for a few minutes . . ." she said.

"We could both use the fresh air," Sol assured her as he guided her towards the door, but there was no freshness to the air outside, just the heavy stillness of a humid summer night. And as for distraction . . . he waited for Elka to talk, to complain about the heat, to ask him about himself, his ideas, his dreams.

But Elka had suddenly become aware that she was alone with a man for the first time in her life, an older man, no less—he had to be twenty-three at the very least—and in a situation that, had she asked her mother, would have been expressly and unambiguously forbidden to her. She could think of nothing to say, stood silently, like a dark and sweating lump in the night.

"Shall we walk a bit?" Sol asked.

"Okay," she said, and they walked a few blocks in silence. Every front stoop they passed had someone on it, every balcony, every staircase, people escaping the heat of their apartments, talking, playing cards, fanning themselves with newspapers.

"So tell me," Sol said. "How do you and your mother know Lily?"

"We don't," Elka answered.

"You don't? You know my brother, then?"

She shook her head.

"Then how . . . ?"

"We weren't invited."

He smiled. "Well, that's certainly . . . interesting." He thought of the huge plate of cake and herring he had seen the mother helping herself to, the chaser of chickpeas and Scotch. It was one of the more ingenious schemes to fill one's stomach that he'd come across, and certainly less arduous than any he'd managed to dream up until now.

"I thought you knew," she said.

"How would I know?"

"Why did you come over to our table then?"

"Well, certainly not to throw you out."

"Oh," she said.

"Do you get thrown out often?"

"What are you talking about . . . 'often'? You think we do this regularly? Make a habit of crashing other people's weddings? What do you take us for?" And when Sol didn't answer: "My mother had a cousin by the name of Lily Azerov back in Europe—Azerov was my mother's family name before she married my father. We haven't heard anything from her family, not since the war started. She's been waiting for news,

but there's been nothing yet." She looked at Sol, who nodded. His mother, too, was waiting.

"They're still sorting things out over there," Sol said.

"So when she heard from one of her customers that a refugee by the name of Azerov had arrived in Montreal . . ."

"But if it was your cousin, wouldn't she have contacted your mother directly?"

"You'd think," Elka agreed. "But I guess my mother thought she might not be able to find us, or something, that maybe she forgot my mother's married name." Elka thought a little more, then shrugged. "I can't explain what my mother was thinking, dragging me here with her, but your brother's wife is not her cousin. She saw that right away."

Which didn't stop her from staying at the wedding and helping herself to food and drink, Sol noted.

"I don't know why we stayed. I know we shouldn't have," Elka said as if she had just read Sol's thought. "And then the things she said . . ." A blush rose to her face.

"It was a little peculiar," Sol allowed.

"Peculiar" didn't begin to describe it, Elka thought. She had expected her mother to turn around and leave the wedding hall as soon as she saw that the bride was not the lost cousin she had hoped to find. Instead, Ida's eyes had hardened, and her grip had tightened on Elka's wrist. She was transfixed on the bride, and not in the usual, admiring way. Elka could only hope that none of the other guests noticed the expression on her face, a cold, hard expression so out of place at a wedding. It was as if Ida's disappointment had turned into anger towards the bride, Elka thought now as she walked with Sol. As if it were the bride's fault that she wasn't the cousin Ida had hoped she would be.

"I can't really explain it," Elka said again. "Why she would have said those things." To the groom's own brother, no less. And at a wedding she hadn't even been invited to. "She thinks she has a sixth sense about people. You know: what they're like, who they should be with." She glanced at Sol. "For all the good it's done her."

Sol raised his eyebrows in a questioning way.

"Her marriage to my father wasn't exactly a huge success."

Sol smiled. "Maybe her sixth sense works better for other people's business than her own."

Elka smiled, relieved that Sol didn't seem as put off as she'd feared.

"And maybe in this case she's on to something," Sol added.

"What do you mean?"

"It was me the bride was supposed to marry, you know."

"You?"

He told her about the letters he and Lily had exchanged, the arrangement they'd come to—leaving out the part about the payment he'd negotiated. Then the scene at Windsor Station.

"But it wasn't right," he concluded. "I could feel it in my gut." He looked at Elka. "Sixth sense," he added with a wink.

He expected a smile from her in return, agreement from her that he had done the right thing, that the gut never lies. He expected some variety of the nodding, smiling encouragement he was used to receiving during a first encounter with a girl.

"And so you left her there?" she asked instead. "You left your fiancée at the train station?"

"I didn't just *leave* her." What did she take him for? "I called the people who had agreed to host her until the wedding." He remembered his desperate call to Eisenberg—his

boss and self-appointed mentor since his father's death eleven years earlier. "I explained what had happened and asked them to come and pick her up."

"And then you left her? A refugee who travelled half the world to marry you?"

"It wasn't like that," Sol protested, but it was, of course. He remembered Lily's face as she waited to be greeted, the hopeful lift of her eyes at each approaching man, the disappointment, then confusion, as one after another swept past her to welcome someone else. As the crowd around her thinned, she had developed a sudden preoccupation with her luggage— an attempt, Sol knew, to control her rising panic, rein in her darting eyes. She'd bent over her suitcase, a lone, still figure in the swirling crowd, her grey dress too sombre amid the bright summer colours, its classic cut too severe among all the wide skirts and needless flourishes that flaunted the end of wartime restrictions. How long had she bent over that suitcase, he wondered now, fiddling with the leather strap that didn't need adjusting, postponing the moment when she would have to look up again at the emptying hall?

Someone had bumped him, a girl with yellow hair and a wide red mouth. "Sorry, hon," she'd exhaled. Her eyes were blue, her hair crimped into countless perfect, yellow waves. A doll, he thought, like the one his younger sister, Nina, had loved so many years before. A living doll that would leave on his arm if he would just give the signal. She smiled encouragement, her mouth a blur of red. While across the hall on the periphery of his vision, the grey blot he was meant to marry.

What kind of man . . . ? he wondered now, remembering Lily's shadowed face, the dress, all wrong, that had obviously been chosen with care. *What kind of man . . . ?* he heard Elka

think, and a hot shame filled him, a shame charged with anger
at the silent girl beside him through whose eyes he had just
glimpsed a distinctly unpleasant view of himself.

What Elka saw, though, didn't seem to her unpleasant.
She liked how Sol kept to the outside of the sidewalk as they
walked, as if what menaced her resided in the empty street.
She liked the light touch of his hand on her waist as he guided
her around corners and across streets, had begun to wait for it
at each crosswalk, that light, fleeting touch claiming different
parts of her. It was scandalous, of course, that he had left the
woman at the station, but she felt flattered to think that she
had caught what Lily couldn't. Maybe it wasn't so strange that
her mother had insisted they stay at the wedding, she thought
now as she smiled up at Sol. Maybe her mother had a sixth
sense after all.

MAYBE IT WILL BE ALL RIGHT, Bella Kramer thought as she sat
alone at the table reserved for the wedding party and watched
her son and daughter-in-law dance above her in their lifted
chairs. The wedding party consisted of three: Lily, Nathan and
Bella. Nathan's father, Joseph, had died eleven years earlier,
and his sister, Nina, had departed for Palestine as soon as the
war in Europe ended. Sol would normally have acted as best
man and been seated at the table with the rest of the family,
but in this case it was agreed all around that he had no further
role to play in this marriage.

Some head table, Bella had thought when she first sat down,
a small round table with five chairs, the extra two chairs being
for the rabbi and his wife. She remembered the head table at

her own wedding, a long table that extended the length of an entire wall in one of the biggest wedding halls in all of Berdichev, with her large and boisterous family filling one end and Joseph's equally large and boisterous family filling the other. Now *that* was a head table.

Nathan had thought at first that there shouldn't be a wedding party at all, that they should dispense with walking down the aisle, given that Lily had no one to walk with her on the way to the *khupah,* but Lily had shaken her head. "Why should my misfortune rob you of a proper wedding?" she asked. "Then I'll also walk down the aisle alone," he said, to which she shook her head again. She would not have his mother be insulted in such a way.

Nathan had told Bella about that exchange as the two of them sat in the back seat of the car he had hired to take them to his wedding. They could easily have walked over. The synagogue where the wedding was being held was on Hutchison Street, just a few blocks away from their apartment on Clark Street, and it was a beautiful summer evening. But the way a thing starts is the way it continues, Nathan felt, so it was important to him that every member of the wedding party arrive in as much style and comfort as he could afford.

Just how much was this ride costing him? Bella had wondered briefly, but then she dismissed the thought because she knew how proud Nathan felt to be able to hire a car for the occasion. And not just one. Another hired car was travelling through the same streets at that very moment, bringing his bride to the hall where they would soon be united in marriage. It was a gloomy way to go to a wedding, Bella couldn't help thinking. She had been danced through the streets to her own wedding. She had heard the singing and clapping of her

family and friends from a distance and then growing louder and louder as they approached her parents' home. Joseph was already waiting for her at the hall, and they were coming to bring her to him. What a moment that had been. She remembered her joy and feeling of triumph as she was swept through the streets to the man she had chosen for herself and already knew she loved. This quiet drive to her son's wedding felt better suited to a funeral, but she knew Nathan was happy and proud. And she knew he had just told her about that exchange with Lily to paint his bride in the most favourable light to her soon-to-be mother-in-law.

She had patted his knee and smiled.

NATHAN WAS NOT ACTUALLY Bella's first-born; he was her fourth. But he was the first to live past childhood. Her first children had died during the civil war that followed the revolution in Russia. They had not been murdered as so many had been, torn and tortured as each successive band of soldiers reconquered the city; and in that, she supposed, she had been lucky. She shook her head now at that thought, tried to imagine if the hopeful bride she had been would ever have believed what life would soon force her to consider "luck." She wouldn't, Bella knew, but the woman she had become understood the darker shades of good luck. And that's what it had been, a very dark shade of good luck that her children had not been afraid when they were taken. They had gone quietly of hunger and illness while in the embrace of their mother's arms. One after another they had gone, the baby first, than two-year-old Leah, then her first-born, Shmulik, who had been his father's delight.

She had thought then that her life was over, but Nathan had been born just one year later on the passage over to Canada. He had come early, an entire month before the date she had calculated, and neither she nor Joseph had thought of a name for him, neither of them able, at that point, to imagine a happy and usual conclusion to the pregnancy. One of the other passengers had suggested he be named for the ship that was carrying them all to new lives. She smiled now, remembering that passenger—a tailor from Pinsk who was on his way to become a farmer somewhere in the wilds of Saskatchewan or Manitoba. Good luck to him, she had thought at the time, thinking he could farm with a stooped back like that. She wondered now what had become of him.

The man's suggestion for her son's name had been as absurd as his ambition for his new life—the ship was the SS *Vedic*—but it had some appeal to Bella. Not because of any shortage of traditional names—there were all the names of brothers and uncles that were not currently in use, suspended as they were by the premature deaths of their previous owners. But Bella hadn't wanted to plant in new earth what had withered in the old. She wanted a fresh name, one unrelated to anyone she and Joseph had ever known. It was she who had suggested Nathan, from the Hebrew for "gift." It was a name, she thought, that balanced the memories of what they'd come through with their hopes for the future. Joseph, though, had had no hope for the future—his or anybody else's—and had suggested Sol instead, the name of his beloved youngest brother who had died at thirteen of typhus, also during the civil war. Bella, however, was adamant: Nathan, she insisted. Joseph's hope would return. They had been given another child, another chance, and were heading to a new life in a new and distant land. But she had been wrong.

In Russia her Joseph had worked with metal. An honourable substance, he had told her the first time they met. A substance whose history paralleled that of man himself. She smiled to remember it, how cocky he'd been. She had agreed with him, of course. She would have agreed with anything he said at that point—he was so handsome and brash—but her agreement went deeper than that. She was a socialist at the time. She shared the view, prevalent among her co-believers, that the metal industry was by far the most valuable and important of all the industries that would build the socialist future.

In Canada, though, Joseph Kramer had sorted buttons. That was the first job he found when they disembarked in Montreal, and it was a fine job for a newcomer, as it required neither English nor French and paid almost a living wage to anyone who could stand the hours.

Joseph, it turned out, could stand the hours. He preferred the hours, Bella soon came to understand, to those he spent at home, mute and stiff with her and their new child. He preferred the procession of buttons that asked nothing more than to be sorted by colour and size.

Bella had assumed the job would be temporary, a stepping stone to something better, especially when one of their neighbours told her that the Canadian Pacific Railway was hiring Jewish tinsmiths and other metal workers. But the weeks went by, and then the months, and Joseph was still sorting buttons.

"What kind of work is this for a man like you?" Bella began to ask. An endless parade of coloured buttons, and Joseph a man who had once tempered the steel that built bridges and ships.

Joseph couldn't explain it. Not to Bella. Perhaps not even

to himself. "It's calming," he said finally. More calming than the hot milk laced with rum that Bella prepared for him each night before bed. More calming than the prayer he had given up as a youth and resumed again now in the dark mornings before he left for work. He was a man who had thought he would not be able to go on after the deaths of his children, would not be able to find the strength to bear himself through his life. *Forgive me that you and the child are not enough,* he implored Bella, though not in words, never in words. He had found his reassurance, Bella understood, in the meaningless work he now performed. In the ceaseless turning of the conveyer belt: a reminder that life would continue with or without the strength of Joseph Kramer. She had not found it in her heart to forgive him.

Who is that? she wondered now as she lifted her eyes from the past to look around the room. She had noticed the woman earlier; she was the only stranger in the room, she and her sulking daughter, whom Sol had just taken outside. Probably a relative of the Eisenbergs, who had been kind enough to host the bride after Sol's misstep at the station. Everyone else in the room, though, Bella recognized. She had not done too badly, she thought, to be sitting here in a room full of people wishing her and her family well.

"I wish your father were here," she had told Nathan earlier, and she had meant it. There's a force to life that sweeps you along, she thought now, as she watched her son dance with his bride. It was a force not unlike that of the guests who had swept her long ago to her wedding and her future. It would have picked Joseph up again if he had been given more time. It would pick Lily up too, Bella thought. Lily was stricken, Bella knew. She recognized grief when she met it. But

she'll come along. People come along. It's the nature of our species to come along, she thought. Maybe this really would turn out all right.

She rose from the empty table to join the dancing.

CHAPTER 2

The first package arrived on April 27, 1953. I remember the date because it was my sixth birthday. I had learned to read that year, so I could piece together the letters on the wrapping of the little box that the mailman had slipped through the mail slot. *Ruth Kramer,* I read. My name. And below it the address on Cumberland in N.D.G., Notre-Dame-de-Grâce, where we lived at that time, my father and me in the upper half of the duplex, and my aunt Elka and uncle Sol downstairs, with Jeffrey, my cousin, who was a year old then. I remember my excitement. I had never received anything in the mail until then. Not a letter, certainly not a package, and so nicely wrapped. The paper was sky blue with different coloured polka dots, and a patch of white like a cloud on the front where my name and address had been written.

Elka was in the kitchen when it arrived. She was baking a cake for the party we would have that evening. My real party had been the day before, which had been a Sunday. All the children from my kindergarten class had been invited

and they'd all come, except for one or two. It had rained the whole day, so the outside activities that Elka had planned were cancelled—the treasure hunt in the backyard, the game of Red Rover—but we'd played Pin the Tail on the Donkey and we'd watched a puppet show put on by my aunt Nina, who had recently moved back to Montreal from Israel, where she had been a famous actress, and we'd had cupcakes that Elka had bought specially from the kosher bakery because some of the children in my class were more kosher than we were and wouldn't eat the cupcakes with the pink icing and silver sprinkles from Woolworth's that were my favourite. The party we were going to have that night was just for family: me and my father, Elka, Sol and Jeffrey, Elka's mother Ida Pearl, and my grandmother Bella. Nina wouldn't be at this party because she lived downtown and was very busy.

It was still raining—the rain hadn't stopped in two days— which is why I was playing inside instead of in the yard or on the street with Murray or Steven, who lived next door. The package was sitting on the floor by the front door with the other mail that had come that day. I didn't usually pay attention to the pile of letters that lay scattered as they had fallen from the mail slot until Elka picked them up and put them on the table in the front hall, but the sky blue package caught my eye.

When I saw it was for me, I brought it to Elka. To make sure it really *was* for me, I suppose. Or that I was allowed to open it.

Elka was just putting the cake into the oven. The bowl with the last bit of batter was already on the kitchen table for me to lick clean, though she would insist I use a spoon to do that because we didn't live in a barn.

I held out the package to her.

"What's that?" she asked. She examined it closely, gave it a little shake. There were stamps in the upper right corner. One was of a Canada goose taking flight. "It came in the mail?"

I nodded. "Can I open it?"

Elka had a thing she did with her mouth when she was thinking—a bit of a twist. She did that now.

"Let's wait for your father to get home."

SOL ALWAYS ARRIVED HOME from work at five thirty. He was the head of sales for a company that sold buttons. The evening of my sixth birthday was no exception. He came in the kitchen door, which was the back door but the one closest to the driveway, took off his hat and coat and hung them on the hook by the door. He kissed Elka, then picked me right up out of the kitchen chair where I was colouring with the new set of crayons and colouring book that one of my friends had given me the day before.

"How's my angel?" he asked. He always asked that. "My birthday angel. Ooow. You're getting to be so big now, soon I won't be able to lift you."

I told him about the present that had arrived for me and the way he said "Another present?" made me think it was he who had sent it and that it was a bell for the new bicycle—a two-wheeler with training wheels—that he and Elka and my father had given me for my birthday.

In the commotion of Sol coming home, my cousin Jeffrey had pulled himself upright in his playpen, which was in the corner of the kitchen beside the table. He was bobbing up and

down as if jumping, but he couldn't jump—he couldn't even walk yet—and he was squealing. Sol put me down to scoop him up, and as he was kissing the rolls in Jeffrey's neck, my grandmother Bella and Ida Pearl came into the kitchen from the front hall entrance.

I got up from my chair to kiss them both, as Elka had taught me. They were both formal and didn't like a lot of hugging or slobbering. Or noise. Or children, I sensed. But they had each brought me a present, small packages that Elka suggested I put beside my place setting in the dining room, which was where we were eating instead of in the kitchen, because it was my birthday. I put Ida's and Bella's presents beside my plate, and then I went to the front hall to get the present that had come in the mail and I put that beside my plate too.

When my father came home he didn't scoop me up or call me his angel the way Sol did. He wasn't like that. I don't know if we even said anything when we first saw each other at the end of each day. What I remember is the way he would touch my head, his hand half on my ear, half on my hair, and hold it there for a bit. Then he would ask if I had a good day or something like that. On that day, he probably asked if I was having a good birthday. I don't remember his greeting. What I do remember is Elka telling him that something had arrived for me in the mail that day.

What was it about Elka's announcement that brought a sudden quiet to the room? I knew something important had happened and that it had to do with the present wrapped in polka-dotted blue that was now sitting with my other presents on the dining room table. I ran to get it and Elka didn't yell after me *No running in the house,* which was also unusual,

and when I showed the gift to my father, he nodded the way Elka had. I saw Bella and Ida look at each other.

"Can I open it?" I asked.

My father looked at Elka and Sol. Elka and Sol looked at my father.

"After supper," Bella said. "With the rest of your presents."

I don't remember what we ate, what we talked about, the wish I made on the candles. Bella gave me a book, I'm sure. She always gave me books. That year's could have been *1001 Riddles for Children*. (The books she gave me were always a little too advanced for me.) Ida's present was a bell for my new bicycle. I rang it a few times to show her how happy I was with it. And the present in the blue wrapping? When I took off the wrapping there was a little box from Birks jewellers. There was a card too, but I didn't look at that. Elka reached for the card, while I opened the box. I lifted the layer of cotton that lay over the top, and there, sitting on another layer of cotton, was a pink rock.

It was a beautiful rock. Smooth and shiny on top, and almost transparent in places, with jagged little nooks on the underside. A beautiful rock, yes, but it was still just a rock. I was disappointed, and wasn't sure what I was supposed to do with it. I lifted it out of the box to show it to everyone. No one seemed excited. No one said anything, in fact.

"*South shore of Gem Lake, Manitoba, 08:45, April 12th, 1953, clear, 31 degrees F, light wind,*" Elka read out loud from the card that had accompanied it. Not a birthday card with balloons on it like the one that had come with my new bicycle, but an index card of the sort Elka used to write down recipes she found in magazines.

"Let me see it, Elka."

That was my father, asking for the card. He read it. He let out a big breath of air.

Did I already know who had sent it? There was an excitement growing in me as I held the stone. There was something about the way it fit into the palm of my hand, a warmth, as if there were a light bulb inside it.

"Can I see it?" Ida asked. She was talking to me and referring to the rock.

I didn't want to give it to her, was afraid she wouldn't give it back. I was afraid I wouldn't be allowed to keep it, just as I hadn't been allowed to have the rifle I had seen in a toy store. But neither was I allowed to disobey adults. I handed it to Ida. She looked at it the way I had seen her look at jewels in her store.

"Quartz," she said. She offered it to Bella, who shook her head.

Elka took it, and looked at it.

"Who's it from?" I asked. Did I already know?

"It's from your mother," my father said, and as he spoke the words I became a different person.

All my life I had been a girl without a mother. She had left soon after I was born, and no one knew where she had gone. She had not stayed in touch, she would never be back. In a way it was as if she had never existed for me. I didn't miss her, had never missed her. I would not have known what to miss. Her absence was more a background to my life than anything else. It was a given, a stable fact of life that was definitional, not dynamic, like the hole in the centre of a bagel, without which a bagel would be something else—a dinner roll, maybe, a *challah*—but which is in and of itself static, not dynamic, certainly not an active force that might exert its own momentum on the dough.

Now, though, I had a mother. She had been at Gem Lake, Manitoba, fifteen days earlier. It had been cold, but clear. There had been a light wind. She had seen a pink rock and picked it up. And when she did, she thought of me.

I could see her pick it up, though I had never seen her before—there were no photos of her in our home. She was dressed in a long black coat with high-heeled boots and a matching black hat with a little half-veil. It was a glamorous look, more suitable for an evening at the theatre in Montreal, perhaps, than an outing to some lake in Manitoba, but it was the first view of her I had ever had, in my mind or anywhere else. I saw her by a lake that looked a lot like Beaver Lake in Montreal at that time of year: half covered with slushy-looking ice, the ground around it bare with patches of old, dirty snow, the trunks of the surrounding trees expanding at the tops into intricate webs of bare branches. She bent to pick up the rock—it must have been the colour that caught her eye, the only pink in all that white, brown and grey. She held it in her hand—that only bit of pink in the whole world around her. She thought of me. My birthday was coming. She must have remembered. My sixth. She slipped the rock that made her think of me into her pocket to take it home. And then she sent it to me.

"Can I keep it?" I asked.

My father looked at me. Had I missed something? Had there been a conversation while I was lost in my daydream?

"Of course you can keep it. It's yours."

It's mine, I thought. He had said it in front of everyone at the table. Elka was still holding it, but she gave it back to me then. Because it was mine. From my mother. And now, for the first time, I wanted more.

I KNEW THE STORY abqut how my mother had left, because neither my father nor Elka and Sol believed there was any reason that I shouldn't. They had talked about that often, I later learned: over coffee late at night at my father's apartment on Côte-des-Neiges in those first months after she left, over smoked meat sandwiches and cherry Cokes at Levitts on the Main. They had planned how they would deal with the issue of my mother having left, how they would talk to me about her in a way that was honest and natural, how they would answer any questions I might have, assuming that they could. Their own parents hadn't been that way with them, but they would do things differently—in a better way—with me.

On that principle they had each recounted their own version of my mother's departure, from which I, in turn, had created my own, the main point of which was that one afternoon during the second month of my life my mother had walked out the front door, ostensibly for a quart of milk, and simply not returned.

Elka had been over. My mother had invited her for coffee. It had been a nice surprise, that invitation, because Elka had thought until then that my mother didn't like her. (My mother was sad, my father told me, and often when people are very, very sad it's hard for them to act friendly all the time. She was sad because her whole family had died in the war.) It was a warm day in June, one of those days when the house fills with warm, heavy air and opening the windows doesn't help because the air outside is just as warm and heavy. My father and mother lived on the third floor, and the stairway to their apartment was even warmer than outside. Like an oven, Elka said. She was sweating so much by time she climbed to the

third floor that she had to stand outside the door for a few
minutes to try to cool down, because it's not nice to arrive
somewhere dripping with sweat. It's also not nice to arrive
anywhere, ever, without a little gift for the host or hostess, so
Elka had made sure not to arrive empty-handed. She had a
rag doll for me—the one Bella had just sewn up for me when
her belly split open and her stuffing started falling out—and
flowers for her hostess, irises that she had bought at the flor-
ist next door to her mother's jewellery shop. "May Flowers,"
Elka elaborated. That was where we still bought our flowers
every Friday afternoon those eight months of the year that we
couldn't cut them from our own garden.

My mother welcomed Elka with a kiss on both cheeks.
"That's what they do in Europe," Elka explained. She also
thanked Elka for the doll and flowers. "She was always very
polite, your mother. You could tell she'd been well brought up."

"Please," my mother said, indicating the couch in the living room where Elka should take a seat as my mother went
into the kitchen with the flowers to arrange them in a vase.
There was a cake on the coffee table, which surprised Elka,
she had to admit. My mother wasn't much for cooking or baking. There were evenings . . . and here Elka hesitated, but it
had to be said. For the sake of honesty and full disclosure.
Quite often my mother would slice a tomato and a couple of
hard-boiled eggs, place them on the table with a pitcher of
iced tea and call that dinner, Elka revealed. (Quite often when
people are very, very sad they lose their appetites and it's hard
for them to eat, my father said.) "It's possible she had servants
growing up," Elka said.

Elka didn't have a seat. She went over to the crib by the
window, where I lay sound asleep like a little doll. That's

how I seemed to Elka, at that time: like a little doll, perfect and beautiful. My mother brought the flowers into the living room, placed them on the coffee table beside the cake, smiled at Elka, and then went back into the kitchen to put the coffee on. She may have exclaimed when she opened the fridge, may have slapped her head for dramatic effect, may even have made some comment about her own absent-mindedness. Elka was too noisily cooing at me to hear what was going on in the kitchen, did not become aware of my mother again until she re-emerged from the kitchen apologizing for her forgetfulness. She had run out of milk, she explained, and would have to dash across the street for a minute to buy some.

"I can go," Elka offered.

"Don't be silly," my mother said. "When I invite you for coffee I don't send you out to buy your own milk. Will you be all right with the baby for a few minutes?"

(She may not have said it exactly like that—she was from Europe and had only been in Montreal a year by then. But she also might have, because she was an expert at languages, even English. On that point everyone in my family agreed.)

Elka was a little nervous to be left alone with me. She had never been alone with a baby so young before. With any baby, actually. "You'll never have that problem," Elka assured me. Because of Jeffrey, she meant. I'd been helping her take care of him since he was born. "She'll be fine," Lily assured her. Me, she meant. "I just fed her before you got here." Elka nodded and said that she too would be fine. And so my mother put on her hat with the veil that covered half her face, pulled on the long gloves without which she never ventured out into the sun, tucked her purse under her arm and left.

And at first everything was fine. I slept. Elka waited. She

was sure it wouldn't be more than fifteen minutes or so. But fifteen minutes passed, then a half-hour. I was still sleeping, but Elka was beginning to wonder what was keeping my mother. Maybe there was a really long lineup at the store, Elka told herself. Maybe there were a few other things my mother had to get once she was out. But finally, when a whole hour had passed, Elka knew something was wrong. She called her mother, who did not say *Don't worry*. She said she would be right over, though it took her an entire half-hour to close up her jewellery shop and make her way over to the apartment, by which time I was awake and crying and Elka was crying too and my mother had still not returned with her quart of milk.

My father was called. The police. The apartment began filling up with family, friends and neighbours, every one of whom knew that a young mother who did not return to her baby after going out to buy a quart of milk was a young mother lying dead in a ditch or abducted by a maniac or pinned under the wheels of a streetcar.

In the meantime I was still crying, so Ida Pearl went to the kitchen to see if there was any formula. She opened the fridge and it was then that she saw the full quart of milk, as well as several bottles of formula arranged neatly behind it, a finding she reported to the police officer, who didn't have time to listen to a busybody's meddlings when there was a young mother missing and a possible maniac on the loose.

"Excuse me," Ida Pearl said again to the investigating officer, who was asking Elka about any suspicious-looking characters she might have noticed lurking around the street or building when she arrived. It could well have been me, Elka thought, sobbing now at the thought of her own near miss, her

close encounter with the dark force that had brushed past her just moments before sweeping Lily into its deadly embrace. "Excuse me," Ida Pearl interrupted yet again, quite a bit louder now, and she drew the police officer into the kitchen towards the fridge, which she opened. The police officer still didn't see why Ida had interrupted him, so she pointed to the full quart of milk that stood right in front of the bottles of pre-measured formula. A different line of investigative inquiry was immediately launched, one that led, not much later, to the bedroom, where resting on my father's pillow was a note. *Forgive me. Yours, Lily.*

A FAIRY TALE. That's what that story had always felt like to me. Now, though, it became the only story I wanted to hear. And the old versions no longer satisfied. What did she look like? I wanted to know. What did she say? Tell me again. Why did she leave? What do you mean she didn't say, you don't know for sure? What do you know *not* for sure? Who was the note to? How could everyone be so certain she wouldn't come back?

CHAPTER 3

Lily sat on the bed and listened. It was three o'clock on a hot summer day and it was quiet, as quiet as it ever got before midnight. She and Nathan had been married almost three weeks now and were still living with Bella and Sol in the family apartment on Clark Street. "It's just for a few months," Nathan promised her. Soon they'd have a place of their own. She smiled as she thought of that promise; he repeated it every night. "I don't mind living here," she responded every time he said it. "It's your poor brother who won't relax until you remove me from his home." At which Nathan too would smile.

Sol was so ashamed of what he had done that he barely showed his face. He ate his evening meal out and then stayed out until late at night, creeping in under the cover of darkness to sleep on the cot behind the piano in the living room that had become a bedroom for both him and his mother while Nathan and Lily occupied the real bedroom. "He'll get over it," Nathan would say every night about Sol.

Through the open window she could hear drifts of people's voices, children calling, the clanging of the streetcar from a few blocks away. From inside the apartment: nothing, though Bella was home. Bella would be in the kitchen this time of day reading the afternoon paper over coffee or tea. Lily knew she should join her. She knew she should get up off her bed, open the door and join her mother-in-law in the kitchen, but she couldn't force herself to take those actions. She pulled the notebook from under the mattress where she kept it and began to read.

October 1943
I begin with a dream. I'm running through a city.
It's a city I don't know. I'm running along streets
of stone, trapped between the high stone walls that
rise on either side of the street. It's not the white
stone of Jerusalem that cousin Sonya wrote about
in her letters, white stone tinged pink by the sun
that's kissed it for centuries, by the blood spilt for
it and absorbed, over centuries, as its own. No,
it's the cold, grey stone of Europe that entraps me.
Sun-starved stone under a low, grey sky. It will
have my blood, but refuse to absorb it. My blood
will puddle on its surface until a dog laps it up,
until marching boots carry it to another place of
butchery.

I'm running for my life through a nameless city
of Europe, running through a city of death. I'm
running for my life, but death is gaining. I hear its
boots behind me, its song, a drinking song. I turn
blindly down an alley, a blind alley I see too late.

Alongside me, two high walls of stone, and ahead a wall, also stone, with a heavy wooden door. The door is weathered grey. It matches the streets, the walls, the sky of the city. The markings on it are familiar, the scratched indentations to the left of the keyhole. I throw myself against it but it doesn't yield. I hurl myself against the unyielding door as death approaches, its marching boots, its laughing, singing voice. I press my cheek against the door, and then it opens.

Have I died, then? I don't know. Can a person die in her dream and then wake the next morning to recall it? They were upon me, the door wouldn't yield, and then it did. To Aunt Lottie's courtyard in Krakow, where my mother would take me every summer, the clucking chicks and summer warmth, the notes of a piano filtering through the leafy cover.

Is that what awaits me? A fragrant courtyard and summer warmth? The scent of ripening fruit and drifting fragments of music? If yes, then I fear I have no hope of survival. For why would I choose this, this fear and cold and hunger and mud? Why this pain, this futile task, if the summer courtyard of my childhood awaits me when I fail?

Lily closed the notebook as she heard footsteps on the front stairs. She had already started to slip it under the mattress when she realized the steps weren't Nathan's. They were too heavy, too slow. Mr. Hausner from upstairs. He stopped briefly on the landing outside the Kramer apartment, then continued up the

final flight, where she would hear his tread again later, pacing over her head half the night, back and forth, back and forth, more of a shuffle than a walk. She reopened the girl's notebook, leafed past the pages she had already read, had read so often already since she had found it—taken it—that the images in them seemed to rise from her own memory.

Who am I? A mound of mud in an autumn field. A pile of leaves to the side of a forest path. I tuck my hands beneath me as you pass, press my face into the earth. I'm a blur of motion out of the far corner of your eye, utter stillness by the time you fully turn your gaze. In your cities I'm a rat scurrying beneath the surface of your life. I hide in your sewers. I infect your dreams with pestilence. Vermin, you call me. Insect. Cur. Swine. Once I was a girl.

Who are you? he asked me. He had uncovered me as I slept, pushed aside the layers of mud and leaves and lies to reveal me.

He scraped the last of the leaves from between the blades of my shoulders, swept the crumbs of soil from my neck. I knew his touch, the brush of his fingers on my skin. I turned from the earth to face him and my entire field of vision filled with light, the dreadful day, the indifferent Polish sky. In the centre was a shadow, an absence in the shape of him, his broad shoulders, his curls in silhouette against the sky. He held something towards me. A potato? A piece of bread? I reached out to take it but my fingers closed on my own empty fist. I

reached farther and my entire hand disappeared,
my arm.

    A crack had appeared in the Polish day, a draw-
ing back of the world along a ragged seam. I nar-
rowed my eyes to make it out, this parting in the
shape of him, this opening to someplace else.

    Get up, he said. Quick.

Lily sat on the edge of the bed as she read. The room was warm—stuffy, Nathan would complain when he got home from work—but she enjoyed the warmth on her shoulders, bare except for the straps of her slip. She'd been reading for a while, had lost track of how long. She closed the notebook as she heard footsteps again, lighter and quicker than Mr. Hausner's. She slid the notebook underneath the mattress, touched up her lipstick in the mirror, fixed her hair, put on her dress.

"Hello," she said to her mother-in-law as she appeared in the kitchen doorway.

"Hello," Bella answered.

Both women paused then, Lily in the entrance to the kitchen, Bella at the counter. It was the first they had seen of each other since breakfast.

"I've made hamburgers for supper," Bella said. An attempt at conversation that sounded—to both—like accusation.

"I should have helped you. I'm sorry. I started to prepare something before I lay down for my nap, but then . . ."

When Bella opened the icebox earlier she had seen, on the lower shelf, the full extent of the supper Lily had prepared: a plate of sliced cucumber, three hard-boiled eggs, also sliced and sprinkled with paprika, a bowl of blueberries with sour cream.

"I don't know what came over me," Lily said. "I was suddenly so tired."

It was the same thing that came over her every day. The moment Lily finished the minimum allotment of chores and shopping that she deemed necessary to fulfill what was expected of her, she retreated behind the closed door of the bedroom. And to do what, exactly? Bella wondered. To nap, she said. To hide, it seemed to Bella. And from what? Or rather, from whom, more to the point, since Bella was the only other person in the house all day. But Bella was trying not to take it personally, trying not to see the closed bedroom door as a slap in her face, as a rejection of her overtures, of her offered friendship, kinship.

"You feel better now?" Bella asked.

Lily looked at her as if she had already lost track of the conversation they were having. She hadn't, but how could she explain the feeling of strangeness that overwhelmed her when she was out of her room, trying to interact as a person normally would when buying bread in a store or talking to her mother-in-law in the kitchen or going about any other business of everyday life? She couldn't, not even to herself. It was as if the world outside her bedroom was a stilted play she'd walked into and couldn't walk out of again, a dream she couldn't wake from, where everything was menacing in an intangible, slightly surreal way. She hadn't felt this way during the war, when the dangers that she faced were real. Had she felt it then, she would not have survived, she thought; she would have given herself away with the sort of anxious glance or gesture that had been fatal to so many. Why now, then? she wondered. Was it a normal response to what she'd seen and been through, to the difficulties of a new marriage to a man

she didn't know, a new life that could not yet be expected to feel like her own? Perhaps, but nothing about her existence felt normal. She was beginning to think the problem might lie elsewhere, in the very life she was trying to make, the life of another that was stolen, not really hers, not ever meant to be her own.

"Since your nap . . ."

Now she really had lost track of the conversation. "Yes," she said automatically. "Thank you." She glanced at the hamburgers that were sitting on the counter. She could no longer stand the sight of raw meat. The very thought of it in her mouth, the dripping fat, the charred, ground flesh . . . If she had to eat it she would vomit, she was certain.

It was grief, Bella knew, watching Lily. It had nothing to do with not liking Bella. It was a shocked sort of grief that demanded time, space, patience and understanding. And a firm hand in equal measure. "You might feel better if you got out more," Bella said. "It might help you to—"

"Thank you," Lily said again automatically, not really meaning to end the conversation with those two curt words, but ending it nonetheless.

And with that ending—abrupt, imposed, as insulting to Bella as the closed door of the bedroom, as her husband's closed face had been day after day, night after night for years—Bella surged again with a familiar, useless anger. And just beneath that anger, the vaguer, more uncomfortable unease she'd felt since the first moments she'd watched Nathan and Lily together. It was there almost constantly, the feeling: when she awoke in the night to the sounds of her sleeping household, Mr. Hausner's pacing overhead; when she was out shopping, questioning the butcher about the true age of the chicken he

claimed was last spring's, or commenting to the fishmonger about the cloudiness of a particular carp's eyes; when she was standing in the peace of her own kitchen shaping raw, minced meat into hamburger patties. Unease so heavy it felt more and more like dread. It was not that she felt she knew the specific disaster that was coming, the specific form her son's pain would take. It was more a mother's vague but certain dread as she feels the rumbling of the approaching truck that is still invisible, around a bend, but already bearing down on the little boy who is running happily out onto the street after the ball.

"Hi, Ma," Nathan said as he came into the kitchen.

Bella was sitting at the table by now, fanning herself. Lily was standing at the counter by the sink, her back to them both, slicing and salting a tomato. Nathan lifted Lily's hair and kissed the moist nape of her neck.

"It's hot," he said, pulling off his tie and jacket.

The apartment was—by coincidence and unfortunate turns of luck—the same one Nathan had lived in as a child. There had been others in between, some slightly better, some slightly worse, but now this one again, this cold-water, one-bedroom walk-up on Clark Street with its dark kitchen opening onto the back fire escape, and the airless bedroom, now occupied by Nathan and Lily, where Bella's hope for her own husband and marriage had died.

Nathan remembered a night—how long ago was it? He couldn't have been more than five. Sol was about three, Nina no more than nine or ten months. It was a winter night. Joseph came home from work with a valentine for Bella, a card with a man dressed in the fashion of the times and peering hopefully at the reader:

I'm looking for a Valentine
But none of those Jazz gluttons
I want a handy little miss
Who can sew on a few buttons.

At the bottom were two buttons sewn right into the card, two little disks of red plastic that Joseph himself may well have sorted. Bella looked at the card, then tore it into pieces and walked out of the room.

Sol and Nina were already at the table—it was suppertime—Nina in her high chair, banging the tray with her spoon. Sol slipped out of his chair and ran out of the room after his mother. Nathan stayed with his father, retrieved the pieces of the card that his mother had torn to shreds and brought it back to the table. A red and white checked oilcloth covered the table, the red slightly darker than that of the two buttons that had been sewn into the shredded card.

He worked quietly, aware of but not distracted by the cold draft at his back where the heat of the stove didn't reach, his father's silence across the table, the rising racket of Nina's beating spoon and increasingly impatient vocals. His father rose from the table to get one of the potatoes that was cooling on the counter. He broke it in the palm of his hand, put it on Nina's tray and then sat back down. The card came back together, but it was painstaking work, the letters and words not providing any clues about which pieces went where, because Nathan could not yet read.

As Nathan worked and Nina ate her potato, their father began to speak, his voice a low murmur. He described the properties of iron, lead and zinc, explaining the reasons you might use one as opposed to another, or might choose another

metal entirely. Tin, for example. Aluminum. He explained how
carbon combines with iron to make steel, the various ways to
combine zinc and aluminum for die-cast. He spoke in the same
tone of distant wonder with which he might have recounted a
dream, with which his own father or grandfather before him
might once have described the fruits of the Galilee on which
they would sate themselves in the world to come.

"Do you know what lies at the core of the earth?" his
father asked him.

"Rock," Nathan answered.

"Iron," Joseph said. "Molten iron. That's what keeps us
rooted to this world. Why do you think we don't go flying off
into space as the earth spins around like a wild woman? Did
you ever wonder about that?"

Nathan hadn't, had never perceived himself to be spinning.

"You think it's gravity that keeps us here?" his father asked
him. "It's not gravity, believe me. In a hundred years gravity
will be as much an accepted part of science as the flatness of the
earth. As Divine Revelation at Sinai. As nothing more than the
half-baked rantings of another false prophet. It's magnetic force
that keeps us here. Magnetic force, do you understand me?"

"What does the valentine say?" Nathan asked. The reassem-
bly was complete, but he couldn't see what might have made his
mother so angry, unless it was in the words.

"Stupidities," Joseph answered.

"Is that why Mama tore it up?"

"In part." Joseph came over to Nathan's side of the table.
"Are you finished with this now?"

Nathan wasn't finished. He had planned to turn over each
piece and tape the whole thing along the back so it wouldn't
fall apart again. But he nodded yes.

"May I put it where it belongs, then?"

Nathan nodded again, and his father gathered the pieces in his hand and tossed them back into the garbage. Nina started banging her tray again with her spoon, gleeful now, bits of potato smeared all over her face, her tray and on the floor beneath her high chair.

"Your mother's a good woman," Joseph told Nathan. "A faithful woman. She's faithful to the man she married."

Nathan shook away the memory now, put his briefcase on one of the kitchen chairs. It's just for a while, he had promised himself when he first rented the apartment. The war hadn't been over that long; housing in Montreal was still very tight.

"It's just for a while," Nathan had promised Bella, which had touched her. It was the sort of promise a man made to his bride, not his mother, and she had not expected to hear such a promise out of the mouth of a man again. She had boarded at Mrs. Pozniak's during the war, and while she had hoped she might have a home of her own again one day, or at least be invited into one of her children's homes when and if her sons returned alive to Montreal from the war or her daughter, Nina, returned from Palestine, where she was teaching school, she had tried very hard not to expect it.

"Did you have a good day?" Bella knew the question was one better asked by his wife, but Lily never asked, didn't seem to care.

"Not bad." He opened the icebox to take out a beer, saw the supper Lily had prepared. Then he saw the hamburgers sitting on the counter. Which would it be? he wondered. Who would be the victor of this particular skirmish? "Is Sol coming home for supper?"

"He didn't say," Bella answered.

"He has a date," Lily said.

Bella looked at Lily.

"He told me last night," Lily said. "I was up when he came in."

So, Sol she talks to, Bella thought.

"You couldn't sleep again?" Nathan asked. He knew about Lily's insomnia but usually slept through her comings and goings in the night.

Lily shrugged. "Not too well."

"It's so hot," Nathan said.

"You're late getting home today," Bella said. This too seemed to her an observation that should have been offered by his wife. Did Lily even notice the length of Nathan's workday? Bella wondered.

"I had a meeting."

"A good meeting?"

"Good enough," Nathan said. He winked at Lily as she set the table.

Lily smiled, lowering her eyes. She had noticed he was late but hadn't commented. A man doesn't want his comings and goings commented on by a woman, her mother had taught her. She put the hamburgers in the frying pan, looking away as she did so, breathing through her mouth to avoid the smell of dead flesh. It permeated the room, that fresh-kill smell with just the faintest underpinning of rot. She glanced at Nathan and Bella. Was it possible they didn't notice it?

"A business is always slow at the beginning," Bella was saying. "It takes time to build a base of customers, to find suppliers who aren't out to cheat you."

Nathan's business was building fast, faster than anything he had imagined possible when he'd told Eisenberg that he wouldn't be returning to his old job once he was discharged

from the air force. It was hard work, yes, but steady. More and more metals were being released from war production every day. Steel, iron, aluminum—everything that had been in such short supply. And more and more customers were lining up to buy them. It wouldn't be long before he would need his own truck for deliveries, rather than borrowing and renting as he'd been doing until now. And soon he would also need an office of his own. A rented corner with a desk and telephone wouldn't do for much longer.

"Business isn't slow, Ma."

Bella and Lily both looked up at the confident tone of his voice.

"Business isn't slow at all."

"Don't get cocky," Bella warned him. His father had been cocky once, she remembered. It was an attractive quality in a man, but dangerous. No man was stronger than life, Bella thought.

CHAPTER 4

It was a full year and a half before the next package from my mother arrived. October 17, 1954. The date is recorded in the scrapbook about her that I started soon after the arrival of the first package. I was in grade two by then, so I wasn't home for the mail delivery; Elka gave it to me when I was having my after-school snack. Jeffrey (two and a half then) and Mitch (eight months old that October) were upstairs having their nap, so it was just me and Elka in the kitchen. Girls' time, Elka called that brief period of time between my arriving home from school and the boys waking up from their naps.

This time the package was wrapped in plain brown paper, which wasn't as nice as the blue, but I would still save it, I thought, and put it into the scrapbook. The scrapbook didn't have anything in it so far except the blue dotted paper, the Canada goose stamp that Elka had steamed off the paper for me, and the index card that told me, in my mother's own writing, where she had gotten the piece of pink quartz that now sat on top of my desk in my bedroom.

The stamps on this most recent mailing were all of Queen Elizabeth, which presented a dilemma. They should more properly go into the scrapbook I had made about the Queen's coronation, a scrapbook I still added to all the time because I had expanded its scope to include ongoing stories and photos of the Queen's family, her corgis and the trips she took with her husband, Prince Philip. But the Queen's scrapbook was already full to bursting and my mother's was all but empty, so I decided I would put the stamps in my mother's. I would cut them from the corner rather than steam them, because I needed help to steam and Elka was busier since my cousin Mitch was born, and not always as interested in helping me with my projects.

Elka was cooking something at the stove while I unwrapped the package, but I knew she was watching me as she stirred whatever she was stirring. I ran my finger over my name. It was written in block letters, so it was easy for me to read. Then I unwrapped the paper, careful not to rip it. It was another little box, though not from Birks, and when I opened it there was the same layer of cotton. Beneath it, another rock.

"What is it, honey?"

I lifted it from the cotton, carefully, as if I could harm it with rough handling. But I couldn't harm it; it was solid. A smooth, flat grey stone shot through with veins of other kinds of rock. It was beautiful, I thought, and this time I wasn't disappointed.

"Is there a card?"

I pulled out an index card and started to read it, but Elka had to help me. "*Rainy Lake, Ontario, 14:00, October 9th, 1954, overcast, 56 degrees F, light breeze,*" we read together.

"Well . . ." Elka said.

I looked at her. She was doing that little thing with her mouth.

"Your mother likes rocks, I would say."

In retrospect I can see that that was the response of a woman at a temporary loss for words, but at the time it seemed like a perfectly reasonable observation to make. And it gave me an excellent idea for the scrapbook. I would have a page where I would list all my mother's likes. "And lakes," I added. "She likes lakes."

"Yes, that's true. The last one was also from a lake, wasn't it."

"Gem Lake," I said.

"Right."

"Where is Gem Lake, Manitoba?"

"Far away."

"And Rainy Lake?"

"Also far away."

I liked the name Rainy Lake. It would smell nice there, I thought. We had been to a lake the previous summer, Trout Lake up in the Laurentians. I'd learned to swim there but had felt a little afraid every time I went into the water after Sol told me to be careful not to let the trout nibble at my feet. Nothing would nibble at my feet at Rainy Lake, I thought. I would float on my back and the rain would fall softly on my face.

"How far away?"

"She's not there, sweetie. That's just where she was that day."

"Is it closer or farther from here than Gem Lake?"

She thought about that awhile before answering. "Closer," she said.

SHE DIDN'T COME ANY CLOSER, though. Or if she did, she didn't let me know, because another whole year passed without anything from her.

And then one Sunday evening my father told me to go put on a dress because we were going out to eat. We usually only went out to eat for special occasions, but it wasn't unheard of for Elka to announce that she didn't feel like cooking on a Sunday night, or for Sol to announce that he was taking us out on the town. Then we'd all pile into Sol's car or my father's and we'd drive either to Ruby Foo's on Decarie, which wasn't kosher, so we could only eat the fish or vegetable dishes there, or farther, all the way across town to my father's and Sol's old neighbourhood to go to Green's, which was kosher, so we could eat anything and everything that was on the menu, though I always ate the same thing, chicken fricassee, and always made Jeffrey cry by telling him that the chicken's necks in the dish were the fingers of little boys who had snooped in their older cousin's things.

"Stop that," my father reprimanded me. We had gone to Green's that night and, like always, I told Jeffrey that he was eating a little boy's fingers.

"She's just fooling with you," Sol told Jeffrey, but Jeffrey was still snivelling.

My grandmother Bella and Ida Pearl hadn't joined us that night, which was unusual, because we always stopped to pick them up when we went out to eat. My aunt Nina never joined us because she was very busy.

I wiggled my fingers at Jeffrey in a creepy crawler sort of way, which set him wailing again, but no one saw me do it, so no one knew what had set him off. Sol told him sharply that that was enough now, which made him cry harder.

"Really, Sol. Do you think that's a help?" Elka asked, but she was busy with Mitch, who was two then and also making a racket. She shoved a large piece of a dinner roll into Mitchell's mouth just as he opened wide for a good howl and pulled Jeffrey over onto her lap.

While Mitchell was busy trying to figure out how to chew the big wad of bread in his mouth, and Jeffrey was leaning into her chest sucking his thumb, Elka looked at me and asked how I would like to have my own room with flowered wallpaper. The last time Elka had talked to me in such a babyish way had been two and a half years earlier when she asked me how I would like a beautiful little baby girl cousin, a few months after which Mitchell had been born.

"I already have my own room."

"I mean at our house."

There were only two bedrooms in their part of our duplex, so I had to share a room with Jeff and Mitch when I slept over.

"Sol and Elka have bought a new house," my father told me. It was on Alpine Avenue in Côte-St-Luc, not very far from where we lived now, but newer, better. I was supposed to be happy, I knew. That's why we had gone out for dinner, because it was a special occasion, and the new house was what was special.

"And we'll stay on Cumberland?" I asked him. I didn't want Sol and Elka to move away, but I could stand it, I thought, as long as we stayed where we were. I knew all the kids on the street. My school, Talmud Torah, was just a few blocks away on Chester. There was a willow tree in the back that Sol had planted when we moved in, and we had a swing set and a jungle gym. But most of all, paramount to any other thing: my mother knew how to find me there.

"No. We're moving too," my father said. Into an apartment on Côte-St-Luc Road a few blocks away from Sol and Elka.

"A really nice apartment," Elka said. "Way up on the tenth floor with an elevator to ride up and down."

"What about my jungle gym?"

"We'll take that with us," Elka said. "And the swing set. It will all be set up in our yard, which is much bigger than the yard we have now. And you'll come over every day. Just like you do now."

I thought about that for a while.

"You'll like it, you'll see," Elka said.

I thought about it some more, stabbed one of the giblets in my chicken fricassee with my fork and put it in my mouth. "I'm not going," I said.

I saw the adults exchange glances.

"I know it's not the same as living in the same house all together," Elka said. "But it's really not far. You'll see. And you'll still come to our house every day straight from school, like I said. And you'll still eat supper with us. And Carrie lives right down the street."

Carrie was my best friend. We saw each other every day at school and had never had any problem going over to each other's houses after school while I lived on Cumberland, where my mother could find me.

"I'm not going," I said again. I stabbed something else in my stew, some indefinable part of a chicken. "I don't want to live in a stupid apartment, with a stupid elevator, with stupid flowered wallpaper." The flowered wallpaper was actually going to be in my room at Elka and Sol's, not at my father's, but that was an irrelevant detail at that point. "I'm not going!" I shouted.

"Keep your voice down," my father said.

I saw Elka rest her hand on her belly, where the new baby had probably just turned or given her a kick. The stupid new baby, who would probably be another boy and was probably the whole reason we had to move. "I'm not going."

"You *are* going and you're to calm down right this minute."

That was my father, and I noticed Elka laid her hand on his for a minute as if he were the one who needed calming down.

"I'm not going. I'm not going!" I shouted, my voice getting louder and more hysterical with each repetition. "I'm not going, I'm not going, I'm not going!" I cried hysterically as my father lifted me from my chair and carried me out of the restaurant.

THE MOVE TOOK PLACE over a weekend in the middle of March. It was decided that Bella and Ida Pearl would take me, Jeffrey and Mitchell for that weekend. To make things easier. Ida Pearl and Bella lived in adjoining apartments in the building on Decarie Boulevard that Ida Pearl had bought just after the war. Her jewellery store was on the ground floor, along with May Flowers, and she rented out the two storeys of apartments above. Until Elka got married Ida Pearl lived in a duplex in N.D.G., like we did, but not in such a nice one as ours—older, smaller. Once Elka and Sol got married, though, Ida Pearl moved into one of the apartments in the building she owned, and Bella moved into the one next door.

I spent a lot of time at my grandmother Bella's, but not at Ida Pearl's, because Ida Pearl worked all day at her store and she didn't really like me. I don't mean in the more general sense

of her not really liking children. Bella didn't really like children either, but in her case that general distaste broke down when a specific child that she loved was right in front of her. Me, for example. Bella regularly overcame her distaste for noisy, snivelling children to grab me in a big hug, or read a book to me, or tell me stories about being a little girl in Russia and getting buried in a snowdrift or some other such disaster. Ida's distaste for me was something different, more particular. I sensed it, though she was never actually unkind to me in any way. It was her coldness, I think, the lack of pleasure she derived from seeing me. "You're too sensitive," Elka told me, tousling my hair. Which was different from saying there was no truth in what I was sensing.

I assumed, of course, that if Bella and Ida were taking care of us for the weekend, I would be sleeping at Bella's, but that was not the plan. It was Jeffrey and Mitchell who were going to Bella's. I would be going to Ida Pearl's.

"Ida Pearl's?" I asked when I heard the terrible news. It made no sense. But I couldn't say outright to Elka that her mother hated me, so I put it another way. "She's not even my grandmother."

"She's as good as one," Elka responded. Because she was Elka's mother and Elka was as good as a mother to me. That's what Elka meant.

"But she doesn't really like me." It had to be said. I'd been pushed to the wall.

"Don't be a goose," Elka said. "This is a perfect chance for you two to get to know each other better."

Elka, though, obviously had her own concerns about the bonding weekend ahead. As she got me ready she scrubbed my face so hard that my skin hurt, and she pulled my hair so

tightly into pigtails that she caught half my scalp in the grip of the elastic bands, and all the while she kept reminding me that her mother didn't like a lot of noise and fuss and that I was to eat whatever was put before me and to remember to say thank you. But whatever nervousness Elka felt couldn't match my own as she deposited me at Ida's door, flowered suitcase in hand.

Ida greeted me with a brisk hug and ushered me into the den, where she had made up the couch to serve as my bed. I placed my suitcase on top of the blanket, then worried it was the wrong place—the bed was so tidily made up, the blanket pulled flat as a skating rink—so I removed it to the floor. Then I worried that might also be wrong, so I cast about for the place that might be right, and while my mind was occupied with that I peed my pants. I had not peed my pants for years by that time, not even in sleep—I was eight years old, almost nine—and my mortification as I felt the spreading warmth was compounded by fears more specific than the heavy but vague sense of dread that I had felt about the weekend until then. I worried that Ida would yell at me, that Elka had not packed spare clothes and I would have to spend the rest of the weekend bare-bottomed or in my pyjamas. But Ida wordlessly extended her hand and led me to the bathroom, where she stripped off my pants and underwear and lifted me into the sink as if I were as light and small as a three-year-old. And when I was clean and dry and had a towel wrapped around my bottom half, we returned to the den to decide together what would be the best outfit for our next activity: tea in her living room, a room that I had never been invited into before, the den and kitchen having been designated as the only domain appropriate for a child.

When Ida opened my suitcase—whose proper place turned out to be the ottoman beside the couch—I was relieved to see that Elka had packed several changes of clothes, including my favourite yellow turtleneck that went with my favourite black stretchy pants with the stirrups that went under the arches of my feet, and my favourite skirt: a green plaid kilt that was held together with a gold pin. The mere sight of these familiar things lifted my spirits, and Ida must have sensed that, because she patted my hand as I patted my yellow turtleneck and said, "Sometimes things can feel like friends."

A few minutes later, dressed in my green kilt and yellow turtleneck, I made my debut in Ida's living room. It was a formal room, decorated in shades of blue, with scallop-edged blinds behind layers of drapery, and lace-scalloped lamp-shades and a gilt-framed mirror hanging over the powder blue sofa that Elka referred to as the Louis Quinze sofa and that didn't look like anything I should be sitting on but was the only object in the line of Ida's pointing hand, so I sat there as she had indicated I should, hands folded on my kilt, and waited for her to bring in the tea. She brought it in on a large silver tray that was crowded with pots of various sizes, placed it on the coffee table in front of the sofa and poured out two cups. She poured the tea from the largest of the teapots, placed a slice of lemon in one cup and poured in some amber fluid from a smaller pot, then stirred a spoonful of raspberry jam into the other cup and handed it to me as if it hadn't crossed her mind that I might spill the scarlet-tinged liquid onto her powder blue sofa. As if I were no longer the same girl who had peed her pants ten minutes earlier.

"*L'chaim,*" she said, lifting her teacup to me in a toast.

"*L'chaim,*" I echoed back, and she smiled.

She threw back her tea unmindful of its heat, poured herself another cup and smiled at me again, as if my presence
suddenly pleased her.

"So I hear you don't want to move," she said.

"No," I said. I wondered if she had also heard that I had
been carried out of Green's Restaurant screaming and crying
like a four-year-old.

"You like your house. You like your street."

I nodded. I had not told anyone the real reason I didn't
want to move, not even Carrie, and I was not about to make
Ida Pearl my first confidante.

"You think that if your mother comes back for you she
won't be able to find you if you've moved."

Now I was afraid. Ida could obviously read my mind. But
I was amazed too. No adult had ever voiced my deepest wish.
I didn't know what to do. I was afraid if I nodded she would
tell me I was being silly, that my mother was not coming back.
But if I shook my head she would know I was lying because
she could read my mind.

I gave a little nod. Ida nodded too, as if she had, in fact,
known my answer and was just waiting to see if I'd admit it.

"She's a very smart lady, your mother. She'll be able to find
you."

"You know her?" It was hard for me to piece together the
chronology of things. On the one hand, my mother had left
before Elka and Sol were married, so Ida Pearl hadn't really
been part of our family yet at that time, so how would she
know my mother? But on the other hand, Ida Pearl had been
the one who came over right away and showed the policeman
the full quart of milk.

"Not well, but she came to my store once."

"She did?" An image formed in my mind of the inside of Ida's store, which I knew so well, Ida standing behind her display counter, her loupe hanging from a chain around her neck. And there on the other side of the counter, a woman in a long black coat, wearing a black hat with a little half-veil. My mother. "Was she pretty?"

Ida smiled, but then she thought for quite a while before answering. It was a pause that confused me because the question I had asked wasn't exactly difficult.

"A woman can be beautiful without being pretty," Ida finally said.

I nodded as if I understood what she meant.

"You have her eyes," she told me.

"I do?" My eyes were my best feature, my aunt Nina had told me. When I got older she was going to show me how to make them up to take advantage of them. I glanced instinctively towards the gilt-framed mirror on Ida's wall now, and saw my mother's eyes looking at me.

"What's her hair like?" I asked Ida. Mine was brown and wavy, though in the summer it was more frizzy than wavy.

"I don't remember her hair."

"You don't?"

"She usually wore it pulled back."

"In a ponytail?"

"A bun."

"A bun?" Now I was disappointed. Buns were what old ladies did with their hair.

"A twist," Ida elaborated. *Tveest* is actually how she would have pronounced that word—she was from Poland—but I didn't notice her accent very often. Hers or my grandmother Bella's or my teachers' or that of the parents of half of my

friends. I was used to it, used to the *v*'s where *w*'s should be, the *ee*'s for *i*'s, the *r*'s that made my name sound like something they had to dislodge from somewhere deep in their throats. "A French twist."

I didn't know what a French twist was, but it sounded more like the sort of arrangement a beautiful woman like my mother would decide on than a bun.

"Why don't we have any pictures of her?" I asked Ida.

Another long pause, but this one didn't confuse me because the question I had just asked was actually a very hard one. No one seemed to know the answer. ("Sometimes when people are very, very sad they don't like the way they look," my father had told me, which made no sense at all. "Not everybody likes to have their picture taken," Elka said, which also wasn't an answer but the lead-up to another question, "But why don't they?" which led straight to the dead end of "I don't know.")

"There are some people who believe that a camera can see what the human eye can't."

"Really?"

Ida nodded.

"And can it?"

"Of course not. But maybe your mother had that belief."

I thought about that as I sipped at my sweet red tea. "What was she afraid the camera might see?"

And here Ida smiled, but it wasn't a happy smile. It was as if something about me had finally pleased her—the question I had asked, the fact that I could understand the conversation we were having—but there was no happiness in the pleasure. "Who she was inside."

I thought about that. "Like an X-ray?"

"In a way," Ida said, and I thought immediately of the machines at Kiddie Kobbler, not far from Ida Pearl's in Snowdon, where they X-rayed my feet to make sure my saddle shoes, loafers and oxfords fit properly. I liked to see my bones, though, liked how my insides looked.

"But she was a smart lady," Ida said, as if someone had just said she wasn't. "A person can have certain superstitions and still be very smart, and your mother—I could tell from the conversation we had in my store that day that your mother is a very smart lady. But you want to know something?"

I nodded, breathless with expectation about what she was going to tell me next.

"Even if she wasn't so smart, your phone number and new address are going to be in the phone book just the way they're in the phone book now, so if she's looking for you she'll be able to find you just like she's been able to find you on Cumberland."

It wasn't quite the next new fact about my mother that I had been hoping to hear, but at that moment it seemed better than that. Relief filled me like a blast of heat.

"Which isn't to say that you won't be sad to leave your house and street."

It suddenly didn't seem quite so sad to me any more. The relief pushed the sadness away, and Ida must have sensed that, because she smiled that same smile again and poured two more cups of tea, added the same raspberry jam to mine, and the same amber fluid to hers, which was whisky, I realized, from the smell that drifted my way. She lifted her cup to me as she had for our previous *l'chaim*.

"Life is change, my dear, so we might as well enjoy it, don't you think?"

CHAPTER 5

Elka was waiting outside for Sol when he went to pick her up for their first date. An odd behaviour, he thought when he saw her standing there on the street. She lived just west of Decarie, in N.D.G., in a brick duplex that looked small but well kept, with a bit of lawn in the front. So what inside could be so shameful, Sol wondered, that she wouldn't even let him in the door?

"It's hot inside," she said at once, as if reading the question in his mind.

"Outside's not much better."

"It's better. Shall we go?"

The August heat had raised a thin sheen of sweat on her skin, a look, he noted, that not every girl could carry off quite so sweetly.

"Don't you think I should say hello to your mother? Let her know I'll bring you home in one piece?"

"My mother doesn't like you. She's forbidden me to go out with you, to even talk with you on the phone."

"I see," said Sol, more surprised at that point than insulted, half pleased, in fact, to imagine Ida Pearl taking his measure and recognizing that he was a man to contend with.

"She's like that." Elka shrugged. "She thinks no one's up to our standard, and hasn't noticed, of course, that we're not up to it either. Our standard, I mean. That our situation in life, the circumstances in which we find ourselves are not exactly—"

"Wait a minute. Slow down. You mean . . . she thinks I'm not good enough?"

"*Not our type,* is how she'd put it."

"And that's what you came out to tell me? That your mother doesn't like me? That I'm not up to your family's standard?"

"I came out to take a walk. It's stifling in our house. And you can walk beside me if you choose."

"Big of you."

A faint smile now. The dimples. "You can walk wherever you want. My mother doesn't own the sidewalk, after all."

He was angry, insulted, but to turn and leave without another word would be a hollow victory, he felt, more her mother's victory than his own.

"I could use the exercise, I suppose," he said as he fell into step beside her on the sidewalk her mother didn't own.

IDA PEARL WAS LOOKING OUT her living room window when Elka walked away with Sol. She had known as soon as she had prohibited the meeting that Elka would go against her wishes—and why? Ida wondered. Why this man and not another? Why this mediocrity instead of a nicer or wealthier

one? Why not a mediocrity who was not already in love with his brother's wife? Was she so starved for attention? Ida wondered. Have I so starved her that she follows the first man whose eyes actually linger for a moment on her face?

It had been a mistake to suggest Sol take Elka out onto the dance floor, Ida thought. A mistake to ever show up at that wedding, which had not been quite the mission of dashed hope that Elka imagined.

Ida and Elka were at the wedding because of a letter Ida Pearl had received from Sonya, her sister who lived in Palestine. Letters from Sonya came regularly and Ida usually skimmed them with impatience. They were litanies of complaint, nothing more, about the humid heat in Tel Aviv in the summer, the damp in the winter, and the ailments those conditions produced in Sonya, her husband, Leo, and their ever-growing brood of children; about the lack of culture in Palestine—she'd been a poet back in Poland and had belonged to a literary circle there; about the British, the Arabs, the price of eggs, the growing violence . . . None of which dissuaded her from encouraging Ida Pearl to move there. *Why should you and Elka sit alone in Montreal like two dogs that have lost their master?* she asked at the end of each letter. *You can starve here as well as there. Your loving sister, Sonya.*

Sonya's letters always found their way to the garbage within ten minutes of entering the Krakauer household, but the foul mood they invoked in Ida Pearl persisted well into the evening and following day. The most recent letter, however, deviated from all those that had preceded it in that there was actually something of interest in it. A woman had turned up on Sonya's doorstep in Tel Aviv claiming to be their paternal cousin Lily.

She wasn't their cousin, Sonya wrote to Ida. She bore no resemblance at all to the Lily that Sonya remembered, a brash and freckled little girl who used to visit from Antwerp every summer. *I know people change*, Sonya wrote. *And G-d knows what she's been through would change anyone. But such a change? So extreme?* Could an experience change a person so much that there was no hint left of the person she'd once been? Sonya wondered.

She didn't know. How could she know, never having been exposed to such an extreme of human experience? This alone gave Sonya pause, made her invite the young woman into her home.

Was it possible, then? Sonya wondered as she made tea, prepared the platter of cake. But when they started to talk, she knew that it wasn't. The girl was an imposter, a thief. Maybe worse. She didn't even know the names of her own family, her beloved parents, brothers . . . *all of whom I now fear are lost*, Sonya wrote.

She confronted the girl with her lie, expecting a confession, a plea for mercy that Sonya fully intended to extend. *She's still a living soul, after all, a living, breathing, Jewish soul that managed to escape an inferno the likes of which you and I cannot understand. I would never expose her, never turn her in, and was prepared to reassure her completely.* But the young woman didn't flinch, didn't ask for reassurance. Confronted with her lie, she maintained it, maintained with perfect calm that she was Lily, despite not knowing any fact of her own past.

This is what confused me, Sonya wrote. *Why the pretence? "I won't expose you,"* I promised. *But neither would I take her in. "It's not like we're family,"* I told her.

"We are family," she said. Then she related a dream in which she was running through a town, fleeing for her life. She came to a door. It was a heavy wooden door the colour of stone. She described it to me, its colour and markings, the scratched indentation to the left of the keyhole. It was the door of our childhood home in Krakow.

It wouldn't open to her no matter how hard she pushed. She threw herself against it—her life depended on its opening—but the full weight of her was as insubstantial as a pebble bouncing off its surface. That's what she told me. She leaned against it, resting more than pushing now, knowing these were the last moments of her life. She leaned her cheek against it, the flat palm of her hand. It opened easily then—into peace: a leafy courtyard, clucking chicks, strains of piano trickling through an open window.

Our own courtyard, Sonya wrote. She was describing to me the courtyard of our childhood, this imposter who looked nothing like Lily, yet knew the summers of her childhood, this stranger who had never stepped foot in our home but could bring it back to me with such force that I lost myself in it. I lost the present moment of my life to a summer afternoon heavy with the scent of ripening apricots, the sound of Mama's voice mingling with the notes of Mrs. Gamulka's piano. Do you remember those afternoons?

Ida did.

I don't know how long I rested there in the dappled shade of that courtyard—such a deep, contented rest. More than a few moments, I suspect, for there was a note of alarm in the voice that pulled me back, dragged me to the present by asking if I was all right.

I became aware at once of the noise of Tel Aviv, the nause-

ating smell of the sea, the weight of the grief that for one brief moment had lifted from my chest.

"Close the windows," I begged her. There was nothing to be done about the smell—it's everywhere, always, that briny rot that swells the walls and permeates even the soft, fine curls of my children's hair—but the noise could be blocked. I couldn't bear the noise.

And what were the sounds that so upset me, sounds so offensive that I experienced them as an assault? People talking on the balconies below me, motorcars and the hum of the city, the high, laughing voices of children in the playground, my own three children among them.

"Please, the window," I said, but she wouldn't do as I asked. She brought me water, cooled my forehead, encouraged me to drink.

I was in danger at that moment, I'm telling you the truth. I was standing on an edge, the balls of my feet still firmly placed on the hard, cold surface of my present life, but my heels unsupported, sinking deeply into memories, the past, a surface that yielded like billowing cloud. I wanted her to stay now, this woman who wasn't Lily. I wanted her to stay and return the dead to me, return me to the dead that felt more like life at that moment than my own children laughing and calling to one another in the playground outside my open windows.

"Please," I said again. Stay, I meant. Tell me your dreams. I wanted to fall back into the void that was waiting to receive me.

But she wouldn't tell me anything more. She's practical, this new Lily of ours. She had arrived just that morning and her status was still precarious.

"Help me," she said.

I sent her over to the Zlotnik woman who arranges things for

people like this—papers, marriages, jobs, whatever is needed.
No problem, Mrs. Zlotnik said. She could have something
arranged that very afternoon, but—are you ready for this?—a
new life in Palestine wasn't good enough for the imposter.

"Canada," she commanded Zlotnik.

"Canada?" Mrs. Zlotnik could only laugh. She was still
laughing, I believe, when the woman pulled out a diamond.
Not a cut diamond, mind you, a rough one, and a good size,
apparently, its source as untraceable as its bearer—I can only
fear it belonged to our dear cousin Lily, that it was one of
Uncle Chaim's, from his workshop.

Zlotnik told her to put the diamond away. There must
have been something she would find easier to resell, gold coin,
maybe—what does a woman like Zlotnik know about assess-
ing the value of an uncut diamond?

"It's all stolen," I reminded her when she was telling me
the story.

"Who are we to judge?" she responded, my moral instruc-
tor, the righteous Mrs. Zlotnik, who gets richer with every
refugee that she helps. She told the woman to leave it with her
for a few days.

It was more like a few months, and then a little longer to
get things properly arranged, but she's on her way over right
now as I sit here on my balcony. She's travelling more quickly
than these words I write to you. The lucky bridegroom's name
is Kramer. Go to her wedding and weep.

Ida had read the letter, shaking her head.

"What?" Elka asked, watching her.

"Nothing," Ida said. She could not quite absorb what her
sister was telling her, could not quite believe it was true.

"Is she still trying to get us to move there?" Elka asked.

Was it Sonya's tendency to embellish that had made Ida doubt what she had read? Or was it a reluctance to face the implications for her family if what Sonya said was true? She'd gone to the wedding fully informed that the bride was an imposter, yet expecting, somehow, to see her cousin Lily walk down the aisle. *I forgive you,* she'd been prepared to tell her, though her cousin probably wouldn't even have known there was anything about her or her family that required forgiveness. Lily had been a girl of just eight or nine when her father, Ida's uncle Chaim, had thrown Ida out of his workshop in Antwerp. *What's past is past,* Ida had been planning to say, though as she prepared her small speech she knew that wasn't quite true. Just receiving the letter had been enough to stir the hurts from the past that she had thought long dead, extinguished, not merely hiding within her.

Still, she couldn't deny her hope. It had been fifteen years since she'd last seen anyone from her family. She was in the process of trying to calculate just how old Lily would be now when the bride appeared at the head of the aisle. A complete stranger.

"ARE YOU MAD AT ME?" Elka asked Sol as they settled into a booth at Miss Montreal. She shouldn't have told him what her mother thought of him. She had thought he would understand, that it would make him sympathetic to the sorts of difficulties she had to put up with every day of her life with her mother. Every hour. Instead, he'd barely spoken the whole way over to the coffee shop.

"No," Sol responded. "What would I be mad about?" He

was as affronted as he was furious, thinking how wrong the
mother was, how obtuse in her assessment of his character
and prospects. Yet he wondered how Ida Pearl had come to
her low opinion of him, on what basis she'd decided he wasn't
good enough for her daughter.

"It's not really my mother's fault," Elka said, looking for
ways to soften the blow, to soften Sol, salvage the evening
somehow. "She's . . ." But here Elka hesitated. How to soften
the fact that she had already told him that her mother didn't
think he was quite up to her standard? "She was famous once,
you know. In her youth."

"Right." Sol made a show of studying the menu, though he
already knew it off by heart. He took a different girl to Miss
Montreal every other week.

"Really." Elka looked at Sol to see if he was still upset, but
he was now studying the menu with such complete concentration it seemed he thought the future of the world could be read
from its offerings. "Her work was famous, anyway." Still no
response. "She was a diamond cutter," Elka went on, though
there had been no indication from Sol that he was even listening. "Among the best in all of Antwerp. Who were the best in
the entire world, of course."

"Uh-huh," Sol said. Like my father was a skilled metal
worker once upon a time, he thought, and my mother a radical who lit fires of enlightenment in the hearts of every factory
worker she encountered. "Ice cream?" he offered.

"Please. And cherry Coke. No, make that coffee." Coffee
was a more sophisticated choice, she thought.

"So . . . your mother's Belgian, then?" No wonder she was
such a snob. They were almost as bad as the German Jews, the

Belgians, thinking they were better, more cultured than their Russian and eastern European brethren.

"She was from Krakow originally. That's where she was born. But then after her father died, she moved to Antwerp. She didn't want to, but she had to. She had an uncle there, her father's brother Chaim, who was willing to take her in."

"Her mother couldn't keep her?" How high-class was that? Sol thought.

"Her mother had six other children to take care of. Not that her uncle didn't, but he could afford another. He was in diamonds. And anyway, my mother worked for her keep."

"He took her in and then put her to work?" Nice family, Sol thought. And she thinks I'm not up to *her* standard.

"He didn't put her to work. She wanted to. She didn't want to be a charity case."

"Still . . . How old was she?"

"Seventeen." Just a few months older than Elka was now. "She started as a polisher. That's what the women in his workshop did. But somehow she ended up learning to cleave and cut. Which was almost unheard of for a woman. And her uncle tried to keep it unheard of. All her work was under his name, his reputation. And he paid her *babkes*." Elka took a sip of her coffee, poured in three creams and half the container of sugar.

Sol smiled, watching her, took another sip of his own, black, as he liked it.

"She got better and better. Her uncle got richer and richer. But then they had a falling-out. Over pay, supposedly, but really over the fact that the secret was out, that more and more dealers were beginning to demand my mother's work by name."

"So what? He was still the one who was collecting on it."

"My great-uncle Chaim had five sons of his own who also worked in that workshop. Five sons who also cut diamonds."

"I still don't see . . ."

"Mediocrity always lives in fear of excellence."

"Ah."

"He fired her."

"Nice guy."

"He not only fired her. He sent her into exile."

"Exile?"

"Well, maybe not quite exile. He bought her a passage to Montreal."

"So she wouldn't go to work for one of his competitors."

"Exactly," Elka said, rewarding him with a full smile.

"But why Montreal?"

"He knew some people here."

"And he just sent her off? With nothing?"

"With some cash to get started and the names of a few people he knew. Not that she ever contacted any of them. She didn't have any of their addresses and had just started asking around when she met my father. Arthur Krakauer." She looked at Sol to see if he knew him. "She thought he was a gentleman. Because he bought her dinner a few times and helped her with her English." Elka shook her head. "Talk about naive."

Sol smiled.

"What's so funny?"

"Nothing." He couldn't very well tell her how young she seemed to him at that moment, how green, how naive, calling her mother—that warhorse—naive.

"Do you find it amusing that he walked out on us?" There, she thought. I've said it. Her gaze was cold and steady.

"Not at all. I didn't mean . . ."

"He was gone before I was even born."

"I'm sorry."

"Along with all the cash Uncle Chaim had given her for her new start."

"He took her money?"

"Along with her honour."

"No," Sol said. "He didn't take her honour."

A faint blush of colour flowed in beneath the steady gaze.

"But all the same, if I ever meet him, I'll spit in his face."

"He's not worth the spit in your mouth," Elka said, but she was pleased with his response, Sol could tell. He had redeemed his earlier smile.

"She tried to find work after he left but there were no diamond workshops in Montreal. Or jewellers who would hire her. I guess they didn't think an abandoned woman with a bawling infant was good advertisement for engagement rings and wedding bands."

"I guess not," Sol agreed. There was a courage to her honesty, he thought. He admired it. Most girls would have left out the details of such a family background, waited until the hook of their charms was more firmly planted in his flesh before revealing abandonment, poverty, the whole sordid picture. "Here," he said kindly. "Eat some ice cream. It's melting."

He's probably looking for the nearest exit, Elka thought. But better now than later. She had already had a disappointment when a boy she'd liked had disappeared after discovering that the upper storey of the duplex in N.D.G. didn't represent quite the rosy picture he'd imagined. At least, she assumed that's why he'd disappeared. She risked another quick glance at Sol's face.

"But she has a good business now," Sol said, encouraging her to continue. "Good" was perhaps a bit of an exaggeration,

but Ida was certainly managing to keep herself and her daughter fed and housed, and in a good neighbourhood, no less, which was no mean feat for anyone, let alone a woman on her own.

"Pretty good," Elka agreed. "She started it when I was still a baby. Uncle Chaim set her up. Mr. Generosity."

"Set her up?"

"With diamonds. He provided them on credit."

I should only have had such an uncle, Sol thought.

"Diamonds cut in his workshop by his sons. Inferior diamonds, in other words. Diamonds inferior to the ones she would have cut." Elka shook her head remembering how her mother would point out the flaws to her when each new batch of diamonds arrived, the dullness one revealed when turned a certain way, the dark centre of another whose pavilion had been over-angled. The fire that could have been created here had this angle only been broken in a different way. Elka could hear her mother's voice in her mind. Or the brilliance there had the light only been bent to a greater degree of refraction. As if Elka had any idea what she was talking about.

"So all she had to do was find a shop to rent." Sol sighed.

"And build a business from nothing, with no contacts, no experience, no friends, no support from anyone." The gaze again, cold and steady.

"Of course. I didn't mean . . ."

"And she's strange, my mother."

Like I hadn't noticed, Sol thought.

Elka sighed, licked the last bit of ice cream off the maraschino cherry. "Do you want this?" she asked before popping it into her mouth.

Sol shook his head, smiled. He signalled to the waitress for more coffee.

"She's not naturally . . . friendly. You know? She couldn't find customers. Not at first. It was so bad we couldn't even afford a proper place to live. She couldn't come up with rent for both the shop and an apartment, so we had a room in someone else's flat. One small room. No privacy, of course. Not that I cared about privacy then, but she did. My mother. No hot water. And the shower six blocks away. That's how we lived until I was eight. And my mother knowing all the while that she was one of the best diamond cutters Antwerp ever produced."

"That was the thirties," Sol said with a shrug. "She's lucky she didn't lose her shop." He thought it best not to mention just yet that he still had to walk over to the Y for a shower, had done so, in fact, just that evening, in preparation for this date with Elka. "It wasn't so great for us either."

"What does your father do?"

"Nothing now," he answered with a lightness that fell flat. "He died in '35."

"I'm sorry."

"Hit by a streetcar on the way to work. The number 55," he added, as if it mattered whether it was the 55 or the 83, or the 29 that he had taken just that evening to see Elka. "He was in buttons."

"Better Made?" Her mother had made the ring for one of the Better Made weddings.

Sol shook his head. "Button King. Better Made makes the buttonholes. We make the buttons."

"So you're in buttons too, then?" Her face flushed again as she realized she hadn't thought to ask until then what he did for a living, had been too busy talking about her own life. Not even her own life. Her *mother's* life. How immature.

He saw her heightened colour and assumed it had to do

with his job, with her disappointment over discovering the disparity between what she wanted for herself and what was actually sitting across the table from her. "It's just for now," he said. It had been eleven years at that point, excluding his years in the service. "Nathan and I took my father's job when he died. Two sets of hands for the price of one—and we were supposed to be grateful."

Sol remembered the look of gratitude on his mother's face when Eisenberg showed up at his father's funeral and made his offer of employment. It was a gratitude that seemed to reset the very lines and features of Bella's face. And when Eisenberg assured her that he wouldn't be a mere boss to her two boys, but a guide and mentor as well, Sol barely recognized her, his mother, who until then could have been faulted mostly for an unforgiving sharpness, but who was now transformed before his grieving eyes to a soft-eyed cow grateful for a day's reprieve from the slaughter. It was a moment so shaming to Sol that he swore he would avenge it, a vow he had not yet honoured. Though Eisenberg—it had to be admitted—had made good on his own vow of that day.

"Which Nathan was, of course," Sol continued. "Properly grateful. He *tukhes*-licked his way off the assembly line within a year. Right into bookkeeping and accounting. But he could—he had the education, had already finished high school by the time my father died. Or just about, anyway. He only missed the last four months. I missed the whole last two years and four months."

Elka hadn't realized that she, having already finished grade ten, was the more educated of the two.

"I wasn't going to go back after the war, was going to strike out on my own, but Eisenberg made me a good offer."

"Eisenberg?" Wasn't that the name Sol had mentioned calling from the station to come pick up his rejected bride?

Sol waited for her to ask what his boss's offer had been, but Elka's attention had stalled temporarily on the fact that Sol's boss had been the one to dig him out of the mess he'd made with Lily—how secure could his job be after that? That and the fact that he hadn't finished high school. She was imagining how all of this would go down with her mother. If it came to that. If he ever asked her out again.

"Sales," Sol said. "Head of sales, actually. Which would be great if I was the kind of *shmo* who wanted to spend his whole life working for someone else."

"Head of sales," Elka repeated. This was good, she thought. Unexpectedly promising. Definitely something she could present to her mother in Sol's defence. "How many in the department?"

The question surprised him. He hadn't thought she would know to ask that. She was still in high school, after all, didn't have experience in the workforce. "For now it's just me. But that's part of my job. To build the department. Something from nothing. Like your mother did. Except that she had diamonds to sell, of course, not buttons."

"Buttons are better."

"Come again?"

"People always need buttons. You can't rely on diamonds to pay the rent when times are bad."

"Your mother did."

"No she didn't. We would have lost the shop had she not developed a sideline."

"A sideline?"

"Matchmaking."

"Are you serious?" He could see that she was. "But people don't even use matchmakers any more."

"They do when my mother sets her sights on them."

He remembered Ida's peculiar and off-putting comment about the stench of Nathan and Lily's match, could not imagine what sort of loser would seek out her services. "Was she any good at it?"

"As good as fate." A hint of a smile, which Sol met with his own.

"And let me guess where all the happy couples bought their rings."

"Bingo." A full smile now.

"I like that," he said. "I like a woman who can think on her feet."

"She can think lying down as well, my mother."

CHAPTER 6

I had my own room at Elka and Sol's new house, as promised, with flowered wallpaper, a red carpet and white furniture embossed with gold, and I liked both the prettiness of
it and the fact that the door to it could be shut. If it was shut,
people had to knock before entering. This was a new rule I
had announced when we moved, and to my surprise neither
Elka nor Sol told me that they were the ones who made up the
rules in their home and that I was acting spoiled. The sudden
privacy was a giddy pleasure. I could do whatever I liked in
my room and think whatever I wanted to think, and no one
asked me if they could have a turn (Jeffrey) or offered me a
penny for my thoughts (Elka).

What I liked most about the move, though, was that Carrie lived just down the street on Bailey, which was by the train
tracks. Most afternoons she and I climbed the fence behind
her house so we could play on the tracks that ran behind it
or in the large empty fields that had not yet been developed
into tracts of apartments and single-family housing. In colder

weather we trudged through the snow drifts pretending we were explorers trying to reach the North Pole, setting up forts along the way so that our competition—usually the kids from Saint Richard's—couldn't claim they had been there first. As the weather warmed we would lay our ears and pennies on the tracks and thrill to the vibrations of the trains we could hear from miles away and to the flattened images of the Queen after a train had rolled over her.

One afternoon one of the girl's from Saint Richard's taught us how to hitch a ride on a slow-moving freight train that was coming through. "It's easy," she said. We just had to know that the train was moving faster than it seemed, so we would have to run along it as fast as we possibly could to get up enough speed and momentum to land correctly when we jumped. We had to grab hold of the metal handle exactly right and if we got it wrong we would fall under the train. It had happened to another girl from her school. She'd lost both her legs. "I was there and saw the whole thing," the girl assured us. "The blood was"—she dropped her voice a little—"terrible."

My terror made it all the more enticing and exciting. I looked at Carrie. I don't think fear was even part of her mix. She had just heard that someone else had failed at something, so she was going to succeed. I'm sure that's what the gleam in her eye was about, though I wouldn't have put it that way then. I only knew, at that moment, that she was too competitive. That's what Elka thought. "Winning isn't everything," Elka had told me at supper one night after I hurt my back trying to jump over a skipping rope that Carrie had kept tying higher and higher between two trees in our yard. ("It's not going to hurt her, Elka," my father had answered.)

So we ran exactly the way the girl had instructed us and

grabbed hold of the metal bar and hauled ourselves onto the train.

"Well done," the girl said. I felt a glow of accomplishment and external approval beginning to warm me. "For a couple of Jews," she added with smirk.

I was a bit stunned at first. We lived in an almost entirely Jewish world. Our school was Jewish, our neighbourhood was Jewish—so much so that some people called it Côte-St-Jew—and I had not encountered that sort of comment before. I had heard of anti-Semitism, of course, but it was from somewhere else (Russia, Europe, the part of town my father, Sol and Aunt Nina grew up in) and another time (before I was born). My first thought was how stupid the girl was. I hadn't quite moved to my second thought when Carrie hit her. More than hit. She punched her right in the stomach. It looked to me like a hard punch, the sort of punch that, if there were an audience and they weren't on a moving freight car, would have led to a fight. But they were on a moving train and there was no one else around to witness any loss of face, so the girl just gave Carrie a funny sort of grin that was different from her smirk and then proceeded to jump off the train. We followed quickly, automatically, but though we knew to push as far out away from the train as we could, we had no sense of the physics of the thing, and both had hard falls followed by some rolling.

"You okay?" the girl from Saint Richard's asked. She had also rolled, despite all her experience, and we were all lying where we had come to a stop, not far from one another, at the bottom of the rise of the tracks.

"I think so," Carrie said.

"I think so," I also said. I was lying on my back looking up

at the sky. I felt more than okay. I felt wonderful. The ground was cool and damp against my back—it was spring and the earth hadn't warmed yet. The sky was a pale and gauzy blue with white clouds moving across it. I had just escaped certain death, and the thrill of it was pumping through my veins.

"What happened?" Jeffrey asked when I came into the yard. He had been playing on the jungle gym, but jumped off when he saw me.

I already knew my face was bleeding, because Carrie had told me.

"Carrie and I were attacked by some Indians," I told him.

His eyes widened. "You were?" It actually came out as *you wuh* because he hadn't quite gotten the pronunciation of his *r*'s down at that point.

"Yeah. By the fields behind Carrie's house. But it's okay. We fought them off."

"You did?"

"There were just two of them. Not big ones," I added. "But don't tell your mother. I don't want her to worry."

Jeffrey nodded, eyes still wide. He wouldn't tell her, I knew. He might still be a baby, but he didn't want to be. He was almost five and would rather be in my camp than be grouped with his little brother Mitchell, and his baby brother, Chuck, who had been born just a few weeks after the move the previous spring.

"I'm going to go home to wash up before she sees me," I said.

"I won't say anything, Wootie. I pwomise."

"Scout's honour?"

He nodded solemnly.

I went home—to my father's home—and looked in the

mirror. The damage to my face wasn't too bad, nothing that would require much of an explanation, but I didn't feel like going back to Sol and Elka's that afternoon. I wanted to stay where I was, alone in the quiet of the apartment I shared with my father. I'd never spent time alone and that afternoon, for the first time, I wanted to. I called Elka.

"Hi, hon," she said. "You at Carrie's?" Quite often I called from Carrie's at that time of day to ask if I could eat supper there.

"No, I went home. To my dad's."

"What happened?"

"Nothing, I just remembered that most of my stuff for that science project is here, so I thought—"

"I don't like your voice. Did you and Carrie have a fight?"

"No," I said.

"What then?"

"I want to stay by myself today."

"By yourself?" A long silence. "You mean for supper too?"

"I can make a sandwich." I was almost ten already. Just two more weeks. Elka knew I could make a sandwich.

"You're not afraid?" she asked. She had been left alone so often in her childhood that she swore her own children would never know the meaning of the word until they wanted to. I wanted to now and she could tell, I thought. Or maybe, on that particular afternoon, she was just so tired from her own three kids and her Passover cleaning that there was some relief in having one less child at the table.

"Okay, sweetie, but if you change your mind you call right away. Uncle Sol can drive up to get you."

It wasn't true that I wasn't afraid. I was, a little. Not of anything happening to me, or anyone coming in to kidnap

me. It was the silence of my home. That was what I found unnerving that first afternoon and evening. I felt very small within that silence. But also a little bit excited. It wasn't still, the silence. It seemed as I sat there on the leather couch in the living room that it moved in and out, sort of like an accordian, compressing and expanding around me. I stayed on the couch for a while, nervous about what might happen if I got off it and walked around, but then I did.

I started with the living room. We had already lived in that apartment for a whole year by then, but it felt different exploring it alone, without my father home. There was his chair, a recliner, in black leather like the couch. I ran my hand along the leather. And there was my father's little table right beside his chair where he piled his newspapers and magazines and where he put his glass of Scotch and little dish of salted almonds when he got home from work. I went through the pile of papers—*The Montreal Star* from the day before, *Time*, *Life*. Then I moved on to the cabinet where we had our hi-fi.

Sol and Elka's hi-fi no longer sat in their living room but was downstairs in the newly finished basement that was now the family rec room. They had a TV, too, which we didn't have yet. It sat right beside the record player on a special piece of furniture that took up half the wall and that Sol called the entertainment centre. Their records were mostly Frank Sinatra and Peggy Lee and the Barry Sisters, though they also had Beethoven's Nine Symphonies and Brahms' Symphonies 1 and 2 and *Kiss Me, Kate,* which was a musical they had seen when they went to New York City for their honeymoon. And Chuck Berry, of course. I say "of course" because one night the previous spring, soon after the move, we were all in the rec room, where Sol and my father were setting up the ping-pong table bought specially

for the new house. Elka put on a song she said she had heard on the radio and it had reminded her so much of Sol that she had to run out and buy it. It was "Brown-Eyed Handsome Man" by Chuck Berry. As soon as Elka put it on, it made her want to dance, she said. It made me want to dance too, I said, so she pulled me off the couch, where I had been wiggling to the music, and she started teaching me how to jitterbug.

"Careful, Elka," Sol warned her. She was in her ninth month of pregnancy then.

"Don't be such a square," Elka said, and she pulled him away from the ping-pong table to dance with us.

He laughed a little but then he started dancing. Then Jeffrey started dancing and Mitch also—though his version of dancing was just to stand in one spot turning round and round and round, laughing the whole time. My father didn't join the dance but he leaned against the wall smiling as he watched us. And then Elka said, "Ooh" in a sharp sort of way and put her hand on her stomach, and Sol said, "What? Oh my God." And she said, "It's okay, I'm just going to sit down for a minute," which she did, with Sol standing beside her going, "What? What?"

When the song ended Elka was still sitting with her hand on her stomach, though Sol had stopped saying "What? What?" by then.

After a little while she said, "You know, I think we'd better go to the hospital."

My father and I stayed at their house to take care of the boys until Ida Pearl and Bella could get over, but even before Ida and Bella arrived we had a call from Sol that the baby had been born. It was that fast.

"Good thing they left for the hospital when they did," I

said, to which my father smiled, tousled my hair and agreed, "Good thing."

They were going to name him Chuck, my father said. After Chuck Berry.

"They are?" I asked, and we both laughed.

He told me then about how his mother wanted to name him for the ship he was born on.

"She did?"

"What's wrong with that?" he asked. "You don't like the name Vedic?"

I told him I liked Chuck better, and we laughed again.

Ida Pearl, though, didn't think naming a baby was something to laugh about. (Not to mention that it was bad luck to tell the name of a boy before his *bris*.) "Chuck?" she asked as soon as she and Bella arrived and heard the news. "What kind of name is that?"

"I think his official name will be Charles," my father said, which seemed to help a little. We didn't tell her about the Chuck Berry part.

My father's record collection included Beethoven's Nine Symphonies and Brahms' First and Second Symphonies just like Elka and Sol's. (There had been a period of time a couple of years back when Bella was giving records of symphonies for presents.) He also had records by Duke Ellington and Ella Fitzgerald and Artie Shaw and Art Blakey and Charlie Parker and a whole lot of other jazz musicians. And then there were the two records of Israeli folk songs and *Peter and the Wolf,* which were mine.

On the bookshelf beside the record player was my set of Childcraft encyclopedias, my father's *siddur,* the Soncino book of the weekly Torah and Haftarah portions, and some art

books that had been a present from a lady named Joyce that my father had dated for a few months when we still lived on Cumberland. (She was very nice when she came to dinner—it was she who had given me my records of Israeli folk songs— but after a while she stopped coming.) On one of the lower shelves there were a few novels from when Elka had signed my father up for the Book of the Month Club. My father didn't read novels—he read newspapers and magazines—so I wasn't sure why Elka would have signed him up unless maybe there had been a two-for-one deal when she joined herself. And beside the Book of the Month Club selections, the notebooks.

They had always been there, the notebooks. In plain view, in the centre of our living room. It was an odd place for them, in some ways, but where else was my father supposed to keep them? In a box at the back of his closet as if they were some- thing to be ashamed of? There was nothing about my mother anybody needed to feel ashamed of, Elka had told me, and my father obviously agreed, so her notebooks sat in plain view, in the middle of our living room, in broad daylight (light that was slowly damaging them, though I wouldn't know that until years later when I studied conservation).

There were two. The older one had once belonged to a girl my mother had known in Europe. And right beside the girl's notebook, my mother's.

The girl's had a soft leather cover that had been fawn- coloured at one point. You could still see the original colour deep inside the seams when you pulled it off the shelf and opened it, which I did now. But the outside was mostly stained and discoloured. Inside, its pages were filled to the very edges with handwriting, Yiddish words so tiny I could barely make them out, a crowded mess of words that I couldn't understand.

I closed it, put it back on the shelf, and pulled out the other one. This one was my mother's. She had bought it not long after she and my father were married, but she had not taken it with her when she left. It was also leather-bound and was in good, almost perfect condition. And it was empty.

Why hadn't my mother written anything in her book? I wondered. Why had she left it behind? ("I don't know," my father had said. "Maybe she couldn't think of anything to write," Elka said.)

I had never been alone with my mother's notebook before. This was very different from looking at it with someone watching me. I opened it and ran my fingers along the empty pages, wondering if my mother had run her hand along those same pages. I ran my fingertips along the pages and then the surface of my whole hand, wondering if I was touching where my mother's hand had touched. I closed my eyes to see if I could feel anything unusual, and I thought maybe I did, but I couldn't tell what, for certain. I did it again, and, yes, there it was again, a strange, pulsing feeling. It was a bit like when my aunt Nina had brought over her Ouija board and we sat with our fingers on it (lightly, Nina warned me) and then all of a sudden, it began to move a little. I sat for a long while with my fingertips resting on the first page of my mother's notebook, and there was definitely a pulsing coming from it.

One more package had arrived from my mother by that time, bringing the total to three. All of them rocks. The most recent one had come to our new apartment, so Ida Pearl had been right about how smart my mother was. Or that she was smart enough, at least, to know how to use a phone book. The wrapping paper on the third package was green; one of the stamps had another goose on it, nesting this time. Both the

paper and the stamp went into the scrapbook and I also was able to add a line to the page about my mother's likes: *Birds,* I wrote. Then I crossed it out and wrote, *Geese,* which was more specific.

The rock was as beautiful as the other two. This one had a fossil in it, an entire little skeleton like a mini-dinosaur embedded within it, as if a baby dinosaur had lain down on a rock for a nap one afternoon while his mother and father went out hunting. (For what? I wondered. What did dinosaurs eat?) And then when he woke up he was trapped inside his bed and nobody could ever get him out.

It was a sad rock, then, but also a very special rock that I was happy to have and would take special care of because it had something in it that had once been alive, so in a way it was almost like a grave, and I knew how important it was to take care of graves. (My father and Sol and Nina went to visit their father's grave twice a year.) But I was also disappointed with the present. More disappointed than happy, I had to admit. Was it that I had thought at first that the rocks were the beginning of something, and now I understood they might not be leading to anything but more rocks? Was it that the most recent rock was, in fact, a grave?

The accompanying card said: *Oldman River, Alberta, 13:00, May 7th, 1956, clear, 58 degrees F, still.* The name was as evocative to me, in one way, as Gem and Rainy lakes had been. I immediately saw craggy rocks all around it, their faces like those of old men, with fossils embedded in them. (I would be surprised years later to see just how accurate my mental picture of that landscape had been.) But I didn't see my mother in that landscape. I just saw the rocks and the river. And a bigger problem with the river was its location. There was no

doubt that Alberta was farther from Montreal than Manitoba or Ontario. Which meant she was getting farther from me, not closer. Which was another source of disappointment.

I pasted the index card into the scrapbook but couldn't pretend the scrapbook was a project that was going well. Its pages remained mostly empty, and the ones that had something pasted in were not anything anyone else would find interesting: scraps of wrapping paper; stamps; index cards with place names, dates and weather conditions written on them; a page with the heading *LIKES,* and then three words below that heading: *Rocks, Lakes, Geese.* Four words if you counted *Birds,* which was crossed out. The Queen's scrapbook, by contrast, was full to the brim with fascinating pictures and articles. Just a few weeks earlier I had added a photo of the entire royal family, Princess Anne looking particularly beautiful in a dress that must have been caught in a slight breeze at the moment the photo was snapped, because it billowed all around her in a swirl of light, cottony blue.

There was no question that my scrapbook about my mother was becoming boring to me. Even my fantasies about my mother had started to dry up. It was not that I was no longer curious about her. I was very curious. But curiosity does require something to feed it, and the pickings on that front were decidedly slim. I was famished. Hence my excitement when I felt the pulsing from the empty notebook that had once been my mother's. Maybe it wasn't as empty as it seemed. The thought came to me like a jolt. Maybe she *had* written in it. And maybe that's why she had left it behind, because she had written in it, but in invisible ink, which she knew, somehow, that I would figure out.

The phone rang. That too hit me with a jolt. I wasn't sure what to do. It was as if I had been caught doing something

I shouldn't, even though it was just someone calling on the phone who couldn't see me, and I wasn't, in fact, forbidden to look at the notebooks. It was not only permissible for me to be doing what I was doing, but natural. ("It's natural to be curious about where we come from," Elka said.) But things that were natural could still be embarrassing, like being caught by Carrie's mother with no clothes on when she came into Carrie's room while we were playing doctor. And I wasn't sure that the pulsing I felt from the book was the same kind of natural as the curiosity Elka had been talking about. So I put the book away before I went to the phone and by the time I got there it had stopped ringing.

It started up again almost immediately, and when I answered it Elka asked, "Where were you?"

"In the bathroom."

"You gave me such a fright. I was about to send Uncle Sol over."

"I was making a pee."

"Are you okay?"

"Yes."

"What did you eat for your supper?"

"A cheese sandwich and a glass of milk." That wasn't much of a lie because I was really hungry by then and was going to go make myself my sandwich as soon as I got off the phone.

"I called your father to let him know you're home. He said he'll be home soon."

It was six thirty. He was almost always home by seven on weekdays, except for Wednesdays, when he had supper with Melinda, who he was dating that year and who had a daughter my age, which we were both supposed to be excited about—Melinda's daughter and I—but we weren't, particularly.

"Okay," I said.

"You're sure you're all right?"

"Yes."

"And you'll come straight here after school tomorrow?"

"Yes."

"Well, then I guess I'll wish you sweet dreams."

"You too."

"And remind your father to make sure he calls me as soon as he gets in so I know he's home."

"Okay."

When my father came home fifteen minutes later I was on the couch in our living room, my empty plate and empty glass on the coffee table beside me.

"Call Elka," I told him before he even had time to shut the door.

"Yes, ma'am," he said, and he did that before he even poured his Scotch and got his little dish of salted almonds.

Once he was settled in his chair with the newspaper and the other magazines that had arrived in the mail he asked how my day had gone.

"Fine," I said.

He looked at me for another few seconds to see if I'd go on. When I didn't, he asked if I had any homework to do.

"Did it already." Which was true. The following year Carrie and I would be switching from our school to the Young Israel Day School because it was better, harder and stricter, according to Carrie's parents. For now, though, our homework didn't occupy much of our after-school time. "That's why I came home. I worked on it all afternoon."

My father nodded. I don't think it ever occurred to him that I might lie to him. Just like it may not have occurred

to him that my mother might lie to him, I suppose. And I didn't think of what I was doing as lying. (Maybe my mother hadn't either.) I thought of it as privacy. That new concept. It wasn't just the door to my bedroom I was learning to shut that year, but other doors that guarded places deep within myself that were my own and that I didn't want to share. So I didn't tell him about learning to jump up onto a moving train. I knew that if I did, Carrie and I would be forbidden to cross the fence to the tracks and the field beyond. And I didn't tell him about the girl from Saint Richard's saying "Jew" as if it were a bad word, because I knew that he and other adults would make too big a deal out of it. And I didn't tell him about the time I had spent with my mother's notebooks, because the pulsing I had felt was something between her and me that other people wouldn't understand.

"You know what I was thinking today?" I asked him.

"What?"

"How neat it would be to have a chemistry set."

"A chemistry set!" The idea obviously pleased him. "What kinds of experiments do you think you might want to perform?"

"Oh, I don't know. Litmus tests, maybe." We had just learned about that in science class. "And stuff with ink. You know, invisible ink."

My father nodded. Then he said, "I don't suppose we have any baking soda in this house, do we?"

"Elka might."

"Lemons," my father said. He always had his tea with lemon. Milk and lemon were the two things we always had in the fridge.

He got up from his chair and we went to the kitchen, where

he sliced a lemon. We didn't have a squeezer like Elka had, so he just used his hand and squeezed the juice into a little bowl.

"Okay. Now go get a sheet of paper and a Q-tip."

I ran to get them. My father never cared if I ran in the house.

"Good," he said when I returned. "Now I'm going to go back to the living room and you're going to write a secret message using the lemon as ink. When you're finished, bring it to me."

What to write? I thought about writing my name, but he had said I should write something secret. I finally decided what it should be.

"Don't forget to let it dry before you pick it up," my father called, just as I was about to lift the dripping wet paper.

I waited a few minutes and when it seemed like the lemon juice had dried I brought the paper to my father.

"Ah. A blank piece of paper," my father said.

It really did look blank. As blank as the pages in my mother's notebook, except a little wavy now, from still being damp with lemon juice. My father held it up to the light bulb in the lamp by his chair and as he held it there I saw my letters begin to emerge in brown. *Mrs. Lazaar is mean,* I had written. Mrs. Lazaar was my ballet teacher, and just that week she had assigned our parts for the end of the year performance. I had hoped to be one of the swans but I wasn't chosen for that. I would be a bulrush, Mrs. Lazaar had told me, a role that was just as important as a swan, she said, and one that would require lots of hard work because it wasn't easy to learn to sway the way a bulrush does. But I knew it wasn't as important or as pretty as a swan. Carrie would be a swan dancing across the stage while I would stand swaying in a corner being

a stupid bulrush. I saw my statement emerge in brown and then begin to fade as the rest of the paper also turned brown.

"It's the acid in the lemon juice reacting with the acid in the paper," my father explained.

He didn't ask about Mrs. Lazaar, the way Elka would have. I don't know that he even noticed the secret message I had written. He was more interested in why the heat revealed the writing and in explaining that to me. If I were to mix baking soda with water, we could do the same thing, he told me. And we could also use grape juice then, rather than heat, to reveal the writing.

I didn't care that he hadn't asked about Mrs. Lazaar. Or if I did, just a little. I could hardly wait to be alone in the apartment again, and as soon as I was I went straight to the bookshelf, pulled out my mother's notebook and held it to the light.

Nothing.

I held it closer.

Still nothing.

I held it on the light bulb itself and the paper turned warm without revealing anything.

"ROCKS?" my aunt Nina asked.

We were all at Elka and Sol's for the Passover Seder and I had told her about the fossil in the rock my mother had sent me. She hadn't heard about any of the packages my mother had sent to me, probably because she lived downtown and we didn't see her much.

"She's sending her rocks?" Nina directed her question to Elka.

Elka nodded, and the look exchanged between Nina and Elka during that nod was not unlike the look exchanged among all the adults the evening the first rock from my mother arrived.

"What kind of rocks?"

"Beautiful ones," I said. It was not that I didn't know by then that there was something strange about my mother sending me rocks. I knew. But strange could mean many things, and since Nina and Elka's exchanged glance was pushing its meaning towards nuts, I was pulling it back as hard as I could towards special and beautiful.

Nina jumped right on board with me. She asked me about the latest rock, and made admiring sounds as I described it to her. So much so that I felt encouraged to describe the scrapbook to her as well, as if I still thought it was a wonderful project, which I didn't, but it became a little less boring when Nina took such an interest and said she absolutely must see it that very evening and was going to come right over to our house after the Seder.

She didn't end up coming over that evening—the Seder went on longer than expected, as it always did, and by the time we had helped Elka clean up it was late and time for bed—but she told me that she would definitely come over soon to see it. On my birthday, for sure, which was just two weeks away.

I wasn't to get my hopes up about Nina's visit, Elka told me. It wasn't that she didn't mean to come. She did mean it when she said it, but often things got in the way for Nina.

"Yeah, like Nina," Sol said, meaning that Nina was selfish.

That was what my father and Sol thought about Nina: that she only thought of herself. That that was the real reason she had gone off to Palestine right at the end of the war, when my father and Sol still weren't home from the service and their

mother, Bella, who was a widow (not that Nina cared) was all by herself in Montreal. Not because she was an idealist or a Zionist or wanted to teach war orphans to read, like she said, but because she thought she could do whatever she wanted over there ("Must be nice to have no one to answer to," Sol said), including trying to be an actress.

"Your aunt Nina's a dreamer," Elka told me, which was why I wasn't to let it hurt my feelings if she didn't come over to see my scrapbook on my birthday.

Which she didn't.

"I'm so sorry," she said when she called to tell me she wouldn't be coming. She was a little breathless, as if she had just run in the door from something very important. And it turned out she had. A really, really important acting part had come up for her and if she didn't take it her whole career might fall apart. ("What career?" my father asked.)

She did come for Jeffrey's birthday though, which was in late June, stopping at our house first to see my scrapbook. Another rock had arrived from my mother just the previous week. That brought the total to four. This one was black with swirls of green that Ida Pearl thought might be olivine. My mother had found it on the west bank of the Fraser River, near Boston Bar, British Columbia, which was farther yet from Montreal. The wrapping paper was blue. "Exactly like your eyes!" Nina said, and it was true that the colour was a sort of greyish blue very much like my eyes. Which meant it was also like my mother's eyes, if what Ida Pearl had told me about my eyes being like hers was true. The stamp had a picture of the explorer David Thompson standing beside a map of western Canada.

Nina admired the scrapbook and told me it had given her an idea for my birthday present, which she still hadn't gotten me.

"What kind of aunt am I anyway, forgetting to get my favourite niece a present for her birthday?" she asked. (I was her only niece.) I showed her the birthday present my father had given me: a chemistry set. "Our own little Madame Curie!" she said.

Nina brought her present over the following week: a map of Canada attached to a bulletin board, with different coloured pins that I could stick into the places where my rocks came from. Which were, of course, the places I knew for certain my mother had been.

I knew when my father was happy and when he wasn't, and as I unwrapped my present from Nina and she explained what it was for, he definitely wasn't happy. That didn't stop him from helping me and Nina stick it up on the wall in my bedroom, but after, when I told them I wanted to find the places on the map by myself and they left my room and walked down the hall, I heard him ask her if she really felt she should be encouraging me.

Encouraging me in what? I wondered. What was wrong with encouraging me? Wasn't "encouragement" a good word? But they were far enough away that I didn't hear Nina's answer.

CHAPTER 7

Who are you? he asked.

I had been walking for days. My skin was caked with dust, my hair a mat of grime, but it was not the black soil of the fields that clung to me, or the red clay of the riverbed or the yellow sand of the paths and roads I had walked. It was the grey dust of ruin, of homes destroyed, of entire towns pummelled to a fine dead powder. I carried it with me. I felt its weight with every step.

I'm a walking graveyard, I told him. The dead are buried in my skin. Look at my face. You'll find your father in its pores. Your mother rests in the creases at the corners of my mouth.

He wet his shirttail with the spit from his mouth and cleared a swath of skin.

Don't, I said. You'll disturb them.

My cheek, a clearing now in the dust. He licked the flesh of his thumb and drew it along

my brows, uncovered the sloping curves of my
face. I felt the groove above my lip exposed by his
touch, the tender skin beneath my eyes, the mole
on the corner of my mouth that my grandmother
promised would one day cast a spell of love on a
man. Hours passed. Days, I think. His eyes were
black but they reflected light. My face emerged,
revealed itself to him.

There was no truth in this notebook, Lily thought as she snapped it shut. It was just the fantasies and dreams of a desperate, heartbroken girl, a girl who was perched on the edge of her death at the very moment that her life should have been opening before her. It was sad to read, but it wasn't truth.

IDA PEARL had just flipped the sign on the door of her shop from PLEASE CALL AGAIN to RING TO GAIN ENTRANCE when the buzzer rang. It was 10 a.m. on a warm September day. She hadn't expected a customer so early, hadn't expected a customer all day, in fact. It was the Friday before Labour Day; people were savouring the last fleeting bit of summer, thinking no further than the three days of leisure ahead. No one was going to buy a ring that day. Ida had opened her shop resigned to filling the hours with bookkeeping, inventory and the inevitable arguments with Elka. The girl had not heard back from Sol since their first date—a month ago now—and had decided, it seemed, that it was the fault of her mother, her mother who had ruined, once and forever, any possibility that she, Elka May Krakauer, might someday know happiness and the love of a man.

"I hope you don't expect me to hang around here all day," Elka had just spat, which, of course, Ida hadn't.

She had hoped, rather, that Elka might find some way to amuse herself on this, one of the last remaining days before school started up again, that she might go for a walk with a friend, have a picnic on the mountain . . . do something, anything other than sit in the shadows of the shop with her nose in a book and a scowl on her face, waiting for the phone to ring.

"Do you want to get the door?" Ida asked when the buzzer rang.

"No," Elka said, though she did then rouse herself from the chair by the back wall where she had set up her camp for the day. She slid the keys off the hook under the counter and ambled over to the door, at which point her demeanour changed entirely.

"Oh! Hello!"

Ida heard the change in Elka—the current charging through her, straightening her back and animating her voice—and her stomach sank. The mediocrity, Ida thought.

But the voice that answered Elka's wasn't Sol's. "May I enter?" A woman's voice.

"Oh! Of course! I'm sorry!" Elka jumped aside, freeing the entrance she had been blocking.

Ah, Ida thought, as she saw who it was. She rose from her desk to stand behind the counter.

"Mrs. Krakauer?" If Lily had noticed Ida's presence at her wedding, she didn't let on.

"Yes. Come in. Please."

"Thank you." Lily closed the door behind her and approached the counter. "Lily Kramer," she said.

"Yes," Ida said. She would not pretend she didn't know who was standing before her in her own store. "How are you?"

"Very well, thank you. And you?" She was speaking in Yiddish.

"Very well." Ida answered, also in Yiddish. "Thank you."

And now Ida waited. She did not jump in with small talk to ease the way, did not ask how she might be of assistance, did not even allow herself to consider the range of possible reasons that might have impelled the woman to come to her. She waited, observing the fine bones of the face before her, the fine cut of the dress, the same grey dress—though Ida couldn't know this—that Lily had been wearing when Sol rejected her at the station.

Wool, Elka thought. In this heat. A light wool, true, but still . . . And yet, if Lily was warm or uncomfortable in any way, she gave no sign, not a drop of excess moisture on the surface of her skin, not a hint of heightened colour in her cheek. She showed nothing, Elka thought, but a smooth countenance of untroubled elegance.

"Is it getting hot out there?" Elka asked.

"Not unduly," Lily answered, a response that insulted Elka, who felt her attempt at conversation snubbed, and impressed Ida, who mistrusted histrionics of any sort.

Lily placed her purse on the glass countertop, her gloved hands folded, for the moment, on top of the clasp.

Kid gloves! Elka thought. That must have set her husband back a bundle. Her own naked hands looked childish in comparison, and her dress—a lively cotton print—flimsy and inappropriate to the season, which was early fall, after all, even if the weather did not yet reflect the change in the calendar. No

wonder he hasn't called me, she thought with new despair, her prospects for future happiness sinking ever lower.

Lily unlatched the clasp of her purse and reached two long, gloved fingers into the dark mouth that opened.

Ida felt the hammering of her heart, the slowing of time as she waited for what might emerge.

A velvet bag, Elka imagined. Black velvet, as befitting the glamour of the fingers reaching for it. Black velvet and tied with scarlet string. Never mind string: satin. Scarlet satin, a long narrow strip of it, and tied in an elegant loop. So caught up was Elka with the packaging she expected that she didn't recognize what was actually between Lily's fingers when they did re-emerge from the purse. And how could she have been expected to recognize the small grey crystal that her mother had been wondering about ever since receiving her sister Sonya's letter? Elka had never seen a rough diamond before. Nor did she know the contents of her aunt Sonya's most recent letter.

"I have reason to believe this might be . . ."

Ida waited, looked at the woman who had the gall to come into her store with her stolen diamond as she had gone to her sister Sonya's with her stolen name. But Ida was stronger than Sonya. Surer. She would outplay this woman at her perverted game.

. . . *yours,* Lily had thought she might say. That's what she had imagined on the way over. But would she have, really? she would wonder later. Even had the woman not been looking at her like that, so coldly, as if there could be no good in her. Would she really have put her fate in this woman's hands?

". . . a diamond," she said.

Ida placed a small square of paper on the countertop.

"Please," she said, gesturing towards it.

Lily placed the stone on the paper.

Ida picked it up first with her fingers, rolled it between them, placed it on the back of her hand, examined it with her naked eye, then put it back down on the square of paper. Next she reached for the loupe that always hung from a chain around her neck and brought it to her eye, picked the stone up with her tongs and brought it to the loupe for a closer look. She put it down again, removed the loupe from her eye.

"It's a diamond," she said.

Lily nodded, swallowed audibly, the first and only indication that she might be nervous.

"As for its value . . ." Ida looked again at the stranger in front of her, who met her eyes, waiting, it seemed to her, but for what? For Ida to sink into a faint as her sister had? "Value is not a simple matter to determine."

Lily nodded again.

"The size is good. The weight. But the surface is cloudy, as you can see for yourself, so we don't know what's inside. It's possible that once a window is cleared—to take a look inside, you understand?—that the inclusions found there, the flaws, will require a cutting that sacrifices much of the weight. Even the surface is flawed. Look at this . . ." She passed a loupe to Lily as she would to any customer, picked up the stone again and pointed with her tweezers to a tiny rust-stained crack. "Iron oxide," she explained. "It's been forced into the crack by the movement of the earth or water. On the surface such a flaw presents no problem, of course. A surface flaw is polished away, but interior flaws, if the interior is riddled with—"

"The Pohl was riddled with flaws," Lily said. As any customer might.

"The Pohl." Ida laughed. "Oh my. Now you begin to remind me of my neighbour Mrs. Kaplan. Her son Hyman was expelled from school last spring for bad behaviour. Terrible behaviour, from what I've heard. Well, it seems that Einstein too was once expelled from school, also for bad behaviour, so Mrs. Kaplan reasons that if Einstein was expelled for bad behaviour and Hyman shares the same flaw it must mean that her Hyman is another Einstein in the making."

Lily received this comparison with a cold stare. "My reasoning couldn't be more unlike your neighbour's."

"And your diamond couldn't be more unlike the Pohl."

It must be an extremely valuable stone, Elka thought. She had never seen her mother feign quite such a level of indifference. If indifference was what she was feigning.

"The quality of the stone is . . . potentially . . . good. *Potentially,* you understand."

Lily nodded.

"But if it's value that interests you, that will depend first on whether you can find a buyer who doesn't care about . . . the circumstances in which it was acquired." At this she brought her eyes again to Lily's. "There's no value if there's no buyer, after all. And then, if you do find a buyer, and that's a big if, Mrs. Kramer . . . people do care about the provenance of the goods that pass through their hands."

They do? Elka wondered.

"I apologize," Lily said. "I had heard, had been led to understand . . ."

Elka remembered how she had gone on to Sol about her mother's skill and former fame. Had he talked about that to Lily, then? Was it Sol who had led her to understand that Ida was the person to whom she could bring a diamond to cut?

"I see," Ida said. "You want me to cut this stone, which may well be stolen . . ." But now Ida hesitated. She had arrived at last, at the moment to confront the woman, to demand that she explain who she was and how she came to possess the name, the memories and the diamond that she was claiming as her own; but her instinct told her no, not now. There was strength to the woman standing before her, she thought, but it was a hard, brittle strength. It would not yield to direct confrontation, would shatter before it would yield. It needed softening.

And besides which, Ida suddenly felt afraid, though of what, exactly, she couldn't say.

"Not that I'm accusing you of theft, you understand, but in the absence of any information whatsoever about how this stone came into your possession . . ." She waited until it was clear that no further information would be forthcoming. "You'd like me to cut this diamond, which may well not even be yours, so that you can then turn around and sell it, at a good price, a far better price than you can get for it at this stage, given the circumstances."

And now, without responding, Lily made motions of leaving, reaching for the diamond, enfolding it in the paper on which it lay.

"I'm sorry," Ida said. "But you must understand, Mrs. Kramer . . ." Ida knew she had misplayed the encounter, but didn't know how, to what effect, or how to shift it. "I can't simply . . ."

"That's fine," Lily said. She picked up the diamond and put it back in her purse. "I do understand," she said. And with that she snapped shut the clasp of her purse, wished good day to mother and daughter and swept out of the store.

IT WAS NOT STRICTLY ACCURATE to say that Ida Pearl had been among the most renowned diamond cutters of her entire generation. She had been good, yes, and would no doubt have become even better had she not had the disastrous falling-out with her uncle so early in her career. But she *had* fallen out, and she had not, in the relatively brief period of her active working life, been able to achieve quite the heights that Elka had ascribed to her in her conversation with Sol. Certainly she had never worked with a stone anywhere near the size and calibre of the one that had sat, for a few precious minutes, on her counter. Her dusty counter, she noted in those first stunned moments after Lily left her store.

"Elka!" she shouted, as if Elka were somewhere out of reach, rather than hovering, as she was, just behind her mother in the dimly lit back recess of the shop.

"What!" Elka jumped, startled by the sudden harshness in her mother's voice, half afraid she was about to be ordered to run down the street after the woman that Ida had all but called a thief, in order to bring back the stone that Ida had all but accused her of stealing.

"The counter's filthy. A disgrace. Did you not even bother to wipe it down this morning?"

"I'm sorry." Elka managed to convey in those three spare syllables all the injustice she felt at the false accusation—the counter was merely dusty, not filthy—as well as at the many equally wounding injustices she had suffered in her life thus far, the betrayal by Sol merely the most recent.

He had told that woman everything, she thought again, as she wiped down the counter. My mother's background, our

private business . . . He ran from his date with me, the impression of his lips still warm on my forehead, to tell her everything I'd confided. She imagined Sol and Lily at a café somewhere, a smoky café with a long brass bar and windows hung with lace curtains. The sort of café she'd seen only in posters. A chic café, in other words, not like any of the snack bars, soda shops and delis that she frequented. She saw them deep in conversation, their heads inclined towards each other, a carafe of red wine between them. Did they share a laugh at my expense? she wondered. Were they amused by the silly teenage girl running to tell her secrets to the first man who pretended to take an interest in her? She heard them whispering, heard them laughing at the childish girl who had a crush on Sol.

SOL HAD NOT RUN home to Lily immediately after his date with Elka. He had walked instead through the humid city streets for hours, precisely to put off the moment he would have to return to the home that he temporarily shared with Lily. Thoughts of Lily had been muted during the hours he'd spent with Elka, but only muted, never absent, and now he faced another night on the cot behind the piano in the living room, his interim "bedroom" until Nathan found an apartment for himself and his new wife. Sol would lie for hours sleepless, sweating, aware of Lily's presence just behind the closed door of the bedroom, or down the hall, through the open window of the kitchen that opened onto the fire escape stairs, where she spent part of every night, smoking and staring into space.

He stopped in at a snack bar. The coffee there was scalding and like acid in his mouth, but he drank it anyway, thinking it

might clear his mind. Then he drank a second cup, and he might have drunk a third had a girl not slid onto the stool beside him remarking that he looked like he needed cheering up.

"Thanks but no thanks," he said, glancing her way only long enough to take in the heavy makeup and puffy skin around the eyes and jaw. He smiled to soften the rejection, though he knew her concern for him was only professional, and she sidled up closer, misunderstanding his smile as indecision.

"I'm sorry," he said.

"You won't be if you take me home."

He left a dime beside his empty cup, and a dollar for the girl, and left.

"Hey, mister." He heard the sound of high heels trotting after him. He turned and she was right behind him, holding out his dollar. "I'm not a charity case," she said. "Just lonely."

Now he was thoroughly depressed as well as agitated. At the pathetic pride of the girl who either was or wasn't a whore, at the uselessness of his own instincts which he had once believed would carry him to a better life.

He thought about Elka with fondness. There was a spirit to the girl despite the superficial first impression she gave of a personality soured by resentment. And she had brains as well, and certainly was pretty, with her brown eyes and adorable dimples. On a feature by feature basis she could even be said to be prettier than Lily, but he couldn't deny the terrible pull he felt towards Lily, the battle he was fighting within himself. It was a battle that would only worsen the moment he stepped into his home, and then intensify in the long hours to follow.

She was there, of course. He sensed it the moment he stepped into the dark stillness that was the front hall of his home. It had been warm outside but inside it was stifling,

the heat of the day trapped within the close walls. And it was dark, the single yellow bulb in the ceiling fixture casting a dusk in the long, narrow hallway. Beyond the stagnant shadow, though, he felt her presence. Beyond the stillness of the hall and the staleness of the air closing in around him. In the kitchen at the end of the hall a window was open to the night, and beyond that open window through which no air or light passed, she waited, a folded figure on the stairs.

He took off his shoes so as not to wake his mother or Nathan and walked as lightly as he could down the hallway. He felt the smooth warmth of the linoleum under his feet, the hideous brown linoleum with its blooms of pink roses that his mother still waxed faithfully every week. He passed the opening to the living room, where his mother was asleep on the fold-out sofa, passed the closed door of the bedroom, behind which his brother also slept.

When he reached the kitchen he saw her through the open window. She was sitting just as he'd known she would be, smoking a cigarette, staring into the night. He knew he should leave. He knew he should walk back down the hallway to the living room he shared with his mother at night, to his cot behind the piano, the hated piano that had been a gift to his sister, Nina, from a man who couldn't give her a ring because he'd given one already to the woman he would never leave despite Nina's many and varied charms. But Sol had done that already. Every night since the wedding he had exchanged no more than brief greetings and superficial chit-chat with Lily, retiring immediately to his cot, where he had lain restlessly, miserably, his condition not improving, only worsening. Tonight he took a beer out of the icebox, slipped through the window and sat down beside Lily.

She didn't move, didn't greet him, just continued to sit there

as she had been, staring out into space and smoking her cigarette as if she were still alone and undisturbed. Now he was at a loss. Had she greeted him, as basic decency dictated she should have, he could have returned her greeting in kind. Then one thing could have led to another, to a simple inquiry on his part, for example, about how her day had been, a brief response followed by a similar inquiry on her part. A normal conversation, in other words, which might lay the groundwork for further normalization of the relationship between them. But there was no greeting from Lily, just the cold wall of her indifference.

"Does Nathan know you smoke?" he asked finally, a less-than-stellar opening, to which she dragged deeply on her cigarette and turned her head away from him to exhale.

She thought if she ignored him he would leave. What man would stay when a woman made it as clear as she was making it that she didn't want him there? What man would insinuate himself into a woman's private moment, as he just had, practically depositing himself onto her lap? The same man, she supposed, who would invite a woman to cross two oceans to marry him and then leave her at the station because she didn't suit his mood on the day of her arrival.

Sol floundered, unsure how to proceed. He had planned to tell Lily how his date had gone. Wasn't that what a normal brother-in-law would do? Wouldn't he tell his slightly older sister-in-law about a young woman he found attractive? And wouldn't that offered confidence typically solicit a teasing and sisterly smile? He had thought so when he mentioned it to her the night before, but Lily hadn't even seemed to hear him.

"Filthy habit," he said, lighting up a cigarette of his own. He glanced at her to see if she'd caught his tone, which was meant to be humorous.

She looked out to the backs of the houses across the way, a sight as familiar to her by now as the four walls of her bedroom. It was quiet this time of night, and mostly dark, but there was one room where the light was always on no matter how late she stayed up. Who was in that room? she wondered. An insomniac like herself? A poet at his work? A harried woman who did piecework in her kitchen while the rest of her family slept? Night after night she wondered about that light, that other sleepless soul keeping her company in an existence that felt more like a vigil than a life.

"The girl I took out tonight . . . You know that mother–daughter pair who came to your wedding? Ida Pearl and Elka Krakauer?"

Lily shrugged. "I was introduced to a lot of people that night."

"They weren't invited."

"But you just said they were there."

"They were, but not because anyone invited them. It seems that Ida Pearl—the mother—had a cousin with the same name as yours, and I guess she hoped, you know, when she heard—"

Now Lily looked at Sol. "A cousin?"

"Back in Europe. And I guess when she heard about you arriving—"

"But how would she have heard?" Lily interrupted him, her indifference replaced now by a sudden tension. "Who would have told her?"

"I don't know. I think a customer of hers had heard—"

"Heard what? Who are these people?"

"Lily, relax." Sheesh, he thought. Talk about tightly wound. "It was just a simple mix-up. Ida Pearl's maiden name was Azerov. Like yours. And she had a cousin Lily. So when she heard that you had arrived in Montreal, that you were

marrying my brother, I guess she thought maybe . . . But it was just a coincidence, you having the same name. She saw that right away."

"Who are these people?" Lily asked again.

"The daughter is the girl I took out tonight. That's what I've been trying to explain to you."

"And what did she say, exactly?" Lily asked.

"I already told you."

"Tell me again."

Sol repeated what Elka had told him, about her mother having heard from a customer about the arrival of a refugee by the name of Lily Azerov, her mother's hope that the bride might turn out to be her cousin. A mistaken hope.

"It's not a big deal."

"Not a big deal," Lily repeated, as if learning a new phrase. She looked away, trying to absorb this. Could it possibly be coincidence? she wondered. Another Azerov, another Lily?

"For all I know it's a cockamamie story. She told me another story tonight about how her mother was a famous diamond cutter."

Lily turned to him sharply. "A diamond cutter?"

"The best in all of Antwerp, apparently. Who were the best in the entire world, didn't you know?"

Lily turned away from him again, but not before Sol had seen a face so stricken that a sickening feeling took hold of him.

It was no coincidence, then, Lily thought. She closed her eyes. To calm herself. For a moment's rest and reprieve from what Sol had just told her.

"I think you may be making too big a deal of this," Sol said. And when she didn't respond: "It's not like it's a crime to have the same name as someone's cousin."

Isn't it? she thought as she turned to him again. She knew it was not a customer who had told Ida Pearl about her arrival in Montreal. It had to have been the girl's cousin that she had gone to see her first day in Tel Aviv. Sonya Nemetz must have written to her relative in Montreal, this Ida Pearl Krakauer, about the unexpected visit she'd received.

"Did you . . . know her cousin?" It was instinct that made Sol ask, her expression when he told her of the coincidence of names, the heightened tension and alertness he sensed.

"No," she said, with an answering instinct to hide anything that might endanger her until she had a better sense of what she faced.

She had not planned to go visit the cousin in Tel Aviv, had not even planned to keep the name. She had taken the name for one purpose, and one purpose only: as a temporary mantle under which she could slip across borders that might otherwise be closed to her.

But then that terrible moment of her arrival in Palestine, the cavern opening within her as she recognized that this was it, this arrival, that this was both the culmination and beginning of all that she had struggled so hard to reach: this bleak dawn, this gaping emptiness that was now, and from now on, her life. There had been no one to meet her, of course. No one waiting. Nowhere to go. She had stepped into a café and had sat there, drinking cup after cup of black coffee. For how long? She couldn't say. The waiter informed her they were closing. A lie, she suspected, a ploy to move her on. But to where, and to whom? The waiter looked at her as if he knew she had no place to go, no one she belonged to or who belonged to her. She stood up, walked outside. She turned left. There was a bus. "Tel Aviv?" she asked the driver. "Where in Tel Aviv?"

She oriented herself towards the only feature that rose from the wasteland within her, a name and address from the notebook she had taken: *Sonya Nemetz, Rehov Hayarkon 7, Tel Aviv.*

It was madness, she knew. Desperation. But it had propelled her forward when she might have fallen back. And it hadn't felt like deception at the time. Not entirely. The name Lily Azerov had seeped into her during the months that she had worn it. It had grown tendrils and found a foothold in the scoured wasteland of her life, taken root. She answered to that name and only to that name; there was no one left who had known her by any other. And yet she knew it was deception. It was madness.

She remembered the keenness with which Sonya had looked into her face, searching, hoping despite her doubt, despite the evidence of hope's futility that was standing right in front of her. And with that memory, another rose, another person looking at her, another woman with the same desperate keenness.

"I remember that Krakauer woman now," she said to Sol, though it was not the woman she remembered, but the look, a fleeting impression she had noted at her wedding but dismissed—she had seen that look so often by then. "I remember how she looked at me when I was dancing." *That look*—that's how she thought of it. "I've seen it in so many others, the way she looked at me." In Europe, in the chaos after the war, on the roads, in the train stations, in the centres they set up. And then in Palestine as well, once she arrived there. But how to explain it to Sol? It was the look of people desperate to find some trace of their dead, following rumours, even the faintest hints of rumours, in the hope . . . almost always futile in the end, of course.

She hugged her knees to her chest and rested her chin on them as she continued. She slipped into Yiddish. "In Tel Aviv once—this was a few weeks after I got there—I was sitting at a café and I saw a man looking at me, staring at me. I felt uncomfortable. There was such intensity to his stare—a ferocity, almost. I couldn't relax with him staring at me like that, was afraid that at any moment he would approach me, grab me . . . I wasn't sure what. I quickly paid for my coffee, and left. He followed me. I turned onto the street, walking quickly—I was quite nervous by now. I quickened my pace and he started to run after me. 'Gabi!' he called out, and immediately I understood. I stopped, turned to him, and his face fell. It fell so completely, it was as if my face was, in itself, the bearer of his terrible news. Do you understand what I mean?"

Sol nodded, though he wasn't entirely sure that he did.

"'I'm sorry,' he said to me. 'There was something in the way that you stirred the sugar into your coffee . . . and then when you lifted the cup to your mouth, the way you held it . . . Forgive me,' he said, and then he turned and left. I watched him walk away, a normal-looking man from that viewpoint. There was no hunch to his shoulders, no obvious dejection in his gait. No one would guess that he was a man who chased women out of cafés in his desperation to see in them . . ." She paused, shrugged. "Who was this Gabi, then? I wondered. A girl he had once had a crush on? A sister of a friend? A cousin?"

Lily remembered her own disappointment at that moment, her wish that her face could have been the one that man sought, could have produced in him, in Sonya Nemetz, in anyone still alive, an expression of joyful recognition.

"Everyone is looking for their dead," she said. Sifting through the wreckage, she thought, looking for some trace,

some fragment . . . a familiar gesture, a fleeting resemblance, a name. "Does your friend's mother think she's the only one?"

Sol didn't answer.

"I'm sorry I can't be the Lily she was hoping to see at my wedding."

Sol nodded again now. He believed her. He also sensed that there was something not quite right. With Lily? With what she'd just told him? He didn't know, could not account for the discomfort that he felt.

And now what? Lily wondered. They sat in silence for a while. "It's getting late," she said. The light was still on across the alley. "Who lives there?" she asked.

"Where?"

She pointed.

Sol shrugged. "I don't know."

She would try to sleep, she decided. She'd know better in the morning what to do. She brushed her hand across her thigh as if to sweep away crumbs that had accumulated there while they had spoken, then she rose to leave, the soft fabric of her dressing gown brushing his cheek as she moved past him.

CHAPTER 8

I was twelve before I saw an adult cry. I'd seen adult eyes fill with tears before then, the time Elka was wearing a brand-new black dress when Sol came home from work, for example, and he looked at her and said, "What's that?" But if Elka's tears spilled over into crying when she fled the kitchen that day (Sol hot on her heels, apologizing) I didn't see that. Nor did I see anything but moistness in my father's eyes when Old Yeller died or when the dreaded doctor's call came for Bella and the news turned out to be good. When the adults in my life cried they did it behind closed doors. Until Mr. C, my sixth grade teacher, who handed out a quiz one November afternoon, then stood by the window with tears running down his cheeks.

I didn't notice at first. He was utterly silent, and I was concentrating on the quiz, so I wasn't looking his way. I might not have noticed at all had Carrie not poked me and indicated with a lift of her chin that I should look in his direction. And even then I didn't know why she was nudging me. I was used

to the sight of Mr. C leaning against the sill of the window, looking out. We all were. That was how he stood even when he spoke to us. "Children," he would say, his eyes not on us but on the scene outside: our schoolyard with its hopscotch and champ boards chalked on cracked asphalt and enclosed by chain-link fence, the row of brick duplexes across the street. "Take out your Humashim and turn to the third verse of the second chapter of Exodus," he would say in his Hebrew that was still infected with the Yiddish inflections and pronunciations of Europe, entirely different, that is, from the Hebrew we spoke or aspired to speak, which was the modern—which is to say, Israeli—form of the language. And all the while he'd be looking outside, at the cracked asphalt, the chain-link fence, the duplexes across the street.

What? I mouthed to Carrie.

She lifted her chin a second time and this time ran her index finger down her cheek so that when I looked again I saw his tears.

We had all been talking and joking around when he walked into the classroom that day and had not stopped even after he called us to attention. "Children," he said several times, "*Banim, banot!*" each time a little louder until at last he was no longer calling us children in English or in Hebrew, but yelling at us in Yiddish, a language only half of us understood, his face red with anger, the vein in his forehead engorged and hammering in a visible and disturbing way. At which point, on that particular day, we did stop talking, returned to our seats and prepared to begin our class, though there had been many times during that school year when even his explosions had no effect on us, not on our behaviour, in any case, and it was not until our principal, Rabbi Loffer, was called in—usually by a

neighbouring teacher—that order was restored and class could begin. It was not that we went out of our way to be rude to him. We didn't. We were simply doing what comes naturally to children: making life a torment for any teacher who cannot control them. But there was something about Mr. C that wasn't quite natural.

He was a small man, no bigger than some of the boys in our class, and lost inside the crumpled grey suit that he wore every day, a crumpled grey suit that was several sizes too big and that fell in folds around his shoes, which were also too big, more like planters than shoes, as if his feet had gone ahead and reached their full potential before fate and history stunted the rest of him. He was small, but he wasn't weak, as those of us who had felt his grip on our wrists or the backs of our necks could attest. There was a strength to him, a hard, dry strength. He was dry and hard and as spare in manner as in build, petrified, it seemed—like the wood we had just learned about, wood that used to be a living tree—except for those moments when anger rushed through him, a flash flood of anger that filled out the cavern that was his face, flushing its greyness with oxygenating blood.

Mr. C had come from Europe after the war. That in itself wasn't unusual. A lot of our friends' parents had come after 1945. (The school that Carrie and I now attended was a half-hour east by bus across the city, close to where my father, Sol and Nina had grown up and where newer immigrants still lived.) And a lot of these friends' parents exhibited certain peculiarities of behaviour related to the war, problems with nerves, temper and mood. Mira's father, for example, would come into her room late at night just to sit at the foot of her bed and watch her sleep, which was why she never felt com-

fortable having her friends spend the night. She would feel his presence, sometimes for hours, his gaze so intense that it would pull her from sleep. And Helen's mother hid and hoarded food. And Lena's father had a temper with the force and staccato rhythm of a machine gun. With the parents of our friends, though, those peculiarities stood out from the rest of their personalities like the lines of quartz that stood out from the black granite face of one of the rocks my mother had sent me. With Mr. C, peculiarity was the rock face itself, shot through with fragments of humour, kindness and other scattered bits of who he used to be.

"He's a damaged person," Carrie's mother said one afternoon after we told her about one of his explosions, and it was her use of that word—"damaged"—the tone of it, that made me start to wonder about my mother in a way that was different from my earlier curiosity—because my mother too had been damaged, I knew. "Shattered" was the word Elka sometimes used, but until then the word had always brought to mind the teacup that sat on the highest shelf of Elka and Sol's dining room high board, a white porcelain cup with a delicate pattern of blue flowers that had shattered once from a fall through Sol's fingers, had been carefully repaired, but was too fragile now for the rigours of holding tea and being transported from saucer to mouth and then back to saucer again. My mother was like that teacup, I had come to think. She could not withstand the rigours of the life she was trying to live, a normal life of love, marriage and family. My birth had re-shattered her, and it was a sad story, to be sure, but it was also a story with a certain prettiness to it. Pretty things shattered, did they not? Glass, crystal, fine china. Mr. C, though, was not in any way pretty.

I saw his tears that day and Carrie's mother's words came back to me, because only a damaged person would stand by a window in a classroom full of children with silent tears rolling down his cheeks. And then for a second I saw my mother standing by a window. She was less glamorous than I'd envisaged her until then, but not because she wasn't nicely dressed. She was very nicely dressed in a skirt and blouse not unlike the brown wool skirt and silk blouse I had seen on my friend Helen's mother, and her hair was pulled back into a French twist held in place with a tortoiseshell clip. It was more how she felt to me than how she looked that was different. It was the same feeling I picked up from other immigrants that I knew from her part of Europe, people with thick accents who were either too severe or held your gaze for too long or simply felt too dense to me, too concentrated, somehow, as if the very cells in their bodies were heavier and more compressed than ours. I couldn't see her face—she was staring out like Mr. C, out onto the city that was now her home—but I could see the tears streaming down the side of her face.

Mr. C's tears were caused by his damage; I knew that. But had we not also played a role? That's what I began to wonder as I watched him. He had called us to attention and we had ignored him. We had made him aware in countless other ways how little we respected him, how unpopular he was as a teacher, referring to him by initial only when we were talking amongst ourselves, as if he didn't even have a name. I imagined him in his grey suit entering an apartment at the end of his workday, hanging his hat—a grey homburg—on a peg by the door, then shuffling down a dingy brown hall to a dingy beige kitchen where he would make himself tea that he would drink out of a glass like everyone from Europe drank it, with

lemon and sugar, and hard cookies on the side, and I resolved at that moment to show him kindness and respect, a resolution that I committed to paper and passed in a note to Carrie, who rolled her eyes and wrote back asking for the answer to one of the questions on the quiz, which I gave her, and which Mr. C didn't notice because he was still staring out the window, though the tears had stopped by then.

"This is a classroom, not a mental ward," Carrie told me at recess. That was a direct quote from her mother, I knew, because her mother had said the same thing to Elka when she had called her a few weeks earlier to enlist her support in having Mr. C removed from our classroom and shifted to a job that was less sensitive than classroom teaching. No one was suggesting he be fired, Carrie's mother had assured Elka.

"I still think we should be nicer to him," I said to Carrie, more because I had conflated him with my mother in my mind, I think, than because I was an inherently nicer person than Carrie. But before I had a chance to enact my good intentions—that very afternoon, in fact—Mr. C unleashed his fury at me for giving a wrong answer in class, as if I had deliberately misunderstood the text for the sole purpose of enraging him. I didn't understand the exact content of his tirade—he had switched into Yiddish—but I understood his fury, his outrage that it was me and my ignorant and boorish ilk that he was forced to teach instead of the vastly superior boys and girls who had perished fifteen years earlier in Europe—no one ever *died* in Europe, they *perished*—and even though I knew he was damaged, and that that was the real cause of his tirade, I still felt the heat of deep shame rising in my face, which is what prompted Carrie to send me the note that called him a murderer.

In Carrie's defence, she was referring to a passage in the Talmud that we had learned earlier that year, that Mr. C himself had taught us, which said specifically: "He who publicly shames his neighbour is as though he shed blood." The shedding of blood in the passage refers to the internal flow of blood in the shamed person's face as it changes colour—though the reference is to a whitening of the face, rather than the reddening I exhibited that day—and that is all that Carrie meant. It was her attempt to comfort me in my shame, a shame that Mr. C had caused but which was not really his fault, so it felt at that moment like my fault entirely. It was an exaggeration, it's true, to leap from the shedding of blood to outright murder, but it was in Carrie's nature to overstate whatever point she was making, and no harm would have been done had Mr. C continued looking out the window as he had been when she first set the note into motion. His tirade at me finished, he had taken up his position by the window and seemed to have forgotten about the class for the moment. Carrie dropped the note on the corner of Freddy's desk—he sat between us—and then Freddy dropped it on the corner of my desk as he had so many times before, but unfortunately he did so at the precise moment that Mr. C turned back to face us. I saw the note land on my desk and glanced up to see that Mr. C had noticed as well. For a moment, though, he said nothing and I did nothing, and the note sat, untouched and unopened, where it had landed.

"*Nu?*" he finally said. His voice was quiet, as it always was after one of his rages. "Aren't you going to read your mail?"

I should have eaten it, Carrie told me later. I should have stuffed it in my mouth and swallowed it, as we had seen done in countless movies and as she would have done, she assured

me. But I had neither Carrie's presence of mind nor her flair for the dramatic, so I opened the note as ordered and read it aloud.

"'He's the one who should be ashamed. He's a murderer,'" I read, and as I did, the blood drained from Mr. C's face in precisely the manner described by Rav Nachman bar Isaac in the passage Carrie had referred to: "You say well because I have seen it [the shaming], the ruddiness departing and paleness supervening."

Mr. C didn't speak, couldn't speak, it seemed. His face was grey and still as stone. The class was quiet too, so quiet that I heard the hand of the clock on the wall behind me advance a minute in its hourly cycle. We were all suspended in the same moment, the same horrible silence until finally, after some time, Mr. C told us to take out our readers and read to ourselves, which we did, or pretended to. I tried to keep my eyes on the meaningless letters and words that swam in front of me, but after a while I had to look up, to see him. He was looking away from us, out the window, but I could see enough of his face to know that the blood that had drained from it had not returned. It was a cadaver's face I was looking at, or could have been if not for the lone muscle working in his jaw, clenching and unclenching in a rapid, repetitive motion.

He was not at school the next day, or the rest of that week, and the word was that he had had a breakdown, one caused—obviously—by me and Carrie. Though he had never been a popular teacher, the sympathy was all with him, even after Carrie explained herself repeatedly and eloquently. If our principal or any of the teachers were aware of what had happened, they didn't intervene. I think they probably didn't know, because as quick as our classmates were to blame me

and Carrie, they felt ashamed of themselves as well, impli-
cated in the unspeakable act that they had witnessed. That
one of us—safe, spoiled and pampered in every way—could
accuse one of *them* of murder, and Mr. C, no less, who was
the embodiment of the walking wounded, was so inexcusable
that it tainted anyone who had heard the words that Carrie
had written and that I had given voice.

He did return to school the following week and to my great
relief he looked no different than before: the same hard com-
pactness inside the same grey suit, which fell in the same folds
over the same oversized black shoes. He removed his hat—the
same grey homburg—as he always did upon entering the classroom and ran his hand across the crown of his head, as was
his habit, to make sure his black *kipah* was where it should be
before placing his hat on his desk.

"Good morning, children," he said.

"Good morning, Mr. Czernowitz," we answered in uni-
son, because it was we who were different, or thought we were,
changed by our shame about what we had done, and by our hope
that our repentance—in the form of unwavering courtesy towards
him from that moment on—might suffice, if not redeem us.

Mr. C began the class by having us read aloud, each of us
in turn, from a text we were learning. We read as we always
did, some of us fluently, some of us not, Mr. C interjecting
corrections as necessary, and interrupting now and then with
questions that the smart and more diligent among us fought
to answer by waving their hands in the air, some going so far
as to grunt while they waved in hopes of attracting Mr. C's
attention, and the stupider and less studious among us looking down to avoid Mr. C's eyes, which had regained the sharp,
almost beady focus that the blow—mine and Carrie's—had

knocked out of them the week before. Mistakes were made, corrected. Mr. C did not explode.

We began to relax, to imagine that no harm had been done—no further, permanent harm, that is—and then Marc delivered the correct answer to a question Mr. C had posed. It was not a brilliant answer. It was not even a particularly interesting answer. But it was correct, entirely adequate—this from a student who had been caught once with *Playboy* slipped inside the tractate of the Talmud he was poring over with such fervour—and in the shocked silence that followed, Mr. C began to cry.

This time he did not turn away from us. He stood at the front of the class, facing us, with tears running down his cheeks. He was not sobbing, was completely still, in fact, so still that I was not certain at first that what I was witnessing was actually crying, an activity I associated with at least some facial move-ment, some exhibit of bodily will. His arms were at his sides, his palms out, facing us, his face tilted slightly upward. He seemed almost to be listening or waiting for something, and I might even have called his expression hopeful had it not been for the tears. And then it passed. We saw it pass, a tremor of self-consciousness like the shadow of a cloud moving rapidly across his face, and then a quick, furtive flurry of activity—a white handkerchief wiping, drying his cheeks. He blew his nose, one loud honk, as if he had just come in from the cold, then he called on the next student to read.

And so it continued. There was no pattern to the crying, no way of knowing what might set him off. It would be a stretch to say we got used to it, but over time we felt less afraid, were no longer frozen as we had been when it began. It became almost normal to us—normal for Mr. C, that is.

The crying had started in November and while it seemed at the time to go on forever, it was, in fact, over—finished—within a few weeks. We arrived at school one morning just before the winter break, and it was our principal, Rabbi Loffer, not Mr. C, who walked into our classroom. Mr. Czernowitz was ill, Rabbi Loffer informed us, and wouldn't be returning to our school. Ever, we understood. A new teacher had been found and would be starting later that day, a teacher who had just arrived in Montreal from Israel. Rabbi Loffer smiled at us then and said he knew we could be trusted to behave in a responsible and respectful manner—which, of course, we and Mr. C knew we could not.

Was it his damage, then, that had driven him from our classroom, or something about us? Or some terrible combination of the two? That's what I wondered long after the rest of my classmates seemed to have forgotten about him. Certainly no one ever mentioned him again, though Carrie did tell me once, about a year later, that he had gotten a job at the kosher bakery over on Victoria, that her mother had seen him at the back of the store where the baking was done, pushing a tray of loaves into the oven. "It's a much better job for him," Carrie concluded, and that seemed to be the end of the matter for her.

For me, though, it lived on, raising new, different questions about my mother. Not just what it was within her that made her unable to stay, but whether there might have been something about my family, about her new community in Montreal, some terrible interaction between her and them, between her and us—like the reaction I saw once when I mistakenly added water to the sulphuric acid in my chemistry set—that might have driven her away.

IT WASN'T LONG AFTER that Carrie let slip to our friend Mira that my mother sent me rocks in the mail. It was a slip that wasn't technically a betrayal, because there was nothing about my mother that was supposed to be cause for secrecy, but I felt it as one, and as the word quickly spread and some of the girls in our group agreed that my mother was obviously off her rocker, I felt a deep sense of shame.

On one level our friends' response was simply a pun that was too easy and obvious to resist, their taunts no more mean-spirited than any of the arrows that regularly flew across the classroom and schoolyard, but I couldn't brush it off because it was clear to me by then that my mother wasn't right. And me, by extension. I knew I also wasn't right. Because of the rocks, yes. That was obviously strange behaviour. Both the fact that she sent them and my response to them. I knew that by then, knew enough to hide how special each one felt, each one a secret, unique communication between my mother and me. I knew enough also to hide the anxiety I felt when too long went by without a new one arriving, an anxiety that was nagging at me that year because I hadn't received one for two years.

Deeper than that, though, was that she had left me in the first place. That's what moved her—and me—into a terri-tory set apart from that of other parents and children I knew, because no woman I had ever heard of had left her baby, and especially no woman who had already lost her entire family in Europe. That should have made her even more desperate to start a new family, like my friends' parents were. Mira's, Helen's, Lena's. The peculiar behaviours, habits and moods

that those friends' parents exhibited did not interfere with their love for their children. If anything, most of them hung on too tightly, watched their children too closely, like Mira's father, staring at her late at night. None of them walked away.

I didn't tell Elka or anyone in my family what had happened at school. The shame I felt in the face of the initial taunts persisted long after my friends had moved on to other targets. It swelled like a noxious gas within me, leaving little room for other feelings, smothering any confidence I had once possessed. One evening at dinner Jeffrey teased me about a pimple on my face. I told him he looked like a pug, and he then retorted that I had a face only a mother could love. It was a line that we had both heard on *The Honeymooners* a few nights earlier, but when he said it I ran from the table in tears, slamming the door to my room behind me.

A few minutes later Elka knocked and asked if she could come in. I didn't answer, buried my face in my pillow, but she came in anyway and sat on the edge of my bed, her hand on my back.

"Is there anything going on at school?" she asked me.

"No," I muttered into the pillow.

"Nothing you want to talk to me about?"

I shook my head no again.

She waited a few minutes, then she said that thirteen was a hard age, that she too had had a hard time when she was thirteen.

My misery had nothing to do with being thirteen. All my friends were thirteen and none of them were miserable.

"I know your father's been busy with Naomi recently."

I didn't answer.

"It's perfectly natural to feel a little bit uncomfortable when your father—"

"I couldn't care less about my father and Naomi."

Naomi was pretty and had been spending a lot of time at our house in recent weeks, but the thought that I might be jealous of her relationship with my father was ridiculous. She had given my father the soundtrack to *Exodus* for his birthday because she thought a lot of the music he listened to had no tunes, and before we ate the chicken cacciatore or salmon à la king that she had cooked we had to go around the table, each of us talking about one nice thing that had happened to us that day. Nothing much was going to happen between my father and Naomi.

"I also only had one parent," Elka said, trying a different tack.

That was true, I knew, but her situation, while difficult and shameful in its own way, hadn't been as abnormal or unheard of as mine.

"You always feel like you're different from everyone else."

It wasn't a feeling, my difference. It was a fact. There was no one else whose mother had lost all her family in the war only to walk out on the infant daughter who should have been the most precious thing in the world to her.

"You feel like there could be something wrong with you," Elka went on, recalling her own experience at thirteen.

I didn't answer, didn't dare to pull the stopper on the torrent within me.

"There's nothing wrong with you, I can promise you that."

It was my mother that there was something wrong with. That's what I understood Elka to be saying. And while I knew that, of course—there would have to be something really wrong with me if I *didn't* know that by then—I felt a surge of protectiveness towards my mother in the face of what sounded like yet another insinuation about her failure to be a normal person.

"Not everything in life is somebody's fault," Elka said, as if sensing my thoughts.

When I still didn't answer, didn't even let on that I had heard her, she began to get irritated. Her hand on my back was no longer resting there in a comforting way, but beginning to move about, restless, tapping impatiently. And sure enough, no sooner had I registered the change in her hand than she said that moping never helped anyone and it was time for me to get up and help her with the dishes.

Though Elka acted like there was nothing left to discuss, I suspect she may have talked about it to other members of the family, because at the Seder a few weeks later my aunt Nina took my hand, studied my palm with an expression of great seriousness and then whispered in my ear, as Sol was droning on about the ten plagues, that I would be blessed with deep and long-lasting love in this life, that it was etched on my palm by God himself or by one of his angels, and was therefore the truth, irrevocable and final, as only God's truth can be.

I knew that Nina was probably only saying that because Elka had talked to her about my recent moodiness (that was the catch-all word to describe my sudden plunge into misery) and that the future couldn't actually be read from a person's palm, and that Nina was in fact an atheist who wouldn't recognize God's truth if it slapped her in the face, but I still felt a surge of hope.

"Oh, I don't know," I said, flushing with something other than mortification for the first time in weeks.

"Well, I do," Nina said.

I wanted to believe her, but already I remembered that Carrie had recently started going over to Mira's house most afternoons, leaving me to take the long bus ride across town

with only Jeffrey for company, and that the two of them, Carrie and Mira, had gone bowling the previous weekend and not invited me along. And then there was my ongoing anxiety about how long it had been since the last rock had arrived from my mother, a non-event that felt more like active rejection with every day that passed.

"What?" Nina asked, seemingly reading my face as she had just read my palm, and with such sympathy in her own face and voice that without thinking, I blurted out my thoughts.

"Carrie hates me."

"What?" Nina asked, at which point both my father and Elka glared at us because we were disturbing the Seder.

A little later, though, during the meal, when we were allowed to have conversation, I told her that Carrie had told Mira about the rocks.

"And that's why you think she hates you?"

"For starters."

"She's just jealous."

"Jealous?"

"Her mother can't think of anything more interesting than which golf club to join, and she sees you getting these amazing rocks from your mother—"

"Who's jealous?" Jeffrey asked from across the table.

"Her friend Carrie," Nina said. "She can't stand that Ruthie has a more interesting mother than she does."

"She's not jealous," I snapped, as angry at Nina now for revealing my private business to the whole family as I was at myself for confiding in her in the first place. "No one's jealous of someone who doesn't have a mother."

There was momentary silence around the table, until Jeffrey said, "But you do have a mother, Ruthie."

"But she's not here," I said.

"That doesn't mean she doesn't exist." That was my father.

"Then why isn't she here?"

An uncomfortable silence fell over the table. Elka busied herself with cutting Chuck's brisket. All the other adults
looked at my father. This was clearly his to handle. My father
gave me his usual answer.

"We don't really know."

I knew that was the truth, that he wasn't lying to me, but I
also felt for the first time that he knew more than he was letting on, that everyone knew more than they were admitting.
"Then maybe I'll have to find her and ask her," I said, and as I
did so I knew, also for the first time, that that was exactly what
I was going to do.

"Really?" Jeffrey asked, his eyes wide with interest.

It wasn't that I hadn't imagined meeting my mother before
then. Of course I had. But my fantasies up until that point
had been all about my mother finding me as she had when she
sent me the rocks, about her seeking me out, the infant girl
she had abandoned for reasons she would finally explain, stoi-
cally, without tears or drama, the pain of her life etched in her
face but not gushing out in her manner. (She was not a gushy
type, my mother, I'd decided. It would have been hard to reach
any other conclusion.) I had often imagined the phone ringing, and the voice at the other end, a low, calm voice, lightly
tinged with a Jewish-Polish accent. *Is that Ruth?* she would
ask, with just a slight, almost imperceptible roll of the *r* that
was nothing like the guttural *r* of my grandmother Bella and
Ida Pearl, more like Ingrid Bergman in *Casablanca. Speaking,*
I would say. Then the invitation to meet for ice cream somewhere. Murray's, I imagined, a Waspy coffee shop that I chose

partly because I liked their ice cream cake roll with chocolate sauce and partly because no one else in my family would be likely to walk into the fantasy (too much mayonnaise in their egg salad sandwiches, Elka thought). But I had never imagined that I might be the one to take the initiative, to call her up, seek her out.

"But how will you find her?" Jeffrey asked me.

It was a good question, one that brought me back to reality, because nobody knew where my mother had gone. It was greeted with another silence, as uncomfortable as the first one.

"I don't know yet," I said to Jeffrey.

No one jumped in with encouragement or suggestions, until Bella said, "If Ruthie decides she wants to find her mother, there will be time enough to try to do that when the Seder is over."

She had addressed her comment to Jeffrey, but everyone looked at me, and I think I was as relieved as the rest of them to let the topic rest for now. I felt myself alone on one side of the discussion, as if the chasm that had opened between me and everyone else in the family during my weeks of misery had just deepened and widened. I wasn't sure why I felt so alone, was sure only of the discomfort all around as we broached for the very first time the possibility of my wanting to look for my mother.

"I'll help you find her, Ruthie," Jeffrey said.

"I'll help you too," Mitchell said, and even though I knew he was like a parrot who had imprinted on his older brother, copying everything Jeffrey said and did, I still felt as touched by his offer as I had by Jeffrey's.

And then Chuck, who wasn't even five yet, looked at me and said, "I help too."

But I knew they couldn't really help me. I was completely alone in some indefinable way. I had probably always felt it, but that was the first time I was conscious of it, aware that while part of me would always be a member of the family that surrounded me, the family that I loved and who loved me in return, another part of me would forever feel alone in some way, set apart. It made me think of the glaciers we had been learning about in school that developed chasms so deep that pieces of them broke off as icebergs that were then too small to resist the current sweeping around the larger glacier. Though they would always be made of the same material as the glacier that spawned them, they floated fast and far away.

CHAPTER 9

My father worked with light, I told him. He captured light with stones. He bent broken light into beauty.

To which he shrugged and said his father was a butcher.

And on my mother's side I descend from kindness, I said, to which he shrugged again, and told me not to be nostalgic.

If you had known my mother's father you wouldn't call my grief nostalgia.

I knew him, he said. I knew a hundred men like him. A thousand.

He was a man so kind that migrating birds came to rest on his shoulders. I saw them, I told him. With my own eyes.

But not so kind that he would ever allow me to forget my mother's shame, he replied.

His mother was not married to his father, it seems. Worse than that: his mother had been married to someone else, but then left her husband to run off with the butcher.

She had seven little bastards of whom I am the youngest, he told me. If you were still your father's daughter you would cross the street to avoid my glance.

I wouldn't, I assured him. We were fated for each other.

There was some truth mixed in with the girl's fantasies, Lily knew—but how much? Was there a message or answer she was meant to understand? Was it really accidental that it had been left for her to find, or was there purpose in what had seemed to her, at first, to be mere chance? These were just some of the questions that filled her mind as she read it, repetitive questions, questions whose answers she didn't know but that were there—she felt them—nudging at the back of her mind. She put the notebook down, waiting for what might become clearer if she looked away from it for a moment, but it was Ida Pearl Krakauer's face that loomed, Ida's cold, hard face, suspecting her, accusing her.

It was a week now since Lily had been to see her. A week, and she could still hardly bear to think about it, the woman's suspicion, her wary, accusatory manner that made it clear she thought there could not possibly be any good in Lily's intentions. It was hard even to remember why she had gone to that woman's store in the first place, hard to recall the feeling of hope she had felt when she had awakened that morning after the conversation with Sol, the sense of purpose that had filled

her. It had felt that morning as if the madness of what she had done to date was not madness at all, but part of a plan, a higher plan to return to the living what could be returned to them. She would go to Ida Pearl Krakauer, she had known when she awoke. She would show her the diamond. She would trust in—what? In what exactly had she thought she would trust? In fate? In God? In some hidden, higher purpose than her base instinct to survive? She couldn't remember, could only remember the coldness of that woman, the suspicion. And worse than that, the fear that Lily had sensed in her, a fear so palpable that Lily had almost glanced over her shoulder to see if something dangerous might be hovering in her own shadow. But there was nothing behind her; she knew that.

A commotion outside interrupted her thoughts, an argument of some sort, Bella's voice, raised against the lower, calmer tones of a man's. Lily could make out no words, only anger. She waited for it to stop, but it didn't. She closed the notebook and put it away, left her room and walked down the hallway to find a delivery man on the landing outside the apartment, and Bella standing in the doorway, blocking his entrance.

"Tell your boss we don't want any more of his disgusting furniture," Bella was saying. "Tell him he can take his filth and . . ."

"Are you Mrs. Kramer?" the deliveryman asked Lily as soon as she appeared behind Bella.

"*I'm* Mrs. Kramer," Bella answered.

"I have a delivery for Mr. and Mrs. Kramer," the delivery man said, still speaking to Lily as he held out a card for her to take. He was the same man—though Lily couldn't know this— who had delivered the hated piano a year earlier, and since this new piece of furniture—a delicate, finely made vanity—was

just as frivolous, just as useless as the piano that fouled their living room, Bella could be forgiven for assuming that this too was a gift for Nina from the same married lout of a suitor.

Lily read the card that accompanied the gift and handed it to Bella: *For my brother and new sister. May your love be long and your life together happy. Mazel tov. Nina.*

This clarification did nothing to pacify Bella, who knew full well that a young schoolteacher in Palestine could not afford to buy such a fine piece of furniture. She assumed Nina had sent a letter to the lout—who owned a furniture store, after all—requesting his help in sending a wedding gift to her brother and his new wife. She did not even want to think what might lie behind the man's willingness to provide that help, to deliver such an offering to the family of a girl who had still been in her teens when he had insinuated himself into her affection and trust. The nature of the offering—a vanity more suited to a preening woman than a struggling couple starting out in life—suggested to Bella lingering intentions on the part of the sender.

"It's filth," Bella said. "Take it away."

But Lily laid her hand on her mother-in-law's arm. "Please," she said.

It was the first time that Lily had touched Bella. Until then there had been the obligatory kisses dictated by convention, the required scrapes of dry lips against cheek, but there had not been this: the light, warm touch of the young woman's hand on her skin, the life Bella felt pulsing behind that warm touch. She turned now to look at her daughter-in-law's face and she saw in it emotion that she couldn't name. Desire, possibly, though it looked like pain. Grief, though she was smiling. Later Bella would think, *She loves the wedding gift more*

than the husband, but at that moment she had no thought, just awareness of a surging life within the shell that her son had married. She stepped aside and indicated to the delivery man the hallway that led to the bedroom.

When Nathan came home he found the bedroom dresser in the front hallway. In its stead, according to his mother, was the latest from Nina. For a second he imagined a cradle, complete with Nina's laughing, bouncing illegitimate baby tucked into it, and he was surprised when he realized that what his mother was so worked up about was nothing more than a new piece of furniture.

"Does she think this is a warehouse?" Bella asked, indicating the dresser's looming presence in the hall.

"I'll speak to Lily about it," Nathan promised.

Lily was sitting at the new vanity, her back to Nathan, when he entered the bedroom. She had been sitting at it all afternoon, according to Bella. Doing what, exactly, God only knows, Bella had said. At that moment she was doing nothing more mysterious than rubbing cold cream into her skin. Its scent, mixed with her own, shifted something inside him as he kissed her shoulder in greeting. She met his eyes in the mirror and smiled. He took off his shirt and lay on the bed in his trousers and undershirt.

"Long day?" she asked. She leaned closer to the mirror to inspect an imagined flaw that her fingertips had detected.

"Long enough."

She knew he was watching her, knew he liked the sight of her in her slip, her upper back exposed to him, one spaghetti strap slipping off a bare shoulder.

"Do you like it?" she asked.

"What's not to like?"

"I meant the vanity."

"It's lovely."

"You haven't even looked."

He smiled. "I'm too tired. Describe it to me." He closed his eyes and listened to her talk about the fine grain of the wood—mahogany, she thought—the subtle pattern of the inlay, the bevelled oblong mirror, the delicate turn of the legs.

"Mmm," Nathan said. "Now describe yourself. The slip you're wearing. Satin, isn't it?"

"Silk."

"Grey silk."

"Pearl, Nathan. The lingerie of the woman you love is never grey."

He heard the smile in her voice, opened his eyes. She was applying lipstick now, a deep, rich burgundy that probably went by another name.

"I know the dresser can't stay out there," she said.

"My mother's not too pleased."

"Neither was the delivery man when I asked him to move it."

"Why on earth did you have him move it all the way out into the hall?" He was not looking forward to moving it back. It was a large piece, heavy as well as bulky. "You could have just asked him to shift it a few inches down the wall."

She didn't answer.

"There's plenty of room for both pieces."

"It's ugly," she said.

"Ugly?" He sought her eyes in the mirror, but she was intent now on her lips. "It may not be to your taste, but . . ."

"It's not a matter of taste, Nathan. The dresser is ugly."

He remembered his mother's delight, his father's pride the night they brought the dresser home. Pure maple, his father

had said, knocking the wood with his knuckles. His mother's smile at that moment had seared into his mind the impression that maple was the most valuable of all the woods.

"Maybe so," he allowed. "But that doesn't mean we can ban it from our bedroom."

"I was just taking a break from it, enjoying one afternoon . . ."

He wondered if she'd been spoiled once. There was something in her tone . . . It made it possible for him to imagine her as a girl who had ruled a rich father with a stomp of her foot and a petulant toss of her hair.

"I didn't realize it bothered you so much."

"It didn't. But when this arrived . . ." She stroked the surface of the vanity with her full open hand.

"We'll have our own place soon," Nathan promised. "Just another few months. Half a year at most. You'll be able to choose all the furniture. Every piece. It will all be what you like."

"It's not that," she said. "It's how I felt when it arrived. To think that your sister could have known exactly what to send me. As if she knew me."

"But . . . she doesn't know you."

"I felt like she did."

"Because she sent you a vanity that you like?" He was trying to understand, but was worried too. Was Lily losing touch with reality, spending all her days alone in her room as his mother described? It had been a week since she had last offered to do the shopping, his mother had reported, a week since she'd left her room during the day for anything other than the required appearances at meals and the walk alone on the mountain that she took every morning after breakfast. "I doubt Nina was even the one who chose it." Although he and

his mother had not discussed it, he too suspected that Nina's role in the matter had been limited to contacting Levine's Fine Furniture, and that it was Nina that Levine had in mind when he chose it, not the anonymous bride to whom he was sending it. "It was Levine, that piece of—"

"My mother had a vanity just like this."

Nathan stopped talking. It was the first image from her childhood that she'd offered him.

"I used to watch her making herself up before my father came home. She was like an artist, my mother, remaking herself every evening. So many pots of cream, so many colours— and she never forgot to dab some of her magic on our lips and cheeks as well. On all of us—there were four of us, all girls. No brothers, my poor father." She smiled in a way that suggested her father felt no lack at the absence of sons, was never anything less than delighted to be greeted by his freshly painted collection of girls every evening. "It was the lipstick I liked the best. Though it wasn't a stick at all. It came in a pot, like her rouges. She used a brush to apply it to her own lips, but for our lips, she always used her finger." She closed her eyes for a moment as if summoning the layered scent of her mother's skin and the feel of her mother's finger as she applied cream to her daughter's lips.

And she was trying to, but nothing came to her. She opened her eyes again.

"The vanity was going to be mine. Because I was the eldest. It was going to be her wedding present to me."

Nathan met her eyes in the mirror.

"So you see."

"See what?"

"It's as if your sister knew me, somehow."

"But, Lily, sweetheart . . ."

"Don't 'sweetheart' me with condescension in your voice."

"I wasn't condescending. I was just . . . Look, it's great that you love it, but it's not like Nina knew beforehand that you would. She doesn't know you, after all. You don't know her."

"I do know her."

"You do?"

"Not personally, but I know who she is. I saw her in a play once."

"You saw Nina?"

"Do you have another sister?"

"No. I'm just surprised you haven't mentioned it before."

"It was just a bit part."

"Still."

Lily shrugged.

"Was she any good?"

"She wasn't terrible."

"That bad?"

Lily smiled. "She wasn't, actually. It was her Hebrew, her accent. You couldn't tell what she was trying to say. But aside from that she was—"

"Bad enough for you to remember her."

Lily smiled again. "I remembered her because I was expecting a letter at that time from a certain Sol Kramer in Montreal, Canada, who might be interested in matrimony. The woman who was helping me with my arrangements had put your brother's name forward just a few days earlier, so, of course, the name Kramer in the playbill caught my eye. I didn't know anything about Sol yet, that he had a sister in Tel Aviv, but it seemed like quite a coincidence that I should go to a play

where one of the actresses had the same last name as a man whose offer of matrimony I might soon have to consider."

Nathan took this in, this very ordinary fluke that Lily seemed to see as something more. "It's not exactly an uncommon last name, Kramer."

"Maybe not," Lily agreed. "But then I saw her again a few nights later."

"In another play?"

Lily shook her head. "At a café near my apartment in Tel Aviv. I didn't usually go to that café, but it was a terrible night outside. The rain was pouring down the way it does there, driven by the wind that howls in from the sea—it could drive anyone mad, that wind. I didn't want to be alone in my apartment.

"I was sitting on my own, reading a book, trying to read a book, but there was a group at one of the other tables, a noisy group that kept getting noisier. They were about my age but they seemed of another generation, another world almost. Which I suppose they were, in a sense. Their laughter took over the place and I felt more and more uncomfortable sitting alone while they laughed. More and more alone. I tried to ignore them, to concentrate on the book I was reading—leaving wasn't an option; the apartment I was living in had no heat, and I knew the lights would probably be out too in such a storm. But there was no ignoring them. Maybe they were no more brutish than any group of young people anywhere, but their loud confidence seemed to me an insult—I can't explain it—their laughter . . ." She shrugged, remembering.

"And then I noticed a girl among them who seemed familiar to me. Almost immediately I recognized her as the girl from the play. The girl with the last name that soon might be mine.

I felt a connection to her already." She looked at him. "Does that seem strange?"

"Not really," Nathan said, though it did, a little.

"It seemed like too much of a coincidence to be just that."

"What do you mean?"

"It was like it was a sign, almost, seeing her again. I started to think about what the chances might be of such a coincidence, to wonder why I had suddenly decided to go to a café that I didn't usually frequent."

"A sign of . . . ?"

"What I should do, what direction I should take when the letter arrived." She glanced at him again. "Don't look so worried. I know what I sound like."

"You don't sound—"

"I'm like one of those old ladies I used to see in cafés in my childhood, pathetic creatures with papery skin who were so lonely they'd attach themselves—in their fantasies, at least—to anyone who spared them so much as a glance."

"You were so alone," Nathan said.

"Yes. I was so alone," she repeated, as if explaining something to herself. "And there was something about her that kept drawing my eye, not just her name. She was more made-up than her friends. There's a particular style, a plainness of style that's cultivated by some circles there. The girls don't wear a stitch of makeup, for example—that's too bourgeois for them. Or too European—I'm not sure what it is. But this girl, with her plum lips and kohl-lined eyes . . . she brought to mind a bird of paradise who happened to land in the midst of a flock of starlings."

That would be Nina, all right, Nathan thought.

"I wondered if she might have just come from the theatre, from another appearance on stage, but then my musings were

interrupted by a new eruption of laughter, accompanied now
by shouts of greeting. 'Ezra, Ezra,' they shouted, and I turned
to see who had inspired such an enthusiastic greeting. Their
hero stood in the entrance for a minute, shaking the rain off
his coat, removing the drenched newspaper that he had used
as a makeshift hat. They were all still calling out and laughing, with no sense that there were other patrons in the café.
I shifted my glance back to them and saw that the girl I had
noticed before wasn't laughing or smiling, wasn't participating in any way in the elaborate collective greeting. She was
applying fresh lipstick, looking into the mirror of her compact
with such concentration she seemed not to have even noticed
the new arrival. Which made me understand at once that he
was the reason for her made-up face, that she'd been waiting
the entire evening for this moment. I turned to give a second
look at the man who had elicited such a well-planned display
of indifference. He sprawled on the nearest empty chair, one
long arm thrown around the shoulder of the nearest female at
hand—not the bird of paradise, who pretended not to notice.
She rubbed her lips together to smooth her lipstick, snapped
her compact shut and got up to leave."

Nathan could see his sister in the scene that Lily had just
described: the feigned indifference, the snap of the compact.
He'd seen that scene so many times before that there was a
staleness in it for him.

"She wove her way through the maze of tables, towards
the door, holding her head high just in case he was watching
her."

"And was he?"

"No."

Of course not, Nathan thought. "She's the star of her

own play, my sister. She just hasn't noticed that no one else is watching her."

"*I* was watching, Nathan. Am I no one?"

"Of course not. You know I didn't mean it that way. I meant—"

"She kept her head high, her eyes straight ahead, so digni-fied. Like a queen."

"But she's not a queen, Lily. That's the point."

"Oh, hush. She has style, your sister. That's the point."

"She's obviously carrying on the same sorts of debasing love affairs over there that she was carrying on here." Nathan shook his head "Though at least there my poor mother doesn't have to witness them."

"Your poor mother. You see why I didn't tell you this before?" And to Nathan's offended look: "She has imagina-tion, your sister. She has class. She reminded me so much of one of my sisters. Who was actually the one my mother prom-ised the vanity to."

She turned back to the array of lipsticks and creams she had arranged on the vanity over the course of the afternoon. "It wasn't really like what I just described to you."

"What, she tripped on her way out the door?"

Lily smiled. "An actress like your sister doesn't trip in the middle of an exit like that. I meant my mother at her van-ity. It wasn't like I just said to you. I barely ever watched my mother make herself up at the end of the day. I was with my father, helping him with his business. That's where I went after school. By the time we got home, my father and I, they were often already in bed. And even if I had been there . . . We weren't close, my mother and I."

"You fought?"

"Not even. I didn't even bother to fight with her. I thought she was trivial, that I was better than her."

"A lot of girls don't get along—"

"I regret it now, of course, but I didn't have the time of day for her, with her hats for every occasion, and her gloves and shoes to match, and her lipsticks and rouges. She knew it; it must have hurt her." Lily removed the lipstick she had just applied, opened another one, a brighter, redder shade. "I didn't have time for this. Lipsticks, rouges, rules about how ladies do and don't leave the house."

She was describing a woman very much like herself, it seemed to Nathan. Had she not been like this before?

"It was my father I was close to, his world that interested me. His business. His life."

"What was his business?"

"Import–export."

Nathan nodded, imagined exotic carpets from Persia, objets d'art from God knows where, fashions from Paris, style, elegance. A male version of the mother she had just described.

"During busy times his hours were very long."

Nathan nodded again. "But why were you the one who helped him?" Surely a business like that could afford hired help, he thought.

"He had no sons, and I was the eldest, so . . ."

"The honourary son."

"More or less."

Was the father cheap, then, unwilling to pay for hired help? Something about the scenario wasn't quite right, a young girl having to work long hours like that when the family obviously had wealth. "You don't look like a son to me," he said.

She smiled. He got up from the bed to stand behind her, his hands resting lightly on her shoulders.

"Though maybe my eyes deceive me." He moved his hands down from her shoulders along the curves of her upper body. "Mmm. No. You definitely don't feel like a son."

She leaned back against him, her eyes closed. That smile, he thought, that release in her body. It cut through everything he didn't know about her, made her next words seem like a regretful caress: "You know your mother's waiting for us in the kitchen."

"I know," he said. "And she's already not in the greatest mood." Just another few months, he thought, and they'd be able to move into a place of their own.

"We don't need to keep it," she said.

"Keep what?"

"The vanity."

"Of course we'll keep it. You love it."

"No," she said. "I don't love it. It was just when it arrived . . . it reminded me of my mother."

"So? What better reason?"

But Lily was already shaking her head. "It was never meant to be mine, my mother's vanity. It was going to go to my sister when she got married. The oldest after me. She's the one who loved to sit with my mother, watching her."

"But that was your mother's, Lily. This one's yours. Ours. From my sister."

"I found myself wondering today who might have it now. What woman looks in my mother's mirror. What she sees."

"What she sees?"

"I hope she sees my mother." She smiled at him in the

mirror. "Don't look so worried. I don't really think my mother's haunting other women's mirrors."

"I'm not worried," he said, but he was, a little. She'd been trying to summon her mother all day, he sensed, with the lipsticks and creams that she said weren't really her.

The next day when he returned from work the old maple bureau had been moved back into the bedroom and the vanity was gone.

"I called Levine's to take it away," Lily told him. "He let us exchange it for credit towards the dining room table we'll need when we move to our own place."

Nathan was disappointed. In its absence both the room and Lily seemed barer, starker, stripped of something.

"NIE BYLO NAS, BYL LAS. *Nie bedzie nas, bedzie las,*" Lily said to Sol as they sat together on the fire escape a few nights later.

"Come again?" Sol said.

"We were not here, but the forest was. We will not be here, but the forest will be. There's comfort in that, no?"

"Not really," he said. It was depressing, actually. A bit morbid. "It makes it seem like there's no point in doing anything, like nothing we do matters in the end."

It had become their habit to sit together late at night while everyone around them slept. It wasn't that Lily had chosen Sol's company over Nathan's; she hadn't, but Nathan couldn't sit on the back steps talking with her till all hours. He was building his own business; he needed his sleep. He had no time for the kinds of conversations she had with Sol, conversations that stretched for hours, with long silences during which

thoughts surfaced and resurfaced in different forms, and in which everything could be said because, in her mind, there was nothing between them to lose.

"I went to see your friend's mother, you know."

"Mrs. Krakauer?"

"Last week." If she was going to come after me, she would have by now, Lily thought.

"But why on earth?"

"I guess I felt bad."

"For what?"

"I don't know. I guess—"

"It's not your fault you have the same name as her cousin." He was sorry he'd said anything. It would have passed had he kept quiet, but now it was there, in the air, and if he saw Elka again, if he were to bring her home, which he might, he realized, because there was definitely something about Elka . . .

"She seems to think it is."

"What?"

"My fault."

"Why do you say that?"

"I could tell. She kept staring at me."

"Well, forget her. She's an old bat." She was too sensitive, he thought, off balance.

She's not going to come after me, Lily knew, remembering the fear she'd sensed in Ida, a fear as disturbing to her as the thought of Ida coming after her, as if Ida knew something about Lily that Lily didn't even know about herself. As if she saw something, as Sol had when he turned away from her at the station.

"Was that Polish you just quoted?" Sol asked, to get her mind off Ida Krakauer.

Lily nodded. "She wrote that on the first page of the notebook."

She had told him a few nights ago about a notebook she had found near the end of the war. The notebook of a girl who had died.

"Who puts a quote at the beginning of their private diary?" Lily asked.

Sol didn't answer. He was not even going to hazard a guess about the workings of women's private diaries.

"No one," Lily answered. "There's something about her writing, the style of it . . . It's not like a private diary. She was writing for eyes beyond her own. That's what it seems to me. She might have been a writer or an artist. Had she lived, I mean. And so that quote . . . It's like what a writer will put at the start of a book. So why that quote, I've been wondering. And when did she choose it? It's right at the beginning, at the top of the first page, but it could have been written in at any time. She could have written it right before she died."

The girl was already dead when Lily came upon her, Lily had told Sol. The notebook was in the satchel that lay beside her.

"And why is it in Polish, I wonder."

"Why wouldn't it be?"

"Everything else is in Yiddish."

"So she was Jewish, the girl?"

"It would seem."

He waited for her to continue. When she didn't, he took the opportunity to change the subject, shift it to something less morbid.

"Our new man's from Poland," he said. The man who was an insult to him, whose presence was as direct a statement as Sol had ever received from Eisenberg about just how low he stood, how limited his prospects at Button King really were. Not that

he should have expected otherwise, he knew, with two Eisenberg sons waiting like the princes they were for the business to fall into their laps. The business that Sol had helped build. And his brother and father before him. He should never have returned there, he thought. The war had provided a natural break, and he should have taken it. As Nathan had. He should have broken out, moved into new territory. His own. Zippers, maybe.

"He doesn't know his ass from his elbow. How to dress. How to speak. Nothing. And I'm supposed to train him in." *To treat him as my equal* was the actual instruction he had understood when Eisenberg introduced the man as Sol's new partner, a word he then used—overused—every time he poked his head into the office Sol and the new man now shared. "Without missing a step, of course. While increasing sales. With him hanging around my neck like a . . . like a . . ."

"Like an albatross," Lily said.

"Exactly," Sol agreed.

It was his punishment, Sol suspected, though Eisenberg would never admit it. It was the fallout from the debacle of Lily's arrival; Sol had been waiting for it for weeks. Nothing terrible had been said at the time; if anything, Eisenberg had been reassuring—*We all make mistakes, the important thing is how we correct them*—but Sol had felt himself being watched since that day. And now this foisting of a partner onto him, the forced sharing of responsibility and prestige, the insulting implication that the refugee from Poland was Sol's equal.

He was big on charity, this Eisenberg, Lily thought. Nathan had already told her how he had turned up at their father's funeral eleven years earlier, not merely to pay his respects to the mourning widow and sons but to offer those sons employ-ment at a time—the depth of the Depression—when the work

of those two boys, ages thirteen and fifteen, could not possibly have generated the salary he paid to them. And then there was his behaviour towards her, the immediacy with which he and his wife, Bayla, had opened their home to her after Sol's desertion at the station, the sense they had imparted that she was no trouble and that it was of no importance to them how long she might need to rely on their hospitality. She wondered what motivated him and his wife to reach out their hands in those ways, what sins they were trying to expiate. It was a cynical turn of mind, she knew, wearying. She wondered if she'd always been this way.

"He's big on helping refugees, your boss," Lily said.

"His wife was a revolutionary back in Russia," Sol said, and Lily smiled. Every second Jew she met in Montreal claimed to have been a revolutionary back in Russia.

"A terrorist, apparently."

And the richer they were, these Jews in Montreal, the more radical their glorious, revolutionary pasts.

"His sons are useless, both of them."

Lily had met the sons, two handsome men in their thirties. "Useless" wasn't the word that came to her mind so much as "underused." He was at least seventy now, the Button King, but he showed no signs of slowing down. The resentment Sol felt towards the sons was probably nothing, Lily thought, compared to that of the sons themselves, who waited in vain for some transfer of the father's formidable powers and responsibilities.

"A couple of pansies."

Lily's mind filled with the deep colours of the flowers that spilled out of her mother-in-law's window boxes. Such hard colours: purples and yellows as dense and impenetrable as the woman who tended them. Lily's mother had grown pansies

as well, all along the path to the door of their summer home, but she had favoured softer colours: pinks and creams so delicate that all the light of summer flowed through them, yellows more like butter than gold.

"My mother loved pansies," she said.

Sol smiled but said nothing. Nine times out of ten she outsmarted him in his own language, and he didn't mind at all. He liked it, in fact. He liked smarts in a woman. But it was Lily's errors that most endeared her to him, those moments when she slipped that he felt his own desire for her most sharply. It was her not knowing what she was revealing that gave a tender ache to his longing, her not seeing the chink in the armour of her intellect. It was like catching a glimpse of private skin inadvertently revealed when a woman reached overhead on the streetcar and her sweater rode up. That glimpse—stolen and unexpected—was more arousing to him than a sighting of thigh or cleavage freely offered.

Lily had not actually misunderstood Sol's meaning. It was more that the other meaning was so pleasant, the image evoked so precious to her, so unexpected—the darkness of her mind parting, just a crack, to allow the light of her past to stream in. She held it for as long as she could, closing her eyes against the tedious description of Sol's day and resentments that she knew were sure to follow. She saw the path that led from the gate to the front door of her family's summer cottage, the lightly coloured petals fluttering in a summer breeze.

"I didn't know they had pansies in Poland," Sol said, amusing himself, if not Lily, with the cleverness of his double entendre.

"Everything you have here we had," she said.

And it was of a higher quality, he could hear her thinking,

and the irritation he felt in sensing that smugness of hers, that sense of her own superiority, was relief to him. He did not actually want to be half in love with his brother's wife. While he could not resist indulging the feeling, could not seem to stop himself from stepping through the kitchen window every night to join her on the fire escape steps, he did nurse a mild hope each time he walked down the brown hallway to the kitchen that this would be the night when he would be delivered from the feeling, that his attraction to her would break, finally, like other fevers had broken, leaving nothing but a feeling of having been returned to himself.

"It feels to me like a living thing," she said.

"What?" he said.

"The notebook." The words that changed meaning every time she read them. "She's trying to tell me something."

"She's dead, Lily," Sol said.

How could she explain about the souls of murdered people, how different their demands from those of the other dead, how quarrelsome they could be, how frightened, how anguished, how dangerous.

"I'm not saying that it isn't tragic that she died—a young girl with her whole life ahead of her."

Platitudes, she thought. Empty words. Words that only conveyed how little he understood her. And how could he?

"But she did die. She's gone. And you didn't. You lived." He looked at her. She seemed to be listening. "And so you need to get on with your life."

She said nothing for a few minutes, for so long that Sol cast about in his mind for ways to restart the conversation.

"Do you think I'm not trying?" she asked at last.

She had bought another notebook just a few days earlier.

She had awakened one morning—it was the morning after she'd returned the vanity to Levine—with an image of it in her mind: a journal just like the one she had taken, but new, pristine, its pages unmarred by word or mark. She had seen it clearly, its beautiful binding, its empty, creamy pages, an image so vivid she imagined she would be able to find its counterpart in the world in which she was now living. Which was a mistake. She could find nothing in her present world to match her interior life, but she did find a book with a soft leather cover and with paper whose texture and smooth finish pleased her. It was expensive, an indulgence, but she bought it anyway. Until that moment she had thought no further than finding as close a match as she could to the image she had woken with, but once she had found it that image began to change, to merge with the new book she held in her hands, and this too pleased her. It seemed the first instance of something in her new life merging with her internal yearnings, and though it was just an empty journal that had found a foothold within her, she felt a surge of hope that maybe this, at last, was the beginning she had been waiting for, that the other moments she had thought were the beginning—the landing in Palestine, the departure from Palestine, the arrival in Montreal, her wedding to Nathan—had been nothing more than the false starts of a runner who is so eager to race that his muscles push him forward before his ears hear the shot signalling the instant of the true start. She had been too eager to begin anew, impelled by fear and loss and guilt to move forward before her mind and heart were ready. But now, at this moment, as she felt the reassuring weight of the new journal in her hand, a weight that gave substance to what she had dreamed and imagined, she felt she had arrived at the beginning.

"I have my own notebook now," she told Sol, hoping that

the hope she had felt in the store that day would be rekindled in the telling.

"You mean a diary?"

She nodded.

His sister, Nina, had kept a diary. He remembered her poring over it, her left hand shielding from her older brothers' eyes the secrets that her right hand wrote. One of the diaries had a lock, easily picked with a pin. He remembered the disappointment he had felt breaking open that lock only to discover what he already knew: the names of the boys she had crushes on, the degree to which she felt afflicted by her brothers, the fact that their father had died. Why write it down? he had wondered. What was the purpose of writing down events and feelings that had been unpleasant enough in the actual living of them? It was not as if the recording of disaster alleviated its effects in any way. To the contrary, in fact. In Nina's case it seemed to have made it worse: *Papa's 4th yahrzeit today. Mama lit the candle, then yelled at me like it's my fault he walked in front of the streetcar.* That's what she had written on February 15, 1939, the fourth anniversary of their father's death—and why? Their father had not walked in front of a streetcar. He had slipped on the ice, fallen into the path of the oncoming number 55. The coroner's report had been very clear on that point, concluding without question that the death had been accidental, but Nina, wallowing in the contents of her own mind, had created for herself a reality even worse than the one she already had to endure.

"It's enough with the diaries," he told Lily now. "You need to get out more, meet some people. You should think about going to some of my mother's lectures with her."

"Your mother doesn't like me."

"She finds you standoffish, but if you extend yourself,

just a little, she'll come around—you'll see. And it would do you good to get out, meet some new people, hear some new things." Living people, living things, he meant. "Air your brain out a bit."

When she had first brought the new journal home, the empty pages had made her think of fields of fresh snow, those white expanses that she had awakened to as a child when they visited the countryside in winter, flat white surfaces bordered by stark lines of brown and black trees, and stretching out on all sides to meet the white of the winter sky. She had run her hands along the clean surfaces of the book's pages and imagined that words would flow easily onto them, would mark them with the evidence of her continuing life as inevitably as those fields of snow had been marked by her footprints when she crossed them. A page for each day, the filling of it as straightforward as walking across a field—but as she had faced the first page with pen in hand, she had hesitated, hadn't known how to start. With the details of her daily life? The time she awoke? The dream that woke her? The egg that she had eaten for breakfast? And if so, in what language? The languages of her childhood? The English of all that stretched ahead? The pen hovered over the page but didn't land.

"Maybe you're right," she said. The hope she had felt when she bought the book had not returned. The pen, when she held it, was dead in her hand. "Nothing feels real. I can't explain it. I thought if I wrote it down, my life . . . the egg I ate for breakfast, for example . . ."

"You were planning to write in your diary about an egg you ate for breakfast?"

"As a start," she said.

Was it possible, she wondered, that what she felt now, the

lethargy, the sense of being coated in a thick, viscous substance that separated her from her experience, her life, was
an exhaustion and alienation that might pass in time? That
the egg, if she wrote it as *ayer* or *jojko*, might, for a moment,
regain its richness and bring her the pleasure that she had once
enjoyed as a child?

"*Jojko*," she said quietly, allowing the familiar sounds to
roll over her tongue. She waited. Nothing. "That's 'egg' in Polish," she told Sol.

He nodded, also waited. This wasn't good, he thought.
There was little about this conversation that he felt he had fully
understood, except that this wasn't healthy. This wasn't good.

"It's enough with the diaries," he said quietly. What she
needed, he thought, was a baby, a living, crying, laughing baby
whose need for her every minute of every day would root her
to the real she said she couldn't feel.

"You really need to try to get out more."

"Maybe so," she said, but even as she said the words her
mind was absent, travelling back to the notebook, a passage
she had read earlier that day:

> *I'm lost in a city of stone. I've entered through a
> breach in the outer wall. At first I think I've come to
> a place of safety. It's clean and dry, the stones unsul-
> lied by mud or blood or excrement of any kind, and
> worn to smooth, grey surfaces by the countless feet
> that have preceded mine. And it's quiet, so quiet,
> the din of what I've left behind muffled at first by
> the outer wall, then gone entirely as I penetrate the
> inner warren of streets. The city is intact, unharmed
> by the war outside it. It's Canada, I think, amazed*

by the ease with which I've gained entry. Canada,
I whisper, as my father used to whisper, the name
a prayer in his mouth, an incantation that evoked
endless prairies in my mind. Canada, I whisper, run-
ning my hand along the cold grey surface of stone
that bears no resemblance to the dream my father
planted in my consciousness.

It was a dream that could have been her own, Lily thought.
It was like reading her own reality filtered through the dream
of another. A prescient dream: the girl had foreseen the peace
that awaited her if she had lived. The peace I'm now living
in her place, Lily thought. A peace that was not the summer
courtyards of her childhood, or the endless prairies of her
father's prayers, but the lifeless stone of a city in which she
was lost, its featureless surfaces—unsullied, she called them—
a colourless cold beneath her hand.

The streets are empty and I imagine at first that
the people are inside, at home, gathered around
the evening meal, but they're not. They're gone.
They've fled. And I'm alone.

It was her own life she was reading, Lily thought, written
in the hand of another.

I've entered an abandoned city, and I'm alone.
The quiet is unnatural. There's no movement, no
background hum, no rustling of leaves or lives of
any sort. Even my footsteps are silent, the sound
of their impact swallowed by the stones against

which they fall. Frightened, I begin to speak, to reassure myself. I state my name, the names of my family, the city in which I was born and raised, but my voice too is silenced, swallowed by the air into which I project it. The quiet in this place is not a mere absence of sound, but an entity, a vacuum that will swallow me whole if I stay. I turn to leave, but there is no leaving. I feel its presence, the silence at the core of the maze. I feel its power as it sucks at my blood like a moon that pulls a tide. It pulls me to itself, its empty heart.

CHAPTER 10

No one questioned why I started going straight home to my father's after school almost every afternoon. Elka's boys were noisy and rambunctious and always getting into my things; I had homework to do and couldn't concentrate with Mitch and Chuck constantly trying to get me to play with them; I needed to spend more and more time on the phone with friends as my social life began to improve, and Elka didn't like me tying up her line. There were many reasons for me to want to spend the hours between school and dinner somewhere other than at Elka and Sol's. I don't think anyone in the family imagined how many of those hours were taken up with me prowling through my father's home like a cat burglar, combing it for clues about my mother.

I had divided our home into zones. The living room held the two notebooks, one of which was empty, one of which was written in a language I couldn't understand. I knew the girl's notebook could be important, but for the moment it was impenetrable. I had once asked my father to read it to me

but his Yiddish wasn't good enough, and when I asked my grandmother Bella, she said, "What for?" There was nothing in it of interest, they both assured me, and I believed that they thought that, but I wanted to confirm it for myself.

I would sometimes run my fingers over the words I couldn't understand, as if they might bypass the closed gates of language in my mind to enter me through my skin. I did the same with my mother's smooth, unmarked pages, and something did enter me. Not the pulsing I had once felt, something else. I felt its weight—the girl's words, my mother's silence. It was like an animal curled up inside me, its current running within my own. But that wasn't anything that would help me track my mother down.

The bathroom and kitchen were devoid of anything related to her. Although she had chosen and used many of our dishes and utensils, our own use of them in the years since she'd left had taken them over completely, buried any traces of her they once might have held.

In my bedroom were the rocks. What they yielded to me— that she hadn't forgotten me, that she wanted me to know where she was or had recently been, that she was either slightly or severely off her rocker—was no more the sort of information I was looking for than the current I felt from the notebooks.

I still had the scrapbook as well, but that seemed nothing other than pathetic to me by then. It was true I had slipped the wrapping and stamps from the most recent mailing between the scrapbook's pages (a piece of layered shale from Jasper, Alberta, that had arrived two weeks after my fourteenth birthday), but only because it was the most logical place to store it.

And then there was the map, which I still had hanging

over my desk. "What's that?" Mira asked the first time she came over. (Stop being so paranoid, Carrie had said when she invited herself and Mira over, as if the rift between us was entirely in my head.)

"A map," I said.

Carrie busied herself with the orange she was peeling, which was as much of a sign as she'd ever give that she was sorry she had betrayed me once and would not do it again.

"Are those places you've been?" Mira asked, referring to the pins sticking out of places like Rainy Lake, Ontario, and the Old Man River in Alberta and Jasper, Alberta.

"Places I want to go," I answered.

"Neat," Mira said, and Carrie handed her a segment of orange.

Our house was littered with clues about my mother, but none of them added up to anything. Which is why I crossed the threshold to my father's bedroom one afternoon. I knew I shouldn't. My sense of the inviolability of my own and others' privacy couldn't have been stronger, even as I opened the drawers of my father's night table, saw the little candies he kept there for when he got a scratchy throat, his packets of Kleenex, his flashlight, various receipts, some loose change. There were a couple of tie clips and a pair of cufflinks that should properly have been in the tray of his valet, some folded notes to himself, a few of which were grocery lists, others of which were reminders of doctors' appointments, performances or tests at school that I had told him about. On one scrap of paper he had noted the title of a book that I knew he had recently bought for Sally, a woman he had taken out for dinner several times. (She was nice, but not his type, I could tell right away. Too gushy.) I felt silly and ashamed of what I was doing—it was like pawing through

the inside of a woman's purse—but that didn't stop me from moving on to his dresser. What girl of fourteen goes snooping in her father's underwear? I asked myself as I opened the top drawer. I must be truly sick. I saw a pair of ratty old grey wool socks that should have been thrown out years ago, a few singles that also should have been discarded, and then I noticed the edge of something that was neither sock nor undershirt. A card of some sort. I pulled it from its nest of socks with a mix of thrill and dread.

It was a valentine, and an old one at that. It was definitely old enough to have been sent from my mother to my father or vice versa. And definitely the strangest valentine I'd ever seen. Valentines were supposed to be romantic, but it was impossible to see how this one could have represented romance to anyone, ever. The sender was *looking for a Valentine / but none of those Jazz gluttons,* which was odd in itself because my father loved Bill Evans and Duke Ellington and Oscar Peterson and other jazz musicians. Just that week he'd brought home a new recording by John Coltrane. The next two lines were even odder: *I want a handy little miss / who can sew on a few buttons.* A message that was not only corny but insulting, it seemed to me, as if the sender (my father?) seemed to be looking more for a charwoman than a sweetheart. There were even two red buttons attached to the card in case the sweetheart in question (my mother?) felt a sudden urge to start sewing right then and there.

The card had been torn to pieces and then reassembled and taped together again. The tape holding it together was yellow with age, but the two buttons at the bottom were still bright red. There was no mystery to me about why my mother would have torn it up. Were I to receive such a valentine I too

might tear it up, I thought. But why then had it been put back together? Who would take such care and time and effort to reconstruct something that had obviously been a mistake, a disappointment, a failure? And why?

I turned it over, but the inscription was in Yiddish, and while I could piece together the sounds of the letters because Yiddish used the Hebrew alphabet, I couldn't understand the words the letters formed. The name, though, I could read. It was the same in Yiddish as in Hebrew. *Yoseph Kramer.* My father's father.

Had my grandmother Bella been the recipient of this valentine, then? I could not imagine it, could not imagine her in any way other than how I'd always known her: as an old lady who did a lot of cooking and reading, and whose idea of a good time was going to the library or getting together with Ida Pearl for tea and whisky over a game of cards. She was simply not the valentine type, though if she ever were to receive one it would make sense that it would be one like this, and that the sender, her husband, would sign it with his full formal name. Knowing it had probably been given to Bella made me less interested in why it had been torn up and reassembled. I loved my grandmother but was not fascinated by her, wasn't particularly keen to try to imagine aspects of her beyond those I knew, or to envision possible scenarios that had Bella in the starring role.

What I was curious about was what that valentine was doing in my father's drawer. Could it have to do with the fact that it had been his father's at some point, had his father's handwriting on the back? I wondered. Joseph Kramer had died when my father was fifteen, not much older than I was now. As far as I knew, this was the only thing of his father's that he pos-

sessed, besides the *siddur* on our living room bookshelf that my grandfather had used for his morning prayers, and that my father also used for the prayers he said every morning before he left for work. Maybe my father liked to look at his father's handwriting from time to time. Maybe he even ran his fingers over it like I sometimes ran my fingers over the index cards my mother had written to me, and over the pages of her notebooks. I couldn't ask him, not without admitting I had been snooping in his things. In his underwear drawer, no less. And I wasn't even sure I wanted to know. The idea of my father sitting alone in his room at night running his fingers along the lines of the handwriting of his dead father was depressing. Creepy, actually. I put the valentine back, closed the drawer. I didn't want to open another. I felt slightly queasy about what I'd uncovered already, a secret life less interesting than lonely and sad.

Not long after that I asked Bella again to read me what the girl had written in the notebook. This time she didn't say *What for?* or tell me there was nothing in it of interest.

"My eyes aren't what they were," she said.

But they weren't so bad, I thought, that she couldn't read the stacks of Yiddish books and pamphlets that she borrowed every two weeks from the Jewish Public Library.

"The writing is so tiny, hard to make out." And a lot of it was gibberish, she explained, dreams that wouldn't make sense to anyone.

She didn't want to read it to me, in other words. But why?

"Because your grandmother respects other people's privacy," Ida Pearl said when I repeated the conversation to her and Elka a few days later. We were in Miss Snowdon, a restaurant a few doors down from Ida's building, where Elka and I often met Ida if we were doing errands in the neighbourhood.

"No, she doesn't." It was no secret that Bella used to make a regular habit of reading Nina's diaries. That was how she found out Nina was having an affair with a married man when she was still in high school.

"Didn't you just order cinnamon torte?" Ida asked me sharply as I took a second helping of the complimentary coleslaw and pickles that the restaurant provided to every table.

"It's okay, Ma, they'll bring more," Elka said.

"It's not a food shortage that concerns me."

"I'm hungry," I said, to explain the heap of coleslaw on my plate.

"Then you should have ordered a meal."

"Maybe I'll bring it to Mrs. Schoenfeld," I said. She lived across the street from Elka and Sol, and spoke Yiddish.

"You'll do no such thing," Ida said. The sharpness of her reprimand surprised me. "You don't bring family business to strangers."

Mrs. Schoenfeld was hardly a stranger—she'd been my piano teacher for years and we saw her in *shul* every Saturday. And since when was the girl a member of our family? According to my father, she wasn't even my mother's friend.

"I'll just have to learn Yiddish myself, then. Since it's obvious that no one in my family is ever going to read it to me."

Ida changed the subject now, asked Elka about the colour of the new curtains she had just ordered for her living room. I refrained from taking a third helping of coleslaw to avoid irritating Ida further, but I knew she was still annoyed. I could feel her stiffness. And sure enough, a little later, just as I was scraping the last of the cinnamon whipped cream and shavings of chocolate from my plate, she interrupted her conversation with Elka and turned to me.

"You're making more out of that diary than there is."

"Then why won't anyone read it to me?"

"When you're engaged to be married I'll read it to you."

Sex, I thought. There had to be sex in it. Which made it inaccessible to me for the time being because the only people I knew who could read Yiddish were parents of friends, grandparents, people who'd come from Europe, and the very thought of any of those people reading me anything that even hinted of sex . . .

"Maybe it's like Anne Frank's diary, but with sex scenes," Carrie said when she was over a few days later. "If it is, it could be a huge bestseller."

She opened the girl's notebook and pored over the first entry. I knew that she understood Yiddish because that was the language her parents used between themselves when they wanted to have a conversation that Carrie and her sisters wouldn't be able to understand, but I had no idea that she could actually read it.

"*I start with a dream . . .*" she said aloud in English. She started working on the next sentence. "*I'm running . . .*"

"Not a dream part," I interrupted her. "Try to find something better." Worth her effort, I meant, because to say that Carrie could read Yiddish doesn't begin to convey just how slowly she had read that first sentence to me, and with what degree of difficulty.

Carrie agreed that other people's dreams were boring. She flipped through the pages, found another passage and then started:

"*Last night I saw . . . Eva.*" She looked up. "I'm pretty sure that last word is a name. Eva."

I nodded, could not believe we hadn't done this before.

"*The path I was walking had opened onto a . . . clearing.*"

She looked up again. "There's a word before *clearing* that I don't know."

"It's okay. Go on."

"*. . . and there she was—my dearest, closest, prettiest Eva* . . . God, she really liked this Eva. Who was she?"

"How would I know?"

"*She was sitting by the side of a stream, her feet . . . hanging . . . in the water, and it was summer again, the forest around her a . . .* something-or-other . . . I can't make out the word *. . . of greens, the water a different* something-or-other *of sparkling blues and greys.*"

"Mixture?" I asked.

"Could be. *She was wearing her favourite summer dress, a light cotton shift in a green as pale as new leaves. Her hair was loose, falling in waves past her shoulders. She was the Eva I had always loved, the friend I had never stopped loving . . .* Uh-oh."

"What?" Here it came, I thought: the reason no one would ever read it to me.

"You're not going to believe this." She continued: "*My dream repaired the break between us . . .*"

"Another dream?"

"*. . . inserted summer warmth like a ray of sun that pierces a gloomy day.*"

Carrie shut the notebook. It had taken her the better part of an hour to read and translate that passage. "It's just a bunch of dreams."

"And I thought no one would read it to me because it was sexy."

"They just didn't want to bore themselves to death," Carrie said.

We put the notebook back on the shelf beside my mother's.

I had come to a dead end. There was nothing else about my mother to find in our home. But at the same time, the compulsion I felt to do that was easing off. My own life was getting busier and more interesting. Happier, even. It was starting to open up more and more, filling up with matters as pressing as whether or not I would be invited to Lina Tessler's sweet sixteen, or whether Charles Blumenthal liked me or hated me, or whether it was fair that I should have to wait until I was eighteen to learn to drive when Carrie was allowed at sixteen. The separateness I felt in my family continued, but that no longer made me feel unusual. All my friends felt separate from their families now.

When another rock arrived from my mother I felt annoyed by it, uncomfortable. I wondered why she didn't either write me a letter or leave me alone. I was practically an adult, and she was still sending me these packages like I was a six-year-old who could barely read and would thrill to a pink rock arriving in the mail. And yet there was also something about the rock (a gorgeous banded agate from the north shore of Lake Superior, near Wawa) that touched me, the trouble she took with the wrapping, the careful curves of her handwriting. There was something pathetic about her that both touched and repelled me.

So it wasn't really longing that drew me to the phone books in the library one afternoon, so much as serendipity. I was doing a research project for school and happened to notice that there were shelves of phone books from cities all across Canada. Saskatoon was the first one that caught my eye. I pulled it off the shelf on a whim, looked under *Kramer, Azerov, Azeroff*. I couldn't find a Lily with any of those last names, but there was an L. Kramer.

Could it possibly be? I wondered as I jotted it down. My heart raced. Had it been this easy all along? There were phone books from just about every city in Canada, it seemed, a whole long shelf. It would take a while to check each one, and I did have a paper to write, a research paper on the French Revolution that was due at the end of the week, but the French Revolution seemed trivial compared to what I was doing, of almost no consequence at all. I pulled out Lethbridge. Nothing there, but Regina had an L. Kramer.

I was on Winnipeg when I heard, "Ruthie!" I looked up to see my grandmother Bella.

"I thought it was you."

She was always happy to see me, but never more so, it seemed, than at that minute. Probably because I was at the library rather than hanging around the shopping centre with my friends. She had already looked to see what I was reading. I saw the puzzlement in her face as I stood to give her a kiss.

"Bubby," I said.

I felt the way I had five years earlier when Elka found the stash of gum and other candy that Carrie and I had stolen and hidden between my bed and the wall. There was no reason to feel that way now, I told myself. What was the crime in looking through a phone book? But my face was hot and I felt an awkwardness entirely out of place in a meeting between a girl and her grandmother in the reading room of a public library.

"Who do you know in Winnipeg?" Bella asked me, because contrary to Ida Pearl's assertion, Bella didn't actually have a finely tuned sense of other people's privacy. If she sensed my awkwardness at the moment, which she had to, that would only be more reason to pry.

"Oh, no one. I'm just taking a break from a paper I'm

researching." I launched into a long and tedious description of Danton's fate during the Reign of Terror.

"Who are you looking for in the phone book?"

It was possible she didn't actually know, that she was asking the question in a purely neutral, curious way, but I felt she did know. What other reason could I have for looking through the phone book of a western Canadian city? What other person might I possibly be looking for?

"My mother," I said.

She hadn't known, I realized immediately from her response. Her delight at finding me in her favourite haunt was erased, her expression so serious now it seemed pained.

"I found a few L. Kramers," I said, just to try to sound normal, to change the look on her face. "I know they're probably not her." I didn't actually know that, was still racing with excitement that one of them might be.

Bella nodded. "Put the phone book away and come outside with me. I want to talk to you about something."

I was resentful, resistant. I didn't need or want to hear from her the advice she was going to give me, her warnings about cans of worms and Pandora's boxes, but I knew there would be another opportunity to continue working my way through the phone books. I put the book away and followed her to the lobby, sat beside her on one of the benches.

"Your mother's name wasn't Lily Kramer," she told me.

Just like that. No preparation, no preamble about having something to tell me that might be confusing, difficult, whatever. Just that. My mother's name was not what I thought it was.

"Not Lily Kramer. Not Lily Azerov. Not Lily anything."

"What do you mean?"

"I mean that Lily Azerov was somebody else's name that she took at the end of the war. It wasn't that uncommon," she added quickly.

I knew it wasn't that uncommon. I had a friend at school whose father had taken the identity of another person in order to get into Canada. It was a secret I would never breathe to anyone—not even to this day—for fear she and her family could still get deported. But the fact that it wasn't uncommon wasn't the point.

"So . . . what *is* her name?"

That seemed to me to be closer to the point, but Bella shrugged. "She didn't want anyone to know."

"But why?"

"Why did she take another name?"

That wasn't exactly what I had been asking, but I let Bella answer.

"Because she was from Poland, very near to the Soviet border, and I think she was maybe afraid she'd be forced back there when the war ended. The Soviets were the liberators of Poland, don't forget."

"But tons of people came over from Poland after the war." Half my friends' parents, it seemed.

"Whether she really needed a false identity, I don't know. I think she probably didn't, in the end, but maybe she did. I don't know," Bella said again. "But she didn't keep the name Lily once she left you and your father."

I was just wasting my time looking for a Lily Kramer or a Lily Azerov in the phone books, in other words. "How do you know that?"

"I feel it." And then, as if sensing my dissatisfaction with that answer: "You can't explain everything you feel in life."

I thought about what she had just told me, tried to absorb it.

"But wouldn't anyone have told me?" If it was really true, is what I meant. I found it hard to believe that my father and Elka and Sol would have withheld such a basic fact from me all these years.

Bella took so long to answer, it was as if she'd never considered the question before. "I think your father wasn't sure what to do. What was best. For you."

"So he thought that it was best for me to not know that my mother's name was fake?"

"I know you don't understand that now, but maybe you'll understand it better when you're a mother yourself."

"I don't ever intend to lie outright to my children."

"No one was lying to you, Ruthie."

"What would you call it then?"

Bella didn't answer.

"It's lying," I said.

"I shouldn't have taken it upon myself to tell you. Not without talking to your father about it. But when I saw you with the phone books, and then you told me what you were doing . . . And you're sixteen now, not a child any more."

I didn't believe her. My father and Elka would not have withheld this from me. But I didn't disbelieve her either. Why would she make up something like this?

"I probably need to talk to my father," I said.

She patted my hand. "Nothing's really different than it's ever been."

I looked at her and saw she believed that. So what if my mother's name had been Selma or Freda rather than Lily? She had still left; I still had never met her; I still had a family who did love me. That's what Bella meant, I assumed, but if she'd

been speaking Martian it would have made more sense to me at that moment.

"It's different" was all I said.

Initially I felt a bit of excitement. There was an element of mystery about my mother now that had been lacking before. She wasn't simply a woman who had cracked, but a woman who had been hiding behind an entirely false identity. And why? Why would she not want her real name to be known, as Bella had said? What was she afraid of? Who was she, if not Lily Azerov Kramer? I would speak to my father, demand he tell me the complete truth, even if it was difficult. It was time now. I was sixteen, no longer a child.

As I walked home from the library, though, and settled in to wait for my father's return from work, that bit of excitement gave way to anxiety. I was about to accuse my father of having lied to me my entire life, of having withheld from me essential defining facts about my mother that he had always known, my father who had always been a steady and loving presence for me and who was probably just trying to do his best by me in circumstances that were not—no matter how positive a spin one might try to put on them—the best.

He had been a young man when she left him, a young, good-looking, ambitious and responsible man. And as time went on he became a financially successful man as well. He was a catch, in other words, even with a young child in tow, and yet he had never remarried, had never even seriously dated another woman. That was because of me, I sensed. Because I came first in his life. Because he had arranged his life so we could be a family, he and I.

Elka and Sol were also my family, their home my second home, and there were times in my childhood when I spent

more time with them than with my father, but my first home was with my father, always. Throughout my childhood he and I spent the last hours of almost every weekday evening together, and most of the weekend as well. On weekdays, after we moved to Côte-St-Luc, he would pick me up from Elka and Sol's after supper and we would walk the three blocks home together. We didn't have to walk; he could have picked me up in his car. Often—in the dead of a Montreal winter, for example—it would have been more expedient and certainly more sensible to drive. But our walk home together was what we did, he and I, separate and apart from everyone else, and the image of family that developed in my mind as a child was not the nightly suppers at Elka and Sol's, much as I enjoyed them—all of us around their table at six o'clock sharp, eating a good and balanced meal and chatting about our respective days—but that silent walk home later with my father. When I thought about that walk it was always winter. In reality, of course, it was often spring, summer or fall, and the nights were variously warm, cold, rainy or windy, but what remained in my mind, what rose to the surface of all the blended memories of those nightly walks home was one cold winter night, a night so cold that the bones around my eyes ached, and so still that the only sound was the squeak of snow beneath our boots, and so peaceful that the only thing that pressed on me was my father's mittened hand holding my own.

And now I was waiting to accuse him.

"Ah, you're home," he said, when he walked in the door.

A happy discovery, his tone implied, and I felt ill about what was ahead. I pretended to be absorbed in my homework, barely looked up as I returned his greeting. He took off his tie and jacket, poured himself a Scotch.

"There's some meat loaf in the fridge," I said. "Do you want me to heat it up?"

"We can eat later. Unless you're hungry—"

"No, no," I assured him. "Later's fine."

He let out his usual end-of-the-day sigh as he settled himself in his chair with his newspaper. I continued to pretend to be utterly absorbed in my school work. It was quiet except for the rustle of his newspaper and the occasional rumble of a passing bus or truck on Côte-St-Luc Road, ten storeys down.

Was the withholding of this fact the same as lying? I wondered. Did the truth of my mother really reside in this information that he had withheld from me?

I remembered an afternoon, years earlier, when he and I took a walk together in the woods around a cabin in the Laurentians that Sol and Elka had rented for the summer. It was a warm day and the air was thick with buzzing, biting insects. I knew the walk was supposed to be a special time for us—my father was not the type to take time away from his newspapers and business magazines to go tramping through the woods—but the insects were driving me mad. "I thought mosquitoes liked to sleep during the day," I said, slapping my ear, but missing the source of the infernal whine, then slapping my arm, a direct hit, which left a bloody smear. "Do you know what kinds of trees are around us?" my father asked me. "Birch," I said. "What else?" he asked. "Evergreens." I pointed to a clump of conifers. "Yes, but what kind of evergreens?" I didn't know. "And those?" he asked, pointing to a clump of deciduous trees. "I don't know. Can we please get out of here and go for a swim?" He looked surprised then. "Of course," he said, and I felt I had hurt him. We started walking back out

along the trail towards the lake, but then he said, "Stop for a minute. Give me your hand." I did. "Now close your eyes." I did again. He took my hand and pressed it against a tree trunk and held it there for a minute. "That's a birch," he said. I nodded. To say that this was uncharacteristic behaviour for him is an understatement equivalent to observing that it would be uncharacteristic for our rabbi at the time, Rabbi Searles, to come twirling down the aisle of the synagogue wearing a pink tutu. "Now keep your eyes closed," he said. He led me a few steps and placed my hand on another trunk. The bark was rougher, almost corrugated. "That's a pine.'" He released my hand and we kept walking towards the lake. "Your mother could identify trees like that," he told me then, and though I immediately wanted to know more, wanted to stay in the forest the rest of the day so he could tell me more about her and the trees that she knew, I had already spoiled it. In another minute we would be out at the lake, where Elka would be sitting on her lounge chair with her silver sun reflector under her chin and a leaf on her nose to protect it from burning, and my cousins would be flinging sand pies at each other, and Sol would be out in a rowboat, pretending he liked to fish.

Was the fact that her name had not been Lily really more important than what he'd tried to tell me that day in the woods?

"Do you mind if I put some music on?" I asked.

"No, go ahead."

I put on an old Artie Shaw record. A mistake, I realized as soon as I returned to my couch and "Begin the Beguine" filled the room. It was annoying, grating. I went back to the record player, took it off.

"Change your mind?"

"I prefer quiet."

My father lowered the newspaper, looked at me. "You all right?"

"Yes, fine. Why?"

"No reason."

That's how it was between us, had always been. We noticed each other, but didn't pry. (Searching through his private things for traces of my mother was different than prying, I had decided.) In our entire life together neither of us ever once said to the other "A penny for your thoughts," an expression I heard so often at Elka and Sol's that I could have amassed a small fortune had I answered it even half the times it had been directed my way.

"I saw Bubby at the library today."

"Oh?"

"I was researching my paper on Danton."

"How's that going?"

"Fine. Good."

"And how did Bubby seem?"

"Fine."

"Her cold's all cleared up?"

"Seems to be."

"Did she have any light reading to recommend for you? *Crime and Punishment*, maybe?"

I wanted to smile as I normally would, but nothing felt normal. "She told me about my mother's name. You know. That it wasn't hers." I had thought I could be straightforward, but my voice was tight, choked with anxiety and a pent-up mix of emotions I couldn't begin to name.

My father nodded, but in the long silence that ensued he didn't offer anything beyond that non-verbal confirmation. He

didn't apologize as I had expected he would, didn't scramble to offer me the explanations he should have offered long before now. He displayed a reticence that might simply have been a non-hysterical and straightforward response to my obvious distress but that felt to me at that moment like willful withholding.

"Who was she?" I asked him. "Her *real* name, I mean."

"She never told me."

"You don't *know?*"

"Do you think I would have kept it from you had I known?"

"You kept this from me, the fact that the name I know her by wasn't hers."

"Because I had nothing to give you in return."

"What about just telling me the truth?" I asked. And when he didn't answer: "Is that nothing?"

Again he didn't answer right away, but this time I waited.

"I thought that would just make things worse," he said, finally. "Not now, perhaps, but when you were young, a little girl with no mother. To take even that from you, to not even leave you with a name you could—"

"But it wasn't hers."

He didn't nod or agree, but neither did he go on with the explanation I had just interrupted. "It was the name I knew her by," he said finally. Lamely, I thought.

"When did you find out, then?"

"After she left."

I waited for him to go on, to explain something, anything, about the woman he had married, my mother, who had now receded farther from my reach than ever before. I wanted him to open up a new track that might lead me to her to replace the one that had just dissolved, to offer some new piece of information that I might grasp at, but he said nothing.

"No wonder your marriage broke up," I said. "You didn't even know her name, for God's sake. It's so basic. To not even know the name of the person you're married to. I mean, how could you possibly not . . . ?"

But something in my father's face stopped me. He was ashamed, I realized. And why wouldn't he be? He was humiliated to have to admit to me how little my mother had trusted him, how little of her she had let him know. And maybe that was the truth of why he hadn't told me. Not out of a desire to protect me. Not out of concern about taking something away from me without having anything to replace it. But because he was ashamed. Because to say out loud that he hadn't known was to acknowledge how false his marriage to my mother had been, how false his great—and only—love. So false that even the name he had called her at their moments of greatest intimacy—perhaps at the very moment that I came into being—was false, not hers, did not resonate within her any deeper than her outermost layer of skin.

I couldn't keep looking at him, his shame exposed to me as it was. It was like seeing him naked; I had to look away. I got up off the couch, walked over to the bookshelf and pulled out the girl's notebook. "I know you think there's nothing in it," I said, repeating the family mantra. "But she wouldn't have kept it if it wasn't important to her. If the girl who it belonged to wasn't important to her."

Was my father relieved for the break in the conversation we were having? Was he happy for the distraction from the light I'd just been shining on his complete failure as a man? He dropped his usual protest that his Yiddish wasn't good enough, took the notebook from me and opened it to the first page.

"There's a quote at the beginning that I don't understand. It's in Polish." He turned the page, began to read. *"I begin with a dream. I'm running through a city of stone . . ."*

"Read me something that isn't a dream," I said.

He leafed through the pages and began again.

"The afternoon before the war began I went to visit Eva."

That Eva again.

"She had come down with a grippe a few weeks earlier, a lingering grippe that she could not seem to shake off, and I had not visited her yet, a lapse on my part that would have been unthinkable in previous summers."

He translated slowly but easily. Fluently, in fact. So why the pretence, all these years, that he couldn't read it when he could?

"She had been my dearest friend since childhood, a friendship that had been heightened by longing during the ten-month separation we were forced to endure every year and deepened by the impassioned letters we wrote to each other, letters sealed with kisses and tears in which we revealed our deepest selves to one another and planned everything we would do together when the school year ended and we could finally be together again."

I was so angry with him now that I could barely concentrate on what he was reading. That he would have pretended he couldn't read Yiddish. That he had lied outright to me . . .

"All through the grey Antwerp winter I would imagine the coming summer in Krakow, how we would walk hand in hand along the leafy lanes of the Planty, stopping for lemonade or cherry ices at one of the cafés there, or spend entire afternoons lying on the grass near the playing fields by the Vistula, watching the clouds overhead, imagining that the shapes those

*clouds assumed as they drifted over us were auguries of our
future lives and loves.*"

He paused in his reading. I thought at first that he was trying to make out a word, a phrase, but then he looked up.

"This notebook was Lily Azerov's," he said, and I was confused for a moment because the name still evoked my mother
for me. Then I realized he meant the original Lily Azerov, the
girl whose name my mother had taken. Who had been Ida
Pearl's cousin, I came to understand as my father told me about
the letter Ida Pearl had received from her sister Sonya in Tel
Aviv a few days before my parents' wedding.

"But . . . why?" I asked. Why would she have taken someone else's identity, I meant. And why that particular identity?

"I don't know. There are many possible—"

"Did they know each other before?" I persisted, unable
to accept that my father could really know as little about the
woman he had married as he claimed. Was it possible that my
mother was Eva, the real Lily's childhood friend that I had
just heard described in the pages of her journal? I asked my
father, and as I did an image formed in my mind of a girl of
about fourteen walking hand in hand with her friend, lying on
a grassy slope watching the clouds, eating cherry ices, writing
the exact sorts of long, sentimental letters that I had once written to my friends from summer camp, sappy teenage letters
sealed with kisses and promises of unending friendship. It was
the first time I had ever had any kind of image of my mother
as a girl in a specific place, doing everyday things. I wanted to
hear more, could hardly wait to hear more, but my father was
shaking his head.

"Your mother wasn't the Eva the girl wrote about," he said.

"Lily," I said. She had a name, the girl, even if my mother

took it. "How do you know my mother wasn't Eva?" It was a nice name, I thought. Eva. I liked it better than Lily.

"Your mother wasn't from Krakow."

"Where was she from, then?"

"She didn't tell me exactly where, but—"

"If she didn't even tell you the name of her town—"

"Your mother was not the same girl as the Eva in this notebook," he said, then he picked up the notebook, leafed through a few pages and began to read to me again. He was very familiar with the contents of the notebook, I realized.

"But that summer I had changed. I knew it the moment I stepped off the train. I saw Eva waiting for me, but her face, so beloved in my memory, did not bring me the joy I had antici-pated. Her soft brown eyes, which were once windows to a soul I found endlessly interesting, were static, shallow pools now."

My father stopped reading, looked up. "Your mother's eyes weren't brown," he said. "They were blue."

"Oh," I said, exhaling with that one syllable all the anxious excitement that had been building in me since I had started imagining that I had just found my mother in the notebook.

"Like yours," my father said.

Maybe he thought I didn't believe him. Maybe it was easier to read to me from the notebook than to face my continuing anger at him, my disappointment that the mother I thought I had located—that I was now imagining in actual places, doing things like eating ices and drinking lemonade and lying in a field watching clouds drift by—had dissolved again to noth-ing. He began to read again.

"When Eva fell sick, then, it was a relief. There were only two weeks left to the summer, and I was happy to be able to spend them alone—"

"Who was she, this Eva?"

"A friend of Ida Pearl's cousin, it would seem."

But not my mother. No one my mother even knew, most probably. Yet another dead end.

"Why do we still have it, then? If nothing in it has anything to do with my mother. If it belonged to Ida's cousin. Why didn't you give it to Ida when my mother left?"

"I tried to, but Ida didn't want it. She gave it back to me."

"Why?"

"She didn't say." He closed the notebook then. There was a certain deliberateness to the way he did it, as if he were saying, with that gesture: *You see? I wasn't lying. There's nothing in it of relevance to you.* "Maybe it's painful for her to see it. Maybe it's too much of a reminder of things she'd rather not think about."

A hundred questions crowded my mind, but I asked the only one I felt certain he could answer. "So how did you finally find out?"

"Ida Pearl told me. The night your mother left."

I waited for him to go on. It was hard for him to go back to that night, I realized from the length of his pause, the slowness with which he dragged the words out from somewhere inside himself.

"We had just found her note."

Forgive me. Yours, Lily.

"Ida asked if she could speak to me for a minute. We went into the hallway and she showed me the letter from her sister Sonya."

I imagined how mortified he must have been to have Ida Pearl tell him that what he had thought was his marriage was a sham. Again I was hesitant to meet his eyes, but when I did

I didn't see any of the cuckold's embarrassment I expected, none of the bitter shame I had just ascribed to him. What I saw in his face was a sorrow more tender than bitter. He had loved her, I realized, even if he hadn't known her actual, real name and life history. He had loved what he knew of her—the sound of her voice, perhaps, the smell of her skin, the expression on her face when she first woke in the morning. And nothing in the disaster of her subsequent departure had ever robbed him of that feeling.

"I have something for you," he said.

He disappeared into his bedroom and I had a moment where I imagined he would emerge with a letter she had left for me along with instructions that he should wait until I was fully grown before letting me read it. But I swallowed back the fantasy before it even fully formed so that I experienced only the most fleeting sensation of disappointment, just a hint of a bitter aftertaste at the very back of my consciousness when my father handed me . . . a rock. That's what I thought he had given me at first: yet another rock, and the smallest one to date. But it was different from all the ones preceding it in that it was, according to my father, a gem. A diamond.

"It doesn't look like any diamond I've ever seen," I said, though I could see that it was, in fact, a crystal, and a crystal unlike any I'd seen before.

"That's because it's rough, still uncut. It was hers," he told me. "Your mother's," he added, as if I had lost track of the subject of our conversation. "I found it after she left."

"You mean she left it for you to find."

"I suppose," he said.

Had she left it for me, then? I looked at it more closely. It was definitely the smallest stone I had ever received from

her—it was no larger than a pea—but in terms of the diamonds I had seen it was large. In a way it resembled some of the bits of frosted glass that I had found as a kid washed up on the beach at Ogunquit, where I had gone one summer with Elka and Sol, but this was unmistakably a crystal. It wasn't much to look at as it was, but perhaps in the right hands it could be as beautiful as the diamond Sol had given to Elka for their tenth wedding anniversary.

"Did you ever think about having it cut?"

"No," he said. "And you shouldn't either."

Out of respect, I thought he meant, for property that was still, technically speaking, my mother's, that we were just holding in safekeeping, that she still might wish to retrieve at some point.

"It's been sixteen years," I pointed out, meaning that if she hadn't dropped in until now to pick up what she'd left behind, it was unlikely she was ever going to.

"That's nothing in questions of provenance."

I had never heard the word "provenance" used in conversation before—we were not a family that owned art or antiques—but I knew exactly what he meant.

"You think she stole it?"

"I have no idea," he said. "It's not something she ever discussed with me."

"But you think she might have." From the same girl whose name she had taken. Whose family's business had been diamonds.

"I think if the matter of ownership hadn't been problematic for her in some way she would have had it cut or taken it with her when she left."

"So you're not really giving it to me."

"It's not really mine to give."

Yet he did give it to me. Maybe because it was all he had to give me of hers. A rough diamond, and one that had probably been stolen.

"RUTHIE," IDA SAID, peering at me from behind her glass counter as I stepped into the dimness of the store. Her surprise at my unexpected visit was evident in her voice. "Are you coming from your grandmother's?"

I shook my head.

"From Resnick?" Mr. Resnick was a tailor who rented one of the units on the second floor.

"I came to see you," I said.

"Ah. And to what do I owe the pleasure?"

I reached into the envelope in which I'd placed the stone the previous evening and handed it to her.

A brief bafflement knit her eyebrows as she stared at the tiny stone in her open palm, then she nodded.

She looked up to meet my eyes. "Where did you get this?"

"My father gave it to me last night. Well, he didn't really give it to me . . ."

Ida raised her eyebrows now, waiting for me to go on.

"On the one hand he gave it to me, but on the other hand he said it wasn't really his to give, and that I'm not to do anything with it . . ."

"He wasn't intending for you to have it cut, then."

"No, no. He said specifically that I wasn't to—"

"He wanted you to have something of hers?"

I looked at her. "How do you know whose—?"

"She brought it to me."

"My mother brought this to you?"

Ida examined the stone in the same way I had seen her examine countless stones before. First she held it between her thumb and index finger and rolled it in all directions, looking closely at it all the while. Then she placed it on the back of her hand and looked at it from every angle. Finally, she picked it up with her tongs and took a closer look with her loupe. She nodded periodically as if the entire inspection were mere confirmation of what she'd assessed at first glance. With a final nod she put it back in the envelope, folded the envelope in four so it couldn't slip out again, and handed it back to me. "It's the same stone," she said.

Ida's response unsettled me. I had assumed she would be interested, curious, excited even, albeit in a suppressed, disappointed, Ida sort of way. I had thought she might pepper me with questions about what my father had told me about it, at which point we would have a real conversation about my mother. I would tell her that I knew now that my mother had taken her cousin's name, and she would tell me what she knew, what she thought. Enough time had gone by already, more than sixteen years. And if she thought my mother had taken the diamond from her cousin, I would return it to her. That's what I had decided. But instead of everything I had imagined, there was just this offhand disclosure about my mother having been here, and her tight-lipped discomfort as she handed me back the stone.

"I didn't know my mother had already—"

"Why would you?" Ida cut me off. "Your father brought it to me also. After she left. Who do you think told him what it is?"

Now I was at a loss. And worse, I sensed that Ida was as

well. "My father is under the impression that its . . . provenance might be questionable."

Ida shrugged again.

"Don't you think we should try to find out? It could be
valuable."

"And whom might we ask?"

The dead, she meant. My mother. As if.

I had the sense now that the passage of time had sealed
the door to the past for her, rather than allowing for it to be
reopened.

"Aren't there networks or something among diamond
workers? If you showed it around, isn't it possible that someone might recognize—"

She waved me quiet before I even had a chance to finish.
"Put it away," she said.

"What do you mean?"

"Put it back wherever your father's kept it all these years."

"But why?"

She didn't answer.

"What if it's valuable?"

When she still didn't answer, I pressed my point. "Isn't it a
waste to just put it away? It could be cut, made into something
beautiful. A brooch, maybe, a ring . . ."

"It's not a good stone."

I thought she was referring to its physical properties, its
colour, its clarity, some flaw she had detected in its interior.

"There's nothing in it but sorrow," she said.

She unlocked the cabinet beneath her counter and pulled
out a box. "Let me show you something. Close your eyes and
put out your hand."

I did as she told me, extending my hand, palm down, so

she could slip a ring on it, but she turned it over and placed something on my palm.

"You can look now," she said.

I opened my eyes. There was a tear of light on my hand.

"Beautiful, isn't it?"

Did she think I was a child who could be distracted simply by her dangling a bright bauble in front of my eyes?

"You haven't even looked at it. Look at it."

"It's beautiful," I agreed grudgingly, distractedly. I wanted to ask her about my mother, about my mother's visit to her store seventeen years earlier, when she brought Ida the same rough diamond that Ida had just handed back to me.

"When you find a husband I'll get him to buy it for you." A slight pause now, during which I tried to find a way to bring the conversation back to my mother. "You're still with the Blumenthal boy?"

"I'm not *with* him, Auntie Ida. We went to one sweet sixteen together."

"And?"

"And nothing."

Another pause.

"I hear you're looking for her."

"I am very curious about her," I allowed, and why wouldn't I be, I thought. What could be more natural than to be curious about the mother I had never known?

But Ida Pearl shrugged as if to ask, *What's to be curious?*

"She's half of who I am, you know."

"No, she isn't."

"Genetically, I mean."

Ida shrugged again. "You're doing well at school now?"

"Pretty well."

"And your friends? You're getting along with them again?"

I nodded, hadn't realized Ida knew I hadn't been getting along with them at one point.

"You like them?"

"Of course I like them. They wouldn't be my friends if I didn't like them, would they?"

Ida didn't answer. "You're a pretty girl," she said. I was surprised to hear her say it; Ida wasn't the sort to throw the compliments around. "And you have a nice family, nice friends, a good head on your shoulders. True?"

"I guess so."

"I know so," she said. "So listen to someone who knows a little bit more about life than you do. Don't go looking for sorrow."

CHAPTER 11

There was little of monetary value in the stone the woman had brought, Ida Pearl reminded herself as she sat in the darkness of her living room a few days after that visit from Lily, her cup of tea cooling on the table beside her. The market was glutted, first of all—a lot of the refugees had brought them. Every second or third shabby coat seemed to have a diamond sewn into its lining, and those were diamonds that were already cut, polished, fully achieved. Which this stone was not. Even in a good market, its value would lie only in its potential, which at that moment was entirely theoretical. Who knew what flaws might run through its centre? Who could be sure that rough, small stone could become the cut gem that Ida had already begun to see in her mind's eye, though she tried not to see it, not yet, because that, right there, was the first misstep she could take: to form a preconceived notion and force the stone to conform to it, to cut it in the image of something too hastily imagined, a gem that might be adequate, and even beautiful, but that would not be the realization of the stone's

unique potential. To achieve that uniqueness—and there was no point in proceeding if not for that—she would have to allow the stone to guide her. And it would; she was certain. She had felt that as she first held it. She had felt the life in it even before she brought it up to her eye for a closer look, even as she knew that its presence in her store, in the hand of the imposter who had brought it to her, confirmed the destruction of her family, who had once owned it. And she had known at that moment that she would be the one to release its light.

She was no longer a religious woman, would not even say that she still believed in fate, but that diamond was her destiny, she suddenly was sure. Why else would things have happened as they had? How else could she possibly understand the appearance of that woman with her cousin's name and her cousin's diamond, not only in Montreal, but in her own store? Coincidence? No. Destiny, she felt certain, and with that certainty, the seemingly senseless unfolding of her life until then revealed its purpose. The untimely, tragic death of her father, the subsequent plunge into poverty and shame, the cold-hearted expulsion from Chaim's workshop and home—an expulsion that she now knew had ultimately saved her life—Arthur's betrayal, the second plunge into poverty and shame, the birth of her daughter, who so often seemed a stranger though it was her own blood that ran through the girl's veins, the unfolding comprehension of what had happened to her family . . . Even the imposter no longer seemed just the looting, lying thief that she had first thought but the agent of a deliverance the exact nature of which Ida could not yet understand, but that she would . . .

"Oh my *God!*" A high-pitched shriek interrupted her thoughts.

Elka, expressing her surprise at stumbling over her mother sitting alone in the dark.

"You just about gave me a heart attack! What are you *doing?*"

"I'm having a cup of tea."

"In the dark? It's pitch black in here. Haven't you noticed?"

It was not even close to pitch black, merely dusk, Ida thought.

And since when did tea smell like booze? Elka wondered. And just how long had her mother been sitting here alone in the dark drinking the whisky that she persisted in calling tea despite the ever-shrinking proportion of the latter in the mix?

Elka flipped the light switch on the wall, and in the harshness of the electric light that flooded the room Ida could no longer see the purpose of her life that she had glimpsed just a moment earlier. Instead: a middle-aged fool with a ruined life sitting in her armchair drunkenly murmuring to herself that everything happens for a reason. And her daughter's face—the light revealed that too. Her daughter's swollen, tear-streaked face, which she knew she couldn't ask about, because Elka would interpret any inquiry from her mother—no matter how kind and well intentioned—as snooping, the underlying purpose of which was to ruin Elka's life. And so they sat in silence for a few moments, Elka on the sofa, her long bare legs awkwardly crossed at the ankles, her hands braced against the edge of her seat as if she might spring up and bolt at any moment, Ida in her armchair, trying to affect an expression of bland neutrality.

"What?" Elka asked.

"What, *what?*"

"You're staring at me."

Ida did not point out that she would have to twist her neck into an uncomfortable position to avoid looking at the spot on the sofa, directly in the line of Ida's vision, that Elka had chosen to occupy. She picked up the cup at her elbow, had a swallow of her tea and then, reaching for the most innocuous way she could think of to open the conversation, she asked: "You didn't happen to pick up the *Star* on your way home, did you?"

Elka shook her head, and as she did the fresh tears that had been welling in her eyes slid down her cheeks. "I went to their house," she said.

"Whose house?" Ida asked. Gently. Carefully.

"Theirs."

It wasn't possible, Ida thought. But of course it was. Elka was an intelligent girl, and resourceful, actually, when left to her own devices. And just because she'd stopped asking Ida about her father didn't mean she'd stopped wondering. Why wouldn't she have found him? It wasn't that hard. It wasn't like he had bothered to hide. He was right there in the phone book: *A. Krakauer,* the third one in the list.

"I made a complete fool of myself," Elka said, at which point her sobbing began in earnest. She bent over, face in her hands, rocking back and forth.

Ida moved to the sofa to sit beside her, placed her hand on Elka's back. Elka turned and heaved herself into her mother's bosom as she hadn't done in years.

"It's not you who's the fool, my sweet," Ida murmured, as she held her daughter close.

"I'm hopeless. Utterly useless," Elka sobbed. "If you could have seen his face when he walked in and saw me sitting at his kitchen table with his mother."

His mother? Ida wondered. Hadn't Arthur told her eighteen years earlier that his mother was dead? Didn't Elka mean his wife, the woman he had chosen over Ida?

"And he was with her. That woman. They walked in together."

"What woman, my sweet?"

"The bride. I didn't even know they lived in the same house. She smiled, so superior, when she saw me. Like I'm some sort of lovesick child. Which I must look like to them. I know they were talking about me." A fresh burst of sobs racked her body.

Ida's arms still embraced her daughter, and she still made reassuring clucking noises, but her mind had moved away from the heartsick sympathy she had felt a moment earlier to a cooler mode.

"You went to Sol's house?"

"I'm such a fool," Elka wailed.

She had planned it perfectly, she had thought, allowing just enough time after the end of his workday that she wouldn't arrive the second he walked in the door, but not so much that her arrival would interrupt his dinner. It was a long streetcar ride from Snowdon Junction to his neighbourhood, but she didn't have to transfer and she had a seat the whole way, which she didn't give up as she usually would because she didn't want to be pressed against other hot, sweaty bodies and arrive with her dress creased and smelling less than fresh. The house was closer to the streetcar stop than she'd expected, so she was in front of it at 5:42, three minutes earlier than planned.

It was a building like every other one on the block, three storeys high and attached to its neighbours on either side, with an outdoor staircase leading to the upper-storey apartments. Two girls were sitting on the bottom step of the staircase, playing

jacks. Elka asked if the Kramers lived there. "Second landing," one of the girls answered without looking up from her game. Elka stepped over the girls and climbed the stairs, her heart beating more rapidly as she anticipated Sol's expression when he opened the door. He would probably not be happy to see her, she was prepared for that. *I don't want to impose on your time,* she would assure him in a tone of dignified detachment, and then she would hand him the note she had already written:

> *Dear Sol,*
> *I'm not sorry that we have had no contact with each other since the evening we spent together a month ago. I believe that if people are meant to be together it is obvious to both of them, and that it is both futile and foolhardy to try to force an affection that does not exist. What I am sorry about, though, is to have discovered this week that you lack even the barest modicum of discretion and common decency. For you to have told your sister-in-law the personal information about myself and my family that I shared with you in confidence that evening is a violation of the most basic code of human interaction.*
>
> *Perhaps there is no purpose in bringing this to your attention since you seem to lack the ethical standards of even the most ill-mannered boors of my acquaintanceship, but in the event that you do have a shred of integrity, I ask that you at least acknowledge the wrong you have done to me.*
> *Sincerely,*
> *Elka Krakauer*

The letter had taken her three days to write. She had wrestled with every line and phrase for hours. Sol would see that she was a person with education, intelligence and dignity, and he would be sorry, then, to have let her go, to have treated her like she was nothing, a child. She could hardly wait to give it to him, then to turn her back just as his face registered his recognition of what he had lost.

But Sol was not at home. It was his mother who answered the door—Elka recognized her from the wedding—his mother who looked her over with bemused curiosity, then informed her that Sol wasn't there. How could he not be home? Elka wondered. She had anticipated and developed responses to every eventuality, she had thought, but somehow, not this.

"What time do you expect him?"

"I don't know," his mother said, a simple statement of fact that Elka heard as mockery, and it was that imagined mockery that re-stoked her anger and emboldened her. She met Bella's eyes dead-on, a technique that she had learned early on to combat the whispers—both imagined and real—that accompanied her passage through life.

"May I wait for him, then?"

What was she doing here, this girl who was no more than sixteen? Bella wondered. Had Sol stooped to this now? To schoolgirls as young as Nina had been when her innocence had been violated by the lout? Had he taken to hanging around high schools? To passing time in soda shops, perhaps, where girls like this giggled with their friends over ice cream, excited by but only half comprehending the intentions of the men who leered at them from the next booth? Was he courting his sister-in-law on the back stairs by night only to soothe his ruffled feathers with schoolgirls the next day? And

who was she, this girl? She seemed familiar to Bella, but from where?

"Come in," Bella said, and Elka followed her down the brown hallway—the bloom of pink roses on the linoleum barely visible in the dim lighting—to the kitchen at the back of the apartment, then sat on the bench seat Bella indicated, wedged between the table and the wall, facing the window that opened to the fire escape where Lily and Sol sat every night.

"Something to drink?" Bella offered, pouring a glass of lemonade and placing it on the red and white checked oilcloth in front of the girl. "I don't believe we've met."

"I'm sorry. Elka Krakauer. I'm pleased to meet you, Mrs. Kramer," Elka said, extending her hand in a belated display of the manners she had accused Sol of lacking.

Bella smiled as she took the proffered hand. She was plucky, the girl, if nothing else. Her hand was warm and dry despite her obvious nervousness, her handshake was firm, her eye contact unwavering.

"And how do you know Sol?"

"We're friends."

"I see."

Elka did not glance away, despite the disapprobation she read on Bella's face.

"And how old are you, Elka?"

"Seventeen," she said. "Next March."

"So you'll be starting grade . . ."

"Eleven. Next week."

"And do your parents know that you're friends with a man in his twenties?"

"No."

"I see," Bella said again, and stood with her arms folded across her chest as Elka sipped at her lemonade with a show of calmness.

She hates me, Elka thought. And why wouldn't she? She thinks I'm a tramp and a slut and that I lie to my parents. The parents she still thinks I have . . . which she's about to discover I don't have, because that's where she's heading now, right this minute as she stands here sizing me up like I'm a chicken on inspection at the market.

"Krakauer . . ." Bella said, as if casually musing about the name.

Here it comes, Elka thought.

"Not Lou and Irma's . . . ?"

Elka shook her head. "Ida Pearl." She put down her lemonade to look Bella directly in the eye. "My mother has a jewellery store on Decarie Boulevard. It used to be on Ste-Catherine Street."

"I don't think I know it," Bella said. She did not utter the usual platitudes about Decarie being a good street, a good neighbourhood. She had noticed there was no mention of a father. And given the bravado of the girl's stare at that moment it seemed a fair assumption that that absence had not been caused by something as shameless as death by natural causes.

Elka glanced at the clock on the wall.

"I'm not sure what's keeping Sol . . ."

"I should probably get going," Elka agreed. It had been stupid to ask if she could wait for Sol. She should have just given the letter to his mother and left. Though, had she done that, she couldn't have been sure she would ever see him again—it was so easy to ignore a letter, to simply not respond—and she did so want to see him. She had worn a dress that she thought

particularly flattering—a linen shift in a shade of cream that contrasted perfectly with her late-summer tan. The linen was a little stiff but was a more sophisticated fabric, she thought, than the girlish cottons he had seen her in so far. She wanted him to see her in it. There was a way he had of looking at her as if he wasn't quite looking, as if he didn't want her to know he was looking and liked what he saw. She wanted to see that quick appraising glance that he thought she didn't notice, that private smile that she couldn't quite interpret, which made her yearn all the more to elicit it again.

But the dress was ugly, she realized a moment later when he walked into the kitchen with Lily. It was wrong in every way. A large stiff tent. More nurse's uniform than dress.

Lily was in a form-fitting grey skirt and light blue blouse. The colours reflected the blues and greys of her eyes, the cut flattered the slender lines of her figure. At the sight of her mother-in-law, her hand flew up to push a strand of hair back behind her ear, a nervous mannerism so beautiful in its execution that Elka felt her heart sink.

Lily noticed Elka a second later, but Sol was ahead of her there. He had seen her as soon as he came in and his expression was neither the pleasure Elka had hoped for nor the anger she half expected. Worse than angry, he seemed baffled.

"Elka," he said, the tentativeness in his voice so unlike that of the firm man of her fantasies. His eyes shifted to his mother for some clue about what was going on, a clue that was obviously not forthcoming because he then looked to Lily, whose eyebrows—pencil thin and perfectly shaped—knitted together before she smiled at Elka in a way that could only be interpreted—at least by Elka—as condescending and superior.

Elka might still have been able to salvage the situation, or

at least some shred of what remained of her dignity, had she simply said, "Hello, Sol," and met his look with the gaze she had directed so effortlessly at his mother just moments before. But she hadn't. She had risen clumsily from her spot between the table and the wall, pulled the letter out of her purse and thrust it at him. Then she had beaten a hasty retreat from the kitchen and down the brown hallway, aware the entire time that the back of her dress was soaked with sweat from leaning against the vinyl back of the kitchen bench.

None of which she told her mother later as she wept in Ida's arms. It was enough that she had thrown herself at a man who didn't want her. To have to recount it in all its humiliating detail was too much and would only irritate her mother, who had no patience for histrionics, which was how she referred to Elka's every response to being alive. Her mother would only end up lecturing her. Criticizing her. As if everything was her fault. As if she had asked to be born. Already Ida had placed a hand on each of Elka's shoulders and had pushed her—gently, yes, but it was still a push— away from her bosom, where Elka had been nestling. She was holding her at arm's length and examining her in that way she had that was never prelude to a smile of pleasure or even satisfaction. Any minute now she would comment on Elka's dress, as if Elka didn't already know that it was creased and plastered to her skin. As if she hadn't already fig- ured out that linen is not the fabric of choice for an occasion that's likely to leave one drenched with sweat. Or maybe it would be her mascara that Ida would start with, the mascara she was not allowed to wear that was now collecting in black pools and running down her cheeks.

Was it possible that Elka could really be as stupid about

men as it appeared at this moment? Ida wondered as she looked at her daughter's miserable face. Could her judgment really be as impaired as it seemed, her instincts as treacherous as Ida feared?

Like you were so smart, Elka would fling back at her if she could read the thoughts running through Ida's mind. Ida had not been smart, of course. She had been stupid, disastrously so, but in her own defence she could at least point to the fact that she had been alone in the world when she fell for Arthur Krakauer. She had been new in a country where she didn't understand the language, alone in a city that she had never wanted to come to, where nobody knew who she was or to whom she had once belonged. She had left Antwerp feeling that her life was over. She had shared all of the nervousness of her fellow passengers on the crossing of the Atlantic but none of their hopeful anticipation. For them Canada was to be their new beginning, but for Ida it represented her place of exile. Her Elba, she had thought on the voyage over. Her Siberia, she decided when she saw where she had arrived.

The ship had landed in Halifax, which looked to her like no more than a shabby outpost wedged between a dark forest and the sea. She had boarded a train immediately upon passing through immigration and reclaiming her one bag of belongings, and it was at that point that her trepidation sank into a heavier feeling of depression. She had come to a wilderness, she realized as the train rolled through an endless monotony of trees, and it was one that had neither the magic of the fairytale forests she had imagined as a child, nor the promise of redemption implicit in the wildernesses of Exodus and other biblical ordeals. There was no magic here, she thought. Certainly no promise of redemption of any sort. There was just

forest, trees stretching as far as the eye could see, relieved now and then by outcroppings of rock, forbidding escarpments and the occasional bog or lake. Those signs of human habitation that she did see merely deepened her depression: intermittent towns and settlements that were mere specks in the eye of the desolation that surrounded them. Weariness overtook her. She closed her eyes and slept, but it was a heavy sleep that did not restore her. When the stirrings within the car alerted her that they were approaching Montreal, the sight of the city did not lift her spirits despite the clots of grey buildings as densely built as those she'd left behind, and the traffic—both human and vehicular—that crowded the streets. She saw the forested mountain behind the downtown core, a rump of the same forest she had been travelling through since disembarking at Halifax. It rose like a tumour in the midst of the city, like a remnant of a bad dream that persists in the day.

In retrospect, she knew she should have taken herself in hand at that moment. She should not have allowed her imagination to overheat and distort reality in that way. She was not in exile from her life, she should have told herself; this was her life now. And the forest she had passed through was simply that: a forest. It was more excessive, to be sure, than the forests she had known in Europe, but that's all it was: excessive. Overdone. It was not the desolate wilderness that she had imbued with all manner of mystical and symbolic meaning, meaning that polluted her first impressions of the city that was henceforth to be her home. But she had not taken herself in hand, nor had there been anyone wiser or more level-headed to lead her out of the morass of her own depression. As she realized she was about to step into a city in which her life or death would be of no consequence to anyone who walked its

streets, she felt as empty as the landscape she had had to travel through to arrive there. This was her state of mind when she stepped off the train in Montreal. Was it any wonder then that she was so susceptible to the charms of the first flesh-and-blood man who smiled at her?

But it should not have been that way for Elka, she thought. Elka had never stepped foot outside the city of her birth, let alone her country and language, and she would never know what it was to be alone in the world. Not if Ida could help it. And yet she obviously felt herself alone. Ida knew that, had known it for years, but was at a loss as to how to make it not be so. Ida knew that Elka felt a loneliness so extreme that her own life felt to her like an exile. And that it was a feeling she would never dare express to her mother, for fear of Ida's disdain, her dismissive irritation that Elka could even think of comparing the trivial struggles of her own life with those her mother had endured and overcome.

"Go wash your face," Ida said, "and I'll make you a cup of tea."

LILY HAD LOOKED OUT onto the same forest as Ida Pearl on the train to Montreal, though to different effect. It was July when she landed in Halifax, but even in the sunny sparkle of that day she too had seen the darkness of the surrounding landscape—greens so deep they shaded into bluish black, a sea that had more grey than blue. But it was relief to her: the dark palette of the landscape, the cool wash of northern light. Restful, after the brash, harsh sun of Palestine.

She was exhausted by the time she finished all the formali-

ties of arrival and embarked on the train for Montreal, so she slept for several hours, saw nothing of Halifax and its out-skirts. She slept until awakened by the screech and thrust of the train shuddering to a stop. The stop was too abrupt for it to have been planned; she did not expect to see the platform of a station, people with suitcases waiting for the train to pull in. But neither did she expect what she saw: a moon-washed plain on which a multitude of gnarled forms rose out of a dense low-lying fog. It was an eerie sight—already there were nervous mutterings among the other passengers.

"Not a place one feels inclined to linger," the man in the seat beside her said, his words so inflected with Polish pronun-ciation and intonation that she didn't immediately recognize them as English.

"It's just a bog," she responded. In another soil these same trees would grow straight and tall, she thought, and yet, there was beauty in this too, in the sheer persistence of these twisted forms.

"I can see that it's a bog." His tone conveyed his affront that she should think he hadn't been able to discern that fact for himself. "The question is why we have come to a halt in such a location."

His English was so precise yet so difficult to understand that she wondered if he had learned it entirely from books. He left his seat to investigate and would no doubt return in a few minutes to tell her, in the most pompous locution possible, that he was unable to find out where they were or why they had stopped. In the meantime she kept her forehead pressed to the window, oddly comforted by the gnarled figures that loomed like tormented crones in the moonlight, the blanket of fog that heaved and shifted like a living thing.

"No one knows anything," she heard her neighbour say a few minutes later, as he resettled himself heavily beside her. "Not why we have stopped here in this decidedly unprepossessing landscape. Not when we might begin to move forward again towards our respective destinations."

She turned to him. "It's the fog."

"I don't think so, my dear. It takes more than a little fog to bring a train of this size to a halt."

Did he think the size of the train had any bearing on whether the engineer could see the track in front of him? Did he think she was his *dear*? She pressed her forehead to the window again and, as she cupped her hands around her eyes to block out the light from the compartment that obscured her view outside, she felt a peculiar sensation, a flood of memory in the form of sensation, though she had never set eyes on this landscape before: the rotting, sweet smell of the river she had floated down with her father on summer nights like this, the heavy air filled with the buzzing, gnawing sounds of the marsh, the rhythmic splash of her father's oar, a surfacing fish, a diving frog or bird. She was at once in her seat with her forehead pressed against the hard, cool smoothness of the window, and deep within the scene she gazed onto; at once on the train heading to the stranger she was about to marry, and in her father's flat-bottomed boat, gliding soundlessly past the gnarled, looming trees.

The train lurched, then began rolling forward.

"As I said," her neighbour intoned.

She closed her eyes and drifted off again to sleep, and when she awoke later all she could see was her own reflection in the blackness of the window. The car was quiet now. Even her neighbour had fallen asleep. She slept again, and when the light of dawn woke her they were in a landscape of cultivated

fields, a patchwork of greens and yellows with a wide grey river running through it.

Her neighbour was pouring hot tea from a Thermos and, seeing that she was awake, he pulled another cup from his bag and offered her some. "You slept well?" he asked.

"Well enough." The tea was strong and sweet and surprisingly, pleasingly hot. "And you?"

"Not at all. I don't sleep any more."

She remembered the snores that had woken her a few times in the night, but refrained from smiling, nodded instead in a sympathetic way.

"You're going to Montreal?" he asked.

She nodded again.

"Winnipeg," he said, though she hadn't asked his destination, didn't care. "Boris Ziblow," he said, extending his large, beefy hand, which she shook, noting the calluses on his palm, calluses like those her own father had once pressed against the smoother palms of those people whose social circles he was trying to penetrate.

"Lily Azerov," she said.

"Very nice to meet you, Lily Azerov."

That he didn't ask where she was from seemed to her more a matter of tact than disinterest. They finished their tea in silence and she excused herself to freshen up.

"So tell me," he said when she returned. "Do you have anyone meeting you in Montreal? If you don't mind my asking."

"My fiancé."

"Ah," he said, as if that changed something. As if he had been planning to propose marriage.

And why not, she thought. She knew about as much about

him at this point as she knew about the man who would be picking her up at the station in Montreal. More, in some ways. And they were sharing a cup of morning tea after having spent the night together, in a manner of speaking.

"You knew him from before?" he asked.

She shook her head.

"Ah," he said again, and with that a feeling of dread filled her about who and what exactly was waiting for her.

"I've heard it's a lovely city," he said.

"Winnipeg?"

He smiled. "Winnipeg too. But I meant Montreal."

It suddenly seemed silly to her to be speaking to a man from her own country in a language that was foreign to both of them. "I hope you're right," she said in Polish.

He smiled, answered her in Polish: "And if I'm not?"

She smiled too and they both shrugged at the same moment. He pulled out a bag of almonds and offered her some. She realized how hungry she was as she ate the first few. She hadn't eaten since noon of the day before. As she saw him watching her, though, she slowed her chewing, then refused his offer of more.

"There's no shame in being hungry," he said in a voice so kind that he seemed a different person from the pompous windbag of the night before.

She took a few more almonds, then accepted a second cup of tea.

"I had a friend who moved to Canada," she told him. "This was several years before the war, when we were still in school. I pitied her terribly at the time. We all did. Having to leave her friends, her house. We went to see her off at

the station. She was crying so much she threw up. I told her she could live with me and my family, that she didn't have to go. She threw her arms around me as if I had saved her life, but she went with her family and I never heard from her again. I interpreted her silence as a sign that she was so happy that she had forgotten all about us, but maybe I was wrong. Maybe she was so unhappy that she had to force herself to forget all about us." Why this ridiculous outpouring? she wondered.

"Neither of your interpretations is correct," Boris said, with a smile so benevolent she was willing to believe him. "She never forgot you."

"Oh, I don't know . . . I was wondering last night if maybe I'll meet her again here, though I don't even know what city she went to—it was a meaningless detail at the time. I'd like to see her, I think. Though, of course, she might not even recognize me. And she has a whole new life, by now, after all."

Boris placed his hand on hers for a moment, his hand that was just like her father's had been, the slight pressure of his calluses as familiar as a face she had known and loved.

"Do you have anyone in Winnipeg?" she asked.

"A cousin of my father's that I've never met."

She nodded. They watched the passing landscape.

"It's a good country," Boris said at one point.

"And if it's not?"

His answering smile was rueful.

By late afternoon they were in Montreal. "It does look lovely," she said when she saw the green mountain that formed a backdrop to the city centre. Yet she felt nothing inside but a low, tugging anxiety.

Boris got her suitcase down for her. As she picked it up with her right hand, he took her left hand in both of his. She remembered how her father had carefully cupped his hands around the occasional frightened bird that had flown into their house, carrying it to the door in that way to release it.

"Good luck to you, Lily Azerov," he said.

"And to you, Boris Ziblow."

CHAPTER 12

I met Reuben at McGill's Redpath Library the winter that I turned nineteen. We were sitting at the same table, studying. My leg was moving up and down in a sort of nervous tic, a movement that disturbed him, or would have, he told me later, had he not liked the looks of the girl to whom the offending leg was attached. He sent a note across the table: "Your leg seems nervous. Would a cup of coffee help?" I liked his approach, his face, the beginning of the smile lines that were forming around his eyes.

We went to the student union and drank thin, bitter coffee out of Styrofoam cups. I complained about the coffee. "It's hot," he said, as if that were enough. I asked him if his apparent satisfaction was a sign of a positive attitude or just a lack of standards, and he laughed. "I save my standards for things that matter," he said. He met my eye and I felt he was talking about me.

He took a sip of coffee and made a face. "It *is* awful," he said. "But I hate the stuff even when it's supposedly good."

"So why did you ask me for coffee, then? If you hate it, I mean."

"What should I have asked you for instead?" he responded, a question that, had it been delivered with a suggestive smile, might have carried us to a very different place. Reuben, though, asked it with a complete absence of innuendo, as if he were just trying to determine my tastes.

"I don't know," I answered. "A rum and coke?" And when he didn't respond with any visible enthusiasm to that: "You don't drink alcohol either?"

"Not really," he admitted.

"So what are you, a Mormon?"

He smiled. "Just a boring Jew."

We talked then about the usual things: where we lived, where we'd grown up, our respective majors—chemistry in my case, biology in his, though what he'd really wanted to study was music, a choice that his parents had vetoed on the basis of it not leading to anything. Chemistry was what I'd always wanted to study, I told him, but I wasn't as sure about that now.

I remembered my family's pride the previous spring when I had told them I was going to major in chemistry. We were all gathered at Bella's for a meal. It was a special dinner to celebrate my admittance to McGill, so instead of the usual roasted chicken, Bella had cooked a brisket in her famous sauce of ginger ale and ketchup, and we were all drinking sweet Hungarian wine, a straw-coloured syrup that was Bella's libation of choice for happy events. "Chemistry!" Elka responded to my announcement, her pride evident in her face and her voice. Most of the girls in my class were going into sociology, even Carrie, though she was a better student than I (and would

ultimately become the first female among our cohort to gradu-
ate McGill law school.) "Our own little Madame Curie,"
Nina said, just as she had when my father had given me my
first chemistry set, and my father refilled our glasses as Sol
proposed a toast to the future winner of the Nobel Prize for
Chemistry. Bella, allowing herself a proud smile, had gone
so far in her celebratory abandon as to clink her glass with
everybody else's instead of warning us all about the pitfalls of
counting unhatched chickens. And Ida Pearl actually winked
at me as she lifted her glass to her lips in my honour.

"It's not anything like what I expected," I told Reuben now.

"What did you expect?"

"I don't know," I said, thinking about the experiments I
had performed with my childhood chemistry set where solutions changed colours before my eyes. "Poetry, I guess."

He smiled. "Maybe you just haven't learned the language yet."

"Maybe not. Do you like biology?"

"I will," he said. He seemed remarkably unconflicted for
someone on a forced detour away from what, presumably, had
been his real passion.

"But you wanted to study music," I said. "What instru-
ment do you play?"

"Piano."

"And your parents didn't support you continuing in that?"

"Not as a profession. No."

"And you don't mind?"

"That they're paying for my entire education and would
just as soon not throw that money down the toilet? No, I don't
particularly mind." His smile at that moment, though charm-
ingly rueful, didn't convey any of the bitterness of deep regret.
"The truth is, I'm not good enough and never would be."

"How do you know that for sure? Without even trying?"

"What makes you think I didn't try?" And then, before I could answer, before I could even identify and adjust to the subtle shift of his tone: "Shall we move on now from my failed aspirations to our continuing exchange of basic facts about ourselves?"

"I'm sorry," I said.

He was the eldest of seven he told me. Three boys and four girls. "Religious," he added, possibly to explain his parents' fecundity. "And you?"

"Agnostic. Though I was raised religious. For the most part. I went to day school, anyway. Young Israel."

He smiled. "I meant how many brothers and sisters."

"Oh. None. My mother left when I was a baby." I looked to see his response to the fact that my existence had been insufficient to bind my mother to me, that I had failed utterly and completely at the first task of personhood, which is to make your mother love you enough to stick around to care for you. "She wasn't entirely normal," I said before he could state the obvious.

"What's normal?" he asked, the way people do when they come from normal and think it's boring and overrated.

"Loving your own baby, for starters."

"Why do you assume she didn't love you?" His tone was so purely curious that I answered without the usual self-consciousness I felt when I talked about my mother, without my usual alertness to the possible responses of others.

"The evidence," I said.

"The evidence," he repeated. "And is there some . . . *evidence* that you haven't mentioned?"

"You mean apart from walking out when I was three

months old and never coming back? No. Not really. A few rocks over the years."

"Rocks?" Now he looked quizzical, so I found myself describing the rocks she'd sent me. He listened, nodding, no longer smiling but not grim or pained either. When I was finished he was quiet for a minute before responding.

"It's like the stones people leave when they go to visit a grave," he said.

"But I'm not dead," I pointed out.

"It was just the first thing it made me think of."

"She was from Europe," I told him. "She lost her whole family in the war."

He nodded. "So you don't have any family?"

"I have my father's side."

He nodded again.

"Are your parents from here?" I asked him.

"My mother is. My father's from Poland, but he came when he was young. Before the war."

Neither of us said anything for a while as we watched another student put a quarter into the machine that had just dispensed our coffee, then shake the machine and finally kick it as it failed to deliver the wretched liquid we had just ingested.

"He should be thanking that machine," I said.

Reuben smiled. "Did you ever think about trying to find her?" he asked.

"I've thought about it."

Reuben nodded, but didn't push for more.

"I used to get teased in school about her being off her rocker," I said. "Because of the rocks . . . Off her *rock*er."

"I get it."

"Which made me think I must be off my rocker too."

"Why?"

I remembered how I would hold each rock when it came and how an image of her would come to me. And how at night sometimes, when I couldn't sleep, I would take out the rocks and pick each one up and imagine her holding the same rock in her hand. Images and sensations rose in me then and I felt comforted, calmed somehow just to think that my mother had held the same rock and had shared the same sensations. I told Reuben about that. "It's like I could feel her presence through each rock that she sent me. It's almost like she was talking to me in her own language that no one else in the world could understand, but she knew I'd understand."

Reuben nodded as if he also understood, and I didn't go into my usual routine about how strange I knew it all was, how bizarre.

A silence opened up between us then. I say opened, because that's how it felt: spacious somehow, comfortable, like the cool, dark air pockets I used to create and inhabit during the summers of my childhood and early teens by capsizing a canoe in exactly the right way and swimming up from under the surface of the water into the domed quiet space. A few minutes passed in that way. There was no feeling of awkwardness, no pressure to speak, to re-emerge into conversation.

"Just how religious are you anyway?" I asked after a while. I had known the second I saw him that the wool cap he wore—had not removed despite the adequate level of heat in the student union building—served a function unrelated to warmth or style.

"Enough that I won't mention your agnosticism when I tell my mother about you."

"So you're already planning to tell your mother about me?" I asked, flattered but also a little taken aback.

"I'm planning to marry you."

"Right."

"I'm serious," he said.

"We just met."

He shrugged as if that were a minor detail.

"You're being crazy," I said. "You don't even know me."

"I know you," he assured me. "My first instincts are infallible."

IT WAS THE SORT OF MARRIAGE PROPOSAL that would have put off some women. Carrie, for example.

"What an arrogant jerk," she said. We were in her bedroom, propped up by pillows on opposite ends of her bed.

"He's not a jerk."

"He has one conversation with you and decides on that basis that he knows you and is going to marry you—never mind that he hasn't even bothered to find out if you have any feelings whatsoever for him—and you don't think he's a jerk?"

"I know he isn't."

"So what would you call him, then?"

"I'd say he's someone who trusts his instincts."

Carrie looked at me for a moment. "Only a psychopath trusts his instincts in that way," she said.

"Not necessarily. *You* did."

"*When?*"

Carrie had walked up to me on the first day of grade one, as I stood against the chain-link fence, surveying but not yet ready to enter the mob of yelling children who would henceforth be my classmates and friends, and announced that she would be my best friend. It was an opener not entirely unlike

Reuben's in its certainty, its instant and unambivalent embrace of me—but when I pointed this out to Carrie, she looked at me again as if I'd lost my mind. "We were six then, Ruthie. Remember? There's supposed to be some level of psychological and emotional development between the ages of six and nineteen."

She reached for her cigarettes, took one out and started tapping the end of it on her night table, the first step of a ritual that would go on now for about ten minutes.

"Do you love him?" she asked me.

"I don't know yet. I just met him, remember?"

"If you were falling in love you'd know it."

There was no sensation of *falling*, I had to admit, just a feeling of extraordinary calm and comfort in his presence.

"That would be great if he were a shoe," Carrie said when I tried to explain this to her. "But we look for different things in men than in shoes. *Comfort,* for example, is supposed to come later with potential husbands, *after* the falling in love part."

How could I explain to her that the comfort I felt with him was more compelling to me than the sensation of falling over a cliff? How to explain the appeal of his instant and unambivalent embrace of me, to Carrie especially, who loved the thrill of uncertainty because she had never known the dread of real doubt? I couldn't because I didn't fully understand it myself at that time, had always imagined *the real thing* would be more of a thunderbolt than a feeling of safe arrival.

Carrie had now moved on to the actual smoking of her cigarette, an act she would manage to perform in its entirety while technically adhering to her parents' rule of no smoking in the house. She would do this by holding the cigarette out the open window of her bedroom, extending her head outside

every time she inhaled or exhaled, and waving around her free hand—which was inside the room—to disperse any smoke that had blown back in. I waited to speak until her head was in the room.

"I trust it," was all I said, and she nodded as if she understood, but I knew that she thought her own first instincts were as infallible as Reuben found his, and that nothing had budged her from thinking he must be an arrogant jerk.

"I HEAR YOU'VE MET SOMEONE," Nina said when I met her for coffee a couple of weeks later. I had started seeing her more regularly now that I was downtown every day for school. Often we met in her apartment, which was just a few blocks from McGill, but that particular afternoon we were sitting in one of the Hungarian cafés downtown where they served flourless tortes and coffee so strong and rich that it bore almost no resemblance to the watery beverage we brewed at home.

"Word travels fast," I said. Reuben and I had just had our fifth date the previous Saturday night.

"Elka said it's serious."

"She hasn't even met him. He's only ever picked me up at my father's."

"She says she sees a big change in you."

"What kind of change?"

"She thinks you seem happier, more mature."

"Talk about wishful thinking."

Nina smiled. "She just wants you to be happy. Isn't that why people have children in the first place?"

"So they can make them happy?"

"So they can push their own failed hopes onto the next generation."

"What failed hopes?"

Nina looked at me as if she couldn't understand my question. "I wouldn't exactly call Elka's marriage to Sol the romance of the century."

Now it was my turn to look at Nina in wonder. Did she think Sol and Elka had an unhappy marriage? "They may not be Zhivago and Lara," I allowed, "but that doesn't make them unhappy."

Elka had spent most of her early childhood lying on the waxed linoleum floor behind the counter of her mother's shop, playing with her dolls while her mother stood above her, arranging and rearranging the diamonds her uncle Chaim had sent her on consignment that nobody came in to buy. Then, when she got older and went to school, she had to rush home to serve tea and sweet wine to her mother's matchmaking clients while the other girls in her class got to play outside or go over to each other's houses for milk and cookies. She would listen to her mother discuss with her clients the compatibilities of background and affinities of character that form the basis of a good match, and at night, as she lay sleepless in her bed, staring into the darkness of the room, she would wonder about those affinities and compatibilities—or equally powerful aversions—that her mother claimed held the world together or could tear it apart. She knew that she was the product of disharmony, that her moodiness and other bad qualities were expressions of the incompatible union she embodied. And she wondered more and more about her father, a man she had never known. She made up fantasy fathers comprising bits and pieces of her

mother's customers and of the heroes of the novels she read and the movies she went to, but whenever and whatever she asked her mother about him, Ida Pearl claimed she couldn't remember.

"How could you possibly not remember the colour of his hair?" Elka finally demanded of Ida Pearl when she was twelve or thirteen.

"What difference does it make?"

"No difference. I'm just wondering."

"What's to wonder?" her mother responded. "Do you think he wonders about you? He doesn't, I assure you. A man like that is too busy saving the world to wonder about a daughter he's brought into it."

He left for Russia soon after Elka's birth, Ida Pearl had told her. "To be with all the other Bolsheviks."

"He's a communist?" Elka asked.

"Absolutely," Ida Pearl answered. Though, once she had let drop that it was actually Palestine he had gone to, to be with all the other Zionists.

"You're lying," Elka accused her. "How can he be in Russia and Palestine at the same time? He's probably in neither. He probably never left Montreal in the first place." And when her mother didn't answer: "He's probably been here all along."

"Do you see him?" Ida countered, sweeping her arm around the dreary apartment that she had worked so hard to attain. "Have I missed something? Has he been here all along and I just haven't noticed?"

"And whose fault is that? Whose fault is it that I have no father and no one invites me to their parties?" Elka cried, throwing herself on the couch. She would never know peace, not in this life, and she raised her head to tell her mother that.

"No one needs a peaceful heart," her mother answered. "It's enough to have one that beats."

"I might as well die," Elka wept into her pillow.

"Enough with the dramatics. You have homework to finish."

What Elka had wanted from marriage—from life—it seemed to me, was to be part of a family that looked like other families, to have a husband who would come home every night, and to live in a house that was decorated in the style of the other houses in the neighbourhood and that was filled with children so confident of their parents' love that they dared to be noisy and to misbehave. All of which she got. And it thrilled her and changed her and opened her in all the ways that transformative love is rumoured to thrill and change and open a person up. I could attest to this because I lived in her home and saw the satisfied smile on her face when she complained on the phone to her friends about the domestic chaos caused by her ever-present husband and their three boys, or the pleasure it gave her to playfully swat Sol with a dishtowel in the way that Lucy and Ethel and other wives in the TV sitcoms that we watched swatted their husbands for similar husbandly misdemeanours.

None of which I could say to Nina without feeling I was betraying Elka in some way. "Elka seems happy enough," I said.

Nina looked at me with her clear brown eyes that always seemed to see more than she was saying. "And what about you? Are you as happy and mature now as she says?"

"Can't you tell?"

She smiled and began to tell me about an audition for a TV commercial that she had been to the previous day. "It's not exactly a Greek tragedy," she admitted, "but it pays a lot better than the radio ads I've been doing. And maybe it will lead to something."

To yet another TV commercial, I feared. "Were you ever in a Greek tragedy?" I asked her.

"Not on the stage." She stirred the sugar into her tiny cup, then drank back her coffee in a single swallow. "Don't look like that. I'm just kidding. My life has hardly been a Greek tragedy."

But was she happy? I wondered

I knew so little about her, I realized. She had left for Palestine in the spring of 1945, a couple of years before I was born, to teach teenage survivors from Europe the *ABCs* that they had missed learning because of the war. It was unclear to anyone how she had gotten in, since she possessed none of the qualifications the British required for the purposes of issuing visas to Jews, or what her life had been like there, or why she had wanted to go there in the first place just when war was ending and life beginning everywhere else. But none of that really mattered to anyone in my family. What mattered to them was that she had left for Palestine as a pretty and talented girl of twenty-one, and when she returned from Israel in 1954 she was an old maid of thirty, and even more out of step than before with everyone around her.

"Why did you go to Palestine?" I asked her now.

She thought about that, then shrugged as if it was so long ago she could barely remember. "For the same reasons Elka married Sol, I suppose. To escape an unhappy home life. To find the piece inside me that was missing." She looked at me as if to let me know that I didn't have to say out loud what she had already seen for herself about Elka. "For the same reasons you'll probably marry this Ronald."

"Reuben," I said. "And I don't have an unhappy home life that I'm trying to escape. Nor do I think he's a fairy tale prince who can magically—"

"I didn't mean to offend you. I just meant that that's what we do when we're young. We look outward for answers and solutions for our lives. We look to other places and other people. In my case, it probably wasn't the smartest thing I ever did."

"Why not?"

"I wanted to act more than anything in the world. So I went to a country where I didn't speak the language. How smart was that?" She signalled the waiter to bring her another coffee.

"Did you find it?"

"Find what?"

"The piece inside you that was missing."

"Not there. No. And the sun was ruining my skin."

The waiter brought her coffee.

"Do you want a piece of cake?" she asked me.

"No, thanks."

"Bring her a piece of cake," she told the waiter. "The one with the walnuts and apricot jam."

"Did you know that Elka found her father?" I asked Nina.

She looked at me as if she wasn't sure she had heard me right.

"She went to his funeral."

"She did?"

"Uh-huh." I said, feeling the sick drop in the gut that accompanies the betrayal of a confidence, though I knew I hadn't, technically, betrayed Elka's confidence since attending a funeral is a public act that anyone can witness.

"How do you know?"

"I went with her."

"And?"

"There's no *and*. She took me out of school, we went to

the funeral, then we went out for ice cream afterwards. I was wearing a blue and white seersucker dress."

I supplied the detail about the dress as a way of proving the truth of my memory, and as I did, the image of myself in that dress pulled with it to the surface of my mind another memory: lilacs sitting on my teacher's desk, a vase full of purple, mauve and white lilacs whose scent I inhaled as I walked to the door of the classroom where Elka was standing.

"So, what? Tell me."

"That's all I remember." The dress. The lilacs. The hard bench at the rear of the chapel. The hat Elka wore with the half-veil that covered her eyes. There had been a grimness to her—something about the way she clutched my hand as we entered and left the funeral chapel, the set of her mouth. And a furtiveness. She had bowed her head as if to hide her face at the moment the coffin was carried past. And as we slipped out immediately following the mourners, her hand like a vise around mine, I had the feeling that we were fleeing.

"How did she explain it to you?" Nina asked.

"She didn't. Not then." She had turned up at my classroom door and spoken in a low voice to my teacher, who then told me to gather my things because there was an appointment I had to go to. But I knew already, before Elka said anything to me, that she wasn't there to take me to a doctor or dentist, though I couldn't say why. Her grimness, perhaps. Her dark suit that I associated with the High Holidays and other sombre, formal occasions.

We would have driven to the funeral in her blue Rambler— that's the car she and Sol had when we first moved to Côte-St-Luc—but I didn't remember the car, just Elka in the driver's seat after we had parked at our destination. She turned the

rear-view mirror towards herself and put on her hat, a little black dome with a frill of black lace attached to its edge that hung down to veil her eyes. She applied a fresh coat of red lipstick, looked at me—her eyes were obscured but not entirely hidden by the veil; her lips, exposed, were vivid, red—then she looked back in the mirror and rubbed off all the lipstick with a Kleenex. When she looked at me again her mouth looked leached of life as well as colour.

"She had to have told you something."

"She told me we were going to a funeral and I had to be very quiet and very good and sit absolutely still, and she would take me out for ice cream afterwards. It was only a few years ago that I figured out whose funeral it had been."

Nina nodded and we sat without talking for a while. Nina toyed with an unlit cigarette; I toyed with the cake the waiter had brought.

"We can't escape it. None of us," Nina said.

"What?"

"Our need to know where we come from, to connect it to who we are and where we're going. That's what makes us human, what sets us apart from all the other animals."

"I thought it was opposing thumbs," I said.

"Monkeys also have opposing thumbs, my dear. It's origins and destiny—our obsession with that. That's what defines us."

"You think so?"

"It's not just me who thinks so. What do you think all the rigmarole in the Torah is about? Ultimately, I mean—all those lists of *begets* and *begats* that they made you sit and learn at that school they sent you to? What do you think the whole idea of God is about?"

I don't know that I had ever heard God referred to as an *idea* until then.

"The nexus of origins and destiny. That's what God is," Nina said.

"I always thought of him more as a big bullfrog sitting on a throne with a long purple gown and a jewelled crown and a sparkling crystal sceptre."

Nina smiled. "It would be worth finding your mother if only to find out if she's responsible for your unique sense of humour."

I looked at her for a moment. No one else in my family ever brought up the possibility of me looking for my mother any more. I wondered sometimes if they thought I'd gotten over it. "No one ever talks about her sense of humour," I said.

"No."

"All I've ever heard is how withdrawn she was. How frozen . . ."

"I'm sure she wasn't a barrel of laughs at that time in her life."

But my father had loved her, I thought, and they'd managed to conceive me, so she couldn't have been frozen and withdrawn all the time.

"I remember her laugh," I said. Just like that. It was something I had never told another person, and had thought I never would. People didn't remember things from so early in infancy. I knew that. But Nina didn't seem to. She was different in that way too: in what she knew and didn't know. She responded now as if I had said something eminently reasonable.

"Tell me more," she said.

"There's not really anything to tell. It's just that sometimes

when I'm sleeping I hear a peal of laughter. It's so vivid, so *real,* that I'm sure there's someone in the room with me. And I wake up."

"It wakes you?"

"Yes."

She nodded, as if the fact that it woke me was significant in some way.

"I know it's just a dream, but it feels real. It feels like—"

"It's memory," she declared. "It's memory so deep you can only access it in your dreams."

I knew that. Believed it, in any case.

"Sometimes I imagine that one day I'll be out on a street in a crowd somewhere, and I'll hear it." That familiar laugh. "And I'll turn around . . ."

But at that point my imagination always failed me. As it did at that moment. Which Nina must have seen in my face.

"Can I give you a bit of advice?" she asked me.

"Do I have a choice?"

She smiled.

"Don't make the same mistake Elka did."

"Marry Uncle Sol, you mean?"

"I'm being serious now, sweetie."

"I'm sorry. Go on."

"Don't wait for your mother to die before seeking her out."

"Elka didn't *wait,*" I said. "She tried to find him for years, but Ida lied to her outright about who he was and where he was living."

Elka's father had, in fact, never left Montreal. Elka told me that soon after I found out about my mother's name, when I was angry and unsettled and looking for an explanation from

all the adults around me about their omission that amounted to a lie. All the years of Elka's childhood, her father had worked in a shoe store on Ste-Catherine Street, just a few blocks west of Ida Pearl's first jewellery store. He had remarried soon after leaving Ida Pearl and had then fathered four children, all of whom he had stuck around to raise to adulthood. He had, in a sense, then, been there all along, just not for Elka.

"Was that something I would have been better off knowing when I was a little girl?" Elka asked me pointedly. "Was my mother really wrong to have kept it from me?"

Better to have blamed and raged at a mother who was present, a mother who could absorb Elka's anger and temper it with the reality of her love than to have let Elka loose too early in the wasteland of her father's inexplicable indifference. That's what I understood Elka to be saying, despite all her talk over the years about being open with me and answering any questions I might have about my own missing parent.

It was not until Elka had children of her own that Ida divulged the identity of the man who had fathered her, admitted, that is, that he was not the Arthur Krakauer who was roaming the world in search of a revolutionary or otherwise heroic cause—there was no such person, and never had been— but was one of the A. Krakauers easily found in the Montreal phone book, the third one listed, in fact. And it was only at his funeral—a typical funeral like others Elka had been to, with a grieving widow and children in attendance, and friends and neighbours talking about how nice he had been—that she fully understood just how banal his abandonment of her had been.

"Ida deliberately threw Elka off the trail to her father," I said to Nina.

"I'm sure that's true. But when she was ready to find him she did find him."

As if the only barrier between me and my mother was my own state of unreadiness.

"I just hope you don't wait until it's too late. That's all I'm saying."

"Too late for what?"

"That's not for me to answer," Nina said.

CHAPTER 13

Bella had just made herself a cup of coffee and was settling in with the newspaper at the kitchen table when she heard the front door open. She had thought Lily was home because the door to the bedroom was shut—the only indication, still, of Lily's presence in the house during the day—but obviously she had slipped out without Bella's noticing and was returning now. She would glide down the hallway like a ghost, without a glance towards Bella, never mind a word of greeting. The door to the bedroom would open with a creak, then click shut, and there would be no further activity, none that Bella would be able to discern, until five o'clock, just before Nathan's return from work, when she would emerge nicely dressed and made-up, just like any housewife who had passed a regular day.

It wasn't right to blame her, Bella knew, but she did. She knew plenty of people who had suffered shocking and grievous losses, but they still managed, somehow, to accord their in-laws a civil and pleasant greeting when they passed them

in the hallway. Bella herself, for example. Had she not also lost everything? Her whole life, it had seemed. Her past, her future. Her children. It had all been taken, leaving her only a present to be endured, a present as thin as the edge of a razor and set in a void. But she had inhabited what was left to her to inhabit. And she not only would have accorded her mother-in-law a civil and pleasant greeting given any opportunity to do so, she would have carried her mother-in-law onto the ship on her own shoulders had the woman not died of typhus before they even left Berdichev.

Though it wasn't really fair to say that Lily wasn't civil. She was very civil if forced into contact. Unfailingly civil and courteous, in fact. It wasn't that, but another sort of absence. Of mind. Of heart. And Nathan trying to coax her back, to rouse her to life, to love, just as Bella herself had tried to coax his father back, not realizing the futility . . .

"You?" she said when Nathan appeared in the door frame of the kitchen.

"Nice to see you too, Ma."

"What happened?" It was three o'clock on a Thursday afternoon.

"I was fired."

"What!"

"I'm just kidding, Ma. Relax. Who's going to fire me?" He took a cookie off Bella's plate. "I'm my own boss now, remember?"

Hanging off the crook of his arm was a woman's coat of black lamb's wool. A stylish coat, Bella thought, as she took in the trim of fur around the collar and sleeves. A beautiful coat. A coat so exactly to her taste that for a moment she thought Nathan had suddenly been granted second sight, that he had

seen past the frowsy, frumpy woman she'd become to the dangerously chic young woman she'd once wanted to be.

La Belle was the *nom de guerre* she'd made up for herself once. Even from a distance of thirty years it embarrassed her to remember that ridiculous moniker which, thankfully, she had never said aloud to anyone. And the equally ridiculous fantasies she'd concocted: "La Belle seems overly concerned about which of the latest styles from *Paree* are appropriate for the metal workers' strike, and which are more suited for teaching female factory workers to read," she had imagined one of her comrades commenting, a jealous girl who couldn't stand that Bella's beauty and fashion sense didn't compromise in any way the seriousness of her class analysis and her commitment to the cause. And of course in her fantasy she had the perfect rebuttal: "I'll soon show the world a new meaning for the term 'femme fatale,' she would hiss, a promise of violence imbued with such erotic charge that when she added, "Watch me," no one would be able to resist.

"What?" Nathan asked, seeing Bella's distant smile.

"Nothing," Bella said.

Was there any of that young woman in the woman she'd become? She couldn't say for sure. If she were to encounter that other Bella in the street, if the two women were to confront each other now, to stare at each other across the ravine of time and experience that lay between them, would the younger recognize the older version of herself? Or would she simply walk right by, mistaking the older woman for a stranger?

She would walk, Bella thought, because what was left to recognize?

And would Bella then call after her: *Wait! Let me prove to you who I am . . .* ? That she didn't know, because how could

she prove it? What could she point to as evidence of continuity through the course of her life? What gesture or mannerism
or turn of thought or emotion remained of the self she'd once
embodied, that younger, better self that she felt staring at her now
in confusion and disappointment? Her ideals had not changed, it
was true, but she had lost the nerve that had once undergirded
them, the courage without which ideals are mere indulgence and
self-delusion. The closest she ever got to mass action now was
the weekly melee at the fish market, the Thursday morning crush
of women trying to beat each other to the freshest, plumpest
carp. She, who had come to hate her husband for his weakness.

And yet, here was Nathan with a coat for that young
woman. As if he felt her presence. As if he had seen through
the layers of his mother to the original girl who lay in ruins
at her core. He laid the coat carefully along the bench seat
against the kitchen wall. Oh, what it must have cost him, Bella
thought.

"Where's Lily?" he asked.

LILY WAS ALSO SURPRISED by Nathan's appearance. She had
heard footsteps bounding up the front stairs but she hadn't
imagined they could be his. He was never home in the middle
of a workday.

"It's you," she said, looking up. She was sitting on the bed,
her back against the headboard, pen in hand, a book open on
her lap.

"Expecting someone else?"

She smiled and closed the book. It was the journal she had
bought a few weeks earlier.

"Any room for me?" he asked.

She moved over a few inches, and he sat down, feeling for a moment like a doctor sitting on the edge of his patient's bed, an image he dispelled by leaning over to kiss her mouth.

"You're freezing," she said. The cold from outside still lay on his skin.

"It's gotten cold," he agreed. "They say we might even see some snow."

"Already?" It was just the first week of October. "Is this usual?"

"Not usual, no, but not unheard of either. We need to get you a winter coat. I've been thinking about it. I saw one at Eaton's . . . lamb's wool with a fur collar, and a strip of fur around the cuffs." He ran his finger around the circumference of her wrist to demonstrate the bracelet of fur on the coat. "Do you think you'd like that?"

"Why wouldn't I like it?"

He smiled. "Wait here."

A moment later he was back.

"Oh, Nathan . . ." She ran her fingers over the soft black wool, the fur collar, the lining that was so smooth it felt to her like satin.

"You don't like it?"

"It's beautiful. Too beautiful."

"Try it on."

She did.

"It's you who's beautiful," he said. "Turn around."

She turned slowly, enjoying his gaze.

"Shall we take it for a test drive?"

Her brow furrowed slightly but she would not ask what he meant. She never admitted what she didn't understand, waited

instead for clues, for more context, and he liked that: her pride, her wiliness, the way she hid herself. He also liked that she didn't ask about the coat's cost, about whether they could afford it. It was probably a bad quality in a wife, impracticality about money and expense, but it attracted him, excited him: the implication that factors other than cost could determine his actions.

"Let's go for a walk," he said. "To show you off in it."

She smiled, picked up her journal from the bed and slipped it into the top drawer of the maple dresser, where she kept her lingerie. She had not written anything in it yet, but even its emptiness was not something she wished to share with her mother-in-law should Bella happen to see it lying around and be unable to resist a quick peek inside its cover.

"What were you writing when I came in?"

"Nothing. A few notes to myself."

"Nothing? Or a few notes to yourself?"

That same smile. Sometimes it felt to him inclusive, conspiratorial, erotic. Other times, like now, it seemed evasive. But the smile itself never changed, he realized.

"Shall we show off my new coat?" she asked.

BELLA WAS STILL RELAXING over her coffee and the newspaper when Nathan retrieved the coat to give to Lily. Now she was standing at the counter, grating onions, her back to the kitchen entrance. Beside the growing mound of onion was a larger mound of ground fish.

"Ma! What are you doing?" Nathan asked.

Bella didn't bother to answer. What did he think she was doing?

"You didn't even finish your coffee." And beside the half-drunk cup of coffee, the newspaper was still lying open. "Leave it. Finish your coffee. Lily will help you when we get back."

Bella continued grating.

"Don't you want to see the new coat I bought for Lily?"

Bella turned around. "Very nice." She turned back to her task.

"I'll help you when we get back," Lily promised.

There's a comfort, Bella thought. But she said nothing aloud. She was determined not to become that sort of mother-in-law. There was no sweetness to be squeezed from bitterness.

The previous week Lily had returned home from one of her outings and had not slunk back into her room as usual, but had hovered at the kitchen door instead, clutching her shopping bag to her chest like a child holding a sack of kittens. "I bought apples and honey," she'd announced. "For Rosh Hashana," she had added, as if Bella wouldn't have known why they needed apples and honey. As if Bella didn't already have a chicken soaking in a tub for the meal they would all sit down to the following evening, and hadn't spent most of the morning grating mountains of onions, potatoes and carrots for the kugels, gefilte fish and *tsimmes* that still had to be made. Lily had unpacked the jar of honey and six apples onto the table and smiled at Bella, an expectant smile, it seemed to Bella—was she awaiting Bella's gratitude for the enormous effort she had just undertaken on behalf of the household?—and Bella's mind had flashed then to Mrs. Pozniak's new daughter-in-law, whom Bella had run into just that morning at the entrance to the fish market.

"Mrs. Kramer!" the girl had greeted her. Shirley was her name; she'd had her eye on Nathan once. "It's a stampede in there," Shirley had said, laughing. "You stay right here and let me get your fish for you."

Bella had started to protest but Shirley insisted. "Don't you dare move! Why should we both risk life and limb?" When she'd emerged a few minutes later she'd wished Bella a *gut yor* and given her a warm hug and a kiss.

A lovely girl, Bella had thought, as she tucked her package of fish into her shopping bag. But Nathan had not been interested in Shirley, not in the least. Why would he want a nice, healthy girl who brimmed with energy and love of life when he could marry the broken bird who was now perched at the edge of her kitchen?

"We'll just be out for an hour," Nathan added.

"Have a good time," Bella said, her back to them both.

"See you soon," Lily said, smiling politely at Bella's back. She was determined not to become the sort of daughter-in-law who becomes a wedge between her husband and his mother.

"IT'S FREEZING," Lily said as they stepped outside. The temperature had dropped dramatically over the course of the day.

"Poor Sol," Nathan said.

"What now?" Lily asked. She slipped her hand into his as they descended the staircase from their landing to the street.

"He was all excited about the game tonight. He's taking a girl."

"He is?"

"And now they're going to freeze half to death." Nathan shook his head. "The whole evening will be a bust."

"Who's he taking, do you know?"

"Some girl who apparently crashed our wedding with her mother."

"Elka?" She dropped his hand.

"You know her?" He nodded at Mrs. Beler, who was out on her front porch, beating a rug.

"She came to our house."

Nathan smiled. "Must be serious, then. He's never had a girl over before."

"He didn't have her over. She came over uninvited. He didn't call her after taking her out, so she came calling, chasing after him."

Nathan smiled. "A girl who knows what she wants and goes after it. Sounds like just the ticket for Sol. Is she pretty?"

"You saw her. She was at our wedding."

"I know, but I don't remember her."

"That's how pretty she is."

"Lily Kramer," he said, still smiling. "If I didn't know better I would think you're jealous."

"Of that?"

"What's wrong with her?"

"Nothing."

"Nothing?" He was still smiling, more amused than disturbed by her annoyance at having her place in Sol's affections usurped. He knew about Sol's longing for Lily. He'd seen it on his brother's face at the wedding. He hadn't minded; it had pleased him, in fact, to see Lily avenged of the shame Sol had brought her.

Jealous? Lily thought. The very idea was an insult. Did Nathan not realize how beneath her it would be to compare herself to that teenage girl? A girl with no depth or shading. A girl who didn't even know how to choreograph a scene with a man who had spurned her . . . Or did she? Lily remembered the tenderness in Sol's face as he read to her the stiff, pompous letter Elka had written, a letter that touched him, it seemed

to Lily, for the transparency of the emotions that drove it, the transparency of the girl who loved him and was offering herself to him.

"She doesn't lack spine, you have to give her that," Sol had said, and Lily had understood from the pride in his voice that he already saw Elka as part of himself, was already claiming her qualities as his own.

He might cast Lily longing looks any time he had the opportunity, might continue to desire her, but he would marry this Elka, she now realized, a girl who had nothing wrong with her, nothing within her to make him recoil as he had instinctively recoiled the first time he saw Lily.

And then what, she wondered. What would be said between herself and the girl's mother, who would become, through the marriage, a relative? She couldn't think about it yet.

"Your mother seems to like her," she said.

He took her hand again. "My mother doesn't dislike you."

"Doesn't she?"

Just a week earlier Lily had done some shopping for Rosh Hashana. She was trying to make more of an effort, as both Nathan and Sol had advised her, each in their different ways. And Bella had been pleasant enough, had thanked her for the apples and honey, and then invited her to sit down and join her for coffee, which she had done. They had made small talk for a while, had tried to, but as Lily tried to summon an interest in what her mother-in law was telling her—the people she'd run into that day while shopping, the price she had paid for the chicken that was soaking in the tub—as she had tried to offer a response in kind, she had felt a weariness so extreme it was like a physical entity bearing down on her, the air itself thickening into another element. She felt like she was speaking in

slow motion, trying to project her words through an element more like water than air, a distorting element that slurred her words, blurred them.

Bella seemed to sense it, because she didn't ask further questions or offer further chit-chat. She reached out to touch Lily's hand and the warmth of her touch was shocking, the immediacy of the sensation despite the thickness in which Lily felt herself encased. Bella had told her then about her own first Rosh Hashana in Canada. She described a bleak, joyless holiday, her husband, Joseph, barely noticing her and Nathan barely noticing the meal she had worked so hard to make festive. At the conclusion of the holiday she had stood by the window with Nathan in her arms, looking at the moon—the new moon of the new year—and singing a song to the baby. "It was such a lonely moon," Bella said, describing the thin, cold sliver of light suspended in the vastness of the night sky. And Lily had understood the analogy at once, the implication that Bella's life too had been stripped back to nothing but then had waxed again over time. As Lily's could. Over time. But the moon, even full, was still a cold, lonely light in a vast darkness, Lily thought.

"She'll come around," Nathan promised.

They crossed the street that divided their neighbourhood from Mount Royal and started along the wide gravel path that edged the playing fields before rising to the wooded upper slope of the mountain.

"That was my father's bench," Nathan said. They had passed that same bench many times on their evening and Sunday afternoon walks, but he had never pointed it out to Lily before. It was occupied now by an old couple, the woman wrapped in a duffle bag of a coat, the sort his mother would

wear, the man in a peaked cap with the ear flaps extended.
They sat side by side, arms crossed, looking out at the world
together but not exchanging a word. "That's where he was
when he wasn't at work. Summer, winter . . ."

"Doing what?"

"Nothing. Daydreaming."

"Nothing? Or daydreaming?"

Nathan smiled. "I don't really know."

More than once he had ignored his father when he walked
by—though that he didn't mention to Lily. He would play
games of catch with his friends just a few yards away and
pretend he didn't see him. His own father. And why? When
he had told another girl about it once, a girl he had liked, she
concluded that Nathan was ashamed. "I wasn't ashamed," he
spat back, as angry at himself for telling her as at the simple-
mindedness of her response. "It's normal for a boy to be
ashamed of a father who does nothing but sit on a park bench
all day," the girl had assured him—Shirley was her name;
she was married now to Pozniak. "He didn't do nothing. He
worked. All day," Nathan answered. "Sorting buttons," Shirley responded, as if that would be cause for shame. As if her
own father were a brain surgeon instead of a butcher who was
known for the weight he added to each purchase by pressing
his pinky—just a little, just a few cents' worth—on the scale.
"Supporting us," Nathan reminded her, to which Shirley had
shrugged, letting the matter drop.

It had not been shame, but something else. How to explain,
to understand that the man Nathan saw on the park bench each
afternoon seemed to him a stranger in his father's body, a man
with a different life from the one in which Nathan was his son.
He was sunk so deep into that other life that he didn't even

see Nathan. That's how it seemed, how it felt. And when they sat at the same supper table in the evenings, he never gave any indication he had noticed Nathan in the park just a few hours earlier. Except for once. Nathan remembered it now: an evening meal, Nina and Sol bickering over something, their mother yelling back at them, giving them each a sharp slap. In the ensuing chaos of offended crying and accusatory howls of who started it, his father had looked up from his bowl and met Nathan's eyes with the clearest and most focused of gazes. It was just the two of them at that moment, Nathan locked into his father's gaze by the force of it. "That was a good save," his father said, the calm quiet of his tone cutting through the surrounding noise. Spoon in hand, he had mimed perfectly the overhead catch Nathan had made earlier that day. Then he hunched back over his soup, gone again, for the rest of the meal.

"I had a dream about him the other night," Nathan said. He almost never remembered his dreams; they dissolved with consciousness. Sometimes, though, fragments lingered like wisps of smoke, wafting through his mind throughout the day.

"What did you dream?" Lily asked.

It started coming back to him, filling in: his father, sitting in sunlight on the top step of their landing. It was spring sunlight—clearer, harsher than the thick, melting light of summer. He was wearing a red and black plaid flannel shirt—Nathan hadn't seen it in years, hadn't thought of it once—and his sleeves were rolled up to the elbows, revealing his strong, muscled forearms. He described his father's forearms to Lily, the remarkably smooth skin of his inner arms, skin as smooth as a child's, but with ridges of muscle just beneath. He could feel his father's inner arm as he described it. He described that to Lily too: the odd sensation he was having—right then,

as they walked together on the mountain, his father dead ten years already—of the soft skin of his father's inner arm beneath his fingertips.

"They say our deepest memories are in our fingers," Lily said.

He looked at her.

"I think it's true," she said. Sometimes at night, as she lay in bed, her hands felt estranged from her, enlarged, warmer than the rest of her body, alive to sensations to which the rest of her felt numb. It was as if they had a life separate from her, might take wing and fly off without her.

"He was sitting on the top step, whittling," Nathan said. "He used to whittle toys for us: soldiers for me and Sol, dolls for Nina, spinning tops . . . He made Nina a horse once, a stallion."

"A stallion?"

Nathan smiled. "It looked more like one of the old nags who delivered our milk, but that's what he called it. A stallion."

Nothing Lily had heard about Joseph Kramer from either of his sons would have led her to imagine a man who would whittle a stallion out of a block of wood for his young daughter.

"My father tried to make me a *dreidel* once," she said. She smiled. "It didn't work."

"What do you mean, it didn't work?"

"It didn't spin. You'd give it a nice twist and it would just fall over dead."

Nathan smiled too. "He wasn't good with his hands?" Ever since she had told him her father was in import–export, he had imagined a wealthy man with a fancy store who did nothing with his hands but run them over the soft Persian carpets he imported.

"He was very good with his hands; he just couldn't whittle. He could tell the bark of an oak from a beech with his eyes closed, just from the texture. He taught me when he took me out in his boat."

"He had a boat?"

"Of course he had a boat. He was a ferryman."

"But I thought you said . . ."

"He transported goods for import and export."

"What sorts of goods?"

"It varied," she said, "depending on the market."

"Which market?" he pressed on. He didn't understand her reluctance to reveal the most basic details of her life before the war.

"Russia," she said.

"Russia?"

"The Soviet Union. We lived near the border," she explained. "Our river became the new border after 1920."

"But . . . I didn't realize there was trade with Russia after the revolution. I thought they closed the border."

"There was trade."

He waited for more, some detail, explanation.

"You didn't finish telling me your dream," she said.

"I did. That was it."

"You saw your father on the front stoop, whittling, and . . . what about you? What were you doing?"

"I wasn't in the dream."

"You were outside it?"

"That's right. Looking in. Tell me more about your father's business."

"I told you. He had a boat. He brought goods across." She glanced at him. "Why are you looking at me like that?"

"I'm not looking at you any differently than I ever do."

"He was a ferryman. Just like his father, and his grandfather before him."

"Except that when his father and grandfather ran their ferries it was legal," Nathan said, careful to keep any note of censure from his voice.

"Everybody benefited," she said.

"Wasn't it dangerous?"

"It was a little risky," she acknowledged. "Less so when he took me with him."

"He took you with him?" Was that what she had meant when she said that she worked with him like the son he hadn't had? What kind of father . . . ? "What if you were caught?"

"I wasn't going to get caught. They were very well paid not to catch us."

"But surely not every border guard . . ."

"There was much more leniency shown for women and children."

He nodded.

"Don't look so shocked."

"I'm not shocked."

"Disappointed." As she'd known he would be. Here he'd thought he'd married class, found a bargain in the bin of refugees delivered up by the war, only to discover . . .

"Not at all." He was actually relieved, he realized. It was the first information she'd offered that made sense of her secrecy, of the evasiveness that had begun to worry him, to make him wonder what might be hiding in its shadow, but that was now revealed to be nothing more ominous than shame about her origins. He took her hand. "Are you warm enough?"

"Perfectly. It's the perfect coat, Nathan. Thank you."

They walked in silence again for a while, their path in the forest now, climbing gradually towards the lookout over the city.

"So, if you closed your eyes and I led you to a tree and placed your hand against it, you could tell me what it was?"

"Try me," she said. She closed her eyes and immediately became aware of the feel of the path beneath her feet, the areas of spongy softness where layers of rotted leaf had accumulated over years, the harder patches of bare trampled earth, the jutting bits of rock and root that broke through the surface. He stopped walking and placed her open hand against the trunk of a tree. She held her hand without moving it, as if absorbing the bark through her skin.

"Maple," she said.

"Good guess," he responded, to which she laughed.

They walked farther, the trail skirting a cliff of exposed rock. She ran her hand along its face as they walked past.

"I suppose you can tell me what that is too."

"Gabbro," she said.

He looked at her, surprised.

"Was it nice to see him?" she asked.

"Who?"

"Your father."

"It was," he admitted, feeling slightly self-conscious to be talking about his dream as if it were real life.

"You're lucky," she said. "I never see anyone."

"It's not like I *actually* saw him."

"My dead don't come to me," she said.

"It was just a dream, Lily."

"There was one time I thought I heard them. It was in the desert. I had gone down there with a man I had met.

An Englishman, on leave. I should never have gone with him, I know . . . our terrible enemies, the English. Though in Europe they'd been our great friends." She shrugged. "It was November—"

"Is that how you learned to speak English so well?" Nathan interrupted. "From this . . . Englishman?"

"No, no. I already knew it. I studied English in gymnasium. I was the very top student."

"When you weren't helping your father smuggle?" He heard the sarcasm in his tone and didn't care. It was jealousy, he knew—just who was this Englishman?

"I only helped him after school. I was a student at the most prestigious gymnasium in the entire district—one of only three Jewish students allowed to attend."

"And what did your prestigious friends think of your father's occupation?"

"They didn't know. I told them he was an exporter."

As she told me, Nathan thought. "So you went with him, this Englishman on leave from sending our people back to Europe—"

"To Cyprus," she said softly.

"So, what—you thought this might be a good opportunity to practise your English?"

"He told me it was the most beautiful place he'd ever been. That's why I went. Actually, he didn't say it was the most beautiful place, but the most lonely. He said it was the most lonely landscape on earth. The only place on earth that he didn't feel lonely."

She looked at Nathan. "I felt an affinity."

Nathan felt her gaze searching him out, but he kept looking straight ahead.

"It was November, so the days were warm but no longer hot, and the nights were cold and clear. So clear—you can't imagine the emptiness, Nathan, the vastness of it. We saw no one for three days. We barely spoke. We sat outside our tent and watched the light change, the sand shift in the wind, the stars appear . . . And then, on the third night, I heard whispering. It woke me in the night—a dream that didn't end when I awoke. It was a distorted whispering—there were no words I could discern—but just the fact that they were there, calling to me, letting me know they were still mine and I theirs . . ."

Nathan heard the emotion in her voice, an opening, but all he could wonder was who the man was who had taken her to the desert.

"In the morning, when my friend made our coffee, he asked me if I'd heard it during the night. 'Heard what?' I asked. 'The whispering,' he said, and then he explained. It seems that whispering sand is a phenomenon particular to that region of the Sinai. It has to do with the composition of the sand there, which is pure quartz. Other sands are composites of different minerals," she explained, "but in that part of the Sinai there's a purity of composition, and when it rubs together as it shifts . . ." She shook her head. "That's what I had heard." She looked at him. "Quartz."

Who was this friend? Nathan wondered, ashamed of his jealousy, of the small-mindedness of his own response. He took her hand to cover his internal agitation, his inadequacy as a husband to her. "I'm sorry," he said.

1944
Last night, a hot meal, a stew of potato and some sort of meat that Andre swore was squirrel but

*was not. It was cat, I knew, and not because of the
taste—for how would I know squirrel from cat?—
but from the quick flicker of Andre's eyes as he
lied. A chivalrous lie—I would have eaten the stew
regardless, and to pretend that I wouldn't was to
transform me from the creature that I am to the girl
that I once was: a girl with sensibilities, a girl who
would rather die from hunger than eat a stew of cat,
licking every last drop of its juices from her bowl.*

*I loved him for his lie, I told him after we had
eaten. You love me for the meat, he answered, but
he was pleased.*

*I felt a surge of strength as we sat with full
stomachs. It was a woman's strength, which is
not muscular but sensual, an opening of all my
senses so that I could smell the river that is still ten
miles away—a faint fishy smell with a hard tang of
metal—and I could hear the shallow rapid heart-
beats of every mouse and mole that hid in the forest all around us. I heard the slower rhythms too,
the hearts of wild boars at rest, of bears preparing
for slumber. I told Andre, and he smiled. It's the
meat, he said.*

*I slept lightly and poorly at first, my stomach
a contracting knot of pain, but I was awakened
later in the night by quietness. It was a quietness so
extreme that I thought at first I had died, but as I
lay there in that quiet I realized it was the absence
of pain and of hunger and of fear and of cold that
I was experiencing, a cessation that was a stillness inside me. And within that stillness I felt the*

warmth of a glowing light, and I remembered what our neighbour once told me when she was pregnant with her first child, that it is said of a child in a womb that a light burns above his head and he can see from one end of the world to another, so that a child sleeping in its womb in Antwerp can see a dream in Spain.

I knew then that I will survive this and be born into a second life. That Andre is not the agent of death I had thought at first. Or the thief I've feared who will simply take the three diamonds I've offered in payment and leave me, or worse kill me. He's a flesh-and-blood man who is as he appears to me. He will take me across the river I can smell from ten miles away.

CHAPTER 14

"Jonathan's back," Carrie said.

We were in my bedroom at my father's home. I was sprawled on the bed, a stack of glossy magazines by my side, looking for ideas for bridesmaids' dresses and flower arrangements for my wedding. Carrie was sitting in the armchair facing the bed, leafing through one of the magazines she'd taken from my pile.

"He didn't even call me to tell me he's home."

"Why would he?" I asked her.

Jonathan had been heartbroken when Carrie broke up with him. He had moped around for months hoping she'd change her mind, had dated other women in hopes of making her jealous, and then, finally, having accepted the hopelessness of his situation, he had quit school and taken himself off to India for the purpose of finding himself.

"I ran into his mother and sister in Snowdon. They were looking for a grad dress for his sister. Who's gotten fat, by the way. They were both thrilled to see me. They obviously had

no idea he hadn't called me, that I hadn't had a clue he was even planning to come home, let alone that he'd arrived and been home a full week already. A week, Ruthie. What is wrong with him?"

"You broke up with him, Carrie. Remember? You found him boring and conventional. You couldn't stand another second of his hangdog look lurking over your every move."

"What if he's met someone else?"

I looked at her. She wasn't beautiful but she had a charm that drew people to her and a confidence in her own lovability that was utterly convincing to others. No one left Carrie; Carrie did the leaving. That was just a basic fact of her life. And Jonathan had not actually proven the exception to that fact, though I could see there was no point in trying to remind her of that.

"What about this?" I asked, holding up the magazine so she could see the dress I'd found for her.

Carrie leaned closer, shook her head. "I'd look like I have hepatitis in that."

"Not the colour. I mean the style."

"Ruthie," she said. "In all the years you've known me, have you ever once seen me in an empire waistline?" She leaned back in her chair but didn't return to her magazine.

"I think I'll dispense with the clouds of angels' breath," I said. "It's become a bit of a cliché."

"And the white dress hasn't?"

I looked at her.

"The point of a wedding is not exactly originality of expression," Carrie said.

I didn't argue, was not in the mood for another of Carrie's lectures on the many and varied ways in which marriage

represented a failure of imagination and nerve. It was 1967 and the changes in the larger culture had begun to penetrate our world, but mostly in the form of shrinking hemlines, drugs, music and draft dodgers from the States. Carrie's lectures about marriage were inspired less by her politics than by her concern that there was no man she liked well enough to invite as a date to my wedding. She pulled a strand of hair in front of her face to check it for split ends, an inspection that absorbed her attention so completely and for so long that I finally returned my attention to my magazine.

"Have you brought the notebook to Ida yet?" she asked me. I had told her I was planning to take Ida up on her promise, made years earlier, to read it to me when I became engaged. When I didn't answer, she asked, "What are you waiting for?"

"I guess I'm afraid it might affect her badly. She was uncomfortable enough when I brought her the diamond. And not exactly forthcoming."

Carrie nodded. "Maybe you should bring it to Mrs. Schoenfeld. That wasn't a bad idea."

"Too late."

Carrie stopped mid-inspection to look at me through a strand of her hair. "She died?"

"No, no. She's just not all there any more."

"What do you mean?"

"She came out of her house naked yesterday."

"She what?"

Reuben and I had been sitting on the floor of Sol and Elka's den helping Chuck set up his train set when I stood up to get something to drink, looked out the window and saw Mrs. Schoenfeld, stark naked, walking down her front walk to the street. I had known for a while that she was losing her

memory, but I had seen no evidence until then that the loss extended to her entire mind. She still smiled warmly at me, for example, when I walked past her house as she was watering her garden, even if she could no longer remember my name, and she still came to *shul* every Shabbes, dressed in the same unmemorable skirts and blouses that ladies of her age generally wear and draped with a double strand of pearls that her little granddaughter played with and pulled into her mouth as she sat on her grandmother's lap during the Torah reading.

"All she had on were her pearls."

"Jesus," Carrie said half under her breath. "Glad I missed it."

It was the impression of looseness that had most shocked me at first. Her grey hair, which I'd only ever seen pulled into a tight bun, flew out from her head in thin wisps; her breasts flapped like two deflated husks on her chest. Another loose fold of skin—her abdomen—flapped over her private parts but, really, she was all private parts. That's how it had seemed. That what I was seeing in front of me was privacy exposed, being desecrated on the empty but decidedly public suburban sidewalk on which she stood. I don't know how long I stood staring at her. It seemed like no time at all. It seemed like I had barely noticed her, had barely had time to register what I was seeing when Reuben was out there on the sidewalk beside her. He had a sheet in his hand, a sheet that he must have pulled out of our linen closet while I was still staring stupefied at the apparition before me. He draped the sheet over her, pulling the ends together and tightening it, as if he were fitting her for a gown. Mrs. Schoenfeld must have thought so as well, because she took the ends of the sheet in her hands as naturally and elegantly as if she were a bride holding up the train of her bridal gown. Then she placed her hand on Reuben's outstretched palm and allowed him to lead her home.

I told Carrie about it, remembering the surge of love I had felt for Reuben at that moment, the sense I had that I was seeing the core of his character, and that it was a good character: unafraid, kind, strong.

"Saint Reuben," Carrie said.

"What's that supposed to mean?"

"Nothing." She reached into her handbag, pulled out a nail file and began filing her already perfectly manicured nails.

"You don't like him."

"Oh, for God's sake. Of course I like him."

"You never have anything nice to say about him."

"I never have anything nice to say about anyone." She flashed me one of her smiles that was charming and infuriating in equal parts.

"It's not that I think he's *wrong* for you. . . ." Carrie thought about that for a few minutes. "You're just really into being normal right now, you know? The normal Jewish husband, the normal wedding with all the bridesmaids and flowers . . ." She looked at me to see how I was taking this. "And there's nothing wrong with that . . ." she trailed off.

Was there truth in what Carrie was suggesting? I loved Reuben, but I couldn't pretend that I didn't also enjoy how easy it was, how restful, to be like everyone else for once. I couldn't pretend I didn't welcome the easy, comfortable warmth people showed me and Reuben wherever we went, the warmth of people recognizing an attractive reflection of themselves, and I couldn't quite believe just how welcome a change that was from the strained kindness that people had shown me all my life until then. None of which I was prepared to admit to Carrie at that moment.

"I know it's hard for you to understand that I might actu-

ally love a man who has loved me from the moment he set eyes on me, is nice to me, is prepared to make a lifelong commitment to—"

"Oh, don't get so defensive," Carrie said. She returned to her manicure and I flipped through a few more pages of my magazine, but absentmindedly now. "Is your father bringing Sandra to the wedding?" she asked.

Sandra was the woman my father had started dating soon after Reuben and I announced our engagement. I knew as soon as I met her that he felt differently about her than any of the women he'd dated over the years. Sandra herself was different—less chatty, less nice, in some ways, than the others.

"Of course," I said, a little too enthusiastically. I was actually a little jealous of Sandra, the look she brought to my father's face.

It had occurred to me just that week that it was entirely possible the reason my father hadn't met a woman he really liked before now was that he had been looking for one who might be a good stepmother to me, and that the women he imagined being good for me (Joyce, Melinda, Naomi and a few others over the years) were not women he found interesting.

"It makes it easier for you," Carrie said.

"What does?"

"That he has someone. You don't have to feel guilty about leaving him."

"Yes. Exactly," I lied. My jealousy embarrassed me.

"Do you suppose Oscar will be coming to the wedding too?" Oscar was Sandra's dog. He went everywhere with her. He was a huge Newfie that Ida Pearl and Bella called The Pony.

"I'm hoping he'll agree to be an usher."

Carrie smiled. "Sandra was always a little weird. My mother told me."

I looked at her. "Your mother knows Sandra?"

"They went to school together. She's not bad weird or anything. Just different. Her father was an artist. He used to set up his easel by the side of the road in Saint-Donat and paint all day."

"That explains it."

Carrie laughed.

"I guess my father just goes for weird women. What can I say? My mother wasn't exactly regular either."

"True," Carrie said.

"Even the way she abandoned me was weird," I said, remembering the bottles of formula neatly lined up in the fridge, an image I'd been told about so often I felt I had seen it for myself; the meticulously planned departure that insured I would not be unattended even for a few minutes; the rocks that arrived, not regularly but consistently, an ongoing communication over the years of my childhood and teenage life, even if the form it took was a ritual of mourning, the stones we left lovingly for our dead.

"I don't think there's really a normal way to abandon your baby," Carrie said, and as soon as she did I felt the old shame creeping back into me. I had thought I was over it, and there was no reason for me to feel it, especially not with Carrie, but there it was, the shame I felt whenever I entered a new situation and people didn't know me yet, only knew about me, what had happened in our family. I wondered if it would ever leave me completely.

"Don't be mad at me," Carrie said. She was back onto our previous subject.

"Mad at you?"

"For what I said about Reuben, you know—"

"It's okay," I said.

"Are you sure?"

"It's fine, Carrie. Really."

"A hundred percent?"

I wasn't, but Carrie's approach when she was contrite was like that of a puppy wiggling near the mess it had made and then licking your nose for good measure so that you couldn't be mad. "A hundred percent," I said.

"Good. Because I really didn't mean—" And then, like that same puppy, she was on to the next mess to be made. "Do you think I should call him?" Jonathan, she meant.

"I think you should leave him alone."

"Too late." She flashed me one of her winning smiles again.

"You called him?"

"Last night."

"And?"

"And nothing. He sounded happy enough to hear from me. Not that you can tell anything over the phone. Oh, and you'll never guess who his new best buddy is." She paused for effect. "David Czernowitz."

She waited for my response, but the name meant nothing to me.

"Don't tell me you've forgotten Mr. C."

"How could I forget—"

"David's his son," Carrie said.

"He has a *son*?"

"He was in India with Jonathan."

"I can't believe it," I said.

"Yeah, I thought he was in Israel working on a kibbutz.

Though he didn't really strike me as the picking oranges type."

"You know him?"

"He was in one of my classes."

"I can't believe you didn't tell me."

"Tell you what? I barely spoke to him."

"Still . . ."

"Still what? If there had been anything to tell I would have—"

"It's so hard to believe he has a son."

Carrie gave me a confused look, as if to ask what was so hard to believe. That a man who had been our teacher more than ten years earlier had actually had a life beyond what I was able to imagine for him?

"He invited me to a party tonight."

"Jonathan?"

"Who else?"

"Are you going?"

She shrugged. "Want to come?"

THE PARTY CONSISTED of a dozen or so people sitting in a circle on the floor of a basement apartment. Carrie had arranged to meet Jonathan there, and as we entered he rose from the circle to greet us. His hair was long and he'd grown a beard, a style that the boys we knew in Montreal had not yet adopted.

"Hi, Ruthie," he said, kissing me in greeting. "Hello, Carrie," he said to Carrie, who was standing just behind me. I noted the slight reserve in his voice and demeanour, a self-conscious demonstration of the emotional distance from Carrie that he had managed to cultivate within himself, and

of his resolve to not fall back into the pit of his hopeless love for her.

"You look like Jesus," Carrie greeted him in return.

Jonathan didn't respond, but already, immediately, I could see the first signs of misery returning to his tanned, handsome face.

"My false messiah returned from the land of the idol worshipers," Carrie said, taking his face into her hands and kissing his mouth. It was a brief kiss but decisive. I saw his will collapse. I saw the resolve that had temporarily firmed his features dissolve, and my heart went out to him. He was a nice guy and would have been on track for a reasonably happy marriage to a girl not unlike one of his sisters, and a career that would enable him to support his family in a neighbourhood and community exactly like the one he had grown up in if not for the relentless attraction he felt to those aspects of life that most scared him. Carrie, for example, whose grip on him had not loosened from the moment she had blindfolded him with his own scarf and led him out of the party where they had just met; free love, which he claimed to believe in despite his more deeply held belief that there's no such thing as a free lunch; and now, his latest: a spiritual tradition that had no creator at its centre, which is what he talked about as he lit what I thought at first to be a cigarette. It was mind-blowing, he said, to bring his own breath, rather than God, to the centre of his consciousness, which was what he did now when he meditated, a practice that had replaced prayer in his life.

"Sounds like narcissism to me," Carrie said before inhaling the joint that he passed to her. To which someone else—a man I had noticed the minute I walked in—responded that if there was any narcissism on display it was her own, her flip dismissal of an entire spiritual tradition about which she knew

absolutely nothing, based solely on its difference from the one she already knew.

Carrie looked more amused than insulted—she loved the challenge of a good argument—but Jonathan was clearly incensed by the attack on the woman who had dumped him and made his life a misery for years.

"Back off, David," he said, and as I looked to see how the man would respond, I knew I was looking at Mr. C.'s son.

Perhaps, had I not known he was a friend of Jonathan's, had I not half-expected him to be at the party, I would not have been able to place so quickly whose features I was look-ing at. But I had known; I had more than half-expected. What I hadn't expected was to find him attractive.

He wasn't a particularly handsome man, but he was attractive in an unusual sort of way. His eyes were large and deeply set in a face so unpadded with flesh that the contours of his skull were clearly visible. And there was a matching leanness to his body, a spareness that was physical and yet seemed to me a manifestation of character, of a personality that eschewed the extraneous, be it flesh or social niceties.

Jonathan was talking—had been talking for some time already—about whether the universe is ordered by sentience or some other force. After a while other people began to join in. I heard voices raised, lowered, but I didn't hear the content of their words because my attention was entirely on David C.

He was bored, I thought. Bored with the talk, an endlessly proliferating mass of words as thick as the smoke in the room, bored with the company, bored with the party. He took the joint that was passed to him and passed it along without smok-ing it. And then, a moment later, he rose and left the circle.

The talk was getting stupider, people acting the way they

thought they were supposed to act when they were stoned: laughing about things that weren't funny, vacuuming up the bowls of chips and plates of cookies that someone had placed in the centre of the circle. I waited for David Czernowitz to return, but when the joint came around to me a second time, I realized he wasn't coming back, that he might not have just left the circle, but the party. I rose, shook the leg that was tingling with pins and needles from having been folded underneath me for too long, and moved towards the one room that always served as a place of refuge for the awkward and uncoupled at parties like this, the kitchen, which was a fluorescent-lit galley with a low, stained ceiling and mustard-coloured appliances. Bags of chips and pretzels were piled on the counter, paper plates and plastic cups stacked neatly beside them; bottles of wine and soft drinks filled the sink. And at the far wall of the galley, David, facing the wall, his back to the room.

He was engaged in conversation with a woman whom he seemed to have pinned against the wall. He hovered over her with one hand on the wall just above her head and one on the wall beside her shoulder. The pinning was more psychological in nature than physical, since he wasn't actually touching her, but it would have taken a deft physical move on her part to duck and slide out from under him. I couldn't tell whether it was seduction or combat I had walked in on, a flow of rage or lust that was passing between them—the volume of their voices was too low for me to hear the content. I was the only other person in the kitchen and knew I should leave, but my curiosity about him was more powerful than my sense of tact or good manners, so I stayed where I was, telling myself it was public space, after all, and busied myself with reorganizing the plastic cups into shorter stacks.

"As you wish," I heard the woman say, then she lifted his arm—the one beside her shoulder—as if it were a gate and walked out of the kitchen.

He didn't move, was still holding his position, one hand on the wall just above the spot where her head had been a moment earlier, the other arm back in place an inch from where her shoulder would have been if she were still standing there, which she wasn't, so anyone entering the kitchen at that moment would think he was simply leaning against the wall rather than hovering over the emptiness that had been filled just a moment earlier by a living, breathing woman. Anyone just entering the kitchen at that moment might reasonably conclude, in fact, that he was ill or upset, especially since his face was now pressed into his upper arm, a posture that suggested suppressed tears or rage or nausea, or some combination of the three, and was exactly the posture his father had assumed during one of his crying episodes in our classroom almost a decade earlier.

After a moment he dropped his arms and turned around. He pretended not to notice my presence, took a plastic cup from the stack I had just rearranged and poured himself a glass of Orange Crush. I also took a cup and held it out as a way to break into his attention. He filled my cup without looking at me. "I'm Ruth," I said. He glanced at me then. His eyes were brown, calm, uninterested. "David," he said.

"Ruth Kramer," I added.

He drank from his cup, then met my eyes again, his expression conveying to me his hope that with this exchange of information we could bring our conversation to a close. "David Czernowitz."

"Nice to meet you." And when he didn't return the pleasantry: "Was that your girlfriend?"

"I'm hoping she still is."

"I didn't mean . . ."

"To intrude?"

"I was just trying to make conversation."

He was like an electrical wire that had been stripped of its sheathing. I wanted to make contact. I didn't question why. I drank my cup of Orange Crush while casting about for something to say. "Coffee or mould?" I asked brightly, pointing to the light brown stain on the ceiling that was just inches above our heads.

He shifted his eyes upward for a moment, shrugged.

"Do you know whose apartment this is?" I plodded on.

"Mine."

"Ah. Well, it must be nice to have your own place."

"Not really."

"Not really?" I smiled, but he didn't smile back. "So, what, you're being forced to live on your own?"

He gave me a long, bored look. "Who do you suggest I live with?"

"*I* don't know. Your parents . . . your girlfriend . . ."

"She won't even sleep with me, so it's unlikely she'll move in with me."

"Poor baby."

"Do you want to sleep with me?"

The question was like the sting of a wasp, the poison of it taking a second to spread within me. I took his words at face value at first and was merely confused, the question having come out of an exchange coloured by his obvious indifference to me. But then I felt the insult he intended. He found me entirely undesirable, but would sleep with me anyway if that's what I was after and it would put an end once and for all to

this tedious conversation we were having. I looked at him. His face was a hard challenge.

"I'm engaged," I answered, perhaps to let him know that there was a man who did desire me, who loved me, in fact.

"Is that a yes or a no?"

"This really isn't a conversation I want to be having."

"No one's forcing you to have it."

And still I didn't leave. "I knew your father," I said.

And now he looked at me.

"He was my teacher."

He waited to hear what I was going to say. What on earth could I say? We went after him like a pack of dogs who sniff weakness? We ejected him like a drop of pus from a wound that's just beginning to fester, not understanding that the pus is the symptom, not the source of our infection? I looked at his face, at the sharp line of his jaw and the ridges of his bones, which I had wanted to run my finger along from the first moment I saw him, a desire that had not diminished despite what had passed between us.

"You look like him."

No response. Did he know, then? I wondered. Know what? That I had been part of the young, healthy pack who had driven his ruined father from our sight so we wouldn't feel his ruination as our own? "How is he?"

"Fine."

What else would he say to someone like me? Someone with normal parents, he probably assumed. Canadian parents. Someone who couldn't begin to understand what it was like to have been born of a soul-breaking grief.

"I'm glad," I said.

I still wanted to touch his face. So I did. I reached out my

hand and he didn't pull away. I felt the ridge of his cheek and the hollow beneath, cool at first, then warm as blood rushed in beneath my touch. I felt the smoothness of his brow as I swept my open hand across its surface, the fullness of his lips, the mask of his boredom falling away. His face, when I removed my hand, was a boy's. And before it could harden again, I imprinted his mouth with my thumb. "I'm not who you think I am," I whispered.

"AH, YOU'RE EARLY," Ida greeted me, though we hadn't actually set a definite time.

Reuben had presented me with my ring the night before. It was Ida who had made it, and when I had called her to thank her she had invited me over so she could see for herself how it looked on my hand.

Did it trouble me that the same hand that bore that ring had explored the contours of another man's face just a few nights earlier? It did, but I had constructed several rationales for the power of the attraction I had felt for David, most of them relating to the past that I was hoping to leave behind. And I had little doubt that I was moving towards a happy future by marrying Reuben. Still, when Ida took my janus-faced hand in hers, I wondered how she could not feel the treachorous heat of its fingertips and palm as she admired the cool beauty of the diamond that sat so nicely on its back. She didn't seem to. She nodded her satisfaction, then gestured me towards the living room and told me to wait there while she made tea.

Ida had lived in that apartment for most of my life—its spacious size and decor reflecting the improvement in her economic

position since the end of the war—but only one other time had she received me in her living room, that weekend of my family's move to Côte-St-Luc, years earlier. `

"Remember when I spent the weekend with you?" I asked her now as she joined me in the living room.

"Of course I remember." She put the tray down on the coffee table by the sofa. "You were such a peculiar little thing. Cleaning your plate no matter how often I filled it—I was worried maybe you had tapeworm—and thanking me every three minutes for every little thing. And then patting your clothes as if they were your pets."

She didn't mention my peeing my pants, which I appreciated.

The tea set was the same one she had used then, and she placed a slice of lemon in her own cup as she had that afternoon, but instead of stirring raspberry preserves into mine she added the amber fluid from the smaller of the silver pots on the tray.

"You've graduated," she said as I inhaled the whisky-scented steam rising from my cup. She spiked her own cup, then raised it to toast "*L'chaim.*"

I returned her *l'chaim,* raising my cup to her.

"So . . ." she said. We spent very little time together, just the two of us; with the inspection of the ring now complete, she was scrambling for something to say to me. "The plans for the wedding are coming along?"

I assured her they were.

She nodded, smiled.

I reached into my satchel and retrieved the notebook I had brought with me. Ida looked at it, then at me. "Remember you once told me you'd read it to me when I was engaged to be married?"

I expected her to put me off again, but she didn't. Had

enough time finally passed for her? Did she have some reason of her own to want to read through it again? Had she always intended to read it to me when she thought I was old enough to understand the feelings it raised for her? She reached for the notebook, put on her reading glasses and opened it.

"*I begin with a dream . . .*" she read, and a scene formed in my mind of a stone city from which the entire range of human emotion had been cleansed except for terror, and from which every colour had been drained except for the grey of the streets and the blackish red of the fluid that filled the hollows where rainwater had once pooled. I saw a terrified girl running through the maze of streets and coming to a door that blocked her flight. I saw her falling against the door, pleading with it as if it held some residue of mercy in its fibres, and then the miraculous opening: into colour, sunlight, the scent of apricots, the tinkling notes of a piano.

"That was my childhood home," Ida said. "Lily's aunt Lottie was my mother. She doesn't refer to my father because she never knew him. He was her father's oldest brother, but he died when she was a baby. His name was Herschel—I named Elka after him." And to my expression of confusion: "*Hersch* means 'deer' in Yiddish. Elk." She smiled. "It was another thing for her to hate me for when she was a child."

"Elka didn't like her name?"

"She would have preferred Elizabeth." Ida shook her head. "Lily and her family lived in Antwerp—her father was my uncle Chaim." She looked at me.

I nodded, already knew that.

"She and her mother would visit my family in Krakow every summer. The visits continued even after my father died and my mother remarried—there was a deep bond of friendship between

my mother and her mother, and it endured and deepened even when they were no longer sisters-in-law. Lily's mother still had her own family in Krakow to visit as well, but they would stay with my mother. Every summer. They would leave Antwerp in June and not return until September. And I would watch them go, my aunt and my spoiled little cousin, to my home, my family. While I had to stay and work like a servant for her father."

"Why was your uncle Chaim in Antwerp if the rest of the family was in Poland?"

"Antwerp was the centre of the diamond trade. A lot of people moved there. My own father had wanted to move there, but he was the eldest, he couldn't leave. And he might not have been able to leave even had he been the youngest, like Chaim. He had more vision than strength, my father—he could see what should be done without being able to do it."

She picked up the notebook. *"Who am I?"* she read. *"A mound of mud in an autumn field. A pile of leaves to the side of a forest path. In your cities I'm a rat scurrying beneath the surface of your life. I hide in your sewers. I infect your dreams with pestilence. Vermin, you call me. Cur. Once I was a girl."*

"She always had tendencies towards the dramatic," Ida said, peering at me over the top of her reading glasses. "She went through a stage of wanting to be an actress. The Sarah Bernhardt of her generation. But at thirteen she was overcome with shyness. You could see it descending on her, my sister Sonya wrote me." I saw a tight-fitting dress inching down the length of a girl's body, a sheath of shyness binding her in. "But beneath it she was still the same as before. Full of herself. So I guess she decided then that she would become a writer, a fantasy that her parents encouraged just as they had

encouraged every other whim that came into her head, bowing and scraping before her—she was their youngest and their only girl. Their little princess. And all the while I was working twelve-hour days in her father's workshop, providing the materials of life that allowed her to entertain her fantasies in comfort. Including this, I might add." She held up the notebook itself, which had probably been an expensive purchase, I realized, though one made long after Ida had already departed for Montreal.

Ida read a bit further then about a meeting the girl had had with a being who was either a man or a figment of her imagination: *"A crack had appeared in the Polish day, a drawing back of the world along a ragged seam. I narrowed my eyes to make it out, this parting in the shape of him, this opening to someplace else. Get up, he said. Quick."*

"Do you think she was really hiding in a pile of leaves?" I asked.

"More likely it was some sort of dugout. It wasn't a chance meeting she was describing. He was a smuggler. He was going to smuggle her across a river—I'm not sure which river, and I don't know why. I don't even know where the border was at that point in the war. The lair she was hiding in was probably a pre-arranged point of rendezvous."

"A smuggler? You mean for payment?"

"Of course for payment."

I thought about the segment she had just read to me. "If she hadn't lived to write about it, you'd think it was the angel of death she had just met, not a man."

She peered at me again over her glasses. "She didn't live long." She picked up the notebook. *"Who are you? he asked. I had been walking for days. I'm a walking graveyard, I told him.*

The dead are buried in my skin . . ." Ida's voice was strong, but her hands were trembling, I noticed. Just a little, but it made me as uneasy as if the earth beneath me was trembling just a little. *"Hours passed. Days, I think. His eyes were black but they reflected light. My face emerged, revealed itself to him."*

"So you see," Ida said.

See what? I wondered.

She read on. *"My father worked with light, I told him. He captured light with stones. He bent broken light into beauty . . ."*

Her writing in that passage reminded me of some of the poems I had written in high school when I fell for Charles Blumenthal, the efforts I had made to try to elevate the boring details of my life into something more interesting, something that might match the intensity of the feelings I had for him.

"And on my mother's side I descend from kindness . . ." This was a reference to the girl's maternal grandfather. *"He was a man so kind that migrating birds came to rest on his shoulders,"* Ida read, and a vision formed in my mind of a man standing on the edge of a field with exhausted geese resting on his shoulders.

"Wouldn't they be heavy?" I asked.

"What, heavy?"

"The geese," I said, thinking about the Canada geese that migrated every spring and fall, imagining how terrifying it would be to have one fly in for a landing on my shoulder.

"Who said anything about geese? It was songbirds. Tiny songbirds, scores of them, all along his shoulders and arms."

"Like a tree," I commented, and she looked at me as if I had said something right.

"There was something wrong with her grandfather," she said.

"What do you mean?"

"In his head. That's why Lily and her mother stayed with us. It was like he'd gone senile, except that he was too young for that. His mind and personality just dissolved. First memory, then reason, then language, then appetite of any sort."

"Until all that was left was kindness," I said, because that was the impression the girl had created, and while Ida didn't nod or agree, she also didn't disagree.

"And she was a coward, Lily's mother; she couldn't face it. Any other daughter would have used those summer visits to help her mother, to take some of the load onto her own shoulders, but she couldn't . . . And yet, she was a real friend to my mother. Through everything. With all the courage that friendship demands."

Ida's face looked different to me, softer somehow, as she granted me limited entrance to the life and people she had known before, a life and world so different from the one I knew her in. She shrugged, turned back to the notebook. *"If you were still your father's daughter you would cross the street to avoid my glance. I wouldn't, I assured him. We were fated for each other."*

Ida paused now. "Lust always feels like fate," she said. "That's why it's so dangerous."

I felt the colour rush to my face as I imagined that Ida had sensed more than she'd let on when she'd held my hand in hers earlier in our visit, that she somehow knew about the desire I'd felt for David several nights earlier—*lust,* she would call it—that could easily have become my fate. But Ida's comment wasn't about me, I realized. She was thinking about her own past, perhaps. Her cousin's.

She continued reading. Some of the entries were more down-to-earth: descriptions of the food they ate, the texture

of the autumn mud. A lot of it was dreams, as Bella had said years earlier. There was some gibberish, though less than I had been led to believe; a few quotes and verses of poetry; some descriptions of her life before the war—her friendship with Eva, other friends, a favourite dress she had once worn to attract a boy that she liked—but there was nothing, it seemed to me, to merit Ida's refusal to read it to me until now, Bella's refusal to read it to me altogether, the family's general discomfort about it.

"Is it all like this?" I interrupted Ida at one point.

"What do you mean?"

"Does anything *happen*?" A stupid question, I realized, but once again I was disappointed. I wanted to know how she had died, what the connection was between her and my mother, why my mother would have taken her name, pretended to be her.

Ida shrugged. "Nothing happens, no."

"But?"

"There's no but." She flipped through a few pages as if to confirm that she hadn't missed anything. "Do you want me to continue?"

"It's okay," I said.

She closed the notebook and put it on the coffee table.

"In some ways it's the usual story," Ida said.

"Usual?" The word hit me like a slap.

"She misread a man's interest in her. In that she was no different from any rich girl who falls in love with a man who courts her for her money. No different in some ways from my own misreading of Elka's father, though I wasn't rich, of course, just richer than him. And the consequences, in my case, weren't fatal."

"I know that's what happened in your life, but—"

"His interest in her was mercenary, my dear—he wanted her diamonds—but she misread it as love. It's a common enough occurrence, I'm sorry to say."

"And you were there, then? You knew him?"

All the natural colour in her face receded, leaving behind a pallor against which the orangey beige splotches of her makeup stood out to ghastly effect. She was silent for a few minutes, and I worried I had ended the conversation with my challenge, but then she began to tell me about a visit she had made to my mother twenty-three, almost twenty-four years earlier.

"It was just before Yom Kippur. She and your father were still living with Bella then—it was just a few months after their wedding. She was pregnant with you already, though no one knew it yet. She had been to see me a few weeks earlier in my store. With the diamond—I told you already . . ." Ida looked at me.

I nodded.

"When she showed it to me, I wondered how she had come to possess a diamond like that."

Again I nodded.

"I shouldn't have wondered, perhaps, not aloud, but you have to understand, she was presenting herself to me—to the entire world—as my cousin Lily Azerov."

It was not Ida's response that confused me. Why *wouldn't* Ida wonder about the source of that diamond? It was my mother's behaviour that made no sense: showing up at Ida's store like that, claiming to be her cousin.

"When she came to my store I thought she didn't know who I was. My relation to Lily Azerov, I mean. I thought she had come only because she had heard about the quality of my

work. By reputation. But I never had such a reputation, I'm sorry to say. If it were strictly a matter of who was thought to be the best jeweller to go to with such a diamond she would have gone to Grinstein. I'm sorry to say it, but it's true." Ida shrugged. "She came to me because she knew who I was. Elka had told Sol that I had a cousin Lily Azerov, that that's why we had come to the wedding, and Sol then told her, and she put it together." She paused again. "Wait here a minute," she said, as if I were about to run out the door just when someone finally seemed willing to tell me something about my mother.

Ida went into her den and re-emerged with the letter her sister Sonya had written to her about the strange visit from a girl who claimed to be their cousin, a stranger with their cousin's name who was on her way to marry a lucky bridegroom by the name of Kramer. I couldn't read it any more than I could read the notebook—the letter was also written in Yiddish—but I had already heard about it from my father, and again I wondered what my mother could have been thinking, going to the cousin of the girl she was claiming to be.

"When she came to my store, she didn't know about this letter, no one did, but she must have figured out that my sister had written to me. From the fact that I showed up at their wedding. But I didn't know that. All I knew was that this woman with my cousin's name was now presenting me with a diamond that could well have been in my cousin's possession at the time of their . . . encounter. I assumed the worst, I admit it."

And what was the worst? I wondered, afraid to ask, but just as afraid to let the moment pass. "You think my mother might have . . . killed her?"

"She told your grandmother that she didn't, and there's no reason to disbelieve that."

She told my grandmother? Bella, but not my father?

"But at the time, that morning in the store, I didn't know. I knew only that my cousin had disappeared in the war and that this woman had emerged instead." Bearing her cousin's name and a rough diamond of the sort that used to pass through her uncle Chaim's workshop. "What was I to think about your mother's purpose in my store that morning?"

She looked at me as if I might have the answer to that question.

"I assumed her interests were mercenary. I assumed that she wanted me to cut the diamond so she could turn around and sell it."

A diamond that my mother had obviously stolen, and probably from Ida's own relative.

"But I was wrong," Ida said. "I misunderstood her intentions. I came to realize that after she left. She would not have come to me if she simply wanted to cut the diamond and sell it. She had not survived five years of war only to lose all of her common sense with the arrival of peace."

Couldn't she have, though? Weren't there people who only flourished in times of danger?

"No, she knew who I was and that's why she came to me. Because of who I was. Because I was the cousin of the girl she was claiming to be. But why? That's what I wondered in those weeks following her visit. What had she wanted? To see if I intended to expose her? To implicate me in whatever crime she had committed by tempting me with that stone? And it's an excellent stone, incidentally. A superb stone. I was plenty tempted, believe me. Which just goes to show . . ." But her voice trailed off, leaving me to draw my own conclusions about what was shown by her temptation to cut a stone that she knew to be excellent as well as stolen from a girl—her own

cousin—who had not survived to reveal the circumstances of the theft and her own death.

"I would not have exposed her. I knew it the moment she stood before me in my store. It was not a decision, so to pretend now that it was is to make me more of a *tzedekah* than I am. It was more . . . I was afraid, I think, of what might happen if I told her what I knew."

Afraid of what? I waited.

"All of her poise and her superior, cultivated airs . . . It was like . . . the surface of ice you see on a river the first cold morning in late autumn. It looks solid but you know that it's not. You know that if you put too much pressure on it—any pressure—it will crack."

Ida paused again. "It was an instinct, that's all, but then, in the weeks following her visit, it grew reasons like branches on a tree. I wouldn't expose her because what would be gained by ruining yet one more life? I wouldn't expose her because who was I to judge her? I wouldn't expose her because . . . it went on and on. Who knows? Maybe a part of me hoped that if I didn't expose her, eventually I would get my hands on that diamond." Ida allowed herself a small, tight smile at that.

"The point is, her secret was safe with me, and that's what I went to tell her. I would not ruin her life, I would not destroy her. That's why I went, I promise you."

She looked at me as if I had asked her for that promise.

"Why else would I have gone on the day before the eve of Yom Kippur?" she asked me. "We don't visit each other before the Day of Judgment to cast our own judgments. We don't go to accuse. We go to beg forgiveness, to repair what can be repaired among our fellow human beings so we ourselves can be forgiven by God."

Why the religious lecture? I wondered.

"But she wasn't home." A shrug now, as if my mother's absence that day had been fateful in some way.

"It was a beautiful afternoon, very warm. I remember it well. It had been cold earlier that week, just days earlier. I remember it all so well, that fall. It was the fall that Sol and Elka started going out in a serious way. He had taken her to a ball game just days earlier. That coloured man was playing . . ."

"Jackie Robinson," I said.

"That's right. A very big event, winning that ball game. Everybody so excited they practically caused a riot." She shrugged. "But it was cold out, very cold. Elka held her hands out to me when she came home, so I could feel how cold, and right away I knew. I can't tell you how I knew—she never told me anything close to her heart, my Elka—but I knew that she loved him, and I knew also, without any doubt, that your uncle Sol would only disappoint her and lead her into misery, because that was just the sort of man he was. But, of course, I was wrong about him too . . ." Again her voice trailed off.

"So you went to see my mother . . ."

"On the day before Yom Kippur. The weather had changed again. Indian summer. It was warm on the streetcar. Too warm. I was thirsty by the time I arrived at your grandmother's. Your mother wasn't home, but Bella asked me in, offered me a drink. We talked . . . That was the first time we met, your grandmother and I. The beginning of our friendship." Ida allowed herself another smile. "Another reason not to expose your mother. Not that my list of reasons mattered, at that point. Your mother thought I was going to expose her. That's what mattered: what your mother thought were my intentions—and they were never my intentions, I promise you. You

have my solemn vow that I would not have sought to destroy the life she was trying to build. But she thought I would, and that was the pressure."

Could Ida really believe that? I wondered. Did she really think that had it not been for that fateful visit of hers whose purpose my mother misunderstood, my mother would not have left? And could she possibly be right? Or partly right? Was it my mother's fear of exposure that drove her away? Did it crack the thin surface of the new life and identity she was trying to build?

"I intended to return after the holiday, but life became busy. The whole world was getting engaged that fall, it seemed—it was the beginning of the so-called baby boom, and it wasn't just the babies that were booming. Everything was, including my business. Like never before. And the next thing I knew, Sukkos had passed, Simchas Torah . . ."

"I saw her walk by my store one day. They had moved into their own apartment by then, she and your father. The apartment where you were born. It wasn't far from here."

I nodded. I knew exactly where it was.

"It must have been November by then. Cold. She was wearing a beautiful coat, black lamb's wool, and trimmed in fur. I'm not sure what kind of fur. Expensive. A coat that told the world just how well your father was doing. And it was tight on her already—she was showing by then. Another few weeks and she wouldn't be able to button that coat over her stomach, I remember thinking. He offered it to Elka after she left, incidentally. Your father. But what would Elka want with a coat like that?"

A coat that would remind everyone of my mother every time they saw it? Is that what Ida meant?

"And socks too, he offered her."

"Socks?"

"A pair of woollen socks that she had brought with her from Europe. What he thought Elka might want with them I can't imagine."

I remembered the pair of old woollen socks I had found in my father's drawer years earlier. Did he still have them? I wondered.

"But that day, when she walked by my store, she looked like any other young married woman at that time, nicely dressed, her first pregnancy beginning to show, and I thought then that the time to expose her had passed. That she had become Lily Azerov Kramer; that's what I thought. Not my cousin. I don't mean that. I mean a new person. And it no longer seemed so suspicious to me. It wasn't uncommon, after all, for a person to change her name if she had escaped from death. It's not a custom here, I know, but where we were from, if you recovered from a serious illness or escaped death in some other way, it wasn't thought to be such a bad idea to change your name. To confuse death—you understand?"

I nodded.

"So when I saw her walking by that day I thought that it could be as simple as that. She had taken someone else's name at the end of the war. That was all. I didn't know the circumstances, it was true, but why assume the worst? She'd taken the name of someone who was already dead, her thinking being that death wouldn't come looking for that name again. Not for many years.

"But I was wrong, of course. It wasn't that simple. How could it be? A name is not just a sound that our mouths make. It's an evocation. It's bound to the life and soul of its bearer in

ways that we don't fully understand—that's why we're forbidden to utter the name of God, why we call him The Name, The Place, our King, our Lord. It's not just out of respect—you understand? But out of fear of what's bound to His name, what we might evoke in our utterance of it . . ."

She paused for a few minutes, then looked at me again.

"I can't tell you what your mother was or wasn't thinking when she took my cousin's name. I've thought about it often, believe me. And then, why her pretending went as deep as it did. Were the shocks and losses she suffered so extreme that she really no longer felt like the person she had been before the war? Could your mother really no longer remember what it had felt like to be that person, the person she was before? It can happen, I know. People can be shaken from themselves by shock. But to this degree? I asked myself. Why not, I answered. A human being's not an egg, after all, carrying her essence from place to place inside a shell. We rely on our surroundings and the people who know us to remind us who we are. You don't believe me, I know. I see it in your face. You think that who you are is written in stone and that if you were to be torn from your world and flung into another you'd land there the same Ruth Kramer you've always been. But you wouldn't, believe me. I didn't. Your grandmother didn't. Your grandfather didn't, may he rest in peace."

"But you didn't become someone else," I reminded her. "And neither did my grandparents."

"Not in that way, no."

Could a person really lose her very sense of self because the world that had formed and reflected that self back to her was destroyed? I wondered. Wasn't a person's self something more intrinsic?

"Maybe it wasn't because of what she lost but what she did," I said. "Maybe she did something so terrible that she couldn't recognize the person who did that as herself."

"That I can't tell you."

But could the notebook? I wondered.

"All I know is that after my visit the person she had been started coming back to her. And that person . . ."

Who was she? I waited to hear.

"Maybe she felt she didn't have a right to you. To any of it . . . your father's love, his name, his family, the new apartment, the expensive coat . . ."

Was she a murderer, after all? I wondered. A traitor? One of those Jews who had joined forces with the murderers in some way to save their own skins? I reached for the notebook again.

"There are no answers in there," Ida said. "I also thought there might be. When your father brought it to me—he brought it to me after she left."

I nodded. I knew that.

"I thought maybe I would find out what had happened to my family. Not one of them has ever been heard from again, you know."

I knew.

"It's as if God followed my steps through this life with an eraser in his hand." She paused. "So when your father brought me this . . . You can imagine." She paused again. "But there was nothing, nothing and more nothing. Not a word about my mother, my sisters and brothers, except at the very beginning, that very first dream. After that, just page after page of . . . well, you've heard it now. So what was I supposed to do with it?"

She looked at me as if I might know.

"The terrible thing is, I never liked my cousin. She was just a little girl when I knew her, but still I didn't like her. You can see a person's character even as a child, and hers I didn't like. Maybe it was jealousy, bitterness on my part—I'm not proud of it, you understand—but it's the truth And as soon as I started to read it I remembered that, just how much I had always disliked her." She shook her head. In regret, perhaps. Or shame that what had endured over time and unimaginable tragedy was her dislike, her jealousy, her near hatred of her cousin who had died. "I gave it back to him. I had to. What kind of guardian could I be?"

She was still looking at me; I felt an answer was called for. "Do you think we should have it translated?"

"What for?" she asked.

"I don't know. Maybe because that's what she would have wanted? If she was writing for an audience . . ."

"What she wanted was to live."

"I know, but . . ."

"What but?"

She had wanted to live. There was no but. "I wonder if my mother was trying to make it up to her in some way."

"Make what up to her?"

"That she died and my mother lived."

"I don't think your mother was trying to make anything up to her."

"What about the notebook, then? Why did my mother spend so much time reading it?" And when Ida didn't answer: "Because your cousin would have wanted someone to read it."

"Maybe so. I can't tell you what your mother felt about my cousin, what she felt she did or didn't owe her."

"Maybe that's why she bought that other notebook," I continued. "The empty one. Maybe she was planning to translate the notebook so other people could read it. So it wouldn't all be for nothing—your cousin writing it."

"I didn't know there was another notebook," Ida said.

"My mother bought it, but then she never wrote anything in it."

I remembered how I had once thought that maybe she had written in it using invisible ink, and that that was why she'd left it behind. Because she knew someday I'd figure out the solution to making the ink visible, to deciphering what she had written and left for me to find. I told Ida that, about the various attempts I had made to reveal the ink that was invisible to the naked eye, admitting that even when I got older, I sometimes wondered if it wasn't really empty. I knew how ridiculous that sounded, so I hastened to explain. "There were a few times in high school that I tried to write in it. Not as a diary." I didn't want Ida to think I would have presumed to use such a beautiful journal for something as mundane as the fact that Charles Blumenthal was by far the cutest boy I had ever met and I could only hope he liked me as much as I liked him, or that Carrie was being such a bitch that I didn't know why I was still her friend. I had my own journal for the daily trivialities of my own life, a dime-store purchase with cheap lined paper and a faux-vinyl cover imprinted with an image of a young woman bent over an open diary, pen in hand, long hair falling around her head like a curtain. "For poetry and things," I explained.

Ida nodded.

"But I couldn't write in it."

I expected Ida's impatience then. Even Carrie had been impatient with me when I'd told her that. "What do you mean

you can't write in it?" she'd asked. But Ida fixed an interested eye on me and asked me what I meant, so I found myself telling her how it had felt wrong from the start, from the moment I had told my father I wanted it. "You mean for your own use?" he had asked. "Not as a diary," I'd explained. "For something special. For poetry." My father had thought about it, then he said he didn't see why not, but he was hesitant; I could hear it in his tone. He couldn't think of any reason why the book should sit unused, but neither was he comfortable with me removing it from the shelf and filling its pages with my own writing.

"I took it anyway," I said to Ida. I removed it from its long-held place and stowed it in the drawer of my night table. "But then I couldn't bring myself to write in it." Every evening I would sit with my pen poised over the page. Every evening I had just the poem that I thought was perfect but I couldn't bring myself to inscribe it. "It was as if the pages were already filled," I concluded to Ida.

Ida nodded as if I had just said something eminently reasonable and rational.

"When I was a young woman I worked as a diamond cutter," she said. "You know that, yes?"

I nodded.

"I started at the bottom, as a polisher. It was considered routine work, tedious, and in some ways it was, but there was always a point with each stone I handled that I would come to know if it had been realized in the way it should have been. I can't explain how I knew it, I just did. I mentioned it to one of the girls on the bench with me and she laughed at me. She told one of the young men in the shop, my eldest cousin, Theo, whom she liked. She was hoping to impress Theo with

her tidbit, to bring herself to his attention at my expense, but her telling had the opposite effect. He was a skilled diamond cutter, the most talented in the shop. It was he who cleaved the stones. Do you know what that means?"

I nodded.

"No, you don't. How could you? A rough diamond is nothing to look at," she went on to explain. "Its beauty is there, but it's unrealized. It's waiting to be released—but how? That's the question that faces the one who's going to cleave it. As he holds a rough stone in his hand, he has to put himself inside that stone, to walk around inside it, to understand its inner landscape. He has to detect the direction of the grain, which may sound straightforward, but it's not. Diamonds aren't like trees, where what you see reflects what is. That's why the word 'truth' in English is derived from 'tree.' Did you know that?"

I shook my head.

"Oh yes," she assured me. "With diamonds, though, the grain can often be the exact opposite of what it seems at first, and if that's the case, if the cleaver gets it wrong, makes his V in the wrong direction and gives that tap . . ." She mimed a quick tapping motion. "It's over."

"What's over?"

"The diamond. It's finished. It shatters to pieces on the table."

"But I thought diamonds are the hardest substance on earth."

She waved her hand dismissively. "Hard, but not tough, not at all. You want tough you're talking nephrite jade. It's netted with fibrous layers like a web of roots. You can scarcely hurt it with a hammer. But a diamond? Hard, yes, but vulnerable if struck wrong. So there's no room for error." She looked at me. "You think I'm exaggerating."

"I don't," I protested.

"When Joseph Asscher cleaved the Cullinan—this was back in 1908—he had to have a doctor and two nurses in attendance. When he cleaved it, the release of tension, the nervous exhaustion . . . it was too much. He collapsed immediately. They had to put him in the hospital for three months." She smiled. "But he had gotten it right."

This from Ida, who supposedly disapproved of tendencies towards the dramatic.

"So when my co-worker went running to tell my cousin about my oddness—what she thought was my oddness—it worked against her, as I said. He brushed her aside and noticed me for the first time. Noticed me not as his poor cousin who had fallen so far down in the world, but as a kindred spirit. He began to talk to me about his work. He would show me the rough diamonds, have me hold them, examine them, and we would talk about them, how to release their brilliance, how to transform them into what they were meant to be."

She paused.

"That's how I ended up in Montreal, of course, but that's a different story."

"Because you turned out to be better than him?"

"What, better? I couldn't hold a candle to him. Because we fell in love with each other. Two cousins. And even if we hadn't been cousins . . . who was I? A lowly worker in his father's shop. A girl with no money. I was not exactly what my uncle Chaim had in mind for his son."

"But I thought . . ."

"Never mind Elka's stories. I'm telling you now what happened. And that what you think about your mother's diary is right. Not that it's been written in yet, but that what's meant

to be written in it has already been determined. That's why you couldn't write your poems in it. Because that's not what that book is meant to hold. When you discover what it is . . . that's when the words will flow from your pen. Not before."

I was so tired last night that I fell asleep as soon as it was dark. We'd had a bad day. Two bad days. It's the mud. We've left the path we were on, and with it the hard surface of summer that's held us until now. With each step we sink a little deeper; each step costs us twice the effort of the one before. It's as if the earth itself can no longer bear to have us walk upon it. And yet it also doesn't want to let us go. It sucks at us; we have to fight it to free our feet from its clutch. We curse it, this place that doesn't want us on its surface but doesn't want to let us go, this earth that will turn itself into another element just to spite us.

When I woke the darkness was moving. Andre was sitting up beside me, alert. At first I thought it was the earth itself that had woken me, the cursed earth turning to liquid all around us, but it was the air this time that was disturbed. Distant mortar, I thought at first—sometimes its vibration wakes me before I'm aware of its sound—but it was a disturbance of a different sort.

Listen, Andre whispered when he saw I was awake.

Then I heard it too: the fall migration, a thousand wings beating overhead.

CHAPTER 15

Lily returned home one October afternoon to find the door unlocked, the kitchen in disarray, but no sign of her mother-in-law anywhere. A raw brisket sat on the kitchen table, unwrapped but still on the butcher's paper; a handful of carrots had been thrown into the roasting pan beside it. On the stove, a pan full of chopped onions waited to be fried. It looked like Bella had been in a flurry of cooking when she realized she was missing an ingredient and had then run out to buy it.

Lily stood by the counter, by one of Bella's interrupted tasks: a half-sliced potato on the cutting board. She looked at the fan of slices spreading out from the lump that had spawned them and wondered what could have been so pressing that Bella would just put down her knife and run out like that, mid-task.

The weather had changed again; a return to summer after the cold that had frosted lawns and banisters just two days earlier. The kitchen was stuffy. Lily glanced at the window to see if it was open and saw that there was someone on the fire

escape. Her heart contracted and her grip tightened around the handle of the chopping knife that was now in her hand, though she did not remember picking it up. Her fingers ran along the blade of the knife, unconsciously, instinctively, testing it for sharpness. She moved from the counter to the window, saw that it was her mother-in-law sitting on the stairs.

"Are you all right?" she asked through the open window. Her heart was still pounding but her voice was calm.

"Ah, you're home," Bella said.

Lily had never seen Bella out on the fire escape before that moment, would not have thought her agile enough to step through the window, would certainly not have thought her interested in something as frivolous as enjoying the last rays of sun on a beautiful autumn day, which was what she appeared to be doing.

"I couldn't spend another minute in the kitchen on such a fine day," Bella said, which Lily heard as criticism, Bella's way of pointing out that it was the day before the eve of Yom Kippur, and a pre-fast meal had to be prepared, and who did Lily think had shopped for it and done most of the prep work today?

"Can I bring you out a cup of tea?" Lily asked.

There was a moment's hesitation. It was an unexpected offer, unprecedented.

"That would be nice," Bella allowed.

Lily replaced the knife beside the potato on the cutting board, put the kettle on.

"Do you know where to find everything?" Bella called through the window.

Lily ignored the implication that she would not know how to find teacups in the kitchen that had been her home

for almost three months now. She made two cups of tea and placed them on a tray, which she passed through the open window onto the landing, then she stepped through the window and joined her mother-in-law on the stairs. The air was as warm as July.

"It's beautiful, no?" Bella asked.

Indian summer, Nathan had called it that morning, this interlude that wasn't a season so much as a spell.

"*Babye Leto,*" Lily said to Bella, preferring the Russian to the English. Women's Summer. It carried with it the poignancy of this last bloom of warmth before winter, a poignancy not unlike that of the last, late blooming of a woman's beauty before its final ruin.

"*Babye Leto,*" Bella repeated with a smile. It had been years since she'd heard the term, years since she had even thought of it. It brought to mind the hard-working peasant women finally getting a chance to relax and enjoy a few days of summer, this last bit of warmth coming as it did after the harvest, after the first frost, at the end of a long summer of unrelenting work. "We used to go to see my grandparents this time of year," she said, slipping into Yiddish now. "We would take a cart as far as the river, then a boat. Often it was already cold, but sometimes we had days like this, and we'd see the people sitting out as we floated past, enjoying the sunshine, the warmth. We'd be eating our apples . . ." She could taste the sweet, crispy flesh of the apples her mother would pack for the trip, feel the smooth, waxy dome of one in her hand. "We'd wave . . ."

"Which river?" Lily asked.

"The Dnieper."

Lily nodded.

"You know the Dnieper?"

"Of course." Lily thought of the river she used to go out on with her father, that snake of a river with its intricate web of tributaries and side streams. It was not as wide or as grand as the Dnieper. She never saw anyone as they floated along. Quite often they made their crossings at night. "The apples . . . they were Antonovs?"

Bella smiled. "What they call apples here . . ."

"They're still better than the ones in Palestine."

"In Palestine they don't have the climate to grow apples. What an apple wants is a day like this, warmth and sun, to bring out its sweetness, followed by a cold night, but not so cold that it should freeze. That's what makes it perfect, what puts a bit of sour in the sweet."

Lily remembered the plum she and Nathan had shared in the first moments of their marriage, that familiar edge of tartness, the shock of it in her mouth. "Can you get Antonovs here, then?"

"Here they don't have the soil."

"Where I lived we didn't have the soil either."

"So how do you know Antonovs?"

"My father would bring them in from time to time."

It was the first mention she'd made to Bella of her father, of anyone from her family. "So, your father—was his . . . specialty . . . fruit, then?"

"Import–export," Lily said.

Bella waited to see if Lily might say any more, and when she didn't: "I bought you a *yahrzeit* candle." A memorial candle—it was customary to light it on the eve of Yom Kippur.

"Thank you," Lily said.

They finished their tea. The heat on the balcony seemed to intensify as the sun dropped lower in the sky.

"We should go in," Bella said. Nathan would be home any minute.

"Yes," Lily agreed, but neither of them made a move to go back inside.

"Someone came to see you today," Bella said.

"To see me?" Who in this city of strangers even knew of her existence?

"A woman by the name of Krakauer."

She had come that morning, just after Bella returned from her errands. Bella had recognized the woman's face from the wedding, had assumed as soon as Ida stated her name that she had come about her daughter who was throwing herself at Sol, the daughter that Bella had had the mixed pleasure of meeting just the previous week. But Ida hadn't come to talk about Elka and Sol.

"Is Lily home?" she asked.

"Lily?"

An irritated frown creased Ida's forehead at the thought of the wasted trip across town in a hot streetcar. "Does she not live here? I thought . . ."

"No, no, she lives here," Bella assured her. "But she's not home now."

"Ah," Ida said, as if she had not considered that possibility.

In that way the mother and daughter were alike, Bella thought. She remembered the dismay on Elka's face when she discovered that Sol wasn't home, the ill-concealed irritation that made it seem as if Sol's absence was in some way Bella's fault, something Bella had planned for the sole purpose of inconveniencing the young woman who had showed up unannounced on her doorstep. Bella offered the same invitation to the mother now that she had offered to the daughter a week earlier. "You're welcome to come in and wait."

Bella ushered her into the living room rather than the kitchen where she had hosted the daughter. She offered her a cold drink, which Ida declined, but she drank thirstily when Bella brought it anyway. Bella made a return trip to the kitchen to refill Ida's glass, then joined her on the sofa. She wanted to know what this woman's business was with Lily.

"You play the piano," Ida said. It was a statement, not a question. She approved of the piano's presence in that cramped, dark apartment. It spoke to her of aspirations, of sacrifices made for the sake of culture. She saw the cot behind the piano, a makeshift bedroom that only increased her appreciation of the values and priorities represented by the piano.

"My daughter plays."

"I didn't realize you had a daughter." Ida couldn't very well mention that she hadn't noticed a daughter at the wedding that she hadn't been invited to but had attended nonetheless.

"Yes," Bella said.

There was something wrong with the daughter; that much was obvious from the mother's terse response. Not so wrong that she couldn't play the piano, but wrong enough that she wasn't at the wedding and that her mother would prefer no further questions be asked. Though in the photo on the bookshelf the daughter was entirely normal to look at, quite pretty, in fact, if a bit too done up, too glamorous for a girl who would have been . . . what, sixteen, at the time the photo was taken? Which was possibly where the problem lay, Ida thought.

"She lives with you, your daughter?"

The shake of the mother's head confirmed Ida's hunch. The daughter was not living at home, but neither was she living with a husband—such information would have been freely and happily offered. The problem was of a moral sort.

"The daughters aren't easy," Ida remarked in a half-sigh that surprised Bella, the openness of it, the admission she heard in it that Ida's own daughter was also problematic. It was an openness that Bella would not have expected from this overly proud woman who had come to see her daughter-in-law.

"And it's much more difficult without a man," Bella admitted in turn. She, like her guest, was normally not the sort to pour out her life story, not to anyone, but the admission she had heard in Ida's sigh had encouraged her own. "Nina was only eleven when her father died, and her brothers were not much older, still boys."

"Elka also grew up without a father," Ida heard herself saying, surprising herself now with her own outpouring, because that's what it felt like, those seven words—an outpouring. For when had she ever put into words for another person the shame of her circumstances? "He left before Elka was even born."

Bella was well aware of the shame and sorrow behind that straightforward delivery of fact. It was an offering that demanded reciprocation, a response that would place her neither above nor beneath her guest, but beside her. It was the sort of demand Bella hadn't had to meet in years—she had made no real friends here, she realized.

"I've met your daughter," Bella said. Ida nodded, making clear that she knew of Elka's visit the previous week. "She's willful, yes, I could see that . . ."

Ida nodded again, half afraid of what was coming, but hungry for it too. She had been too alone in raising her girl. There had been no one who cared enough to venture an opinion.

"But there can be strength as well as mere stubbornness in will . . ." Bella looked at Ida. "The sort of strength that comes from knowing one's own worth."

Which you and you alone imparted to her, Ida heard just beneath Bella's words. *Which you managed to impart to her without benefit of a husband or social standing.*

"She has her moments," Ida responded. It was the closest she could come to thanking Bella for her compliment, for Bella's tactful way of letting Ida know that she had not failed with Elka as completely as she had feared. "When I think what I was like at her age . . ."

"What were you like?" Bella asked.

Their eyes met. They had embarrassed themselves now, both of them, two mature women feeling like schoolgirls, thrilling to their reflections in the eyes of the other. It was a feeling that lifted them into a type of conversation neither of them had ever expected to have again, and it was that feeling that had sent Bella out onto the fire escape later that afternoon, that long-forgotten thrill of her life being of interest to another. Not her physical life, which of course her children cared about, even Nina, but her inner life, "her soul," she would have called it once. The long-forgotten pleasure of feeling herself come alive under the attentive gaze of another, and seeing that other unfold and reveal herself in turn. It was a pleasure she wanted to savour for a little bit longer before turning herself over to the brisket that needed roasting for the pre-fast meal.

"Did she say what she wanted?" Lily asked. Was it possible Ida had already unmasked her to Bella, had aired to her mother-in-law the accusations implicit in the way she had looked at Lily that day in her store, in her refusal to have anything to do with the diamond Lily had brought her?

"She didn't," Bella said. She wondered how the two women knew each other, was half afraid to ask, but then did ask.

"I brought a stone to her a few weeks ago."

"A stone?" Bella asked.

"A diamond."

She remembered her sense of purpose as she made her way across the city to see Ida that day, a city where she had no purpose but this, she remembered feeling: to return to the living what was left to return, to return what she had been entrusted to return.

Would her madness never stop?

"She accused me of stealing it."

"And did you?"

"I don't know."

"You don't know?"

"The girl was dead. Can you steal from the dead?"

Bella didn't answer. She was thinking about the pair of boots she had taken off the feet of a corpse years earlier, during the civil war that had followed the revolution. It was an act of acquisition that would have been unthinkable, criminal, had the woman been alive to feel the loss. But was it theft to have taken them off of someone who would never take another step, would never feel the ice forming around the soles of her feet? Was it a crime to take from the dead what was needed to sustain the living?

"The girl it belonged to was a relative of Ida's," Lily said.

"You knew one of her relatives?"

There was a calmness to Bella's voice, a matter-of-factness that was soothing.

"Her cousin. I didn't know her. I was charged with bringing her to a place where she'd be safer, but when I arrived at the place I was to meet her . . . something had gone wrong."

Was there truth in Ida's assumption that Lily was just a

common thief? Lily wondered. That it was profit that had motivated her? Acquisition? Had Ida seen in Lily what she herself only feared? An irregularity of conduct that in the light of peacetime revealed itself as sin? A flaw that was not merely circumstantial in nature, but essential to who she was, inseparable from her very character? Did the extraordinary vision Ida was rumoured to have with regard to the quality of a stone's worth extend to the human heart?

She was "charged with bringing her"? Bella wondered. What did that mean? "You . . . helped people?"

"I moved people. I knew the landscape," she explained. "I knew people who would help. From before, my father's work. Whether it was helpful in the end to those I moved . . ." Lily shrugged.

"Your father's work . . . ?" Bella asked.

"He was a smuggler. Though that's not what he started out to be."

Did anyone ever become what they started out to be? Bella wondered.

"He was a ferryman. Like my grandfather, like my great-grandfather. That's what we were, my family. The men. Ferry-men. The river was the source of my family's livelihood for generations. But then the revolution in Russia, the war . . . After the war, the Polish–Soviet war, our river became the new border. Do you know it, the Slutsk?"

"Only by name."

It was no secret, the smuggling along the new state's borders. Even before Bella and Joseph had left Berdichev, smuggling had been identified as one of the major problems facing the new regime. *Contraband derails the decree on the nationalization of foreign trade, turning it into a fiction,* she

remembered reading in a newspaper just months before they left; and at a meeting she had attended in Montreal years later a guest lecturer had told them that the volume of contraband and numbers of people involved in the smuggling during the twenties and early thirties were higher than in any other era in Russian—and perhaps world—history.

"All of a sudden no one was allowed to cross it any more," Lily said. "So, crossing it became lucrative. You can't imagine what they lacked there, between the disruptions caused by the war and then, just a few years later, the redirecting of the most basic goods away from domestic, everyday use . . ."

Towards the collective effort to build a better, fairer future, Bella thought.

" . . . kerosene, matches, shoes . . . They banned artisan production of shoes in 1932 in favour of state production, then underestimated by tens of thousands how many to produce, so half the people in the western regions were barefoot . . ."

Poor children had always gone barefoot, Bella thought. At least now there was no stigma attached to the condition.

". . . leather goods of any kind, religious articles, of course, thread, needles, kettles, cooking pots, any household goods that were made of metal—they redirected all metal for industrial use in the 1930s, it suddenly became illegal to own a pot—" She shook her head at the memory of it. "It provided a living my grandfather and great-grandfather could not even have dreamed of . . . two homes, one of which we used only in summer, education for all of us, fine furnishings, clothing . . ."

"A real entrepreneur," Bella said, immediately regretting the sarcasm, fearing it would shut the small chink that had finally opened in her daughter-in-law's outer shell, but Lily only smiled.

There was relief for her in Bella's sarcasm, a familiar tone, not unlike that of her aunts when they would discuss her father's sudden rise in the world.

"He would take me with him. Against objections from my mother, who didn't want a daughter of hers mixed up in . . . well, you can imagine." She glanced at Bella. "It was my mother who was right, in fact. My father's work was dangerous, difficult. He should not have taken me with him. He should have preferred that I stay safely at home in the soft bed that he could afford to buy for me, benefiting from the education and polishing that his own parents could not provide for him. But at the end of the day it was his bad judgment that saved me. Had my mother prevailed, as she did with my younger sisters, had he not taken me with him, had I not learned from him what he knew . . . Not just the practicalities that he taught me—his knowledge of the land and how to traverse it, the people he knew who would help us—but the withstanding of fear, of bodily discomfort of every sort . . ."

Bella nodded again. "And the girl? Mrs. Krakauer's cousin?"

"I don't know what happened."

"She wasn't there?"

"Oh, she was. She was exactly where she was supposed to be—I was to pick her up in a village I knew. But she was dead."

The word itself—*toit* in Yiddish—forced an ending, Lily thought. That final *t*. There was no hanging vowel or soft consonant that could be rolled or extended, no bridge of any sort to whatever would follow, just that word and the full stop of the mouth that it forced.

"I don't know how she died," Lily said, though Bella hadn't

asked. "She had been robbed . . ." She glanced at Bella again. "The payment was gone."

"What payment?"

"For her passage."

Did the shock show on her face? Bella would wonder later. Her shock that payment would have been required to save the life of a girl whose life had barely had a chance to begin? It must have, because Lily's next words were justification.

"We needed it for food, medicine," Lily said. "Not just for the two of us. There were others. An encampment . . ."

Bella nodded.

"I think she'd been ill. From something she ate, perhaps." The cat. The cat that Andre had told her was squirrel and that could well have been dead, septic, when he found it.

"You think it was illness that killed her?"

"It could have been."

"But you're not certain."

"No." Lily said. "But a person wouldn't have to have killed her to rob her."

The girl had been robbed, it was true, Lily thought, but not everything had been taken. The two diamonds, yes, the two polished diamonds were gone, but not the identity card, the notebook, the last diamond. And why not? Why had he left them?

"There was a stone on her—a diamond. The one I brought to Ida."

Why had Ida come here today? Lily wondered again. To unmask her? But as who? To accuse her? But of what?

"It was rough. Unpolished." Without value, Ida had told her. "That's the only reason he left it behind."

"He?"

"The thief. And her ID card was also still on her. Which is more difficult to explain." She looked at Bella. "As the Germans retreated, a Jewish ID acquired value. Anyone would know that. Anyone would know that it could open certain doors for the right customer." She was still looking at Bella, wasn't sure if Bella understood. "A random thief would have taken it," she explained.

"So . . . it wasn't a random thief?"

"It wasn't. No."

"You know the man who robbed her, then?"

"I do," Lily said.

"It was . . . your . . . comrade?"

"It was," Lily said. "Andre."

"Andre," Bella repeated. The man the girl had trusted to take her to safety.

"He didn't kill her," Lily said.

"But he left her," Bella said, and Lily didn't disagree. "And he left you the diamond," Bella said. The worthless diamond. "For your payment."

Her payment for a job uncompleted, a job for which no payment was due and for which no amount of repayment would ever suffice.

"And the ID," Lily said.

"For you to sell."

"For me to use," Lily said. "I was afraid of the Russians. They had already arrested my father when they took over in '39. We went to bed one night as respected citizens and woke up enemies of the people. They took him away. Andre knew I was afraid of being caught by them—it was the Soviets who were liberating Poland. Of being repatriated. To them. So he left me the ID."

"A thoughtful man."

"He was trying to get rid of me."

Bella looked at her.

"He wasn't just my comrade."

"You . . . cared for him?"

"Very much. But he didn't care for me quite as much, it seems. He betrayed me with her. It's all there. In the notebook."

"What notebook?"

"The girl had a notebook, and he left that for me too. I thought at first he had left it simply because it had no value to him, the ramblings of a girl who'd served her purpose—I'm sorry to be so crude. But I realize now that he left it for a reason. He left it so I could read with my own eyes how he'd betrayed me. So I wouldn't try to follow him, I suppose."

"Follow him where?" asked Bella.

"Into Russia. The Soviet Union. That's where he wanted to live. It's the place he dreamed of—he was of a different class from me. For me there would be no opportunities there, just the opposite. But for him? Why wouldn't he dream of a society like that, where his origins wouldn't always block the path ahead?"

The tide had turned by then, and it was time to turn with it. It was time to take what could be taken to fuel a future. Which is exactly what he had done, Lily thought. He had taken what he had needed. And he had left the rest behind.

"He was a butcher's son. And illegitimate to boot. My parents almost killed me when I brought him home. That they would have worked so hard, only to have me marry someone so clearly beneath us in status, education, manner. They thought it was my little rebellion, I guess, but it wasn't. It was love. It was—"

"You were married to him?"

"I still am, I suppose."

She could have said no, Bella thought, but she didn't. Because she still felt married to him, the first husband, the one she obviously still loved though he had betrayed her with another, though he was neither worthy of her nor decent, though he—

"He didn't kill Ida's cousin," Lily said.

"And you know that for a fact?"

"Not for a fact, no, but she looked peaceful." She had looked like her youngest sister had in sleep. "Would she have looked peaceful had she been murdered at the hands of the man she loved?"

The sun had dipped by then behind the houses across the alley. They were sitting entirely in shadow, though it was warm shadow, pleasant on the skin.

"I don't deny that her death was convenient for me." He had left it for her, the ID that he had freed for her, the ID of the girl with whom he'd betrayed her, with its place of birth so far from the Soviet sphere, its name with an attached history so different from her own family's. His payment to be rid of her, she had come to think. His insurance that she wouldn't try to follow him. "Does that mean I caused it?"

Bella didn't answer. She was trying to understand what her daughter-in-law was telling her, what it really meant to have survived the destruction of her entire world only to be betrayed by the last person standing, the person who perhaps mattered most to her. And what was the scope of the betrayal? Lily didn't seem to know, was afraid to know, perhaps. The love between them, yes, their marriage . . . but what beyond?

"I don't think she suffered in the end," Lily said.

"Maybe not," Bella answered. The only comfort she could offer. "And what was her name?" she asked. The girl whose final payment was the ID card that proved convenient to someone else.

"Lily Azerov."

"Ah . . ." An exhalation more than statement or comment.

They said nothing more for a while, sat in silence in the deepening dusk.

"And your name?" Bella asked.

"It doesn't matter."

"It matters."

Soon, very soon, Nathan would be home. It would be time to go inside, get supper on the table.

"Yanna," she said.

"Yanna," Bella repeated.

How long had it been since she had said her own name? How long since she had heard it? "Yanna Marissa," she murmured. She closed her eyes to be alone with all it carried.

CHAPTER 16

Bella died in September 1972. It was early in the month. The whole family was gathered at Sol and Elka's to watch the first game of the Soviet–Canada hockey series, a contest that we expected to be brutal and sweet, more demonstration than contest, really. We would show the Soviets how the game is played.

I was five months pregnant with my daughter, Sophie, at the time and felt so much movement within me throughout the game that I was convinced I was carrying a boy. We would name him Phil, I thought, after Phil Esposito, who scored for Canada within the first minute of play. As I looked at Reuben, though, I knew that in the matter of naming our children, as in so many other aspects of our life together, tradition would rule.

"I'm not feeling well," Bella said at one point in the second period.

"None of us are," Sol said. The Soviets had pulled ahead by then and were outskating and outshooting as well as outscoring us.

Bella went to my old bedroom to lie down, and when Sol went upstairs after the game to tell her the disastrous final score, she was dead.

She was seventy-seven when she died, and had seemingly been in good health until the end of the first period of that hockey game, but at the *shiva* Ida told us Bella hadn't been feeling well the last months of her life, had been finding it an effort to get her shopping done, to make herself a cup of coffee in the morning. She had been afraid that one morning she simply wouldn't have the strength to get up at all, would not even be able to pick up the phone to call anyone, so Ida had been calling her every morning.

"I didn't know that," I said.

"How would you?" Ida answered, and I wasn't sure if she was accusing me of being a selfish, non-attentive granddaughter or acknowledging that Bella was always someone who had kept her troubles to herself.

"She loved roses," the rabbi said at one point in the eulogy, which I also hadn't known, but then, who didn't like roses? It seemed an oddly generic type of detail to put into a eulogy, one that blurred Bella into a fuzzier, more Hallmark version of herself, rather than bringing her more sharply into focus. I wondered if there was list of safe, generic details that someone had compiled so that rabbis and other clergy could choose from it when writing eulogies for people they barely knew, but when I said that aloud, Ida Pearl shook her head.

"I'm the one who told him."

On summer evenings she and Bella would often walk around the neighbourhood admiring the roses in their neighbours' gardens, she told me. Bella liked the older varieties that hadn't given up their scent for the sake of a more intricate lay-

ering of petals. She thought that showy roses with no sweetness to their petals were like the shaved, deodorized women
that Canada produced.

"She told you that?"

"You think I'm making it up?"

"I never really knew her," I said.

"But you loved her," Ida answered, and again I wasn't sure
if she meant that as accusation or comfort. Was it less important or more important to know someone than to love them?

Bella left me her candlesticks, an enamel butterfly pin that
I had never seen her wear and a sealed envelope with my name
on it.

She had left envelopes for each of her grandchildren. Jeffrey tore his open immediately. I watched his face as he read
it, how full of feeling it was, feeling he tried to make light of.

"So now I know what she really thought of me," he said.

The rest of us saved our letters for when we could read
them in private.

My dear Ruthie, I read when I got home that evening.
Her voice was so clear in my mind that it was hard to believe
I would never hear it again. It was a voice soft and heavy
with the Yiddish she had spoken before she learned English.
She addressed me as a granddaughter, but appealed to me as
a mother. The birth of my first child was still a few months
away, so it seemed Bella had expected to live longer than she
had, long enough to see me become a mother. She appealed to
my own understanding as a mother that there are times when
you don't know the best thing to do to help your children,
the children in this case being me and my father. She told
me about the conversation she had had with my mother on
the back stairs of the apartment on Clark Street that warm

afternoon on the eve of Yom Kippur in the autumn of 1946. She told me about the life my mother had lived before, and of the husband she had loved and still loved three months into her marriage to my father, a man who had betrayed her and then possibly murdered the girl with whom he had betrayed her, the girl—Ida's own cousin—whose name my mother then bore out of Europe. She told me my mother's real name and how the person my mother had been re-emerged in the telling of it—*Right before my eyes, like the chicks I used to watch chipping through their shells*—and how once Yanna Marissa emerged from the outer shell that she had taken on, Bella knew she would stand up and walk away. *She had to,* Bella wrote. *How could she not? How could she stay when she was no longer the person your father had married and no longer the person who had married your father, and when I knew and Ida knew, but your father she hadn't told?*

The way a thing begins is how it continues, my father often said. What begins in deception continues in deception. I knew he believed that, but would it really have been too late three months into their marriage for my mother to correct the deception with which that marriage had begun? Could they really not have made a clean start had she wanted to, given the circumstances of her life at that time, the reality of where and what she had just come from? They could have, I thought. Had she wanted to.

What Bella hadn't known was that my mother was pregnant at the time. She would have left immediately after that conversation on the stairs if she hadn't been, Bella thought. *She would have left that night, or within days, and the fact that she didn't was a credit to her. She didn't have to stay. She could have left at any point, taking you with her in her belly.*

But she didn't, and why? That's what I've had to ask myself. Why did she stay when, in her heart, she was already gone? Because she had morals, your mother, despite everything that had happened to her and what she'd seen and been party to. She had morals and in her heart she was good. She knew you'd be better off with us than wherever she was going and so she left you. To be better off. That was her gift to you, to leave you with a family she knew would love you and raise you as you needed. And you were her gift to us.

It was a nice spin on it, I thought, but I couldn't really buy it. If I had been a box of chocolates, yes. Women gave chocolates as gifts. We gave pretty objects, flowers, books . . . but we didn't give our babies. As atonement, then? Could that be what Bella really meant, but she didn't want to come right out and say that my mother's role in the death of Ida's cousin might have made her feel she had to offer her own baby as atonement? Possibly. But I couldn't buy that either. It had a neatness to its logic that human emotion didn't obey.

As if sensing the turn of my thoughts, my own unborn baby stirred inside me. I rested my hand on her as I read further.

I should have told your father what she'd told me. Not right away. I don't mean right away. She had taken me into her confidence and I'm not a person who breaks another's confidence. And I felt sympathy for her. More than she ever knew. I think she may have thought I didn't.

There it was, then: Bella's confession of her part in driving my mother away. Everyone in my family thought there was something they had done or hadn't done, I'd come to realize. Some failing, a discomfort with her that they couldn't hide. Ida most of all, but all of them, right down to Sol, who had rejected my mother at the very outset of the new life on which

she was trying to embark. Bella was probably telling the truth when she said she felt a sympathy for my mother. When she sensed that my mother wouldn't stay—couldn't stay, Bella stressed—she probably really did hope that my mother would be able to make a new life for herself somewhere else. But she was probably also relieved that that new life would not be lived in the core of Bella's own family. It was a relief that she would not have been able to help but convey, and that then would have compounded the reasons for that young woman to be unable to stay. In Bella's mind, in any case.

But after she left I should have told him. I know that now, but at the time I thought it would only hurt him more. He was still young when she left him and the marriage had been so brief, and based on falseness. It was more a dream than a marriage, your parents' time together. I didn't want to add anything else to the pain he already felt. It would not have changed anything for the better. It would not have brought her back.

So she didn't tell him. She didn't tell anyone—except perhaps Ida Pearl—that she knew my mother's real name and some of the circumstances of her life before and during the war. To protect my father, she said. And it didn't occur to her that sparing her son's pride might be hurting me in some way. She swore that to me.

I wanted you to be happy.

To move forward in my life, in other words, away from the tragedies of the past. As she had done. Could I really fault her for that?

There was a certain cowardice, I thought, in Bella's waiting as she did until she would not have to face my response to her deception. But there was generosity in it too. She could

easily have taken her long, dishonest silence with her to her grave, but she hadn't. She had chosen instead to risk my good memories of her and to incite my anger when she could no longer defend herself against it in order to set right what she felt by then was a wrong she had done to me. Because she was a moral person, I thought, and in her heart she was good.

My response to Bella's revelation was muted. It had been nine years by then since I had received anything from my mother. I didn't know why the rocks had stopped any more than I knew why they had started. I would have liked to know, of course. I wondered if she was all right, if there was something in my lack of response that had disappointed her, if she had hoped, perhaps, that I would take more initiative, as Nina had once suggested, once she had re-established contact with me by sending the rocks, but I had accepted by then that I would probably never know. My mother was like a death that lay buried within me, a muffled mix of sadness, dread and regret beneath the layers of my busy, ongoing, ever-expanding life, but I wasn't tormented by it. I felt an unease within myself that I knew was related to her, though it felt diffuse, unbound to anything that specific. I felt also a sense of incompleteness, but was it any worse than what other people experienced? I didn't know, and I could push it away more easily as my own adult life moved forward, even if there were times those feelings sharpened. The previous spring, for example, when Reuben and I had taken our first trip to Israel.

Was it because we had just made the decision to start our own family and the thought of becoming a mother myself raised the spectre of my own lost, failed mother, the broken chain of continuity from one generation to the next? Probably. We had arrived in Tel Aviv, and I had wanted to retrace my

mother's steps, to stand in places where I knew for a fact that she had once stood. We had sought out the building where Ida's sister Sonya had once lived, only to discover it was gone, replaced by a high-rise hotel, one in the long line of high-rises that had been built along the shoreline and that now blocked the sea breeze that had brought relief to the city from the oppressive heat of the summer when my mother and Nina had lived here.

"I'm sorry," Reuben said as we stood in the fumes of the tourist buses that were idling in the driveway of the hotel.

"It's okay," I said. He took my hand. "Let's go for a swim," I suggested, and we did.

And later on that trip we returned to our room in another of the high-rise hotels that now dominated the shoreline, obliterating any hint of what had been there before, and conceived the child I now felt coming to life inside me.

I took in the information that Bella had given me, but it was not the bombshell she seemed to have worried it might be. I did not read that letter and feel the layers of my present life giving way, my mother's name the proverbial warm blade melting a path to the agitated longing and failure at my core. The acute sadness I felt that fall was actually about Bella, a real person who had been with me every step of my life until then, whose voice and cooking and book recommendations and admonishments and praise and less-than-subtle guidance and awkward pats on whatever part of me was within reach were still so vivid that I kept waiting for her to reappear.

My father too did not seem on the verge of falling apart from Bella's belated disclosure. If he might once have been upset that the wife whom he adored had confided in his mother and not in him, he was over it by then. A quarter-century had

passed. It was 1972, not 1947. He was thoughtful and quiet when I told him, and there was an expression on his face that might have been sorrow, but if it was it could as easily have been sorrow for my mother, not himself. Or maybe it was sorrow for me. I don't know. As for him, he loved Sandra now. They lived together in her house on the Lakeshore, where they listened to music and walked Oscar. (And when Oscar died, they walked Sadie. Also a Newfie. Also huge.) He had learned to read music, and had taken up the cello, which he played for hours after work, Sandra told me, and while she thought maybe he was improving, Sadie always got up and walked out of the room and resettled herself with a sigh as far away from my father and his cello as she could get.

It was with the birth of my daughter that I felt a sorrow so powerful I thought it might pull me under. It was like a dark undertow of the amazed, protective love that flowed into me the first time I held her and looked into her searching, bewildered little newborn face. With each ritual of new motherhood I felt it: the counting with Reuben of ten tiny perfect fingers and ten tiny perfect toes, the discovery of every inch of her newborn perfection, learning how to feed her, to change her, to anticipate her needs, to interpret the timbre of her cries, the gazing into eyes that slowly came into focus and gazed back at me. Could my mother possibly have done the same with me? I wondered. She had to have, I thought. But she couldn't have, I also thought, because if she had she would not have been able to leave me.

When Sophie first smiled at the sound of my voice, I understood that I too had smiled at the sound of my mother's voice, had followed the sound of that voice around the room as Sophie began following mine. And as Sophie began to coo at

me—sooner than I expected, younger—I knew that I too had
cooed at my mother and that it had been a sound as soft and
sweet and melting as Sophie's. I had probably cooed at her the
day she left, maybe as she was preparing the bottles of formula
for others to find. And as I understood this, a grief took hold
of me that was as deep and strong as any love I had ever felt.

I didn't speak about it to anyone, not even Reuben. I felt
too ashamed to be feeling such a deep, pulling sorrow in the
face of the joyful miracle that was Sophie. And I felt afraid,
because it had a life of its own, this sorrow. I was afraid of
where it might take me. But I hoped that if I kept moving forward, caring for Sophie, loving her, living the life that I knew I
wanted, it would recede without pulling me with it. And it did,
over time. As it had receded the first time I had experienced it.

But what had it been like for me, that first grief, I wondered, the desperate longing that I must have felt for the warm
living centre of my world that had simply ceased to be? How
had I experienced it with no way to understand it? Who had
comforted me? Bella? My father? Not Elka, who had only
been seventeen then, too young yet to become the surrogate
mother she would later be to me. Did they even know I needed
comfort? Or did they think I was too young to feel the impact
of what had happened?

I couldn't think about it, didn't want to think about it.
I attended to the ongoing minutiae of my everyday life, and
it was a full, busy life. Sophie was as active and demanding
as any healthy baby and then as any healthy toddler. I was
completing a master's degree, and beginning my work as a
paper conservator. I became pregnant again, sooner than we
had planned, had a son, Joey, then another, Sam. We bought a
duplex in Côte-St-Luc, thought about moving to Toronto like

so many of Montreal's anglophones of our generation, then decided to improve our French instead and take advantage of the depressed real estate prices caused by the city's fleeing English. We bought a house just a few blocks from where I had grown up. I was surrounded by people who loved me and whom I loved in return. I was part of a noisy, boisterous family. I wasn't always happy, but I wasn't unhappy.

IT WASN'T UNTIL 1982 that I decided to find her. It was summer and we were on a family road trip. For reasons that escape me now, Reuben and I had thought it would be fun to drive all the way across Canada and back with three children under the age of eleven. We had been driving for two days when we reached Wawa, Ontario, on the north shore of Lake Superior. Sam and Joey had been bickering for several hours by the time we drove into town. Sophie was pressed up hard against the car door to create as much distance as she could between herself and the rest of us and was reading a comic book, pretending she was somewhere else. I turned around to yell at the boys and utter threats about sending them home on the train, and when I turned back I was looking at a huge goose that seemed to be rising straight out of my dreams. It was a massive statue of a Canada Goose, Wawa's claim to fame.

"Stop the car!" I said. There was such urgency in my tone that Reuben veered to the side of the road.

"Do you have to throw up?" Joey asked me.

"No," I said. "Look at the goose."

It was an impressive goose. None of the children found it strange that I would have commanded Reuben to stop for its

sake. Only Reuben found it odd. He was looking at me, not the goose.

"She was here," I said to him, but it was more than that. It was as if the sight of that goose had released the latch on the place within myself in which she resided and she had shot up through all the layers of my life to its surface.

"Who was here?" Sophie asked.

"My mother."

I had told them about her before, how she had come after the war but not been able to stay, and that I didn't know why and I didn't know where she had gone, and yes it was sad, but having sadness doesn't mean you can't have happiness too. We'd been through the whole story, our own personal fairy tale: the mysterious mother who disappeared and then sent her daughter beautiful rocks from beautiful places. There were times it didn't even feel real to me any more. But at that moment it felt real. I didn't know why, couldn't explain the impact of that stupid goose on my psyche any more than I could explain anything related to my mother.

My children picked up on the opening in me. "Do you miss her?" Sophie asked me. She was still at the age where her worst fear was losing her mother. They all were. Are you sad? they wanted to know. A little, I admitted. Joey thought we should go to the beach and look for a rock like the one she had sent me from there, and we did go to a beach, though I don't know if it was the one she had walked twenty years ago when she sent the last rock to me. We found many rocks, some of them beautiful, but none with the beauty and pleasing shape of the banded agate she had sent me. My children's questions continued. Do you think she's sad? Do you think she misses you? Why did she send you the rocks? Why did she stop? Did

she love you? Do you think she'd like to see you? Would you like to see her? Do you think she'd want to meet us? Is she dead?

Each question was one I wanted to answer. I wanted to answer those questions more than I had wanted anything for a very long time.

WHEN WE GOT HOME a few weeks later I called a friend of Nina's who was a private detective. According to Nina, at least. He was actually a forensic accountant and couldn't help me, but he put me in touch with Paul, who worked for a collection agency.

"Those guys can find anyone," Nina's friend assured me, but Paul was less confident.

"It isn't much to go on," Paul said when I called him. "Two names, neither one of which is a surname, a geographic area that comprises more than half the country . . ."

I pictured him in a grimy office of the Sam Spade variety, but for all I knew he had a sprawl of office space on a top floor of Place Ville-Marie looking over the whole sweep of the city and river. Interest rates were in the double digits then—there was lots of money to be made in debt collection. The sigh at the other end of the line, though, suggested that my first fantasy was closer to the truth.

"Leave it with me and I'll see what I can do," he said.

I didn't expect to hear another word from him, but it wasn't more than a couple of weeks before he called me back. "Yanna Marissa Eglitis," he said. "Birthdate, December 3rd, 1919. Currently residing in Thunder Bay, Ontario. Sound possible?"

I nodded.

"You still there?"

"Yes," I managed to say.

"I can't be certain, but it's all I could come up with. It's the name that helped. Unusual combination, Yanna Marissa. Aren't too many of those around. If it had been Susie Q, forget it."

I smiled as if he could see my polite response to his feeble joke. "Thank you," I said.

"I have an address too. You want it?"

He gave me a street address in Thunder Bay and then there was silence and I knew it was my turn to say something.

"Thank you," I said again. And in the continuing silence: "What do I owe you?"

"Your first-born. Ha ha. Just kidding. You don't owe me anything."

"I'm sure you normally charge for your time. I'd like to pay you."

"If it turns out to be Mom, send me a photo of the happy reunion. That's payment enough."

I took it as a sign, that show of generosity from a man I sensed wasn't generous by nature.

"A sign of what?" Carrie asked me when I called her to tell her. She was exhausted, I could hear it in her voice. She and Charles Blumenthal had three children by then, but they were younger than mine, and she worked full time as a Crown prosecutor in Toronto. She didn't have time for signs. "Eglitis," she said. "I think that's Latvian."

"How do you know that?"

Her deep, familiar laugh. "I get out more than you do."

It wouldn't be hard. My workday involved entering a climate-controlled room to restore old documents corroded by

the highly acidic ink with which they'd been written.

"It's certainly not a Jewish name," she said.

"I'm aware of that."

"So?" Carrie asked.

"So what?" I asked, thinking she was still on the fact that my mother had a non-Jewish last name.

"You think you're ready to give up being motherless?"

I WROTE TO HER that evening. It was not a difficult letter to write, perhaps because none of it felt quite real to me. The most difficult part was deciding what to call her. *Dear Ms. Eglitis,* I wrote. That was part of what made it feel unreal, perhaps. I was not a person who could possibly have a mother called Ms. Eglitis living in Thunder Bay, Ontario. I identified myself to Ms. Eglitis and told her I had reason to believe she might be my mother, and wondered if she might have any interest in meeting me. I could come to Thunder Bay at her convenience. I didn't offer further explanations. If she was my mother, she wouldn't need them. If she wasn't, it didn't matter what she thought of the letter.

I signed it, *Sincerely, Ruth.*

I had a response within a week. When I came home from work I saw the envelope lying on the floor in our front hallway, just as I had seen the first package as it had fallen through the mail slot. I saw the handwriting, the only part of her that was familiar to me.

Dear Ruth, Thank you for contacting me. I would like to see you whenever it is convenient for you. Yours, Yanna Marissa Eglitis, née Chorover.

She certainly wasn't gushy. In that, at least, my lifelong fantasies had been accurate. But then, my letter hadn't exactly been spilling over with long-repressed love and longing either. As for the formal awkwardness of the signing-off, I sensed that had been the hardest part of the letter for her to write. How does a mother sign a letter to a daughter she abandoned thirty-five years earlier? What does she call herself? Especially when the name she had been using at the time of the daughter's birth was false? She'd packed a lot of information into that sign-off: that she was in fact Jewish, had been born with a Jewish surname, in any case; that she had remarried since leaving my father. And in that *yours*—not *sincerely,* as I had written—I read that she still felt herself, in some way, to be mine.

I decided I would go right after the month-long cycle of fall holidays that begin with Rosh Hashana and end with Simchat Torah. I would take the bus.

"Why would you take the bus?" Reuben asked. "That's two days and a night's travel each way. A flight will have you there in two hours."

"I don't want to get there in two hours," I said. I wasn't sure why I needed the trip to take more time than that. Did I imagine a slow shedding of the accumulated layers of myself as the bus tediously covered each of the miles that would take me to my beginning? Maybe I did, and maybe Reuben sensed that—feared at some level just what I might slough off along the way. Certainly he had his own set of concerns about the trip I was about to make. I knew that, which was why I could forgive him the next comment he made.

"It is the very beginning of the school year," he said. He didn't add anything about how busy his practice was, or about

how much the kids needed me to be around just as the school year was gearing up. Not out loud.

"I have to go," I said.

"But do you have to go now?"

"Yes, now," I said.

He didn't argue with that, but neither did he convey the encouragement and support I had expected. I could have interpreted his reticence and hesitation as a sign, just as I had interpreted Paul's generosity to be one, but decided not to.

"You'll be fine," I said.

His answering expression suggested he might not be. He was a man with a medical degree and a thriving practice as a pulmonologist, but he obviously thought it beyond his capabilities to read the instructions on a package of spaghetti. And making a bed also seemed to require higher spatial and physical skills than he believed he possessed.

"How long do you think you'll be gone?" he asked.

"I have no idea."

"I think you need to have *some* idea," he said.

I understood that his concern was not only for himself and how he was going to manage the household and children, that he was worried about me, about sending me off alone into the emotional abyss that was my mother, but I couldn't attend to his worry at that moment.

"Well, I don't," I said.

I DID TAKE THE BUS, and Reuben and the kids accompanied me to the station to see me off. When we got to the station Nina was there, and then Sol and Elka showed up. And then,

just as I was about to board the bus, my father and Sandra arrived. We all stood for a few minutes, trying to act casual, talking about how long the trip might take, with all the stops along the way, and if the weather would hold and if it was possible I might see snow once I got past Sudbury, even though it was still only the middle of October. I suspected that if Jeffrey hadn't been living in Palo Alto, and Mitch and Chuck in Toronto, they also would have booked off work that morning to stand around talking about the weather and bus route.

Finally Sol said, "Okay, go already," and took me into one of his bear hugs, and I kissed each of them in turn, Reuben last, though it was the feel of my father's hand on the side of my head and ear that lingered as I boarded the bus. I felt a bit like a child leaving for summer camp, a mix of dread and excitement in my gut as I smiled bravely and waved at the family I loved receding behind me. And like a kid I tore into my lunch as soon as we hit the highway, though it wasn't even nine in the morning. I ate two cheese sandwiches and all the cookies that were supposed to last for three days, which left me feeling nauseated—but that smothered some of the anxiety I had been feeling. It also made me sleepy. I slept for a few hours and when I awoke I was alone on what felt like a great adventure.

I didn't think about what was ahead, didn't worry about what was behind. I just sat with my face to the window, watching the endless boreal forest. Many of the trees had changed colour, but under a low, grey sky the golds, ochres, reds and oranges of the dying leaves, interspersed as they were with dark evergreens and ragged outcrops of grey rock, looked more bleak and foreboding than pretty. A sign? I hoped not. At every stop, I stepped outside for air that was fresher and crisper the farther north we drove. It didn't snow.

Once my sandwiches and cookies were gone I barely ate again. I drank coffee and water, bought a banana at one of the stations along the way. I wasn't consciously fasting, but I enjoyed the slightly altered state produced by an empty stomach, interrupted sleep and no one but myself for company. It had been many years since I had been alone. The only time I was not in the presence of people whose love for me was both a comfort and a demand was when I sank into the warm bath at the end of each day. I wanted the life I had made, a life that padded me from the sense of separateness and difference from everyone around me that I had felt as a child. I had constructed it every bit as consciously as Elka had constructed hers, but it was bracing to be alone, bracing to have an empty stomach and empty mind and to be travelling along a ribbon of road cut through a vast and unforgiving wilderness.

We arrived in Thunder Bay in the early afternoon of the following day. The sun had come out and the water of the lake sparkled blue in its light. The trees were also suddenly beautiful, glowing like living fires in the sun. I had thought I would go to my hotel, check in and unpack when I arrived—I had promised Reuben I'd call. But instead I took a taxi directly to the address Paul had given me.

The taxi ride took longer than I had expected. "It's on the outskirts of town," the driver told me. It was a quiet area with ranchers and wood-frame houses set on large lots, most of them tidy and well tended. The taxi stopped in front of a one-and-a-half-storey, white clapboard house with black shutters and window boxes filled with orange flowers.

"This is it," the driver said. I realized we had been sitting for more than a few moments outside the house and I had made no move to pay him.

"I'm sorry," I said, fumbling in my purse to find my wallet. I paid him, and he got out to retrieve my suitcase from the trunk. I had forgotten about my suitcase. I should have left it in a locker at the bus station, I thought. It was heavier than I had remembered as I half carried, half dragged it up the front walk—a walk lined with leafy plants, none of whose names I knew, in various shades of autumn golds and reds. Someone was an attentive gardener. My mother?

I had told her what day I was arriving, but regretted now that I hadn't called ahead from the bus station. I stood at her door for a long time, unsure what to do. Finally I rang the doorbell, but I heard nothing from within the house. She could well be out, and then what? I had sent the taxi away and could not make it back into town with the suitcase I was carrying. But as I thought about what to do, where I might temporarily stow the suitcase, I heard the approach of someone on the other side of the door.

The door opened and there she was, a flesh-and-blood woman in her early sixties, with white hair pulled smoothly back to reveal the high Slavic bones of her face, and the eyes like mine that were set within it.

She looked at me, I looked at her.

"Oh my," she said, and her eyes filled with tears, and her hand came up to touch my face, almost as if to check if I were real.

I made no answering touch. I was mesmerized by her face, its angles and planes, the brimming blue eyes, the mouth that was both wide and thin, and that had to have once brushed itself against my skin. I was looking for myself in its structure and expression.

"Will you come in?" she asked, and I stepped into a warm space that smelled of coffee and baking cake.

I left my suitcase by the door, and sat where she indicated I should, on the sofa facing a fireplace where a low fire was burning. She perched beside me on the edge of the sofa, her hands on her knees, her body half twisted so she could face me. She looked almost birdlike, perched as she was, peering at me closely but also poised for flight. There was no excess in her, not so much as a thin layer of fat between the pale, smooth skin of her face and the bones just beneath it.

I had not taken off my jacket and was suddenly too warm. As I started to remove it, she made the self-deprecating gestures of negligent hostesses the world over. The *Here, let me take that from you, what was I thinking asking you in and not taking your coat?* was unvoiced but understood as she took my jacket from me and went to hang it up. Was that how she had acted when she came out of the kitchen that day to tell Elka that she had to run out and buy milk, and that of course she wouldn't allow Elka to run that errand, that she wasn't the sort of hostess to invite a guest over and then send her out to buy her own milk? And as I wondered that, I noticed again the inviting smells of coffee and cake that were the exact smells that must have filled our home the day she left me. I had never imagined that part of the scene before now, the brewing coffee and baking cake that Elka must have smelled when she walked into my parents' living room, that must have hung in the air after my mother had left and Elka sat there with me, waiting for her. Was my mother also aware that she had filled her home with the same smells that had engulfed us the last time we were in each other's presence? I wondered. It was thirty-five years later and a different living room, yes, but with the same smells in the air it could have been the same moment, and it was possible to imagine that in the next moment she

wouldn't tell Elka she had to go out and buy milk, but would
pick me up and kiss my belly, and time and experience would
unfold along an entirely different line of life.

"I've made coffee. Do you drink coffee?"

"I do. Yes. Thank you."

She disappeared into the kitchen and I remained on the
sofa. It was a small house, and the living room had just
enough room for the furniture it held: the sofa I was sitting
on, the coffee table between me and the fireplace, the two arm-
chairs on either side of the fireplace. The window was on the
wall behind me, the door to the kitchen somewhere off to my
right, as was the stairway leading to the upper floor. The floor
was wood, with a large round woven rug covering the area
between the sofa and the fireplace. Beside one of the chairs
was a basket filled with wool and an unfinished sweater or
scarf with knitting needles sticking out of it. Beside the other
chair was another basket filled with magazines. That's where
they sat at night, she and Mr. Eglitis, on those two chairs,
my mother knitting, her husband reading. Maybe he read out
loud to her as she knit. On the mantelpiece: a framed photo of
my mother and the man I assumed was Mr. Eglitis, and beside
it, another photo of a young handsome man that I knew had
to be their son, smiling proudly in his cap and gown. Scattered
around the base of those photos was a handful of rocks.

She came out of the kitchen with a tray heavily laden with
coffee and cake and all the accompanying trappings. I jumped
up to help her.

"I'm all right, thank you. Sit. Please." She put the tray
down on the coffee table, pulled up the chair I had already
identified as hers, and sat down facing me.

"I should have called before coming. I'm sorry," I said.

"I knew you were coming," she said. "I was waiting."

She poured the coffee. Her fingers were longer than mine, more tapered, but stronger. She had the hands of someone who had used them for work all her life, very different from the gloved elegance Elka had described. My own seemed pudgy, in contrast, soft, suburban. She cut the cake, and as she did so she extended her index finger to press against the entire length of knife. It was an unusual way to hold a knife. Had I grown up with her I would have seen her do that all the time, I thought. It would have been just another one of the ways my mother's essence found expression in the countless little tasks of everyday life. I would have incorporated her particular way of holding a knife into my overall sense of her without ever really noticing it, the way I carried within me the particular way Elka brushed her hair, and twisted her mouth when she was thinking, and held her hand on the small of her back when she was tired. She handed me a plate with a piece of cake on it.

"Thank you," I said, and then we just looked at each other again.

We didn't touch the cake sitting in front of us or sip at our coffee. She didn't ask me how my trip had been, or how long I thought I might stay in Thunder Bay. Or how my life had been and was going, for that matter. I didn't comment on her house or ask if the small, rust-spotted apples in the bowl were from the tree I'd noticed in the garden. Nor did I ask the name and age of my half-brother, who smiled at me with my own mouth from the mantelpiece. We looked at each other without self-consciousness, without thought of anything outside the long mutual study in which we were engaged. Her face was beautiful in its starkness; the only colour in it the blue of her eyes. Even her lips were pale. I felt the contrast of my own darker

colouring, the softer, more padded contours of my face. Was she seeing that too, the differences between us, the different way her own eyes looked when set against my colouring and within the fleshier, less austere structure of my face?

I heard the sound of a cuckoo clock from somewhere deeper inside the house, the breaking apart and falling of a log in the fireplace. Did my mother notice?

No, I thought. She was transfixed, the expression on her face one of wonder. Her eyes brimmed with tears again. Like sapphires now, her eyes, not like mine at all. The first tears spilled, slid down her face. She wiped them away, but more followed, and then more. A continuous flow of tears as if a well within her were emptying itself.

"I'm sorry," she said, and I reached my hand out, an instinctive reaching out, to comfort her, and she took my hand in hers.

It was a stranger's hand, strong, weather-worn, not at all like the hands that had comforted and cared for me through my life, but I had known it once, I thought, as I felt it press against my own.

"I'm sorry," she said again.

I had imagined so many scenarios for our first meeting, had lists of questions and possible things we might talk about, things we might do. I had brought some of the rocks she had given me to ask her about them, why she had sent them, if there was something special about each particular one. I had brought the diamond, the notebooks. I wasn't sure I would bring them out, but I had them with me just in case. And then there were the photos of Reuben and the kids, the drawings the kids had made for her, the rock Joey had found in our backyard that he thought I should give her from him.

"I can't explain to you why I did what I did."

"That's not why I came."

"Isn't it?"

I thought about that before answering. "Only in part."

"I'm sorry," she said again.

"It's enough to see you," I said.

"Is it?"

I realized the degree to which that was true. It wasn't that my questions had disappeared or felt irrelevant. It was more that they had been displaced by the comfort I felt in her presence, a comfort I had not expected at all, that settled on me as I sat with her, pushing the noise of questions and explanations to the outer periphery of my mind. I didn't answer, but maybe she felt my answer, because she smiled then and didn't say she was sorry again.

"You're not eating your cake," she said.

"Neither are you."

She smiled again. "You're beautiful."

"No, I'm not." I was nice enough to look at, I knew— "easy on the eye," Reuben liked to say—but I was not beautiful. Never had been, never would be.

"Yes," she said. "Beautiful."

And I didn't argue a second time, because the look on her face, as she said it, was like that of a new mother proclaiming the beauty of the crying, slimy bundle of wrinkled humanity she has just brought forth into the world.

"You have your father's goodness," she said. "I felt it the minute I saw you. And your grandfather's mouth."

And ten perfect fingers and toes, I thought. Was it possible she hadn't done this the first time she had seen me? It was, I realized, for whatever combination of loss and fear and

self-recrimination and bewildered grief and remembered horror, none of which I would ever understand at the level that she had felt them. And though I was thirty-five years old by now, with three children of my own, I basked in her strange, belated, proud inventory of my beauty.

I heard the clock strike again. How long had I been here? An hour? Two? The room had darkened, though it was not quite yet dusk. This time she had also heard the clock. I felt the shift in her.

"My husband will be home soon," she said, and I understood she wanted me to leave before he came.

"Is that your husband?" I asked, looking at the photos facing me on the mantelpiece.

"Yes," she said, without turning around to look.

I knew I should leave, should start making the motions to leave, at least, should ask her what time we might see each other the following day, if she would like to see me, that is, and if she would prefer to meet somewhere else, my hotel, perhaps. We sat a little longer. It seemed like no time, but the clock struck another quarter-hour.

"You'll come back tomorrow?" she asked.

I said I would, reached for my purse.

"Earlier in the day," she said.

We agreed on a time.

"Your husband doesn't know about me, does he?"

"Not yet," she said, and she looked at me then with a look that seemed to beseech me to understand. I was afraid she would say she was sorry, again, but she didn't.

"How old is your son?" I asked, looking at the photo of my smiling half-brother in his graduation cap and gown.

"Twenty-nine."

He was born when I was six, then. The year she sent me the first rock.

WHEN I CALLED REUBEN that evening he suggested I rent a car the next day and take her somewhere we could walk.

"Where?" I asked him.

"Anywhere. Outside. Where you're not just staring at each other. Somewhere she likes. She'll tell you where."

She directed me to a trail that led through forest to a small lake. She told me it was the landscape and lakes in the area that had made her get off the train.

"I just wanted to smell it," she said. She had been in Montreal a year by then and had not been out of the city. And before that in Palestine. The train to Montreal when she first arrived had passed through forest, but she hadn't stepped outside. "I grew up in a forest like this. I thought if I smelled it again, now that time had passed and peace had come, something from before the war would come to me." Some lost memory of her father, of other members of her family whose voices and faces never came to her, she said, not even in her dreams. "No one came," she said, but she didn't get back on the train.

"Where had you been planning to go?"

"I didn't have a plan," she said. "I had a ticket to Winnipeg."

She had found work right away, at a roadhouse, making pancakes. She had liked the customers, men mostly, many of them from the northeastern corner of Europe: Finns, Ukrainians, Estonians, Latvians, Lithuanians, Poles. They worked in the forest, the port. She rented an apartment in a house in Port Arthur. When she wasn't working she walked and skied in the

forest. Often she camped, sometimes for days at a time.

"You weren't afraid?"

"Of what?"

"I don't know. Bears."

She smiled. "I was always afraid. But not of bears."

But over time she became less afraid. The fear started to slip from her. And then after a little more time she met the man who would be her husband. He was a surveyor, one of the customers at the restaurant. One day, four years after first meeting him, she noticed him. *He's a good man,* she thought. She married him, they had a son. She stopped making pancakes, began working as a tutor.

"I have a talent for languages," she said.

The more she talked the further I felt from the woman I had sat with the previous day who had looked at me with wonder through tear-filled eyes, but I was happy to hear some of the facts of her life. She asked about my life. I told her about Reuben, the children, the work I did restoring manuscripts. The more *I* talked, the less I felt I was expressing the truth of my life.

"I can't explain what it was like for me," she said at one point.

I knew that by then.

We sat on a large outcrop of rock overlooking the lake. I showed her the photos I had brought. She commented how beautiful my children were, how handsome my husband. I opened my knapsack again to pull out the drawings the children had made for her. "So talented," she said. I gave her the rock from Joey, and she smiled and wordlessly enclosed it in her hand, and all the words and explanations fell away again and I felt myself in the presence of a deeper part of her.

We sat for a while longer.

"You weren't my first," she said.

I looked at her.

"I had lost a child already."

"A baby?"

"I couldn't keep her alive."

"During the war?"

"Yes. Then." And with an almost imperceptible shake of her head, "I'm not telling you that to excuse what I did, as if that would explain . . ." She paused. "Many people lost children. Your own grandmother."

She looked at me, waiting for my response.

"I'm sorry," I said, and with that, her eyes, which had been dry, almost hard as she told me about my half-sister who had died, softened.

"Tonya," she said. "That was her name."

"How old was she?"

"Five months." She shook her head. "It was madness to keep her with us. There were families that would have taken her, helped us." She looked at me. "Don't believe it when people tell you no one would help us. People helped us. Good people." She paused. "Even not-so-good people. They helped us."

I nodded.

"But I wanted her with us." She looked at me then as if to ask if that was such a terrible thing to have wanted.

I tried to imagine the situation she had been in, the choice she had faced, but knew I couldn't, not really.

"Either way I would have lost her. But she'd be alive."

I tried again to imagine it. "You did what you thought best," I said, which sounded hollow and trite.

"I did," she said. "But I was wrong."

We sat for a while saying nothing. The wind had picked up, raising a light chop on the lake.

She looked at me. "It makes me happy to see you." She smiled. "I know it may not seem that way."

"It seems that way," I said. I knew the undertow certain kinds of happiness could bring.

A few clouds moved across the sky. When they hid the sun the air lost all its warmth. I felt cold sitting there but didn't want to move. She didn't either. She pulled her coat tighter around her. We sat a little closer to each other.

"Why did you go to Palestine right after the war?" I asked her.

"I don't know," she said. "Where else was I going to go?" After a while she said, "It wasn't Europe, and there was a chance of landing there and not being sent back. I suppose it seemed as good as any place to make a start. Why do you ask?"

"I don't know. I just wondered."

"It was the wrong decision. I knew it as soon as I landed."

"How did you know?"

She shrugged. "I just knew."

What was it, I wondered—the heat? the smell of the air?— that somehow made her loneliness harder to bear there? She didn't elaborate and we sat for a while without talking, looking out onto the northern forest that was like the one she had grown up in, the landscape, familiar to her, that had made her get off the train.

"In the end I had to pass through Europe again to be admitted to Canada."

"You did?"

"Because I had come into Palestine illegally, so to leave

it and enter Canada . . . it wasn't something that could be arranged with the British in control."

"So you left it for Europe?" Whoever heard of a Jewish person leaving Palestine in 1946 for Europe?

"Someone I knew was going to Egypt through the Sinai. I went with him to Egypt and from there back to Europe. It wasn't hard to get back into Europe then. And it was easier to make arrangements from there. Everything was still in chaos."

"But after what you must have gone through to get to Palestine . . ." I remembered all the books I'd read about the attempts by Jewish refugees to land there. "Wouldn't it have made more sense to stay and try to—"

Something in her face stopped me mid-sentence.

"Nothing made sense at that time. I had Canada in my mind; I can't tell you why. The word itself raised certain images, a feeling of calmness . . . I really can't tell you what I was thinking."

I felt her shutting herself away from me, or maybe from the memory of that time in her life that I was prodding her to explain and thereby re-experience, to some degree. "I'm sorry. I didn't mean to make you—"

"I'm sorry I don't have a better answer for you."

"It's good enough."

"Is it?"

We sat for a time and just when I thought the sun would never emerge again from the huge cloud that was covering it, it did. It was nice to sit there with her in the warming sun. I think I knew then that I would probably never see her again, but it was okay. This was what I had come for, I thought.

"I remember your laugh," I told her.

She smiled. "Do you?"

I told her how I would hear it in my sleep, that it would seem like a dream but it would pull me from sleep and when I woke I knew it wasn't dream, it was memory.

She nodded; she understood perfectly, and I hoped she would laugh, so I could hear it again, but she didn't.

"You're lucky," she said.

I looked at her. "Lucky?"

"What I wouldn't give to hear my mother's laugh," she said.

EPILOGUE

January 2005

Laughter wakes me. A single peal. It pierces my sleep, scatters my dreams, then it's gone and I'm awake, alone, alert to the bark of a distant dog, the car driving too quickly along the pavement outside. I won't sleep again tonight. Already I can feel the gathering pressure in my chest, a heavy beast awakening inside me. I open my eyes but darkness obscures the life I'll resume in the morning. For the moment there's just the shadow and shape of a room that isn't home and the sweeping lights of cars as they pass in the street below.

I glance at the clock: 4 a.m. I had hoped it would be later. The dog's barking is building, getting desperate. Soon it will turn to howls. This happens every night: an hour or so of barking, then some howls, then—finally—quiet. Or what passes for quiet. No one complains, and when I mention it to my neighbours they look quizzical, barely suppressing their smiles. I'm an oddity to them—my lack of family, of purpose. They don't dislike me, but my presence unsettles. They wonder how much longer I'll stay.

I arrived here last month, intending to stay for a week.

"Purpose of your trip?" asked the border guard.

"I'm delivering a paper," I said. What I was actually delivering was Lily Azerov's notebook. I was donating it to the archive at Yad Vashem, Israel's centre for the memory of those who died in the Holocaust. But I was tired from the long trip over, didn't feel I had the energy for even a minimal explanation of my long overdue delivery of the girl's writing into the public domain. I just wanted to get out of the airport into fresh air.

"Where are you speaking?" the guard asked idly, misunderstanding my vague use of the word "delivering." She was flipping through my passport looking for a clean page to stamp.

"Yad Vashem."

I expected her to ask for more information, but she didn't. The mere mention of Yad Vashem seemed to dispel any possible suspicions of my purpose there. She nodded, then her brow furrowed slightly as the stub of my boarding pass flew out from between the pages of my passport. She retrieved it from the floor, slipped it into my passport and returned my passport to me.

"Enjoy your stay," she said.

It's never really quiet here. Not even in the middle of the night. There's a hum, a humming tension. My own, perhaps. I hear it now, now that the other nighttime noises have finally died away: the barking dog, the footsteps above me, the laughing voices and rhythmic slap of cards. I heard it, felt it the moment I stepped outside the airport terminal. A humming like a rising swarm of bees.

"Jerusalem," I told the first cab driver that approached me. "The Kings Hotel."

"American?" he asked as we pulled away from the curb.

"Canadian."

"You speak Hebrew?"

"A little," I acknowledged. Fluently, actually—I've inherited my mother's facility with language—but I immediately wished I'd pretended otherwise. I wanted to be left alone, in silence.

As the cab pulled away from Ben Gurion Airport, I opened my window. The air was refreshing after the staleness of the airplane cabin. It was a January night, cooler than I had expected, and still dripping from an earlier rain. The driver closed my window and sped onto the highway. I opened it again.

"You have a reservation at the Kings?" he asked.

"You think I need one?"

He laughed. "If I may make a suggestion . . ."

"Let me guess," I said. "You know a much better place. Better price, better location." He met my eyes in the rear-view mirror. "And it just happens to be run by your brother-in-law."

"My cousin," he said, revealing a mouthful of silver as he smiled broadly at me in the mirror. "It's a block from the sea . . ."

"I'm sure it's very nice but I need to be in Jerusalem. I'm delivering a paper there."

"It's just forty-five minutes from Jerusalem. I can pick you up whenever you need and then take you back. Every day." He reached back to hand me his business card. It had his name on one side and the prayer for safe travel on the other. "Whatever time you need, you just call and I'm there. At your service. Yuri," he added, in case I couldn't read his name on the card.

"Thank you very much," I said. "But I'm really not interested. Just take me to my hotel, please."

"It has its own kitchen."

"I don't need my own kitchen. I'm only here for a few days."

"What? You come all the way from Canada to stay only for a few days?"

"I can't stay longer," I said.

I was actually at the beginning of a six-month leave of absence from my job. Stress leave, I was calling it, because my workplace didn't grant leaves of absence for grief. I could stay as long as I wanted, had no return ticket, had told Reuben I would be away for a few weeks. But I had imagined flying out of Tel Aviv for the south of France, maybe Tuscany, where Nina was now living with the girlfriend she had loved for forty years, demonstrating, with that revelation, that she had been a better actor all along than any of her family had imagined.

"It's just perfect for one person," Yuri assured me. He glanced at me in the mirror. "You have a husband?"

I considered not answering but sensed that he would just think I hadn't heard him and would ask the same question, but louder.

"Yes," I said.

"He doesn't like Israel?"

Everything was personal here. I'd forgotten that. "He couldn't get away right now."

He accepted that answer. "I'll tell you what . . . You have a name, Madame Professor?"

"Ruth," I said.

"I'll tell you what, Ruthie. I'll stop along the way so you can have a look—we're going right by there anyway. Then, if you don't like it, I'll take you straight to Jerusalem, no extra charge for the detour."

"I thought you said we were going right by there anyway."

"You'll be happy. I promise."

I HAD NOT SEEN my mother again after our first meeting. It was as I had sensed during the time we spent together. She was my mother, my beginning, but our lives had diverged, we had separate families and she couldn't integrate me into her life. I had hoped for more, and maybe she had too, but it had also been enough to meet her, to sit in her presence, to have a sense of who she was and why she had to leave, and to know that she had a sense of who I was, who I loved, how I lived. I felt more comfortable in the world knowing where she was, being able to picture her in the living room of her home in Thunder Bay, sitting by a fire in the evening, or tending her garden or walking in the forests around her home.

As the years passed, though, I did begin to think more about her again. I wondered how her health was, how her life was now that she was getting old. Did the past sit differently within her now that less of life lay ahead? Had her memories of her family resurfaced in her? Would it give her any pleasure or comfort to meet my children, who were now young adults, finding their own ways into the world? I began thinking about writing to her, asking her if it would be all right to visit again, if she would like that; but then my father became ill, Sophie's marriage fell apart, and Reuben's mother moved in with us while waiting for a bed to become available at an extended-care facility. All that was more pressing.

My father died in November 2004, on a bleak day of a

bleak month. And then, not more than two weeks later, the phone rang after dinner. Reuben answered.

"Yes?" he said. "Yes. I see. Just a moment." He handed me the phone. "It's Anton Eglitis."

She had asked for me. That was my first thought as I reached for the phone. By the time I said hello I had already imagined my mother on her sickbed, surrounded by the family she loved but feeling that someone was missing, me, the daughter she had not been able to raise as her own. She had told them about me, finally, had begged their forgiveness and understanding for her long-kept secret and asked them to bring me to her side. I would leave the next morning, no question. Sophie, Sam or Joey could move back in to help with Reuben's mother.

"Hello?" I said.

"Hello," he said. "This is Anton Eglitis. I know we've never met, but we have the same mother." Did he think I didn't know that? "I'm calling with some sad news, I'm afraid. I'm calling to—she's died. Our mother."

"She has?"

"Yesterday morning. At 10 a.m."

I'd been at work at 10 a.m. the previous morning, had not felt anything unusual. Nor had I noticed any change in the world, just the continuing, grim reality of my father's recent death, Reuben's mother's decline, Sophie's sadness about her broken marriage.

"I thought you'd want to know."

"Of course. Yes."

I felt Reuben standing behind me, his hands on my shoulders.

She had been sick for a couple of weeks with the flu, Anton told me. She just couldn't seem to shake it. And then it moved into pneumonia.

"I see," I said, with what felt like the last bit of air within me.

Anton began to speak then of the funeral. They had buried her within twenty-four hours, in a simple pine box, according to her wishes. "She was Jewish," he explained to me. Did he think I didn't know that? I wondered again. I was her daughter, for God's sake. But then, I hadn't even known her name for years and years, had I?

"The funeral was today, then?" I asked.

"This afternoon. I'm sorry I didn't call sooner."

"I appreciate you calling now. How did you know . . . ?"

That I even existed, is what I meant to ask. I wasn't sure how to phrase it, didn't need to.

"She told us. After you came to meet her."

"She did?" That too felt like a blow. She had kept her distance not out of fear for the stability of her marriage and family, then, her husband's possible response, but for her own psyche. Because to face me was to face a part of herself and her own experience that she felt compelled to rebury.

But what about Anton, this half-brother of mine? Had he not felt curiosity about me, his only blood relative on his mother's side?

"Do you live in Thunder Bay?" I asked him.

"Toronto. But we're all here now, of course."

In the living room that I could picture. But how many of them were there? Who exactly?

"Your family?"

"My wife and our sons."

The family and life that my mother had built atop the wreckage of her former lives and identities.

"How many sons do you have?"

He hesitated. Did he think it was a trick question? That I

wanted something from him, was going to lay a claim on the family that wasn't mine? Had my mother conveyed to him her fear of the place within her in which I resided, the terrible mix of feelings attached to me that I could carry to the surface of her life, blowing it apart as I did?

"Four," he said.

"Nice," I said, and on one level I meant it. It was nice that my mother had four grandsons, but as I imagined them all gathered in that living room where I had sat with her, to mourn her death, their mother and grandmother who had been my mother as well, I felt like the defective puppy who's been pushed out of the warm litter to the lonely coldness of the world. And I felt angry that I should have a half-brother and nephews who were all strangers to me, and that my children had an uncle and cousins who would always be strangers. It seemed a useless, stupid waste of blood relations.

Anton didn't ask me anything about myself, didn't make any noises about how nice it would be if we could meet sometime, how if I was ever in Toronto I should call, come over and meet the family. Was he not even curious? I wondered again. Was he an insensate blockhead? Did he not even know that curiosity about our own origins is what defines us as human? That it wasn't speech, as he might think, or opposing thumbs, but origins, which were inextricably linked to destiny?

"I appreciate you calling," I said again.

"No problem. I thought you'd want to know."

After I put the phone down, Reuben got a razor from the bathroom and made the beginning of the tear in my blouse for me. He made it on the left side of my blouse, over my heart. Then I took the fabric and pulled it apart and Reuben took me into his arms while I wept alone for my mother.

YURI'S COUSIN WAS a woman of indeterminate middle age who had obviously been asleep for the night when Yuri rapped at her door. She greeted us pleasantly, adjusting her housecoat with a tug and giving her hair a quick pat—surprisingly pleasantly, I thought, for someone who had been roused from sleep at eleven o'clock on a rainy winter night to show an apartment to someone who had no interest in renting it.

"I'll just get the keys," she said.

As we followed her up the three flights of stairs, I imagined a dim room smelling of mould, but when she pushed open the door I was dazzled by the whiteness, the blue floor that shimmered like the sea in sunlight even in the middle of the night.

"It's lovely," I said immediately. The entire apartment was one white room with a blue-tiled floor. It wasn't large but it felt spacious. The furnishings were minimal—just a desk against the wall with the window, a bureau made of wood, and the bed, pushed against another wall and covered in a white quilt. The blue of the floor repeated in the tiles of the counter in the kitchenette.

"It's like a ship," I added, which was perhaps a peculiar thing to say because it was nothing like a ship except in the way it made me feel. I felt I could return to it after I had delivered the notebook that I had once hoped might hold the key to my mother's life, could trust that room to carry me through whatever might lie ahead and deliver me to a new harbour.

Yuri flashed a hopeful smile at his cousin. "It's completely remodelled," he said, though it must have been obvious to him by then that no further salesmanship was required. "It's one of the original buildings in Tel Aviv. It was built . . . When was it built, Ayelet?" he asked his cousin.

"Never mind the history lesson," his cousin answered. "She's tired from her trip, can't you see?"

I was exhausted, I realized, as every cramped, uncomfortable moment of the last twenty hours of travel suddenly caught up with me.

"You'll sleep well here," she assured me.

I haven't slept well here, but I don't care. I'm not here to sleep.

It's 5 a.m. now. I know without even having to look at the clock. The first flight of the morning just roared overhead, banking steeply in its turn out to sea. Yuri didn't mention the flight path, would not have thought it worth mentioning. "You'll get used to it," Ayelet assures me. She pities me, it's very obvious. Lost soul, she thinks. Nothing better to occupy her nights than worrying about barking dogs and the noise of airplanes. But she's wrong.

The apartment faces east, away from the sea, and I like how that fault catches the first light of morning. Soon I'll see it, that first ray of light. It will sweep the wall by the desk where I've pinned the photo of Reuben and the kids emerging, laughing, from the freezing cold lake at Wawa on that road trip across Canada in 1982. Then the desk, where I've placed the pink quartz that I've always used as a paperweight.

Lily Azerov's notebook is gone—I delivered it yesterday, along with the diamond, still uncut and unfinished. The curator looked at the notebook for a long time, nodding. She told me how rare this sort of document is, how important, how helpful it will be to future generations. The diamond, though, puzzled her. She raised her eyebrows at me.

"It was found with the girl," I said. "With Lily Azerov."

I would leave it to the curator and those future generations

to determine the role it had played in the life of the girl who hadn't survived to tell us.

What's left on my desk now is the other notebook—my mother's. It's empty still, but not for long. I opened it last night before I went to bed, and it lies open to the first page, where I'll begin this very morning, as soon as the first ray of light sweeps across it. I'll begin with a wedding in July of 1946. I'll begin in a small room off a banquet hall in Montreal.

The first chapter of this book appeared in slightly different form in *Room of One's Own*, Volume 28:2, 2005.

The stanza from Czeslaw Milocz's "Dedication," which appears at the beginning of this book, was translated by the poet and is used by permission of HarperCollins Publishers Ltd.

ACKNOWLEDGEMENTS

I am grateful to the following people, who read early drafts of this novel and offered helpful observations, criticisms and encouragement: Cynthia Flood, Tova Hartman, Sara Horowitz, Barbara Kuhne, Lydia Kwa, Helen Mintz, Janet Ostro, Susan Ouriou, Diane Richler, Dianne Richler, Martin Richler, Carmen Rodriguez, Robin Roger, Julia Serebrinsky, Howard Stanislawski, Rhea Tregebov, Vicki Trerise, Aletha Worrall.

Thanks to Dean Cooke and Iris Tupholme for their faith in this novel, their insights and their patience. The fresh eye that Jennifer Weis brought to the manuscript was also very helpful.

I also wish to thank my parents, Myer and Dianne Richler, for their constant generosity and support.

The Calabria Café in Vancouver, B.C., was my second home during the writing of this book. Thanks to Frank Murducco and sons, who own and run it.

And finally, always, thanks to Vicki Trerise.